Marno Verbeek
Panel Methods for Finance

De Gruyter Studies in the Practice of Econometrics

Series Editor
Marno Verbeek

Volume 1

Marno Verbeek

Panel Methods for Finance

A Guide to Panel Data Econometrics for Financial
Applications

DE GRUYTER

ISBN 978-3-11-066013-5
e-ISBN (PDF) 978-3-11-066073-9
e-ISBN (EPUB) 978-3-11-066081-4
ISSN 2570-0928
e-ISSN 2570-0936

Library of Congress Control Number: 2021943958

Bibliographic information published by the Deutsche Nationalbibliothek
The Deutsche Nationalbibliothek lists this publication in the Deutsche Nationalbibliografie;
detailed bibliographic data are available on the Internet at http://dnb.dnb.de.

© 2022 Walter de Gruyter GmbH, Berlin/Boston
Cover image: gremlin/getty images/E+
Typesetting: VTeX UAB, Lithuania
Printing and Binding: LSC Communications, United States

www.degruyter.com

To Marcella

Preface

Financial data are typically characterised by a time-series dimension and a cross-sectional dimension. For example, we may observe financial information on a group of firms over a number of years, or we may observe returns of all stocks traded at the New York Stock Exchange (NYSE) over a period of 120 months. Accordingly, econometric modelling in finance requires appropriate attention to these two – and occasionally more than two – dimensions of the data. Panel data techniques are developed to do exactly this. This book provides an overview of commonly applied panel methods for financial applications, with a focus on cases where the cross-sectional dimension is large (and the time-series dimension may be limited).

Campbell et al. (1997) is one of the first monographs focusing on the use of econometrics in finance, mostly in the asset pricing area. A few years later, Gourieroux and Jasiak (2001) provide a guide to "financial econometrics" at an advanced level with a strong focus on time-series models (including continuous time models and high frequency data). The textbook by Brooks (2019), with a first edition published in 2002, deals with econometrics at an introductory level, targeted to finance students, emphasizing linear regression and time-series models (including event studies). More recently, Linton (2019) provides an overview of econometric models and methods in finance, again with a focus on financial markets and investments. Cochrane (2005) presents a systematic overview of the asset pricing literature, with an emphasis on empirical methodology. Econometric textbooks with a clear relevance for financial work, particularly in the corporate finance area, are Cameron and Trivedi (2005) and Wooldridge (2010), both paying elaborate attention to microeconometric issues and panel data. For causal inference, the monographs of Angrist and Pischke (2009) and Angrist and Pischke (2015) provide attractive sources for many scholars.

Dedicated textbooks on panel data are Arellano (2003), Baltagi (2013) and Hsiao (2014), while Pesaran (2015) focusses both on time-series and panel data econometrics. Despite these resources, there is not yet a systematic treatment of econometric techniques based on panel data in empirical finance. To some extent, this gap is filled with comprehensive papers focussing on specific issues, for example, Petersen (2009) on the estimation of standard errors in panel data sets, Roberts and Whited (2013) on endogeneity problems in corporate finance, and Gormley and Matsa (2014) and Grieser and Hadlock (2019) on the estimation of models with fixed effects (FE).

My goal with this monograph was to provide an intuitive and relatively non-technical overview of econometric approaches exploiting panel data. Key topics are alternative assumptions regarding exogeneity on explanatory variables and their consequences for model estimation, the inclusion of a variety of fixed effects to control for unobservable differences across units, the incidental parameters problem in nonlinear models, the use of clustered-standard errors as a means of making standard (cross-sectional) estimation methods "panel robust", the problem of having a lagged dependent variable, and the estimation of – potentially heterogeneous –

https://doi.org/10.1515/9783110660739-201

treatment effects. Further attention is given to outliers, measurement error, missing data and other data problems. Along the way, references are given to a variety of empirical papers in finance as an illustration of the employed methods. In terms of methods, I discuss pooled Ordinary Least Squares (OLS), within and between estimators, feasible Generalised Least Squares (GLS), Fama-MacBeth regressions, robust and clustered standard errors, instrumental variables (IV), the generalised method of moments (GMM), (conditional) maximum likelihood (ML), regression discontinuity design (RDD), difference-in-differences methods (DiD), matching and weighting. Apart from linear models with or without dynamics, I discuss models for binary dependent variables, such as logit and probit, models with censoring or truncation, duration models and count models.

Given the length and scope of this book, I had to make many choices of what to discuss. To compensate this, I have included a wide range of references to other sources that go deeper into certain methods or issues. This is particularly true for the area of the estimation of treatment effects, where new papers are coming out almost every day. I hope the readers appreciate the attempt to collect and discuss a wide variety of methods and approaches, at a reasonable intuitive level and as much as possible in uniform notation. Almost all methods discussed in this text are readily available in Stata, occasionally after installation of user-written routines. For convenience, specific details on relevant Stata functions are provided when appropriate. A very useful and detailed guide to microeconometrics with Stata is Cameron and Trivedi (2021).

Rotterdam, The Netherlands   MARNO VERBEEK

July 27, 2021

Acknowledgments

I wish to thank my colleagues at the finance department of Rotterdam School of Management, Erasmus University, for support and inspiration. Particular thanks go to Rómulo Alves, Mathijs van Dijk, Gelly Fu, Francesco Mazzola, Mikael Paaso and Guosong Xu for helpful comments and suggestions. I am also grateful to *#econtwitter*, which has repeatedly alerted me to recent developments and discussions. I also thank Steve Hardman for his continuous confidence and professional support over the past 22 years, and the people at De Gruyter, who have the courage to start new book projects in this turbulent age for academic publishers. Finally, my wife Marcella has been incredibly supportive with her love and patience, also in the presence of COVID-19.

M. V.

https://doi.org/10.1515/9783110660739-202

Contents

Acronyms

2SLS	Two-Stage Least Squares
AME	Average Marginal Effect
ATE	Average Treatment Effect
ATT	Average Treatment Effect on the Treated
ATET	Average Treatment Effect on the Treated
ATU	Average Treatment Effect on the Untreated
BHC	Bank Holding Company
BHHH	Berndt-Hall-Hall-Hausman (estimator)
CAPM	Capital Asset Pricing Model
CATE	Conditional Average Treatment Effect
CDS	Credit Default Swaps
CEO	Chief Executive Officer
CIA	Conditional Independence Assumption
CRE	Correlated Random Effects
CRSE	Cluster Robust Standard Errors
CRSP	Center for Research in Security Prices
CSR	Corporate Social Responsibility
DD	Difference-in-Differences
DDD	Triple Difference (Difference-in-Difference-in-Differences)
DiD	Difference-in-Differences
FD	First Differences
FE	Fixed Effects
FGLS	Feasible Generalised Least Squares
GDP	Gross Domestic Product
GFE	Group Fixed Effects
GLS	Generalised Least Squares
GMM	Generalised Method of Moments
GRS	Gibbons, Ross and Shanken (test)
HAC	Heteroskedasticity-and-Autocorrelation Consistent
HCSE	Heteroskedasticity-Consistent Standard Errors
HML	High Minus Low (factor)
IIA	Independence of Irrelevant Alternatives
IID	Identically and Independently Distributed
IFE	Interactive Fixed Effects
IM	Information Matrix
IMR	Inverse Mills Ratio
IPO	Initial Public Offering
IPW	Inverse Probability Weighting
IV	Instrumental Variables
LAD	Least Absolute Deviations

https://doi.org/10.1515/9783110660739-203

LATE	Local Average Treatment Effect
LSDV	Least Squares Dummy Variables
LTV	Loan To Value
M&A	Mergers and Acquisitions
MAR	Missing at Random
MCAR	Missing Completely at Random
MDR	Market Debt Ratio
MEM	Marginal Effect at the Mean
ML	Maximum Likelihood
NAICS	North American Industry Classification System
NAV	Net Asset Value
NID	Normally and Independently Distributed
NYSE	New York Stock Exchange
OLS	Ordinary Least Squares
QML	Quasi-Maximum Likelihood
R&D	Research and Development
RCT	Randomised Controlled Trial
RD	Recursive Demeaning
RDD	Regression Discontinuity Design
RE	Random Effects
RMI	Risk Management Index
ROA	Return on Assets
ROS	Return on Sales
RSS	Residual Sum of Squares
SEC	Securities and Exchange Commission
SEO	Seasoned Equity Offering
SIC	Standard Industrial Classification
SMB	Small Minus Big (factor)
SOA	Speed of Adjustment
SOX	Sarbanes-Oxley Act
SUR	Seemingly Unrelated Regression(s)
SUTVA	Stable Unit Treatment Value Assumption
TFE	Two-Way Fixed Effects
TLS	Trimmed Least Squares
TNA	Total Net Assets
WLS	Weighted Least Squares

1 Introduction

Financial data are often characterised by two or more dimensions. Think of monthly returns on a group of stocks, annual reporting data for a cross-section of firms, or monthly money flows to mutual funds. Additional dimensions arise when, for example, industry or country dimensions are added, or when stock holdings of mutual funds are tracked over a number of quarters. Econometric models can help to understand and explain the variation across multiple dimensions. Modelling of cross-section time-series data in finance – or simply panel data – introduces a number of issues related to heterogeneity, cross-correlations, and the specification of control variables. For example, intercept terms or slope coefficients in a model may vary over time or over cross-sectional units, and unobservable factors in an equation may correlate over time or across firms. In many cases, this involves specific challenges in models with explanatory variables that are not strictly exogenous, dynamic models and non-linear models.

1.1 Some illustrative examples

In finance we encounter a large variety of econometric models that exploit both the time-series and cross-sectional dimensions of the data. I review a number of illustrative examples here, providing a first inventory of some of the econometric issues that could possibly arise. All methods and techniques are discussed in more detail later.

1.1.1 Predicting the cross-section of stock returns

Asset pricing models, like the Capital Asset Pricing Model (CAPM), impose restrictions on the joint distribution of asset returns. This has implications for both the time-series as well as the cross-sectional properties of returns. One approach, explored in, for example, Brennan et al. (1998) and Lewellen (2015), is to relate stock returns in month t to characteristics of those stocks dated $t-1$ or before, such as firm size and previous return. A simple version of such model is given by

$$R_{it} = \mu_t + \beta_1 \text{logsize}_{i,t-1} + \beta_2 \log \text{B/M}_{i,t-1} + \beta_3 \text{return}_{i,t-2,-12} + \varepsilon_{it}, \quad (1.1)$$
$$t = 1, \ldots, T; \ i = 1, \ldots, N_t,$$

where R_{it} denotes the return on stock i in month t, $\text{logsize}_{i,t-1}$ denotes the log of the market value of equity at the end of month $t-1$, $\log \text{B/M}_{i,t-1}$ denotes the log of the book value of equity minus the log of the market value of equity, and $\text{return}_{i,t-2,-12}$ is the stock return from month $t-12$ to $t-2$, to capture the momentum effect. The terms μ_t denote time-specific intercepts. The number of stocks in period t is denoted by N_t, and we denote the total number of unique stocks as N.

https://doi.org/10.1515/9783110660739-001

In many cases, a model like (1.1) is estimated using so-called Fama and MacBeth (1973) regressions, where the model coefficients are first estimated for each t, using the relevant cross-section of stocks, after which inference is based on the sampling variation in the T different estimates. Alternatively, the model can be estimated as a pooled regression using ordinary least squares (OLS) on all observations. Apart from the usual discussion about which explanatory variables should be included on the right-hand side, and perhaps the functional form, the main issue with regressions like this one relates to the cross-correlations between different error terms ε_{it}. Most importantly, it can be expected that error terms for different stocks in the same month are correlated due to broad market developments that affect all stocks, although not necessarily to the same extent. Accordingly, such effects are not fully captured by the overall time effects in μ_t. In addition, it is possible that ε_{it} exhibits some degree of serial correlation (for a given stock), although this can be expected to be small. This means that any statistical inference should carefully take such correlations into account. Because the predictor variables on the right-hand side are dated $t - 1$ or before, they can reliably be assumed to be uncorrelated with the error term dated t. That is, the regressors in the equation can safely be assumed to be exogenous.

When a factor-based asset pricing models is imposed, regressions like (1.1) would include factor exposures as explanatory variables. A factor exposure measures the sensitivity of a stock to an overall risk factor. The CAPM, for example, implies that the market return is the only relevant risk factor, and the exposure to this factor, popularly referred to as the market beta, would be the only predictor in a cross-sectional regression. Fama and French (1992) and many others use this to test the validity of the CAPM by expanding the set of regressors including additional variables, similar to those listed above. An additional problem with this is that the factor exposures are not observed and need to be estimated first. This introduces an errors-in-variables problem. Different approaches exist to address this additional problem. Fama and MacBeth (1973) and Fama and French (1992) use estimates based on portfolios of stocks so as to minimise the errors-in-variables problem, Shanken (1992) proposes to adjust the standard errors to correct for the corresponding biases.

1.1.2 Explaining flows to mutual funds

A substantive literature investigates money flows into and out of investment funds, for example, to understand how investors interpret information about fund performance. This also connects to fund managers' incentives as their compensation is typically closely tied to assets under management. Sirri and Tufano (1998) estimate a model relating fund flows to fund performance, expenses, fund size and other characteristics. A simple specification is given by

$$\text{flows}_{it} = \beta_1 + \beta_2 \text{rank}_{i,t-1} + \beta_2 \log \text{fundsize}_{i,t-1} + \beta_3 \text{fees}_{i,t-1} + \cdots + \varepsilon_{it}, \qquad (1.2)$$

$$t = 1, \ldots, T; \ i = 1, \ldots, N_t,$$

where flows$_{it}$ denotes the net percentage growth in fund i in year t, and rank$_{i,t-1}$ denotes the performance rank of a mutual fund in year $t - 1$.[1] Models like (1.2) can be estimated using the Fama and MacBeth (1973) methodology, as done in Sirri and Tufano (1998) or Spiegel and Zhang (2013), or by means of a pooled panel regression, as done in Barber et al. (2016). Whereas the equation is similar to (1.1), the econometric issues are somewhat different. Most importantly, the error terms in (1.2) are likely to exhibit serial correlation for the same fund. This is because fund flows tend to be persistent, for example, due to investors reallocating their investments with a delay. There are different ways to alleviate such problems. For example Spiegel and Zhang (2013) and Barber et al. (2016), include lagged flows in the equation. Alternatively, a static model can be used where the standard errors are adjusted for within-fund and within-period correlations. As we shall discuss in Chapter 2, the standard Fama and MacBeth (1973) methodology does not allow for serial correlation in the error terms.

1.1.3 The impact of CEO compensation or board structure on firm value

An interesting question in corporate finance is to what extent firm value is affected by characteristics of the firm's governance (e. g., Gompers et al., 2003), the compensation contract of the Chief Executive Officer (CEO) (e. g., Palia, 2001), or other choices made by the firm. A typical model for this would relate a measure of firm value (often Tobin's Q or the market-to-book ratio) to the characteristic of interest and a set of control variables. We can write this as

$$\text{firmvalue}_{it} = \beta_1 + \beta_2 \text{comp}_{it} + \text{controls} + \alpha_i + u_{it}, \tag{1.3}$$

where α_i captures unobserved time-invariant heterogeneity across firms, and where we have included comp$_{it}$, a variable describing the compensation contract of the CEO, as our key variable of interest. A particularly interesting characteristic is the pay-to-performance sensitivity, often defined as the change in the dollar value of the executive's wealth for a one-percentage-point change in stock price (delta, see Coles et al., 2006). Delta can be interpreted as a measure of alignment of incentives of managers with the interests of shareholders. A higher delta means that managers will deliver more effort because they share gains and losses with shareholders. However, the compensation contract of the CEO is not exogenous. Unobservable characteristics of the firm, such a firm culture, are likely to correlate with both firm value and the incentive scheme of the CEO. The inclusion of α_i as a fixed firm effect can control for these unobservable differences, as long as they are time-invariant.

---

[1] Actually, Sirri and Tufano (1998) employ a piecewise linear specification in rank$_{i,t-1}$; for the sake of brevity we ignore this here.

Equation (1.3) can be estimated under the "fixed effects" assumption, which essentially eliminates α_i by a transformation, for example, by subtracting averages per firm over time (the within transformation) or by first-differencing. The impact of the compensation contract upon firm value is then identified from its variation over time only, within each firm. This makes the fixed effects estimator a popular choice in empirical work. Unfortunately, when the number of time periods is small, one needs to assume strict exogeneity of $comp_{it}$ (Grieser and Hadlock, 2019), which requires that compensation contracts do not depend upon previous firm values, conditional upon the included control variables and the fixed firm effect.

1.1.4 Explaining capital structure choice

Explaining the capital structure of firms is one of the key questions in corporate finance. In their seminal paper, Modigliani and Miller (1958) show that in a frictionless world with efficient capital markets a firm's capital structure is irrelevant for its value. In reality, however, market imperfections, like taxes and bankruptcy costs, may make firm value depend on capital structure, and it can be argued that firms select optimal target debt ratios on the basis of a trade-off between the costs and benefits of debt. For example, firms would make a trade-off between the tax benefits of debt financing and the costs of financial distress when they have borrowed too much. Alternatively, the pecking order theory (Myers, 1984) argues that, due to asymmetric information, firms adopt a hierarchical order of financing preferences so that internal financing is preferred over external financing. If external financing is needed, firms first seek debt funding. Equity is only issued as a last resort.

Lemmon et al. (2008) specify alternative equations to explain a firm's leverage ratio, defined as the amount of debt relative to the market or book value of the firm. One of their specifications is given by

$$leverage_{it} = x'_{i,t-1}\beta + \mu_t + \alpha_i + u_{it}, \tag{1.4}$$

where $leverage_{it}$ denotes leverage of firm i in year t, and $x_{i,t-1}$ is a vector of explanatory variables, including log(sales) and measures profitability and tangibility, observed in the previous year. Further, μ_t is an overall time effect, and α_i is a firm-specific time-invariant effect. Because leverage is highly persistent, the firm-specific effects in α_i have the purpose of capturing firm-level heterogeneity. Lemmon et al. (2008) argue that this time-invariant unobserved component of a firm's leverage ratio is likely to be correlated with the traditional right-hand side variables. Thus, treating $\alpha_i + u_{it}$ as a random error term, uncorrelated with the regressors, is inappropriate, and tends to lead to biased and inconsistent estimators. Instead, fixed effects or other approaches are required to control for this endogeneity problem. In addition to the presence of α_i, there is a year-specific intercept term to capture correlation between different firms' leverage ratios within the same year. Fama and French (2002) argue that this correlation is important. In addition, serial correlation in u_{it} may be present. All of these problems have an impact on the question what is the appropriate estimator for (1.4) and what is the appropriate way to calculate correct standard errors. Different authors make different choices here.

It is also possible, and quite common, to extend the previous model with the lagged leverage ratio, that is,

$$\text{leverage}_{it} = x'_{i,t-1}\beta + \gamma \text{leverage}_{i,t-1} + \mu_t + \alpha_i + u_{it}, \tag{1.5}$$

as is done in, for example, Flannery and Rangan (2006). This creates an additional problem in the sense that the lagged dependent variable is correlated with α_i and $u_{i,t-1}$. This makes standard fixed effects approaches inconsistent and more general instrumental variables or generalised method of moments (GMM) estimators may be used (e. g., Lemmon et al., 2008).

1.1.5 Governance and firm value

An often posed question is whether, and to what extent, corporate governance has a causal impact on firm value (or some other measure of performance). A linear model based on panel data can be written as

$$\text{firmvalue}_{it} = \beta_1 + \beta_2 \text{gov}_{it} + \text{controls} + \varepsilon_{it}, \tag{1.6}$$

where gov_{it} is some measure of firm governance, for example, board characteristics (Fich and Shivdasani, 2006). The problem is that governance is not exogenous. For example, it is possible that an omitted variable (or unobserved heterogeneity) affects both firm value and governance, and not controlling for this would lead to biased estimates of β_2. To the extent that such omitted variable is time-invariant, a fixed effects approach would be able to alleviate this concern, provided gov_{it} is strictly exogenous. One problem with this could be low power, if gov_{it} varies only little over time in the sample. In addition to an omitted variable bias problem, other issues could hamper this model. For example, governance and firm value could be simultaneously determined, or the impact of governance on firm value could be heterogeneous and vary over firms, depending upon observed and unobserved characteristics.

An important line of literature tries to exploit the impact of a credibly exogenous shock, such as new regulation that impacts governance (e. g., the Sarbanes-Oxley Act (SOX), or the adoption of antitakeover laws) to estimate the causal impact of (changes in) corporate governance; see Atanasov and Black (2016). If such a shock affects one group of firms, but not another group of similar firms, the impact of a change in governance can be determined by means of a difference-in-differences approach. One compares the outcome before and after the shock, and then compares the differences between the firms that are affected and those that are not. This requires assumptions. For example, the affected firms should be similar to the unaffected firms, such that the difference can be attributed to the shock and not to other factors. Other approaches that are used in this contexts are, for example, instrumental variables approaches (e. g., Bhagat and Bolton, 2008) and, in selected cases, a regression discontinuity design (e. g., Cuñat et al., 2012).

1.1.6 Dividend policy

In a world without taxes and transaction costs, Miller and Modigliani (1961) have shown that the dividend policy of a firm is irrelevant for its value. The question why some firms pay dividends and others do not has puzzled finance scholars, and several alternative explanations and theories have been put forward. Empirically, it appears to be that larger firms, firms with higher profitability, and firms with fewer growth opportunities are more likely to pay dividends (Fama and French, 2001). When modelling dividend policy, the dependent variable is binary: $div_{it} = 1$ if firm i pays dividends in year t and $div_{it} = 0$ otherwise.

Accordingly, econometric models explaining dividend payments are binary choice models explaining the probability that a firm issues dividends from firm characteristics, such as fund size, earnings, asset growth or book-to-market ratio. A logit regression specifies this probability as

$$Pr(div_{it} = 1) = \frac{\exp(x'_{it}\beta)}{1 + \exp(x'_{it}\beta)},\tag{1.7}$$

where x_{it} is a vector of firm characteristics. To capture the decreasing trend in the likelihood that firms pay dividends, the inclusion of a fixed time effect in the specification appears appropriate (replacing $x'_{it}\beta$ in (1.7) by $\mu_t + x'_{it}\beta$). This implies that the logit equation has a year-specific intercept term. Specified as in (1.7), the probability of a firm to pay dividends is modelled independently of the history of the firm. Empirically, this may be unsatisfactory as most firms either never pay dividends or pay dividends each year (Fama and French, 2001). It can therefore be expected that there is a substantial dependence between the decision of any given firm to pay dividends in year t and that in year $t-1$.

This persistence may be captured by the inclusion of firm-specific heterogeneity in (1.7), or the inclusion of a lagged dependent variable, but in applications this is often ignored. Many papers in this literature (e. g., Fama and French, 2001; DeAngelo et al., 2006; Denis and Osobov, 2008) estimate the logit regression year-by-year, and then present average coefficients in the spirit of Fama and MacBeth (1973). While this may seem appealing, obtaining valid standard errors is challenging, particularly in the presence of a very persistent or fixed firm effect (Petersen, 2009). The inclusion of a firm fixed effect in (1.7) suffers from an incidental parameters problem, and requires nonstandard estimation techniques (such as conditional maximum likelihood); see, for example, Ma (2019).

Alternatively, one could attempt to model the amount of dividend paid by a firm (appropriately scaled), which would be zero for a substantial part of the sample. This leads to a dependent variable that is observed over a limited range, with many zero outcomes. Tobit models are developed to deal with this (see, e. g., Brockman and Unlu, 2009). Again, modelling the persistence may be challenging.

1.2 The structure of this text

Clearly, empirical work in both corporate finance and investments heavily use panel data techniques to model financial phenomena. Despite the popularity, it seems that not all issues are sufficiently well understood. Certain techniques have become very popular, despite the fact that they are not necessarily appropriate. For example, there is an abundance of studies using cross-sectional estimation methods in panel data contexts, with or without combining this with standard errors clustered along one or more dimensions, and with or without the inclusion of one or more variations of fixed effects (e. g., firm fixed effects, year fixed effects or year × industry fixed effects). This occurs both in linear and nonlinear models. Critical assumptions regarding consistency of the estimators, or the validity of the standard errors are often overlooked. Similarly, many studies use estimation methods based on estimating the parameters across subsets of the data and then averaging the estimation results (as in, e. g., Fama and MacBeth, 1973). Studies may include dynamics in the form of a lagged dependent variable, also in cases where this is inappropriate or crucial additional assumptions are required (e. g., the absence of serial correlation in the error terms). Crucial assumptions are often not tested, as if – for example – using clustered standard errors solves all misspecification issues.

The examples from the previous subsections illustrate a variety of issues that play a role with estimating econometric models using panel data in finance. In this text we will systematically review these issues, including assumptions for consistency, dealing with heterogeneity and cross-correlations, small sample biases, obtaining appropriate standard errors, and identifying genuine causal effects.

The next chapter starts with a refresher of the linear regression model, the workhorse of many models in finance, and then extends this to the panel data case to present and discuss a range of basic estimators: pooled OLS, fixed effects (FE) and random effects (RE) estimators, and the Fama and MacBeth (1973) approach. Chapter 3 discusses a variety of topics related to the inclusion of fixed effects in the model, the use of instrumental variables estimators, or – more generally – the generalised method of moments (GMM). It also focusses on critical assumptions, such as strict exogeneity. Chapter 4 collects a number of issues and problems related to the available data. This includes outliers, missing values, panel attrition and measurement errors.

The possibility to estimate dynamic models at the level of the individual firm is a great advantage of panel data, and Chapter 5 focusses on models with lagged dependent variables. The estimation of models with binary dependent variables, or limited dependent variables, in the presence of panel data is often more challenging than with a single cross-section. Chapter 6 discusses how such models can be estimated. The final chapter elaborates upon causal inference in the context of heterogeneous treatment effects. It introduces the potential outcomes framework, and discusses alternative approaches to estimate average treatment effects, such as regression-adjustment, weighting, regression discontinuity, and difference-in-differences (DiD) methods.

2 Linear static models

This chapter starts with a refresher of the linear regression model, its assumptions and how it can be estimated, in the contexts of cross-sectional, time-series and panel data. In case of panel data, models often include fixed effects or random effects. Fixed effects, random effects and pooled approaches, differ importantly in their assumptions about the exogeneity of the explanatory variables, and can yield significantly different results. We review this in Sections 2.4, 2.6 and 2.7. Standard estimators, such as OLS or the within estimator, are often combined with clustered standard errors to allow for correlations of the error terms within clusters (e. g., within a given firm) as well as heteroskedasticity. We elaborate upon this in Sections 2.5 and 2.8. Estimation in first-differences is discussed in Section 2.9, while Section 2.12 pays attention to the Fama and MacBeth (1973) estimator. Tests for heteroskedasticity and serial correlation are discussed in Section 2.10. The chapter concludes with a short discussion of goodness-of-fit measures.

2.1 The linear regression model with cross-sectional data

The linear regression model is one of the important building blocks in empirical finance. In general, a linear regression model relates one variable, typically denoted by y, to a set of explanatory variables, say $x_2, \ldots, x_K$. A population model can then be written as

$$y = \beta_1 + \beta_2 x_2 + \cdots \beta_K x_K + \varepsilon, \tag{2.1}$$

where the coefficients $\beta_1, \ldots, \beta_K$ are unknown population parameters, and typically our interest is focused on them, and where ε denotes an unobserved disturbance term (or error term). As examples, we can think of (2.1) as describing the relationship between firm value and firm characteristics or between stock returns and stock characteristics. The error term ε then includes the role of all other aspects that are not included in the model. A relationship like (2.1) may follow from economic theory or may simply be an empirical approximation to some underlying relationship or mechanism. The interpretation of the model, and its coefficients, depends upon the application and the assumptions that are made. In general, it is assumed that (2.1) describes a large population of (potential) observations.

2.1.1 The linear model and ordinary least squares

Before moving to the panel data case, we start by considering the case where the regression model describes a cross-sectional relationship, and the available sample is

https://doi.org/10.1515/9783110660739-002

a cross-section of, for example, firms, assets or mutual funds. Assuming a random sample of observations, indexed $i = 1, 2, \ldots, N$, we can write the model as

$$y_i = \beta_1 + \beta_2 x_{2i} + \cdots \beta_K x_{Ki} + \varepsilon_i, \quad i = 1, \ldots, N, \tag{2.2}$$

where N denotes the total number of observations. It is convenient to introduce some shorthand notation for the elements in this model by collecting all parameters in a K-dimensional vector $\beta = (\beta_1, \ldots, \beta_K)'$, and all explanatory variables in a vector $x_i = (1, x_{2i}, \ldots, x_{Ki})'$. The first element in this vector corresponds to the intercept term ($x_{1i} \equiv 1$). Later we shall also consider models where the intercept term is excluded from the vector x_i. This allows us to write the linear regression model as

$$y_i = x_i'\beta + \varepsilon_i, \quad i = 1, \ldots, N. \tag{2.3}$$

Typically, the linear model is complemented by a set of assumptions related to the error term ε_i, its distribution, and how it is allowed to relate to the explanatory variables in x_i.

Ordinary least squares (OLS) is an estimation method where the model coefficients are estimated by minimising the residual sum of squares (RSS). That is, the OLS estimator for β is obtained from minimising

$$RSS(\beta) = \sum_{i=1}^{N} (y_i - x_i'\beta)^2. \tag{2.4}$$

The first-order conditions of this problem easily show that the solution is given by

$$\hat{\beta} = \left(\sum_{i=1}^{N} x_i x_i' \right)^{-1} \sum_{i=1}^{N} x_i y_i. \tag{2.5}$$

A requirement for this solution to exist is that the matrix

$$\sum_{i=1}^{N} x_i x_i' \tag{2.6}$$

can be inverted, that is, is nonsingular. This matrix contains sums of squares and cross-products of the regressors x_i. If it cannot be inverted, this means that one explanatory variable can be written as an exact linear combination of the other ones. This case is referred to as (exact) **multicollinearity**: the minimisation problem does not have a unique solution, and the OLS estimator does not exist. A typical situation where this arises is when the data consist of D mutually exclusive categories and a dummy variable is included corresponding to each category. A simple solution is to exclude one of the dummy variables, which makes the omitted category act as a reference group in the interpretation. For example, when we have data of firms from 12 industries, the inclusion of 11 dummy variables is sufficient to capture the differences between industries. The coefficients for each dummy reflect the differences with the omitted industry.

Irrespective of the assumptions that are imposed upon the population model in (2.3), the OLS estimator in (2.5) provides the best linear approximation of y_i based upon x_i. That is, the linear combination

$$\hat{y}_i = x_i' \hat{\beta}$$

provides the **best linear approximation** of y_i, within the current sample, in the sense that the sum of squared approximation errors $\sum_i (y_i - \hat{y}_i)^2$ is as small as possible (among all possible choices for $\hat{\beta}$). This is true irrespective of the true values of β or the interpretation of the model. This result highlights the importance of OLS as an algebraic tool, even in cases where there is no clear population model of interest; see Davidson and MacKinnon (2004, Chapter 2) for an excellent discussion of the geometry of least squares.

The first-order conditions of the minimisation problem in (2.4) imply that

$$\sum_{i=1}^{N} x_i (y_i - x_i' \hat{\beta}) = 0,$$

or, defining the OLS residual as

$$\hat{\varepsilon}_i = y_i - \hat{y}_i = y_i - x_i' \hat{\beta},$$

that

$$\sum_{i=1}^{N} x_i \hat{\varepsilon}_i = 0.$$

This means that, by construction, the residuals are mean zero and uncorrelated with each of the explanatory variables. This result allows us to write

$$y_i = x_i' \hat{\beta} + \hat{\varepsilon}_i, \tag{2.7}$$

which decomposes, within the sample, the observed values y_i into a part that is correlated with x_i (the fitted values $\hat{y}_i$) and a part that is orthogonal to x_i (the residuals $\hat{\varepsilon}_i$). It is important to understand the differences between this equation and the population regression model in (2.3). The latter describes a relationship that has an economic interpretation and characterises a large population of interest, in which β is a vector of unknown population parameters, and ε_i is not observed. In contrast, (2.7) is a decomposition that holds within the sample, $\hat{\beta}$ and $\hat{\varepsilon}_i$ being functions of the observed data (and varying from one sample to the other). Ideally, we would like that $\hat{\beta}$ is a "good" estimator for β and we now move to this question.

We start with discussing assumptions in the context of a cross-sectional data set. With $\{y_i, x_i, i =, 1, \ldots, N\}$ being a random sample (taken from a large population of interest), the OLS estimator $\hat{\beta}$ is a random variable, and its properties will depend upon the assumptions we are willing to make. For each sample, the actual estimate will be different, and the sampling distribution of the different outcomes is used to evaluate the properties of the OLS estimator. To continue, let us write

$$\hat{\beta} = \beta + \left(\sum_{i=1}^{N} x_i x_i' \right)^{-1} \sum_{i=1}^{N} x_i \varepsilon_i, \tag{2.8}$$

which shows that the OLS estimator can be written as the sum of the true value of the population parameter vector β and an estimation error. The properties of this estimation error drive the properties of the OLS estimator. The decomposition in (2.8) illustrates that the key assumptions relate to ε_i and its relationship with x_i.

An estimator is **unbiased** if its expected value equals the true population coefficient. The expected value here refers to the sampling distribution of $\hat{\beta}$ reflecting the different realisations of the estimator across different random samples of size N. Mathematically, this means that $E(\hat{\beta}) = \beta$, where $E(.)$ is the expectation operator. Obviously, this requires that the estimation error in (2.8) has an expected value of zero. A sufficient condition for this is

Assumption EXO1 (ols-cs) : $E(\varepsilon_i \mid x_1, \ldots, x_N) = 0.$ \hfill (2.9)

The notation $E(\cdot \mid c)$ gives the expected value conditional upon the information in c. Assumptions labelled EXO (exogeneity) refer to assumptions involving alternative restrictions regarding independence or absence of correlation between the explanatory variables and the equation's error term. Assumption EXO1 (ols-cs) says that the expected value of the error term in (2.3) is zero, irrespective of the values of all x_i, in other words, ε_i is **conditionally mean independent** of $x_1, \ldots, x_N$. Intuitively, this means that knowing all values of the explanatory variables does not provide any information on the expected value of the equation's error term. With a random sample, the error term of firm i is automatically unrelated to the explanatory variables of firm j and Assumption EXO1 reduces to

Assumption EXO2 (ols-cs) : $E(\varepsilon_i \mid x_i) = 0,$ \hfill (2.10)

which says that ε_i is conditionally mean independent of x_i. Intuitively, this means that knowing the values of the explanatory variables for firm i does not tell us anything about the expected value of the unobservables of that firm. An implication of this assumption is that the linear model in (2.3) describes the conditional expectation of y_i given x_i, that is,

$$E(y_i \mid x_i) = x_i' \beta. \tag{2.11}$$

An estimator is **consistent** if it converges to the true population coefficient when the sample size increases. More formally, it means that the probability limit of the estimator (for $N \to \infty$) equals the true value, mathematically denoted as $\text{plim}_{N \to \infty} \hat{\beta} = \beta$, or – when the limit is clear – simply as $\text{plim} \hat{\beta} = \beta$. A necessary condition for this is

$$\textbf{Assumption EXO3 (ols-cs)} : E(x_i \varepsilon_i) = 0, \qquad (2.12)$$

which says that the error term is mean zero and uncorrelated with the explanatory variables in x_i. An explanatory variable that violates (2.12) is referred to as being endogenous. Assumption EXO3 (ols-cs) is substantially weaker than Assumption EXO1 (ols-cs), and slightly weaker than Assumption EXO2 (ols-cs). To ensure consistency, we also need to impose a regularity condition, which can be written as

$$\textbf{Assumption R1 (ols-cs)} : \text{plim}_{N \to \infty} \frac{1}{N} \sum_{i=1}^{N} x_i x_i' = E(x_i x_i') = \Sigma_{xx} \text{ has rank } K. \qquad (2.13)$$

Assumptions labelled R present regularity conditions. The current assumption says that the symmetric $K \times K$ matrix of cross-products of regressors in (2.5), scaled by the sample size N, converges to a (invertible) positive definite matrix. It requires that there are no exact linear relationships among the explanatory variables (in the population), and it is the population version of the no-multicollinearity condition discussed before.[1]

If an estimator is consistent it means that, if we obtain more and more observations, the probability that our estimator differs from the true parameter vector becomes smaller and smaller. Accordingly, values that $\hat{\beta}$ may take that are not close to β become increasingly unlikely with larger samples. In many relevant cases in empirical finance, unbiased estimators are not available and we focus attention on consistent estimators. Inconsistent estimators are typically considered poor and unattractive, as they may provide misleading conclusions even in very large samples. An estimator can be inconsistent in two ways. The first is that, as the sample size grows, the estimator converges to some nonstochastic limit, but the wrong one. The second is that the estimator does not tend to any nonstochastic limit, and remains a random variable. In this case, the estimator could still be unbiased, also for $N \to \infty$. Often, empirical papers in finance use the term "unbiased" to mean consistent or asymptotically unbiased and thus are thinking about large sample properties.[2]

---

1 A subtle case where this assumption is violated is one where the value of a particular explanatory variable is equal to 1 for only a very small (and fixed) number of observations and zero for the rest.

2 Although in many cases the two concepts are equivalent, a consistent estimator is not necessarily asymptotically unbiased, and an asymptotically unbiased estimator is not necessarily consistent. Consistency means that in large samples, the estimates will be close to the true value; asymptotically unbiased means that in large samples, the expected value of the estimator equals the true value.

In addition to the desire that an estimator is consistent or unbiased, we also care about the precision of an estimator. This is determined by the covariance matrix of the estimator, or – in the univariate case – the variance. Estimators with lower variance are more precise and are referred to as being more efficient. This means that, in repeated sampling, estimates tend to be closer to the true value. Loosely speaking, an estimator is referred to as **efficient** if it has the smallest covariance matrix among all consistent estimators, under a given set of assumptions. In most cases, this argument will be based upon asymptotic theory, and the statement is about asymptotic efficiency. In general, many choices about estimating a model will be characterised by a trade-off between efficiency and robustness. With stronger assumptions, it is often possible to derive a more accurate estimator, but this estimator may no longer be consistent if one of the assumptions is violated. Instead, it may be preferred to focus on an estimator that has a larger variance, but is robust against violations of certain assumptions. Particularly with large samples, as is common in most financial applications, robustness of an estimator is often considered more important than precision.

The asymptotic distribution of the OLS estimator is obtained by writing

$$\sqrt{N}(\hat{\beta} - \beta) = \left(\frac{1}{N} \sum_{i=1}^{N} x_i x_i' \right)^{-1} \left(\frac{1}{\sqrt{N}} \sum_{i=1}^{N} x_i \varepsilon_i \right). \tag{2.14}$$

Assuming that the equation's error terms ε_i are independently and identically distributed with mean zero and variance σ^2, it can be shown that the asymptotic distribution of the OLS estimator, under weak regularity conditions, is given by

$$\sqrt{N}(\hat{\beta} - \beta) \rightarrow N(0, \sigma^2 \Sigma_{xx}^{-1}), \tag{2.15}$$

where $\rightarrow$ means "is asymptotically distributed as". This says that, scaled by the square root of the sample size N, the OLS estimator for β minus the true value has an asymptotic normal distribution with mean zero and covariance matrix $\sigma^2 \Sigma_{xx}^{-1}$. More formally, in addition to Assumptions EXO2 and R1 (ols-cs), the two key assumptions for this are

Assumption ED1 (ols-cs) : $E(\varepsilon_i \varepsilon_j \mid x_1, \ldots, x_N) = 0$ for $i \neq j$, $\quad$ (2.16)

Assumption ED2 (ols-cs) : $E(\varepsilon_i^2 \mid x_1, \ldots, x_N) = \sigma^2 < \infty$. $\quad$ (2.17)

Assumptions labelled ED impose restrictions on the error distribution and typically relate to (the absence of) serial correlation and (the absence of) heteroskedasticity. Assumption ED2 imposes **homoskedasticity** and says that the variance of the equation's error term is finite and does not depend upon any of the explanatory variables. Homoskedasticity is a strong assumption, which is often violated in financial applications. We discuss the problem of heteroskedasticity, when Assumption ED2 is violated, in the next subsection. Assumption ED1 (**no cross-correlations**) effectively requires that there are no common components in the error terms. Oftentimes these two assumptions are formulated with the conditioning set omitted, which makes them easier to interpret. Assumption ED1 then simply says that two different error terms should not be correlated. With cross-sectional data, Assumption ED1 is often satisfied. An exception is when there are common components in the error term of the equation that affect groups of observations similarly, for example, firms in the same industry in combination with unobservable industry-specific effects (that are not controlled for in x_i). Another exception is the existence of spatial correlation, where firms located close to each other are subject to correlated shocks.

The result in (2.15) implies that, in finite samples, the OLS estimator $\hat{\beta}$ approximately has a normal distribution (where the approximation error becomes smaller when the sample size increases) with mean β. Its variance-covariance matrix can be estimated as

$$\hat{V}(\hat{\beta}) = \hat{\sigma}^2 \left(\sum_{i=1}^{N} x_i x_i' \right)^{-1}, \tag{2.18}$$

where $\hat{\sigma}^2$ is a consistent estimator for σ^2 given by

$$\hat{\sigma}^2 = \frac{1}{N} \sum_{i=1}^{N} \hat{\varepsilon}_i^2, \tag{2.19}$$

and where $\hat{\varepsilon}_i$ is the OLS residual, as before. Alternatively, σ^2 can be estimated by the sum of squared residuals scaled by the number of observations minus the number of parameters. That is,

$$s^2 = \frac{1}{N-K} \sum_{i=1}^{N} \hat{\varepsilon}_i^2 \tag{2.20}$$

This provides an unbiased estimator of σ^2 under relatively weak assumptions. The square root of the diagonal elements in the estimated covariance matrix provide the **standard errors** for $\hat{\beta}$, which are important for hypothesis testing and, more broadly, to judge the precision of the estimator. Where needed, we shall denote the standard error of the estimator $\hat{\beta}_k$ by $\mathrm{se}(\hat{\beta}_k)$.

2.1.2 Heteroskedasticity

Heteroskedasticity is a common problem in models using financial data. It means that the variance of the disturbance term ε_i is not constant across all observations (and depends upon x_i). For example, it is very common that large firms have more variation in their characteristics than do small firms and therefore also have a larger error variance. In this case, the variance of ε_i depends upon firm size (and potentially some other firm characteristics). Similarly, the variation of the unexplained component in financial returns (idiosyncratic volatility) may vary across assets. The presence of heteroskedasticity in a linear model does not affect unbiasedness or consistency of the

OLS estimator, as long as Assumption EXO1 or EXO3 are satisfied. It does, however, invalidate the routinely estimated covariance matrix of $\hat{\beta}$ in (2.18), including routinely provided standard errors. It also means that a more efficient estimator for β could exist, for example, a weighted least squares (WLS) estimator.

The appropriate covariance matrix for the OLS estimator in case of heteroskedasticity can be derived from (2.14). Following White (1980), it can be estimated as

$$\hat{V}(\hat{\beta}) = \left(\sum_{i=1}^{N} x_i x_i' \right)^{-1} \left(\sum_{i=1}^{N} \hat{\varepsilon}_i^2 x_i x_i' \right) \left(\sum_{i=1}^{N} x_i x_i' \right)^{-1}, \tag{2.21}$$

which provides a consistent estimator for the OLS covariance matrix in the presence of arbitrary forms of heteroskedasticity. Standard errors based on (2.21) are referred to as **heteroskedasticity-consistent standard errors** (HCSE), or simply White standard errors, and are readily available in modern regression software. Although they could also just be referred to as "robust standard errors" it is recommended to be explicit about what they are robust against. The expression in (2.21) is a special case of a so-called sandwich estimator, where the matrix in the middle is sandwiched between the inverse of two identical matrices. Their use is very common, because they also provide appropriate (asymptotic) standard errors in the presence of little or no heteroskedasticity, and there is little reason to not use them (unless the sample is very small and heteroskedasticity is likely to be weak). In the vast majority of cases, the HCSE are larger than the routinely calculated ones.

Similar to the fact that, in small samples, $\hat{\sigma}^2$ tends to underestimate σ^2 in the homoskedastic case, the White covariance matrix estimator (HC0) tends to underestimate the true covariance matrix in finite samples. Several small sample adjustments to (2.21) have been proposed that are suggested to have better small sample properties (see Davidson and MacKinnon, 2004, Section 5.5, or Angrist and Pischke, 2009, Chapter 8). A popular one (HC1), which is the default in Stata, involves a simple degrees of freedom correction and multiplies the expression in (2.21) by $N/(N - K)$. Despite this adjustment, the calculation of HCSE relies on asymptotic properties, and their performance in very small samples may not be very accurate (see MacKinnon and White, 1985). In financial applications, this is rarely an issue.

White (1980) also provides a specification test based on a comparison of the estimated covariance matrices with and without allowing for heteroskedasticity. When (2.18) and (2.21) are very different, this indicates the presence of heteroskedasticity or some other form of model misspecification (see, e. g., Wooldridge, 2010, Chapter 6, or Verbeek, 2017, Chapter 4).

2.1.3 Hypothesis testing

To test a set of linear restrictions on the model coefficients, the most common approach is to use a Wald test. We write the set of q linearly independent restrictions as

$$H_0 : R\beta = r$$

with the alternative that at least one restriction is violated. Here, R denotes a $q \times K$ matrix of constants, and r a q-dimensional vector of constants. For example, if we wish to test that $\beta_2 = 0$ and $\beta_3 = 0$, we have

$$R = \begin{pmatrix} 0 & 1 & 0 & \cdots \\ 0 & 0 & 1 & \cdots \end{pmatrix}$$

and $r = (0,0)'$. The Wald test statistic is given by a quadratic form in $R\hat{\beta} - r$, weighted by the inverse of the corresponding estimated covariance matrix. That is,

$$\xi_W = (R\hat{\beta} - r)'[R\hat{V}(\hat{\beta})R']^{-1}(R\hat{\beta} - r). \tag{2.22}$$

Under the null hypothesis, ξ_W has an asymptotic Chi-square distribution with q degrees of freedom. Thus, large values of ξ_W lead to rejection of the null hypothesis.

In empirical work we often see the F-test for testing linear restrictions. Its test statistic is simply

$$F = \xi_W/q,$$

and its distribution, under the null hypothesis, is an F-distribution with q and $N - K$ degrees of freedom. This distributional result is exact in finite samples under the strong set of assumptions EXO1, ED1, ED2, and the additional assumption that the error terms in the model are normal, that is,

Assumption ED3 (ols-cs) : ε_i has a normal distribution. $\qquad$ (2.23)

This requires the use of the covariance matrix in (2.18) in combination with the estimate s^2 for σ^2 in (2.20). Under more general conditions, it is possible that the F-distribution provides a better approximation to the small sample distribution of the test statistic than the Chi-square distribution. The expression in (2.22) is generally valid, the asymptotic distribution under the null hypothesis being Chi-square, on the condition that the covariance matrix is estimated consistently.

If attention is focused on one linear restriction, it is more common to consider the t-statistic. For the simple restriction $\beta_k = r$, it is given by

$$t = \frac{\hat{\beta}_k - r}{se(\hat{\beta}_k)}, \tag{2.24}$$

where $se(\hat{\beta}_k)$ is the relevant standard error, obtained as the square root of the (k, k)-element in the appropriately estimated covariance matrix. Under the null hypothesis, the test statistic has an asymptotic standard normal distribution, provided the standard error is estimated consistently. Under the strong set of assumptions EXO1, ED1, ED2 and ED3, the test statistic t follows an exact t-distribution with $N - K$ degrees of freedom. For large N, this distribution collapses to a standard normal one. For realistic sample sizes, the differences between the normal and t-distributions are small. As a rule of thumb, at the 95% confidence level, the null hypothesis is rejected if $|t| > 1.96$ (based on the standard normal approximation) or $|t| > 2$ (formally corresponding to a t-distribution with around 60 degrees of freedom, but often used as a simple approximation for any sample size).

p-values and p-hacking

Most modern software provides p-values with any test that is done. A p-value denotes the probability, under the null hypothesis, to find the reported value of the test statistic or a more extreme one. If the p-value is smaller than the significance level (e. g., 5%), the null hypothesis is rejected. Checking p-values allows researchers to draw their conclusions without consulting the appropriate critical values, making them a convenient piece of information. It also shows the sensitivity of the decision to reject the null hypothesis with respect to the choice of significance level. However, p-values are often misinterpreted or misused, as stressed by a recent statement of the American Statistical Association (Wasserstein and Lazar, 2016). For example, it is inappropriate (though a common mistake) to interpret a p-value as giving the probability that the null hypothesis is true.

Unfortunately, in empirical work some researchers are overly obsessed with obtaining "significant" results and finding p-values smaller than 0.05 (and this also extends to journal editors). If publication decisions depend on the statistical significance of research findings, the literature as a whole will overstate the size of the true effect. This is referred to as publication bias (or "file drawer" bias). For example, investigating more than 50,000 tests published in three leading economic journals, Brodeur et al. (2016) conclude that the distribution of p-values indicates both selection by journals as well as a tendency of researchers to inflate the value of almost-rejected tests by choosing slightly more "significant" specifications. Their analysis is extended in Brodeur et al. (2020), with a focus on inference methods used in causal analysis.

The problem of publication bias relates to the broader problem of p-hacking. Even if the null hypothesis is correct, there is always a small probability of rejecting it (corresponding to the size of the test). Such type I errors are rather likely to happen if we use a sequence of many tests to select the regressors to include in the model. This process is referred to as data snooping, data mining or p-hacking (see Leamer, 1978; Lovell, 1983). As a result, an extensive specification search may pick up accidental patterns in the data and deliver a seemingly "significant" result with no genuine interpretation or meaning. This problem is potentially a serious issue in empirical finance, where many scholars are using the same databases (such as the Center for Research in Security Prices (CRSP) and Compustat). For example, Lo and MacKinlay (1990) analyse data snooping biases in tests of financial asset pricing models, while Sullivan et al. (2001) analyse the extent to which the presence of calendar effects in stock returns can be attributed to data snooping. Harvey et al. (2016) provide a critical account of the literature on factor models explaining the cross-section of asset returns. To accommodate for the inherent data mining, they suggest that a new factor needs to clear a much higher hurdle, with a t-statistic greater than 3.0. However, as argued by Harvey (2017), simply raising the threshold for significance is insufficient, and may unintendedly increase the amount of data mining and, in turn, publication bias. Recently, Mitton (2021) documents large variation in empirical methodology in corporate finance regressions in top finance journals, enabling selective reporting that results from p-hacking and publication bias.

2.2 The linear regression model with time-series data

With time-series data it is common to index the observations by a suffix t, denoting a time period (or a moment in time), and to consider a sample for $1, \ldots, T$. In comparison with cross-sectional data there are two important differences. First, the observations have a natural ordering in the sense that period 1 comes before period 2. Second, strictly speaking it hard to think of a time-series being a random sample from a large population of time periods. Instead, we think of the sample as one possible realisation of the process that generates the data. This is a subtle difference. A key implication of this is that we need to think carefully about asymptotic theory. With time-series data, asymptotic theory asks the question what happens – hypothetically – to the properties of our available data if we continue expanding the sample into the future (or into the past). Depending upon how the data are generated, their long-run properties could be quite different from their short-run ones. For example, if $x_t = t$ it is clear that its sample average increases with every additional observation and that there is no long-run mean around which the data fluctuate.

The linear regression model with time-series data can be written as

$$y_t = x_t' \beta + \varepsilon_t, \quad t = 1, \ldots, T. \tag{2.25}$$

Building upon the results of the cross-sectional case, unbiasedness of the OLS estimator requires

Assumption EXO1 (ols-ts) : $E(\varepsilon_t \mid x_1, \ldots, x_T) = 0.$ $\qquad$ (2.26)

This says that the expected value of the error term, conditional upon the value of the explanatory variables of *all* periods, is equal to zero. If this is satisfied we call the explanatory variables **strictly exogenous.** Compared to cross-sectional data, this assumption is much more a concern with time-series data. For example, if lagged realisations of y_t affect the value of one or more of the regressors in x_t, Assumption EXO1 (ols-ts) will be violated. An important situation where this occurs is when the model contains a lagged dependent variable y_{t-1} on the right-hand side.

The weaker assumption that ε_t is conditionally mean independent of x_t, is given by

$$\textbf{Assumption EXO2 (ols-ts)} : E(\varepsilon_t \mid x_t) = 0 \qquad (2.27)$$

and is actually substantially weaker than EXO1 in the context of time-series data. It only requires that the explanatory variables are **contemporaneously exogenous.** Including a lagged dependent variable in x_t may still satisfy Assumption EXO2 (ols-ts) and lead to a consistent estimator. Unfortunately, Assumption EXO2 (ols-ts) is insufficient to guarantee that the OLS estimator for β is unbiased. Similar to our conditions before, consistency of the OLS estimator requires

$$\textbf{Assumption EXO3 (ols-ts)} : E(x_t \varepsilon_t) = 0, \qquad (2.28)$$

which says that the error terms are mean zero (assuming x_t includes an intercept) and contemporaneously uncorrelated with the explanatory variables. The additional regularity condition in Assumption R1 is now written as

$$\textbf{Assumption R1 (ols-ts)} : \plim_{T \to \infty} \frac{1}{T} \sum_{t=1}^{T} x_t x_t' = E(x_t x_t') = \Sigma_{xx} \text{ has rank } K. \qquad (2.29)$$

Again, this is less trivial than in the cross-sectional case, because it essentially requires that the data are (weakly) stationary. A time-series variable is weakly stationary if the first and second moments of its distribution (mean, variances and autocovariances) do not depend upon time. Additional regularity conditions are typically required, mostly related to the degree of dependence that is allowed between different observations (see, e. g., Hamilton, 1994; Pesaran, 2015). Loosely speaking, this requires that any dependence between ε_t and ε_{t-h} disappears if h becomes very large, that is, if observations are increasingly far from each other.

The key assumptions to derive the (asymptotic) covariance matrix and asymptotic distribution of the OLS estimator $\hat{\beta}$ are similar to those in the cross-sectional case. That is,

$$\textbf{Assumption ED1 (ols-ts)} : E(\varepsilon_t \varepsilon_s \mid x_1, \ldots, x_T) = 0 \text{ for } t \neq s, \qquad (2.30)$$

and

$$\textbf{Assumption ED2 (ols-ts)} : E(\varepsilon_t^2 \mid x_1, \ldots, x_T) = \sigma^2 < \infty. \qquad (2.31)$$

Assumption ED1 (ols-ts) implies that $E(\varepsilon_t\varepsilon_s) = 0$ for $t \neq s$ and requires that there is no **serial correlation** (or autocorrelation) in the equation's error term. With time-series data, this assumption is often violated. It imposes, among other things, that the unobservables that affect the outcome in period t are uncorrelated with the unobservables that affect the outcome one period later. Oftentimes, autocorrelation arises due to model misspecification, for example, omitted variables, incomplete dynamics or the wrong functional form (see, e. g., Verbeek, 2017, Chapter 4). Testing for autocorrelation is standard practice in most time-series models.

Under Assumption EXO3, ED1 and ED2, and several regularity conditions, including R1, the asymptotic distribution of $\hat{\beta}$ is again normal with a covariance matrix that can be estimated similarly to (2.18). With Assumption ED2 dropped, we allow for heteroskedasticity and the appropriate covariance matrix can be estimated as in (2.21). It is also possible to relax assumption ED1 to allow for limited forms of autocorrelation in ε_t when estimating the covariance matrix of the OLS estimator. If we can assume that the autocorrelation is restricted to L periods, that is, if $E(\varepsilon_t\varepsilon_{t-h}) = 0$ if $h > L$, the covariance matrix of the OLS estimator can be estimated as

$$\hat{V}\{\hat{\beta}\} = \left(\sum_{t=1}^{T} x_t x_t'\right)^{-1} B \left(\sum_{t=1}^{T} x_t x_t'\right)^{-1}, \tag{2.32}$$

where B is a $K \times K$ matrix given by

$$B = \sum_{t=1}^{T} \hat{\varepsilon}_t^2 x_t x_t' + \sum_{j=1}^{L} w_j \sum_{s=j+1}^{T} \hat{\varepsilon}_s \hat{\varepsilon}_{s-j}(x_s x_{s-j}' + x_{s-j} x_s'), \tag{2.33}$$

where w_j are known weights, often referred to as the kernel or lag window. Hansen and Hodrick (1980) propose to estimate the covariance matrix with a uniform kernel ($w_j = 1$), which is appropriate if L is small relative to the sample size and the error terms follow a moving average structure of known order. In general, however, there is no guarantee that the estimated covariance matrix is positive definite. To prevent this, it is common to use Bartlett weights (Newey and West, 1987) which decrease linearly with j according to

$$w_j = 1 - j/(L + 1).$$

The use of such weights is compatible with the idea that the impact of the autocorrelation of order j diminishes with $|j|$. Clearly, if all $w_j = 0$ we obtain the White covariance matrix in (2.21).

The covariance matrix in (2.32) allows researchers to determine **heteroskedasticity-and-autocorrelation consistent standard errors** (HAC standard errors) for the OLS estimator that allow for heteroskedasticity of unknown form as well as serial correlation up to a limited lag length. This is available in Stata in *newey* with the option *lag(L)*. The choice of L, often referred to as the bandwidth (or window size), can be done manually if the maximum lag length over which autocorrelation is likely to exist is more or less known (e. g., in the case of overlapping data with moving average error terms, see Hansen and Hodrick, 1980 or Fama and French, 1988), or can be chosen as a function of the sample size (theoretically allowing L to grow with T as the sample size increases). Common choices are to set L equal to the smallest integer larger than or equal to $T^{1/3}$ or $T^{1/4}$, but there are also automatic bandwidth selection procedures (e. g., Newey and West, 1994; Sun et al., 2008).

2.3 Introducing panel data

With panel data, our base data have two different dimensions. For example, we may have quarterly accounting data of publicly listed firms, or monthly returns on all stocks traded at the New York Stock Exchange (NYSE). As before, we index the cross-sectional units by $i = 1, \dots, N$, and the time periods by $t = 1, \dots, T$. The econometrics literature on panel data has broadly developed into different streams depending upon the relative sizes of these two dimensions. The case where N is small and T is large has much of its roots in the time-series literature, and an excellent treatment is provided in Pesaran (2015). In contrast, the literature with large N and (relatively) small T is strongly rooted in the micro-econometrics literature analysing, for example, household or firm behaviour. Cameron and Trivedi (2005) and Wooldridge (2010) are leading textbooks in this area. In comparison with cross-sectional data sets, the availability of panel data has several advantages in this setting (Hsiao, 2014, Chapter 1). First of all, panel data sets typically have larger samples and exploit variation across both individual units and time. This improves efficiency of estimators and eases identification. For example, when modelling we can make comparisons along one dimension (e. g., time) keeping the other dimension fixed. This allows us to model dynamics at the firm level or to control for time-invariant unobservables in the model. At the same time, the availability of panel data introduces some important issues to worry about, most notably cross-correlations and parameter heterogeneity, both of which can have important consequences for the properties of our estimators, particularly so in dynamic models and nonlinear models.

While standard panel models involve two dimensions, it is increasingly the case that finance scholars employ models where the data have even more dimensions. For example, one may wish to analyse quarterly stock holdings data for mutual funds across multiple countries (e. g., Dyakov et al., 2020), or the characteristics of multiple loans per firm per year (e. g., Lou and Otto, 2020). Examples with four of five different dimensions are given in Bertrand and Mullainathan (2003), who investigate plant-level and firm-level data over time across different states of location and states of incorporation, and Gormley and Matsa (2016), who match information on target firms and acquiring firms and distinguish states of location, states of incorporation, as well as industries. In an asset pricing context, aggregating individual assets into portfolios is a way to reduce noise and to reduce one of the dimensions in the data. We illustrate this in Subsection 2.3.2.

2.3.1 Parameter heterogeneity

If the number of time-series observations per unit is sufficiently large, it is possible to specify and estimate a linear regression model for each unit separately. This corresponds to a linear model of the form

$$y_{it} = x'_{it}\beta_i + \varepsilon_{it}, \quad i = 1,\ldots,N; \quad t = 1,\ldots,T, \tag{2.34}$$

where β_i is a K-dimensional vector of unknown coefficients that it is specific to unit i. If no further restrictions are imposed upon β_i, the model in (2.34) can be estimated separately for each i, using observations over $t = 1,\ldots,T$. For small N, it is also possible to estimate the model as a system of seemingly unrelated regressions (SUR).

In the SUR model, the N different equations are estimated as a system allowing the error terms to be correlated across equations. In this case, this means that ε_{it} may be correlated within periods across units. The $N \times N$ covariance matrix of the stacked vector of error terms $(\varepsilon_{1t},\ldots,\varepsilon_{Nt})'$ is given by Ω, where the (i,j)-th element is given by

$$\mathrm{cov}(\varepsilon_{it}, \varepsilon_{jt}) = \omega_{ij}.$$

This assumes homoskedasticity over time and no serial correlation. The estimator is a feasible generalised least squares (FGLS) estimator, where the covariance matrix of the N different error terms is estimated in a first step from the per-equation OLS residuals as

$$\hat{\omega}_{ij} = \frac{1}{T-K} \sum_{t=1}^{T} \hat{\varepsilon}_{it}\hat{\varepsilon}_{jt},$$

noting that different choices can be made regarding the degrees of freedom correction. In the second step, feasible GLS is applied to the entire system using the estimated covariance matrix. Under the above assumptions, the SUR estimator is more efficient than OLS, but it can be shown to be identical to the equation-by-equation OLS estimator if either all correlations across equations are zero, or if the explanatory variables are identical across equations, that is, if $x_{it} = x_t$. Estimation as a system has the advantage that one can directly test restrictions on the coefficients across the different equations. A special case of this arises when one wishes to test whether the intercept term in each of the equations is equal to zero, which is relevant in testing (factor-based) asset pricing models. In Stata, the SUR estimator is implemented in *sureg*. An alternative is to use *suest*, which provides a covariance matrix that is robust to arbitrary cross-equation correlation, after each equation is estimated separately.

A restricted model arises if we impose homogenous coefficients, that is, $\beta_i = \beta$ for each i. This restriction can be tested using an F-test or Chi-square test. In the simplest case where the error terms are uncorrelated across equations, this is a generalisation of the Chow test for structural change. Baltagi (2013, Chapter 4) provides more discussion and a more general version of this test for poolability (allowing for a non-diagonal Ω).

Rather than estimating a separate set of coefficients for each unit, it is also possible to impose a so-called random coefficients assumption. In this case, it is assumed that the coefficients β_i are drawn from a distribution with mean vector β. Denoting this as

$$\beta_i = \beta + v_i,$$

where v_i is a zero-mean random vector, we can write the model as

$$y_{it} = x'_{it}\beta + (x'_{it}v_i + \varepsilon_{it}), \quad i = 1,\ldots,N; \quad t = 1,\ldots,T. \tag{2.35}$$

As long as v_i (and ε_{it}) are independent of x_{it}, this can be estimated using a pooled OLS estimator, which will provide a consistent estimator for the (average) coefficient vector β. Feasible GLS can exploit the specific structure of the covariance matrix of $x'_{it}v_i + \varepsilon_{it}$; see Cameron and Trivedi (2005, Chapter 22) for more details and variations within the class of mixed linear models. Hsiao (2014, Chapter 6) provides an extensive discussion of variable coefficient models. In Section 2.6 we will discuss a special case, where all coefficients, except the intercept term, are assumed to be identical across units. This is known as the random effects model.

2.3.2 Illustration: testing an asset pricing model

Empirical asset pricing models are often formulated as factor models, where the excess returns to an asset are related to the excess returns on one or more factors (Cochrane, 2005). The CAPM implies that there is one factor driving asset returns, namely the return on the market portfolio. In equilibrium, assets that covary strongly with the market should provide higher returns, on average. The three-factor model of Fama and French (1993) adds a size factor and a value factor to the CAPM and has been very influential in empirical work, often complemented with a momentum factor. A wide variety of empirical factor-based models have been proposed since. In general terms, a factor asset pricing model can be written as

$$y_{it} = \beta_{i1} + \beta_{i2}x_{2t} + \cdots + \beta_{iK}x_{Kt} + \varepsilon_{it} = x'_t\beta_i + \varepsilon_{it}, \tag{2.36}$$

where y_{it} denotes the excess return in period t on asset i, x_{kt} denotes the excess return on a factor-mimicking portfolio ($k = 2,\ldots,K$), and β_i is a K-dimensional vector of coefficients. In this context, the intercept term is typically denoted as "alpha" (α_i) rather

than "beta", but we will not follow this convention here. The factor model provides
a valid asset pricing model if the intercept term is zero for every individual asset or
investable portfolio i.

Estimation of the parameters in (2.36) can be done by OLS, separately for each
asset i. Because the dependent variable is an excess return, which exhibits little or no
autocorrelation, a typical assumption is that ε_{it} is not correlated over time for a given i
(Assumption ED1 (ols-ts)). The variance of ε_{it} can be assumed to be constant over time
(but potentially different for each asset i), or can be allowed to be heteroskedastic. The
latter is more important when analysing returns at higher frequencies, for example,
daily returns. To test the validity of the asset pricing model we need to test whether
$\beta_{i1} = 0$. For a single i this can be based upon the t-statistic, given by

$$ t_i = \frac{\hat{\beta}_{i1}}{\text{se}(\hat{\beta}_{i1})}, \tag{2.37} $$

where $\text{se}(\hat{\beta}_{i1})$ denotes the standard error of $\hat{\beta}_{i1}$ based on (2.18), or – allowing for heteroskedasticity – on (2.21).

Typically, asset pricing tests like this are not performed on individual assets but
on cleverly constructed portfolios. For example, Gibbons et al. (1989) use stock portfolios sorted on size, industry and stock-level beta, and Fama and French (1993) use
portfolios based on firm size and book-to-market ratios. In case of N portfolios of assets, the null hypothesis corresponds to $\beta_{11} = \cdots = \beta_{N1} = 0$, which involves the N
intercept terms of the portfolio regressions. Instead of estimating the N equations in
(2.36) equation by equation by means of OLS, we can also treat them as a system of
equations and estimate them as a SUR model, which takes into account the cross-
correlations between ε_{it} and ε_{jt}. Due to such correlations between different assets, the
estimators for the intercept terms $\hat{\beta}_{i1}$ are not independent and the joint test should take
this into account. Because the regressors are identical across equations, the SUR estimator for each vector β_i is identical to those obtained by applying the OLS estimator
per equation. Nevertheless, the cross-correlations matter for the joint test. Gibbons
et al. (1989) show how the standard F-test for $\beta_{11} = \cdots = \beta_{N1} = 0$ can be rewritten
and interpreted graphically. This test, typically referred to as the Gibbons, Ross and
Shanken or **GRS test**, assumes normal error terms and is commonly used to test the
validity of a factor-based asset pricing model on the basis of a set of time-series regressions like (2.36). An alternative Chi-square version does not impose normality, but is
only asymptotically valid. The Stata routine *grstest2* provides a quick way to obtain
the GRS test and some related statistics.

Although the example of the asset pricing model is based on a set of N time-series
regressions, it illustrates the potential richness of panel data and having two dimensions of data. Writing a model as a set of equations allows all coefficients in the model
to vary per asset i, and the estimation is done using a relatively long time-series. Asset

pricing models are also put to test based on "cross-sectional regressions", where either factor exposures (β_i) or asset characteristics (e. g., size, book-to-market ratio) are
used as explanatory variables to explain asset returns. We discuss this in Section 2.12.

2.4 The linear regression model with panel data

In the asset pricing example above, it obviously does not make sense to impose that
all model coefficients in β_i are identical across i. In many other contexts, it can be
perfectly fine to impose that $\beta_i = \beta$ for each i. In this case we can write a standard
linear regression model for panel data as

$$y_{it} = \beta_1 + \beta_2 x_{2,it} + \cdots \beta_K x_{K,it} + \varepsilon_{it}, \tag{2.38}$$

where y_{it} denotes the value of the dependent variable for firm i in period t, and where
ε_{it} denotes the disturbance term. Some explanatory variables may be constant over
time and vary only between cross-sectional units (e. g., the industry a firm operates
in), while others may vary only over time (e. g., variables reflecting macro-economic
conditions). When relevant, we will stress this in the notation by dropping the irrelevant suffix. Compared to the illustration above we now impose that all model coefficients are identical across units.

This linear regression model can be written as

$$y_{it} = x_{it}'\beta + \varepsilon_{it}, \quad i = 1,\ldots,N; \quad t = 1,\ldots,T, \tag{2.39}$$

where T denotes the number of time periods, and N denotes the number of firms. For
notational simplicity we shall typically assume our panel is balanced, in the sense
that all variables are observed for each firm i in each period t. Extensions to the more
relevant case of unbalanced data are often straightforward, albeit that the notation is
more cumbersome.[3] The OLS estimator for β in this case is given by

$$\hat{\beta} = \left(\sum_{i=1}^{N}\sum_{t=1}^{T} x_{it}x_{it}'\right)^{-1} \sum_{i=1}^{N}\sum_{t=1}^{T} x_{it}y_{it}. \tag{2.40}$$

This estimator, often referred to as the **pooled OLS estimator** is simply based on pooling all observations and applying a standard least squares approach. It does not exploit the panel nature of the data, and standard errors would typically have to be adjusted to allow for cross-correlations or heteroskedasticity in ε_{it}. As before, we can
write the OLS estimator as

$$\hat{\beta} = \beta + \left(\sum_{i=1}^{N}\sum_{t=1}^{T} x_{it}x_{it}'\right)^{-1} \sum_{i=1}^{N}\sum_{t=1}^{T} x_{it}\varepsilon_{it}. \tag{2.41}$$

---

3 An exception is the case with non-randomly missing data. We discuss this issue in Section 4.3.

That is, the OLS estimator equals the true value plus an estimation error. Unbiasedness of the OLS estimator, that is, $E(\hat{\beta}) = \beta$, requires that the expected value of the second term on the righthand side is equal to zero. This is obtained if

Assumption EXO1 (ols-p) : $E(\varepsilon_{it} \mid x_{js}, j = 1, \ldots, N, s = 1, \ldots, T) = 0.$ (2.42)

This says that the equation error term has a zero conditional mean, where we condition upon all explanatory variables across the entire sample. This assumption obviously excludes the inclusion of a lagged dependent variable in the model or any other type of feedback relationship between x_{it} and $\varepsilon_{i,t-j}$, for example, a situation where the previous value $y_{i,t-1}$, say firm performance in year $t-1$, affects some firm characteristics in the explanatory variables in year t (e. g., the CEO's compensation contract). To allow for the presence of a lagged dependent variable on the right-hand side of the equation, we can relax assumption EXO1 (ols-p) to

Assumption EXO2 (ols-p) : $E(\varepsilon_{it} \mid x_{it}) = 0,$ (2.43)

which is similar to EXO2 (ols-cs) and EXO2 (ols-ts). This does not lead to an unbiased estimator.

When we investigate asymptotic properties, we need to realise that with panel data there are at least two dimensions of the data: the number of firms N and the number of periods T. Unless indicated otherwise, we focus on the case where N is large relative to T and we employ asymptotic theory for $N \to \infty$. This is the most common situation in corporate finance applications. To appreciate this, let us rewrite (2.41) as

$$\hat{\beta} = \beta + \left(\frac{1}{NT} \sum_{i=1}^{N} \sum_{t=1}^{T} x_{it} x_{it}' \right)^{-1} \frac{1}{NT} \sum_{i=1}^{N} \sum_{t=1}^{T} x_{it} \varepsilon_{it}.$$ (2.44)

Under the assumption that

$$\text{plim}_{N \to \infty} \left(\frac{1}{NT} \sum_{i=1}^{N} \sum_{t=1}^{T} x_{it} x_{it}' \right)$$ (2.45)

is finite and invertible, the OLS estimator $\hat{\beta}$ is consistent if

$$\text{plim}_{N \to \infty} \frac{1}{NT} \sum_{i=1}^{N} \sum_{t=1}^{T} x_{it} \varepsilon_{it} = \frac{1}{T} \sum_{t=1}^{T} E(x_{it} \varepsilon_{it}) = 0.$$ (2.46)

This requires that the equation's error term is mean zero and uncorrelated with each of the regressors in each period t (or, on average, across all periods). For later use, let us summarise the assumption explicitly.

Assumption EXO3 (ols-p) : $E(x_{it} \varepsilon_{it}) = 0, \ t = 1, \ldots, T.$ (2.47)

Even though this exogeneity assumption is much weaker than EXO1 and EXO2, it is still a strong assumption and in many applications it is likely to be violated. For example, unobservable firm-specific characteristics may affect both the dependent variable as well as one or more of the explanatory variables. We return to such cases below.

Under weak regularity conditions, the OLS estimator has an asymptotic normal distribution, as before. To determine the appropriate covariance matrix we again need to make assumptions about the error terms relating to the presence or absence of heteroskedasticity and autocorrelation. Imposing

Assumption ED1 (ols-p) : $E(\varepsilon_{it}\varepsilon_{js} \mid x_{i1},\ldots,x_{NT}) = 0$ for $t \neq s, i \neq j$ (2.48)

allows for heteroskedasticity of unknown form, but does not allow for any correlation between the disturbance terms across firms or periods. Under this assumption, the covariance matrix can be estimated following White (1980), as before

$$\hat{V}\{\hat{\beta}\} = \left(\sum_{i=1}^{N}\sum_{t=1}^{T}x_{it}x_{it}'\right)^{-1}\sum_{i=1}^{N}\sum_{t=1}^{T}\hat{\varepsilon}_{it}^2 x_{it}x_{it}'\left(\sum_{i=1}^{N}\sum_{t=1}^{T}x_{it}x_{it}'\right)^{-1},$$ (2.49)

again with the possibility of applying small sample corrections. Given the nature of financial panel data it is highly unlikely that Assumption ED1 is satisfied. For example, it is quite likely that unobservables affecting a firm's capital structure or dividend policy are persistent over time. Similarly, returns on different stocks tend to be correlated cross-sectionally, due to, for example, overall market movements or industry-specific effects. This invalidates heteroskedasticity-robust standard errors. As a result, standard errors for panel data estimators typically need to account for the panel nature of the data. Depending upon assumptions, this can lead to a variety of different standard errors (Petersen, 2009). A common choice is to employ **panel-robust standard errors**, where the errors terms are allowed to be correlated within a firm, in combination with arbitrary forms of heteroskedasticity. That is, we impose

Assumption ED2 (ols-p) : $E(\varepsilon_{it}\varepsilon_{js} \mid x_{i1},\ldots,x_{NT}) = 0$ for $i \neq j$, (2.50)

while allowing ε_{it} and ε_{is} to have a nonzero correlation. We also do not impose homoskedasticity across firms or time. Under these assumptions, the covariance matrix of the OLS estimator can be estimated as

$$\hat{V}\{\hat{\beta}\} = \left(\sum_{i=1}^{N}\sum_{t=1}^{T}x_{it}x_{it}'\right)^{-1}\sum_{i=1}^{N}\sum_{t=1}^{T}\sum_{s=1}^{T}\hat{\varepsilon}_{it}\hat{\varepsilon}_{is}x_{it}x_{is}'\left(\sum_{i=1}^{N}\sum_{t=1}^{T}x_{it}x_{it}'\right)^{-1},$$ (2.51)

where, as before, $\hat{\varepsilon}_{it}$ denotes the OLS residual. This estimator is similar to the HAC covariance matrix in (2.32); the use of Bartlett weights is unnecessary, given the fixed number of time periods T. This covariance matrix allows for arbitrary forms of heteroskedasticity as well as arbitrary autocorrelation within each firm i. Hansen (2007) shows that the robust covariance matrix estimator in (2.51) is also consistent when both N and T go to infinity. However, when N is fixed and T goes to infinity, the estimator is inconsistent, as it converges to a random variable.

Another variant to accommodate serial correlation in the error terms of the same firm is to generalise the Newey-West approach in (2.33) to panel data (Petersen, 2009). The maximum lag length in this case is one less than the maximum number of periods for a firm. Fixing the maximum lag at L, the central matrix in the covariance matrix becomes (Vogelsang, 2012)

$$B = \sum_{i=1}^{N} \sum_{t=1}^{T} \sum_{s=1}^{T} w_{ts} \hat{\varepsilon}_{it} \hat{\varepsilon}_{is} x_{it} x_{is}', \tag{2.52}$$

where

$$w_{ts} = 1 - \frac{|s-t|}{L+1} \quad \text{if } |s-t| \leq L, \quad 0 \text{ otherwise.}$$

Compared to the clustered case in (2.51), this approach attaches a weight to the covariances that diminishes with the distance between two observations. Whereas this is a necessary step in the pure time-series case (so as to obtain a positive definite covariance matrix), it is not necessary in the panel case (with a sufficiently large number of firms/clusters). Petersen (2009) shows that the resulting Newey-West standard error estimates do not perform very well when the serial correlation in ε_{it} does not die out quickly at larger lags, for example, in the presence of a time-invariance firm-specific component in ε_{it}.

As mentioned before, covariance matrix estimators based on (2.49), (2.51) or (2.52) are often referred to as **sandwich estimators**: there are two identical pieces of "bread" on the outside and a "filling" in the middle (MacKinnon, 2019). Recently, a wide variety of covariance estimators have been proposed, based on different assumptions about the cross-correlations between different error terms and leading to a different filling. We discuss several of these in the next section.

2.5 Clustered standard errors

The panel-robust standard errors are a special case of **cluster robust standard errors** (CRSE) or clustered standard errors, which allow for arbitrary correlation within a given cluster of observations as well as heteroskedasticity of arbitrary form. Clustering standard errors has become very popular in applications where the data have more than one dimension, and panel data provide a natural situation where clustering can be very useful, so as to accommodate for correlation of error terms within the same firm or the same time period. Clustering standard errors can also be more involved, for example, when other dimensions play a role, for example, industries or countries, or when more than two dimensions characterise the data (e. g., mutual fund holdings data with stock level information, or target firms and potential acquirers followed over time).

As stressed by Cameron and Miller (2015) and others, ignoring to control for within-cluster correlation in the error terms can lead to standard errors that are several times smaller than those that do. For example, Bae and Goyal (2009, Appendix), estimating a model explaining loan spreads for a sample of loan tranches across 48 countries, show that White standard errors for pooled OLS are greatly understated compared to standard errors clustered by country. In the general case of one-dimensional clustering, we can write the covariance matrix estimate as

$$\hat{V}\{\hat{\beta}\} = \left(\sum_{i=1}^{N}\sum_{t=1}^{T} x_{it}x_{it}'\right)^{-1} \sum_{i=1}^{N}\sum_{j=1}^{N}\sum_{t=1}^{T}\sum_{s=1}^{T} I_{it,js}\hat{\varepsilon}_{it}\hat{\varepsilon}_{js}x_{it}x_{js}' \left(\sum_{i=1}^{N}\sum_{t=1}^{T} x_{it}x_{it}'\right)^{-1}, \qquad (2.53)$$

where $I_{it,js}$ denotes an indicator variable, equal to one if two observations (firm i in period t and firm j in period s) belong to the same cluster and zero otherwise (with $I_{it,it} = 1$).[4] Given a choice of clustering, standard errors based on (2.53) are referred to as **cluster robust standard errors** (CRSE), or – more precisely – cluster- and heteroskedasticity-robust standard errors. It is good practice to clearly indicate the chosen clustering. Because it is often the case that both the unobservables in the error term as well as the explanatory variables are positively correlated across observations within a cluster, the additional terms in the summation in (2.53) lead to an increase in the covariance matrix, compared to the case where the within-cluster correlation is ignored in (2.49). In general, the bias in routinely provided standard errors increases with the within-cluster correlation of the regressors, the within-cluster variation of the error terms and the number of observations in each cluster. If explanatory variables do not vary within a cluster (so their within correlation is 1), even a small correlation in the unobservables within a cluster can lead to cluster-robust standard errors that are very different from the default ones (Moulton, 1986). Occasionally, clustering could lead to lower standard errors, but this seems exceptional in most finance cases where either within-firm correlation can be expected (e. g., capital structure of firms, or their investment behaviour) or within-period correlation can be expected (e. g., aggregate shocks to asset returns), or both.

Choosing an appropriate level of clustering serves the purpose of restricting the correlation patterns that are allowed among the many error terms. Implicitly, clustering assumes that $E(\varepsilon_{it}\varepsilon_{js} \mid x_{i1},\ldots,x_{NT}) = 0$ unless observations it and js are in the same cluster. That is, any two observations that are not in the same cluster, are assumed to have zero correlation. Having completely unrestricted correlations, that is, having $I_{it,js} = 1$ for all it, js (assuming that all observations belong to one big cluster) is infeasible. In fact, it may not even be possible to consistently estimate β in this

---

4 In some versions, the indicators may be combined with weights (e. g., Newey and West, 1987).

case because the noise in the disturbance terms may not cancel out in estimation (see MacKinnon, 2019). An important requirement for the validity of clustered standard errors is that, asymptotically, the number of clusters, G, say, increases with the sample size. Effectively, this means that the number of clusters needs to be large relative to the sample size. When standard errors are clustered at the firm-level, as in (2.51), G is equal to the number of firms N and this requirement is satisfied with the usual asymptotics of N going to infinity. Effectively, when we estimate the covariance matrix based on clustering, we are taking an average across clusters. If the number of clusters is small, estimation error will be larger, and the small sample performance of clustered standard errors will be poor. In panel data with large N, most would recommend to have at least 20 to 40 clusters.

Alternatively, it is also possible to cluster standard errors by time rather than by firm. This allows for common shocks that affect all firms in the sample, while imposing independence over time. The expression for the covariance matrix is similar to (2.51), but with the roles of the cross-sectional and time dimensions switched. That is,

$$\hat{V}\{\hat{\beta}\} = \left(\sum_{i=1}^{N} \sum_{t=1}^{T} x_{it} x_{it}' \right)^{-1} \sum_{i=1}^{N} \sum_{j=1}^{N} \sum_{t=1}^{T} \hat{\varepsilon}_{it} \hat{\varepsilon}_{jt} x_{it} x_{jt}' \left(\sum_{i=1}^{N} \sum_{t=1}^{T} x_{it} x_{it}' \right)^{-1}. \tag{2.54}$$

Petersen (2009) shows that clustering over time leads to biased standard errors if the number of periods is small, for example, 10 or less. This is consistent with the general requirement that the number of clusters, in any setting, should be sufficiently large (and, asymptotically, grow with the sample size).

Double clustering

As shown by Thompson (2011) and Cameron et al. (2011), it is possible to calculate standard errors that cluster by both firm and time. The relevant estimator for the covariance matrix can be determined as the sum of (2.51) and (2.54), minus the heteroskedasticity-consistent estimator from (2.49). The latter matrix is subtracted because otherwise the diagonal elements would be counted twice in the final result. Such standard errors allow for the presence of firm effects, meaning that error terms may have arbitrary correlation across time for any given firm, as well as time effects, meaning that error terms have arbitrary correlation across firms in any given period. They do not allow for correlations across different firms across different periods, for example, persistent common shocks. Conley et al. (2018) argue that this is restrictive and find it implausible in firm-level panels that there are non-negligible correlations across firms at a point in time, within each firm over time, but no correlations between these same firms at distinct but close points in time.

Clustering standard errors by firms and time is an example of double or two-way clustering (Cameron et al., 2011). In this case, observations belong to two clusters that intersect. As a general recommendation, the number of clusters in either dimension should be sufficiently large for the double clustered standard errors to have good properties. The theoretical properties of multiway clustering are derived in MacKinnon et al. (2021b), who also propose bootstrap methods for multiway clustered data. In Stata, standard errors based on double or multiway clustering can be obtained with the function *vcemway*.

In the standard panel data case, there are two dimensions and clustering standard errors is typically either at the period level, firm level or both. However, it is possible that additional dimensions matter. For example, firms could be located in different countries, or mutual funds could be holding large numbers of stocks over multiple periods. In such cases, other levels of clustering can be chosen. It is possible that different clusters are defined in a nested or hierarchical way. For example, firms and industries or mutual funds and fund families. In such cases, the clustering should be done at the highest level of aggregation. For example, clustering by industries allows all observations within an industry to be correlated with each other. Given the requirement that the number of clusters should be sufficiently large, one should be careful to define clusters too widely. With too few clusters, the cluster-robust standard errors may not work very well.

Double clustering has become reasonably popular in recent years. For example, Diether et al. (2009b) regress individual stock short sales during day *t* on past returns, and estimate standard errors that cluster by both stock and calendar date, and Menzly and Ozbas (2010) estimate a model explaining annual return on assets (ROA) from contemporaneous market-wide ROA and ROA in related industries, employing standard errors double clustered by stock and year, or by industry and year. Other examples can be found in Barber et al. (2016), who estimate a model explaining flows to mutual funds, clustering standard errors over both funds and periods, and in Lei et al. (2018) who use firm-level data covering 24 years and 45 countries, employing standard errors clustered at the firm and period level, in a model explaining cash holdings. Often, such applications also include one or more types of fixed effects, an issue we return to below.

Another variant is to cluster on the interaction of two variables, for example, industries and periods. This would allow for uncorrelated common shocks across all firms within an industry. Note that clustering on the intersection of two variables leads to small clusters and therefore allows for a limited number of nonzero correlations. Also note that clustering standard errors on industries × periods is different than two-way clustering on both industries and periods. Similarly, clustering standard errors on the intersection of firms and periods, in a standard firm-level panel, would result in each observation being its own cluster. Effectively, this means that the standard errors only adjust for heteroskedasticity.

Although double clustering allows for correlation over time within any given firm, and correlation over firms within any given period, it does not allow for correlation over time across different firms. Driscoll and Kraay (1998) have proposed a covariance matrix estimator that allows for autocorrelation at the level of the firm and arbitrary cross-sectional correlations. In this case, the filling of the sandwich estimator is given by

$$B = \sum_{i=1}^{N} \sum_{j=1}^{N} \sum_{t=1}^{T} \sum_{s=1}^{T} w_{ts} \hat{\varepsilon}_{it} \hat{\varepsilon}_{js} x_{it} x_{js}', \tag{2.55}$$

where the maximum lag length is L and, as before,

$$w_{ts} = 1 - \frac{|s - t|}{L + 1} \quad \text{if } |s - t| \le L, \quad 0 \text{ otherwise.}$$

This approach requires large T, because it is based on asymptotics with $T \rightarrow \infty$. The resulting covariance matrix estimator (also referred to as spatial correlation consistent), is robust to general forms of cross-sectional dependence, as well as correlation over time up to lag L. For unbalanced panels some adjustments are required, see Hoechle (2007), who provides an implementation of this estimator in Stata (available in *xtscc*). The choice of the maximum lag L is, in principle, up to the researcher. If the error terms are known to have a moving average autocorrelation structure (for example, in case of overlapping samples), L should reflect this. Alternatively, and more commonly, the lag length L is chosen as a function of the sample size T.

Driscoll and Kraay (1998) standard errors are not recommended when T is small or when the cross-sectional dependence is absent.[5] An example of their use in finance is provided in Kang and Pflueger (2015), who regress international corporate yield spreads against inflation volatility, the inflation-stock correlation, and a range of control variables, using standard errors accounting for cross-country correlation and serial correlation up to $L = 16$ lags (based on a quarterly sample of at least $T = 160$ periods).

Small sample issues

There are two important problems when the number of clusters is small (Cameron and Miller, 2015; Conley et al., 2018). The first problem is that OLS leads to overfitting, with the estimated residuals systematically too close to zero compared to the true error terms. This leads to a downward bias in the cluster-robust covariance matrix, similar to the downward bias in $\hat{\sigma}^2$ in (2.19). Fortunately, this bias is relatively easy to fix. The simplest correction requires multiplying the covariance matrix estimate by a factor $G/(G - 1)$, where G is the number of clusters, or by

$$\frac{G}{G - 1} \frac{NT}{NT - K},$$

where K is the number of variables in x_{it}. The additional adjustment in the latter fix tends to be negligible in most cases. Cameron et al. (2011) and Imbens and Kolesár

---

5 See Vogelsang (2012) for more theoretical considerations.

(2016) discuss a number of other finite-cluster corrections, but there is no clear uniformly best approach.

The second problem is due to the fact that the number of nonzero terms in the middle part of (2.53) is very large if the number of clusters is small. For example, with a panel of 5000 firms over five years, clustering standard errors by time leads to no less than $5000^2 - 5000$, or almost 2.5 million covariance terms. Even if each of these terms is small, taken together they contribute importantly to the estimated covariance matrix and thus make resulting standard errors noisy. As a result of this, standard distributional results, for example, based on the usual t-statistic, tend to be inaccurate. This may lead to finding statistical significance, even when it does not exist (Thompson, 2011). A potential solution for this is to use other distributional approximations (rather than the standard normal one). For example, Bester et al. (2011) propose to use a t-distribution with $G-1$ degrees of freedom (after applying the first adjustment factor given above); see Conley et al. (2018) for more discussion and alternative approaches. Practically, as argued by MacKinnon (2019), the rank of the estimated covariance matrix cannot be larger than G, the number of groups. This makes it impossible or very unreliable to test q restrictions when q is not much smaller than G.

The small sample properties of clustered standard errors may also be poor if there is a large degree of heterogeneity in cluster sizes (MacKinnon et al., 2021a). An example of this is when half of the sample is one large cluster, and all other clusters are small. This extreme case is potentially relevant with firm-level data, because more than half of all publicly traded US corporations are incorporated in Delaware. Consequently, inference based on clustering at the state level may have poor finite sample performance (Hu and Spamann, 2020).

The choice of clusters

The choice of the appropriate level of clustering is often ambiguous. In general, clusters should be defined sufficiently broad so that correlations between error terms from observations in different clusters are zero, or negligibly small. This condition becomes more plausible when there are more observations within each cluster. However, if we choose too few clusters, our standard errors may become very inaccurate. On the other hand, if we choose too many clusters and therefore allow for insufficient correlations among observations, standard errors will be biased. This is the usual bias-variance trade off that characterises many approaches in econometrics. Standard errors can thus be very different depending on whether and how observations are clustered (MacKinnon, 2019). With this in mind, Thompson (2011) argues that double-clustering across time and firms can do more harm than good if either T or N is small. In particular, he advises to have at least 25 firms and 25 periods. Cameron and Miller (2015) essentially advice to cluster within any group if there is reason to believe that there is some correlation within these groups. "The consensus is to be conservative and avoid bias and to use bigger and more aggregate clusters when possible". They also suggest to compare the cluster-robust standard errors with the default standard errors (or with clustered standard errors based on a lower level of aggregation), in the spirit of the White (1980) test. If there is a large difference, the first standard errors should be chosen. However, Abadie et al. (2017) demonstrate that clustering can substantially affect standard errors even in cases where correlations are essentially zero. They argue that "a researcher should decide whether to cluster the standard errors based on substantive information, not solely based on whether it makes a difference". They advocate that the number of clusters in the sample should be small, relative to the number of clusters in the population, a condition that is hard to satisfy in many finance applications (using, for example, clustering across industries or countries). Along these lines, Conley et al. (2018) recommend the use of a limited number of clusters consisting of many observations, so as to accommodate the rich types of dependence encountered in real-world finance data. Ideally, this is combined with modifications to improve the small sample performance. Recently, some literature has developed deriving statistical tests to determine the optimal level of clustering. For example, Ibragimov and Müller (2016) develop a test for one-way clustering against no clustering (or a low level of clustering). More recent results are developed in MacKinnon et al. (2020).

Correlation structures
To better appreciate the alternative ways of clustering, let us consider some specific examples of cross-correlations among the error terms. First, consider the case where the correlation with a cluster, say a firm, is attributable to a time-invariant firm-specific effect, that is,

$$\varepsilon_{it} = \alpha_i + u_{it}, \tag{2.56}$$

where u_{it} is not correlated over time. Both α_i and u_{it} are allowed to be heteroskedastic. In this case, clustering standard errors across firms adjusts for the correlation over time due to α_i. Standard errors will typically increase, because an additional observation on firm i does not provide completely new independent information. However, the clustering across firms allows for more general forms or correlation, for example, we could have

$$u_{it} = \rho u_{it} + v_{it}, \tag{2.57}$$

with $\rho \neq 0$ and v_{it} uncorrelated over time. In this case, the errors are not only correlated over time due to a time-invariant component α_i but – decaying over time – also due to the autoregressive structure in (2.57).

The above structure is still quite restrictive. Clustering standard errors across firms allows for arbitrary correlations over time. However, a key assumption is that both α_i and u_{it} are not correlated cross-sectionally. This means that, conditional upon the explanatory variables in the model, there are no common shocks that affect all firms. This is potentially restrictive, as, for example, exchange rate shocks may jointly affect firms that have similar exposure to exchange rate risk. Thompson (2011) considers the following specification

$$\varepsilon_{it} = \theta_i' f_t + u_{it} + \xi_{it} \tag{2.58}$$

$$u_{it} = \rho u_{it} + v_{it}, \tag{2.59}$$

where f_t is a vector of random factors common to all firms, and θ_i is a vector of factor loadings for firm i. Both ξ_{it} and v_{it} capture firm-specific shocks, specific to firm i in period t. The interactive component $\theta_i' f_t$ generates both time effects and persistent common shocks. If f_t is uncorrelated over time, there are time effects in the sense that observations on different firms are correlated within the same period due to the fact that they are subject to the same common factor shocks, albeit with different sensitivities. Such a structure is potentially relevant when modelling stock returns. Importantly, in the absence of serial correlation in f_t there are no persistent common shocks. Different firms are uncorrelated at different points in time. Nevertheless, unless $\rho = 0$, there are still firm-specific persistent shocks, generating correlation over time for a given firm. This is a case where, apart from small sample concerns, double-clustering across firms and periods is appropriate. With persistent common shocks, Thompson (2011) shows how the previous formulas can be extended to capture this, provided that the autocorrelation in f_t decays sufficiently fast over time (in the spirit of the Newey and West, 1987, approach).

It is important to understand that the impact of clustering is not solely driven by the correlations among the error terms but also depends upon the correlation structure of the explanatory variables. To be precise, what matters is the correlation between $\varepsilon_{it} x_{it}$ and $\varepsilon_{js} x_{js}$. In principle it is possible that within-firm correlation of ε_{it} matters vary little if x_{it} has little or no correlation over time. For many applications, this seems to be an unrealistic setting.

Towards panel methods

If we are willing to make specific assumptions about how the unobservables in the equation correlate with each other, there are alternative ways to adjust for it. For example, if the within-firm correlation is due solely to the presence of a firm-specific time-invariant component, its process can be exploited in the estimation of β using a feasible generalised least squares approach. An example of this is the random effects estimator discussed in the next section. Alternatively, it is possible to add firm-specific dummy variables to the equation, capturing time-invariant firm-specific fixed effects. This has additional advantages, but also some drawbacks, and we discuss this in Section 2.7. Further, it is possible to use sample-splitting approaches. In this case, the standard error of an estimator for β is obtained from the sampling variation across estimates over different subsamples. A special case of this is the Fama and MacBeth (1973) approach, which we discuss in Section 2.12. This allows the error terms to be arbitrarily correlated within each subsample. Another reason to impose more structure on the correlations between the different error terms is because they are of interest themselves, for example, when modelling asset returns with a common factor structure, as in Ross (1976). Sarafidis and Wansbeek (2012) provide a survey of panel estimation allowing for cross-sectional dependence, using a spatial correlation or factor structure approach.

Bootstrapped standard errors

Instead of deriving standard errors (or p-values) using analytical expressions based on asymptotic theory under an appropriate set of assumptions, it is also possible to use bootstrapping. The bootstrap is a resampling method, where new samples are drawn repeatedly from the existing sample (with replacement) to determine the sampling variation in estimators or test statistics; see Cameron and Trivedi (2005, Chapter 11) for a good introduction. In the simplest setting, a total of M random samples of size N are drawn from the existing sample of N observations. Let us denote the relevant estimate from sample m as $\hat{\beta}^m$, so that the bootstrapped standard error for $\hat{\beta}$ is obtained as

$$se(\hat{\beta}) = \sqrt{\frac{1}{M-1} \sum_{m=1}^{M} (\hat{\beta}^m - \bar{\beta})^2}, \tag{2.60}$$

where $\bar{\beta}$ is the average of the M bootstrap estimates. This provides an appropriate standard error under the assumption that the N observations are independent, provided M is reasonably large (e. g., 200 or more).

When observations are not independent, as is likely to be the case with panel data, bootstrapping should take this into account. The standard way of implementing the bootstrap with panel data is to resample units rather than individual observations, which allows for within-firm correlation. This is similar to using parametric standard errors clustered at the firm level. More generally, if observations are correlated within clusters, one can resample clusters rather than observations. Bootstrapping is particularly attractive in cases where the number of clusters is small, or where clusters are very different in size (unbalanced cluster sizes), although this will depend on how the bootstrapping is implemented. The *bootstrap* command in Stata is based on resampling clusters of observations on (y_{it}, x_{it}), and is often called the "pairs bootstrap".

In practice, the implementation of the bootstrap is often a bit more sophisticated than described above. First, it is recommended to use the bootstrap to approximate the distribution of a test statistic one is interested in, for example, a t-ratio, rather than relying upon the estimator having an approximate normal distribution with the bootstrapped standard error.[6] Second, in a regression context it is appropriate to re-sample from the residuals, and use these to construct new values for the outcome variable. The "residual cluster bootstrap" uses the same values for the covariates across all bootstrap samples, and new values for y_{it} are obtained by drawing from the residuals. The "wild cluster bootstrap" multiplies the residuals by +1 or –1 (with probability 50%) first. Finally, it may be better, if one is interested in testing a certain null hypothesis, to impose the null when generating the bootstrapped samples, leading to the so-called "restricted wild cluster bootstrap". Often, this is the most attractive option (see MacKinnon, 2019). Cameron et al. (2008) provide an overview of the different methods of bootstrapping to test a restriction on β, as well as simulation evidence of their performance. Roodman et al. (2019) describes the Stata routine *boottest*, developed to perform tests based on the wild cluster bootstrap.

2.6 Random effects estimators

The pooled OLS estimator provides an easy and attractive estimator in case of exogenous explanatory variables, and, as discussed above, its covariance matrix can be estimated allowing for different types of correlations between the error terms as well as heteroskedasticity. In some cases we may wish to impose more structure on the correlation structure, so as to exploit this in estimation, or to investigate its magnitude. A common approach with individual or firm-level data is to allow for a time-invariant unobserved component in the equation. This component captures unobserved unit-specific heterogeneity that does not vary over time. Dependent variables in finance often exhibit substantial persistence that may be attributable to, for example, company culture, ethical standards, efficiency of operations, or management quality that varies little over time. Therefore, when explaining variables like capital structure, investments, or firm performance, such unobserved components tend to be important. In contrast, when explaining returns on stock portfolios, correlation over time in the unobservable components is not very likely. Instead, within-period correlation may arise, corresponding to commonalities in market-wide shocks.

A common starting point for models with firm-level unobserved heterogeneity is the **random effects model**. In this case, the equation's error term is decomposed into a time-invariant component α_i and a time-varying component u_{it}, both of which are assumed to be uncorrelated with the explanatory variables in the model. Mathematically, we write the random effects model as

$$y_{it} = x_{it}'\beta + \alpha_i + u_{it}, \quad i = 1, \ldots, N; \quad t = 1, \ldots, T, \tag{2.61}$$

---

6 In general, the statistic that is bootstrapped should be "asymptotically pivotal", which means that its distribution should not depend upon unknown parameters. In such cases, bootstrapping may provide "asymptotic refinement", which means that the bootstrap distribution approaches the actual distribution faster than does the asymptotic distribution; see Cameron and Trivedi (2005, Chapter 11).

with $x_{1,it} = 1$, corresponding to an overall intercept term. This model is also known as a (one-way) error components model. Compared to (2.39), it decomposes the overall error term ε_{it} into a time-invariant component α_i and a time-varying component u_{it}, which is assumed to exhibit no correlation over time. The standard assumptions for this model impose

$$\textbf{Assumption EXO1 (re)} : E(\alpha_i \mid x_{i1}, \ldots, x_{iT}) = 0, \tag{2.62}$$

and

$$\textbf{Assumption EXO2 (re)} : E(u_{it} \mid x_{i1}, \ldots, x_{iT}) = 0, \tag{2.63}$$

which is similar to, but stronger than Assumption EXO2 (ols-p): all explanatory variables in the model should be uncorrelated with the unobservables in the model. In fact, assumption EXO2 (re) requires strict exogeneity of the regressors. This not only requires x_{it} to be uncorrelated with u_{it}, but also to be uncorrelated with leads and lags of u_{it}. Among other things, this excludes any model where there is feedback from the dependent variable to future regressors.

Usually the random effects model makes additional, quite strong, assumptions about the distribution of the two components in the error term. In particular, it imposes

$$\textbf{Assumption ED1 (re)} : E(\alpha_i^2 \mid x_{i1}, \ldots, x_{iT}) = E(\alpha_i^2) = \sigma_\alpha^2 \tag{2.64}$$

$$\textbf{Assumption ED2 (re)} : E(u_{it} u_{is} \mid x_{i1}, \ldots, x_{iT}) = \sigma_u^2 \text{ if } s = t, \text{ 0 otherwise.} \tag{2.65}$$

This imposes homoskedasticity upon both error components α_i and u_{it}, and it excludes serial correlation in u_{it}. Note, however, that assumption ED1 (ols-p) does not allow for serial correlation in ε_{it} and thus imposes that $\sigma_\alpha^2 = 0$. Under the above assumptions, the coefficients β can be estimated by means of feasible generalised least squares (FGLS). This exploits the error components structure of the equation's error term in estimation. The FGLS estimator can be written as

$$\hat{\beta}_{RE} = \left(\sum_{i=1}^{N} \sum_{t=1}^{T} (x_{it} - \hat{\theta}\bar{x}_i)(x_{it} - \hat{\theta}\bar{x}_i)' \right)^{-1} \sum_{i=1}^{N} \sum_{t=1}^{T} (x_{it} - \hat{\theta}\bar{x}_i)(y_{it} - \hat{\theta}\bar{y}_i), \tag{2.66}$$

where $\bar{x}_i = T^{-1}\sum_t x_{it}$ denotes the firm-specific average of x_{it} (and similar for $\bar{y}_i$), and where $\hat{\theta}$ is a consistent estimator of

$$\theta = 1 - \sqrt{\frac{\sigma_u^2}{\sigma_u^2 + T\sigma_\alpha^2}},$$

which depends upon the relative importance of the two components of the error term. If θ is known the above estimator is a generalised least squares (GLS) estimator. In practice, the variances σ_α^2 and σ_u^2 are typically unknown and can be estimated using the residuals from two simpler estimators, the within estimator and the between estimator, which we will discuss below. The FGLS estimator is therefore a two-step estimator, where the unknown coefficients characterising the covariance matrix of the equation's error term are estimated first, after which an asymptotically efficient estimator is determined using (2.66).

The within and between estimators are based on an orthogonal decomposition of the variation in the data into variation around the firm-specific means and variation of the firm-specific means around the overall mean. To see this, first write

$$y_{it} - \bar{y} = (y_{it} - \bar{y}_i) + (\bar{y}_i - \bar{y}).$$

The first component captures variation over time, while the second component captures variation between individual units, but not over time. We can use the corresponding transformations to transform the equation of interest. This leads to the within equation,

$$y_{it} - \bar{y}_i = (x_{it} - \bar{x}_i)'\beta + u_{it} - \bar{u}_i \tag{2.67}$$

(with all time-invariant variables eliminated) and the between equation,

$$\bar{y}_i = \bar{x}_i'\beta + \alpha_i + \bar{u}_i. \tag{2.68}$$

The **between estimator** $\hat{\beta}_B$ for β is given by the OLS estimator in (2.68). Effectively, it discards the time-series information in the data set. It is available in Stata in *xtreg, be*. Similarly, the within estimator $\hat{\beta}_{within}$ is given by the OLS estimator in (2.67). These two estimators provide two independent sources of information about β. The between estimator is not frequently reported in empirical work because its assumptions are no weaker than those of the random effects or pooled OLS estimator (although it may be less sensitive to measurement error), whereas the latter estimators tend to be more efficient. An exception is provided in Murphy (1985), who also reports the between estimator based on relating average compensation of executives to their average performance. As shown by Hsiao (2014, Section 3.3), the random effects estimator is a matrix-weighted average of the between estimator and the within estimator, where the weights depend upon the relative variances of the two estimators, the more accurate one getting the higher weight. The GLS estimator, under the current assumptions, is the optimal combination of the within estimator and the between estimator.

To estimate σ_α^2 and σ_u^2, one can use the residuals from the within and between regressions above. Denoting

$$\hat{u}_{it} = y_{it} - \bar{y}_i - (x_{it} - \bar{x}_i)'\hat{\beta}_{within}$$

we estimate σ_u^2 as

$$\hat{\sigma}_u^2 = \frac{1}{N(T-1)} \sum_{i=1}^{N}\sum_{t=1}^{T} \hat{u}_{it}^2, \tag{2.69}$$

where we divide by $N(T-1)$ because the within transformation effectively eliminates one period. The combined error term in the between regression (2.68) has variance

$$\sigma_B^2 = \sigma_\alpha^2 + \frac{1}{T}\sigma_u^2,$$

which we can estimate consistently as

$$\hat{\sigma}_B^2 = \frac{1}{N}\sum_{i=1}^{N}(\bar{y}_i - \bar{x}_i'\hat{\beta}_B)^2. \tag{2.70}$$

From this, a consistent estimator for σ_α^2 is obtained as

$$\hat{\sigma}_\alpha^2 = \hat{\sigma}_B^2 - \frac{1}{T}\hat{\sigma}_u^2. \tag{2.71}$$

These estimates can be used to obtain an estimated value of θ. The resulting FGLS estimator is popularly referred to as the random effect estimator and is also known as the Balestra-Nerlove estimator (Balestra and Nerlove, 1966). If it is assumed that the two error components have a normal distribution, the random effects model can also be estimated by maximum likelihood, which is asymptotically equivalent to FGLS under the current assumptions. We postpone the discussion of this to Subsection 6.1.2.

Under the above assumptions, the pooled OLS and random effects estimators are both consistent for β. The random effects estimator is more efficient, as it exploits the error components structure in estimation, rather than – ideally – just allowing for it when calculating standard errors (in the clustered version). The efficiency gain can be expected to be substantial if the unobserved heterogeneity is important, that is, if σ_α^2 is relatively large. When $\hat{\sigma}_\alpha^2 = 0$, $\hat{\theta} = 0$ and the FGLS estimator is identical to the pooled OLS estimator.

It is possible to test whether or not there is an unobserved effect in the equation's error term, that is, whether or not $\sigma_\alpha^2 = 0$. Breusch and Pagan (1980) derive a Lagrange multiplier test for this null hypothesis, which can be obtained in Stata with the command *xttest0* after *xtreg, re*. Except in cases where serial correlation tends to be close to zero, for example, in time-series of stock returns, it is exceptional for this test to not reject the null hypothesis.

Under the previous assumptions (homoskedasticity, no serial correlation in u_{it}), the covariance matrix of the FGLS estimator can be estimated as

$$\hat{V}\{\hat{\beta}_{RE}\} = \hat{\sigma}_u^2\left(\sum_{i=1}^{N}\sum_{t=1}^{T}(x_{it} - \hat{\theta}\bar{x}_i)(x_{it} - \hat{\theta}\bar{x}_i)'\right)^{-1}, \tag{2.72}$$

where $\hat{\sigma}_u^2$ is a consistent estimator for σ_u^2. Because consistency of the FGLS estimator in (2.66) does not rely upon assumptions ED1 (re) and ED2 (re), it is possible to combine the random effects estimator with robust standard errors, similar to the pooled

OLS estimator. In this case, the random effects estimator may be more efficient than the OLS one, but it is no longer optimal in any sense. Because homoskedasticity and absence of serial correlation in u_{it} are very strong assumptions in most applications, using standard errors that allow for serial correlation and heteroskedasticity may be recommended in cases where a random effects estimator is applied (Wooldridge, 2010, Chapter 10). In fact, this may be quite an attractive approach, as it combines some of the efficiency gains of exploiting some form of correlation in the error terms with the robustness of using clustered standard errors. That is, the resulting estimator may be more efficient than pooled OLS, and still allow for arbitrary forms of heteroskedasticity and within-cluster correlation when making inferences. The random effects estimator is available in Stata in *xtreg, re*, where the covariance matrix can be standard, *vce(robust)*, to allow for heteroskedasticity, or *vce(cluster cvar)*, to allow for both heteroskedasticity and within-cluster variation (where *cvar* is the cluster variable).

In the empirical finance literature, use of the standard random effects estimator is somewhat uncommon relative to pooled OLS or other approaches. An application is provided in Barclay et al. (1993), who estimate the effect of friendly block holdings on the value of closed-end funds using the random effect estimator. Maksimovic and Phillips (2002) use a random effects approach to test the effects of plant-level productivity and industry-level demand on firm industry segment sales growth. Another example is Anderson and Reeb (2003), who relate firm performance to an indicator for family firms and several control variables, using pooled OLS, and compare this to a random effects approach yielding qualitatively and quantitatively similar results.

A particularly strong assumption in the random effects approach (and also in the pooled OLS approach) is assumption EXO1 (re) which says that α_i is conditionally mean independent of the explanatory variables in $x_{i1}, \ldots, x_{iT}$. This imposes that the unobserved heterogeneity that is captured by the error component α_i only affects the dependent variable but is not correlated with any of the explanatory variables in the model. In many cases where firm-level variables are explained, such as leverage or firm value, it can be expected that there are unobservables in the model that also correlate with one or more of the explanatory variables, for example, company sales or cash flows. In such cases, the random effects approach, as well as pooled OLS, are inconsistent, and a fixed effects approach may be more appropriate.

2.7 Fixed effects estimators

The pooled OLS estimator assumes that all coefficients in the model are the same across all firms and periods. An obvious way to relax this restriction is to allow the intercept term in the model to differ across firms. This leads to the so-called fixed effects model. Formally, it can be written as

$$y_{it} = \alpha_i + x'_{it}\beta + u_{it}, \tag{2.73}$$

where the α_i are firm-specific intercept terms, treated as fixed unknown parameters, and where the overall intercept term is eliminated from the vector x_{it}. We can write this in the usual regression framework as

$$y_{it} = \sum_{j=1}^{N} \alpha_j d_{ij} + x_{it}'\beta + u_{it}, \tag{2.74}$$

where $d_{ij} = 1$ if $i = j$ and 0 otherwise. Thus, the equation contains a set of N dummy variables as regressors in addition to x_{it}. The OLS estimator for β based on (2.74) is referred to as the **Least Squares Dummy Variable estimator** (LSDV estimator). This estimator is identical to an OLS estimator applied to an equation where all variables are transformed into deviations from their individual-specific means. Denoting $\bar{y}_i = T^{-1}\sum_t y_{it}$, and similarly for $\bar{x}_i$, this transformed equation can be written as

$$y_{it} - \bar{y}_i = (x_{it} - \bar{x}_i)'\beta + (u_{it} - \bar{u}_i), \tag{2.75}$$

corresponding to the within equation presented above. This is a regression model in deviations from individual-specific means. The transformation producing this is referred to as the **within transformation**. The OLS estimator based on estimating (2.75) is given by

$$\hat{\beta}_{FE} = \left(\sum_{i=1}^{N} \sum_{t=1}^{T} (x_{it} - \bar{x}_i)(x_{it} - \bar{x}_i)' \right)^{-1} \sum_{i=1}^{N} \sum_{t=1}^{T} (x_{it} - \bar{x}_i)(y_{it} - \bar{y}_i). \tag{2.76}$$

This estimator is often called the **within estimator** or simply the **fixed effects estimator** for β. The firm-specific intercepts can be estimated as

$$\hat{\alpha}_i = \bar{y}_i - \bar{x}_i'\hat{\beta}_{FE}, \quad i = 1, \ldots, N.$$

In most applications, these estimates are not presented. When the number of time periods T is fixed, and only $N \rightarrow \infty$, it is not possible to consistently estimate α_i, as their number grows with the sample size N. With fixed T, the firm-specific averages $\bar{y}_i$ and $\bar{x}_i$ do not converge to anything if the number of firms increases, and neither does $\hat{\alpha}_i$. Fortunately, this is typically not a problem, at least in linear models, because our main interest is in estimating β.

The conditions for $\hat{\beta}_{FE}$ to be consistent (for $N \rightarrow \infty$) are both weaker and stronger than those for the pooled OLS estimator in (2.44). On the one hand, the conditions are substantially weaker because the explanatory variables are allowed to be correlated with unobserved components in the error term that are time-invariant. That is, correlation between the time-invariant unobserved heterogeneity in α_i and the observed explanatory variables in x_{it} is not a problem. On the other hand, for fixed T the conditions are somewhat stronger because it is no longer allowed that explanatory variables in period t are correlated with u_{is}, $s \neq t$.

For consistency of $\hat{\beta}_{FE}$ we need to assume that

$$E((x_{it} - \bar{x}_i)u_{it}) = 0, \quad t = 1, \ldots, T. \tag{2.77}$$

Sufficient for this is that x_{it} is uncorrelated with u_{is}, that is,

$$E(x_{it}u_{is}) = 0, \quad t = 1, \ldots, T, \quad s = 1, \ldots, T. \tag{2.78}$$

Following Wooldridge (2010, Chapter 10) and others we reformulate these conditions in terms of conditional expectations, which are slightly stronger. The key assumption is that

$$\textbf{Assumption EXO3 (fe)} : E(u_{it} \mid x_{i1}, \ldots, x_{iT}, \alpha_i) = 0. \tag{2.79}$$

This assumption states that the explanatory variables in x_{it} are **strictly exogenous**, conditional upon the unobserved effect α_i. This not only requires x_{it} to be uncorrelated with u_{it}, but also to be uncorrelated with leads and lags of u_{it}. This is restrictive. It clearly excludes the inclusion of a lagged dependent variable in the model, because $y_{i,t-1}$ is obviously correlated with the error term from the previous period. More generally, it excludes any model where there is feedback from the dependent variable to future regressors. For example, Pastor et al. (2015) relate mutual fund performance y_{it} to the logarithm of the size of the fund, so as to identify the existence of decreasing returns to scale in the mutual fund industry. Their model includes a fixed fund effect to capture managerial skill. However, because fund size is partly driven by past fund performance, size cannot be treated as strictly exogenous and the standard fixed effects approach yields an inconsistent estimator.

Relative to the random effects approach, the fixed effects approach has the advantage that it does not make any assumptions about α_i and how it is allowed to depend upon the explanatory variables in the model. This makes the fixed effects approach much more robust to the presence of unobserved firm-specific heterogeneity that is potentially correlated with the observed explanatory variables in the model.

Whereas the contemporaneous exogeneity $E(u_{it} \mid x_{it}, \alpha_i) = 0$ is testable only in very restrictive cases, the additional requirements of strict exogeneity, $E(u_{it} \mid x_{is}, \alpha_i) = 0, s \neq t$ can be tested relatively easily (see Wooldridge, 2010, Chapter 10). Nevertheless, according to Grieser and Hadlock (2019) the strict exogeneity issue is almost entirely overlooked in the empirical finance literature, except in cases where the model of interest contains a lagged dependent variable. We return to these issues in Chapter 3.

In addition to the strict exogeneity of x_{it}, the standard assumptions of the fixed effects approach impose homoskedasticitiy of u_{it} and the absence of serial correlation in u_{it}. Under these assumptions, the covariance matrix of the fixed effects estimator is easily obtained by applying the standard least squares formulas for the LSDV formulation. It is important, though, to take into account that the number of coefficients that is estimated in this setting is $N + K$, so increasing with the sample size N. The standard covariance matrix can be estimated based on (2.75), assuming that u_{it} is homoskedastic and not correlated across firms and time, and is given by

$$\hat{V}\{\hat{\beta}_{FE}\} = \hat{\sigma}_u^2 \left(\sum_{i=1}^{N} \sum_{t=1}^{T} (x_{it} - \bar{x}_i)(x_{it} - \bar{x}_i)' \right)^{-1}, \tag{2.80}$$

where $\hat{\sigma}_u^2$ is a consistent estimator for the error variance based on the residuals

$$\hat{\sigma}_u^2 = \frac{1}{N(T-1)} \sum_{i=1}^{N} \sum_{t=1}^{T} \hat{u}_{it}^2, \tag{2.81}$$

where

$$\hat{u}_{it} = (y_{it} - \bar{y}_i) - (x_{it} - \bar{x}_i)'\hat{\beta}_{FE} = y_{it} - \hat{\alpha}_i - x_{it}'\hat{\beta}_{FE}$$

denotes the residual from the within or LSDV regression. This estimator is different from the routinely provided one after applying OLS to (2.75), because the variance of the within-transformed error is smaller than that of u_{it}. As in the case of pooled OLS, it is possible to calculate standard errors under weaker assumptions; we discuss this in Section 2.8. In Stata, the fixed effects estimator is implemented in *xtreg, fe*. In the absence of heteroskedasticity and within-unit correlation in u_{it}, the fixed effects estimator is efficient in the class of estimators that treats α_i as fixed unknown parameters (Verbeek, 1995). If these assumptions are not satisfied, the FE estimator is inefficient and a more efficient alternative can be derived (see Wooldridge, 2010, Section 10.5.5, for a GLS version of the fixed effects estimator).

Essentially, the fixed effects model concentrates on differences "within" firms. That is, it is explaining to what extent y_{it} differs from $\bar{y}_i$ but does not explain why $\bar{y}_i$ is different from $\bar{y}_j$. On average, firm i could have much higher levels of the dependent variable than firm j, but this is all captured in the fixed firm effects. The variation around the firm-specific average levels is what matters. The extreme implication of this is that any variable that is time-invariant cannot be included in the fixed effects model. It is simply eliminated by the within transformation (and its effect subsumed by the firm-level fixed effects). As a result of this, the fixed effects estimator tends to have a relatively high variance, as it is exploiting only a limited part of the variation in the data.

The big advantage of the fixed effects estimator is that it controls for time-invariant unobserved heterogeneity between firms. Compared to the random effects and pooled OLS approaches, the fixed effects estimator does not impose that $E(\alpha_i \mid x_{i1}, \ldots, x_{iT}) = 0$. This is an important advantage. In many cases it can be expected that firms have time-invariant unobserved characteristics, related to, for example, managerial quality, or company culture, that affect both the outcome variable y_{it} as well as one or more of the explanatory variables. A classic example of this is the estimation of production functions (Mundlak, 1961). In many cases, especially in the case of small firms, it is desirable to include management quality as an input in the production function. In general, however, management quality is unobservable. Assuming management quality does not vary over time, this leads to a time-invariant component in α_i that positively affects output y_{it} but negatively correlates with one or more inputs in x_{it}.

A good example of this in the financial literature is given in Murphy (1985), investigating the relationship between corporate performance and managerial renumeration. Within any given firm there may be a positive time-series relationship between executive pay and firm performance, but a pooled estimator can even produce a negative relation if, in the cross-section, there are unobservables determining compensation levels in a given firm (e. g., related to firm size) that are negatively related to average stock performance. A similar point is made in Wintoki et al. (2012) in the context of estimating the relationship between board structure and firm performance. Unobserved heterogeneity includes managerial quality and it can be argued that high-ability managers will monitor less and thus, will have less independent boards. As a result, a standard regression of performance on board structure ignoring this unobservable heterogeneity may find a negative relation between board independence and performance.

An illustration of potential differences between fixed effects and pooled estimates is given in Figure 2.1, where α_i and x_{it} are negatively correlated. For each firm, the relationship between y_{it} and x_{it} is upward sloping (the solid lines). When pooling the data (and estimating by pooled OLS), a very different slope is found (the dashed line). Similarly, the random effects estimator will be severely biased. This is because the combined error term $\alpha_i + u_{it}$ in the latter two approaches is correlated with the regressors.

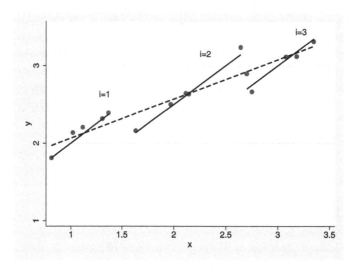

Figure 2.1: Fixed effects versus pooled OLS.

Lemmon et al. (2008) stress that leverage ratios are highly persistent over time, and argue that, when modelling capital structure decisions, firm fixed effects are needed to control for unobservable, time-invariant features of the firm. Yermack (1996) uses both pooled OLS and a fixed effects approach to estimate the impact of board size on firm valuation (Tobin's Q). Firms with larger boards may differ from firms with smaller boards in many ways, and to properly estimate the role of board size one needs to control for these differences as much as possible. Part of these differences is captured by observed variables, such as firm size, but there are also differences between firms that are not directly observable. If these unobservable differences do not vary over time the inclusion of fixed firm effects in the model controls for time-invariant firm-specific heterogeneity. Himmelberg et al. (1999) advocate a fixed effects approach to control for time-invariant firm-specific heterogeneity in models explaining equity ownership by top managers. Palia (2001) compares pooled OLS, random effects and fixed effects estimators in a model relating firm performance to the structure of managerial compensation and concludes that the latter approach dominates the other two, as it controls for unobserved firm-specific heterogeneity, for example, relating to intangible assets or a firm's contracting environment. Bertrand and Schoar (2003) use a manager-firm matched panel data set to determine the role of manager fixed effects in a wide range of corporate decisions, such as diversification and dividend payments. Manager fixed effects appear to be correlated with several firm characteristics, like research and development (R&D) expenditures. Fich and Shivdasani (2006) estimate the relationship between firm value and board characteristics using a sample of 508 industrial companies across seven years. They prefer the fixed effects approach, because it "is robust to the presence of omitted firm-specific variables that would lead to biased estimates in an OLS framework. Given the high correlation between the market-to-book ratio and corporate governance variables with numerous other company attributes, we view the fixed effects framework as offering significantly more reliable estimates than OLS regressions".

The Hausman test

The restriction that α_i is uncorrelated to the explanatory variables can easily be tested. The most common way to do so is by means of a **Hausman test** (Hausman, 1978). In general, a Hausman test is based on comparing two different estimators for the parameters of interest: one that is consistent under both the null and alternative hypotheses and one that is consistent (and typically efficient) under the null hypothesis only. A significant difference between the two estimators indicates that the null hypothesis is unlikely to hold. In the current setting, the Hausman test simply compares the random effects and fixed effects estimators for β (excluding the coefficients of any time-invariant regressors). Under the assumptions of the random effects model, $\hat{\beta}_{RE}$ is consistent and asymptotically efficient, whereas the fixed effects estimator is consistent but inefficient. If Assumption EXO1 (re) holds the random effects estimator is inconsistent, but the fixed effects estimator remains consistent. Under the null hypothesis the difference $\hat{\beta}_{FE} - \hat{\beta}_{RE}$ is asymptotically normally distributed with covariance matrix

$$V\{\hat{\beta}_{FE} - \hat{\beta}_{RE}\} = V\{\hat{\beta}_{FE}\} - V\{\hat{\beta}_{RE}\}. \tag{2.82}$$

This simple result is due to the efficiency of the random effects estimator. As a result, the Hausman test statistic can be calculated as

$$\xi_{Hausman} = (\hat{\beta}_{FE} - \hat{\beta}_{RE})'[\hat{V}\{\hat{\beta}_{FE}\} - \hat{V}\{\hat{\beta}_{RE}\}]^{-1}(\hat{\beta}_{FE} - \hat{\beta}_{RE}), \tag{2.83}$$

where the $\hat{V}$s denote estimates of the covariance matrices of the respective estimators, assuming homoskedasticity and absence of serial correlation in u_{it}. Under the null hypothesis, the test statistic has an asymptotic Chi-square distribution, where the degrees of freedom equal the number of relevant elements in β that are used in the test. The Stata command *hausman fe re* implements this test, where *fe* and *re* are the names of the fixed and random effects estimation results stored from *xtreg*. (Note that the order of the two estimates should not be changed.)

The Hausman test thus tests whether the fixed effects and random effects estimators are significantly different. Computationally, this is relatively easy because the covariance matrix satisfies (2.82). A practical problem when computing (2.83) is that the covariance matrix in square brackets may not be positive definite in finite samples, such that its inverse cannot be computed. As an alternative, it is possible to test for a subset of the elements in β. In addition, the test does not apply if u_{it} is heteroskedastic or exhibits serial correlation. This is because the random effects estimator is no longer efficient in this more general setting and (2.82) is no longer valid. As an alternative, Pesaran (2015, Section 26.9) presents a test based on comparing the pooled OLS estimator and the fixed effects estimator for β. Wooldridge (2010, Section 10.7) proposes a variant of the Hausman test that can also be applied in this more general case, which we discuss below.

Bae and Goyal (2009) examine to what extent differences in legal protection affect the size, maturity, and interest rate spread on loans. They use an extensive sample of loan tranches to borrowers in 48 countries, and include country random effects in their main specification, even though the Hausman test rejects the null hypothesis. They do so because their key variables are the property rights index and the creditor rights index, measured at the country level, and show relatively little variation within countries and much larger variation between countries. Barclay et al. (1993) model the premium to net asset value (NAV) of closed end funds, as a function of block ownership, and report several Hausman tests to defend their choice for the random effects estimator.

Testing for fixed effects

In many cases, the fixed effects are simply added as a set of additional controls in the model, so as to improve robustness of the estimator. With the within transformation, explicit estimation of the firm-specific intercept terms is redundant, and estimated fixed effects are not reported. In some cases, though, the fixed effects, or their impact on the explanatory power of the model, are of economic interest. For example, Bertrand and Schoar (2003) are interested in the role of manager fixed effects in corporate decisions. Matching firm-level data with manager-level data, they can track individual top managers across different firms over time, and are able to separate manager fixed effects from firm fixed effects (focusing on the subsample of managers who change firms during the sample period).[7]

The null hypothesis that fixed effects are irrelevant corresponds to $H_0 : \alpha_i = \alpha$ for all i, which is a total of $N - 1$ restrictions. This hypothesis can be tested by means of a standard F-test in the LSDV approach when u_{it} is assumed to be homoskedastic. Many software packages routinely provide this test. The general expression for the test statistic is

$$F = \frac{(R\hat{\alpha})'[R\hat{V}(\hat{\alpha})R']^{-1}R\hat{\alpha}}{N-1}, \tag{2.84}$$

where $\hat{\alpha}$ denotes the N-dimensional vector of estimated firm-specific intercept terms, and $R\alpha = 0$ summarises the $N - 1$ restrictions under test. That is, R is a $(N - 1) \times N$ matrix of rank $N - 1$, the columns of which add up to zero. The test does not depend upon the particular way the restrictions are formulated, and a convenient choice is

$$R = \begin{pmatrix} 1 & -1 & 0 & \cdots & 0 \\ 0 & 1 & -1 & & 0 \\ \vdots & & \ddots & & \vdots \\ 0 & & 1 & -1 & 0 \\ 0 & \cdots & 0 & 1 & -1 \end{pmatrix}.$$

The matrix $\hat{V}(\hat{\alpha})$ denotes the estimated covariance matrix under the standard fixed effects assumptions. Under the null hypothesis, the test statistic has an (approximate) F-distribution with degrees of freedom equal to the total number of restrictions $N-1$ in the numerator, and the total number of observations (NT in the balanced panel case) minus the total number of parameters ($N + K$) in the denominator.

Recall that with large N and fixed T, the estimators for the unit-specific intercept terms, $\hat{\alpha}_i$, are unbiased but not consistent (under the previously listed assumptions). In addition, the number of restrictions under test is $N - 1$. As a result, it is inappropriate to use asymptotic theory (based on $N \rightarrow \infty$), for example, to allow for either

---

7 In a more recent study, Fee et al. (2013) revisit this question, arguing that – in many cases – manager changes in a firm are likely to be endogenous.

heteroskedasticity or within-cluster correlation in the F-test.[8] This problem is highlighted in Fee et al. (2013) in the context of manager fixed effects. They conclude that the traditional F-tests on the joint significance of fixed-effects dummy variables are highly suspect in many settings typically encountered in corporate finance (e. g., in the presence of serial correlation in u_{it}). "In many cases, there will be no information content in these tests, even when reported p-values are well below 0.001".

An alternative way of examining the explanatory power of the firm fixed effects is to investigate their impact on the model's adjusted R^2 or explained sums of squares. Bertrand and Schoar (2003) focus on the increase in the adjusted R^2 comparing models with and without manager fixed effects. Alternatively, Lemmon et al. (2008) use a more elaborate analysis of covariance framework to determine the contribution of firm fixed effects to the explained sums of squares in models explaining a firm's capital structure.

2.8 Clustered standard errors with fixed effects

As with the pooled OLS and random effects estimators, it is possible to calculate standard errors for the fixed effects estimator for β under weaker assumptions than homoskedasticity and absence of serial correlation in u_{it}. Because the fixed effects estimator is a least squares estimator in a transformed model, its covariance matrix, in general, has the typical sandwich shape, now given by

$$\hat{V}\{\hat{\beta}_{FE}\} = \left(\sum_{i=1}^{N} \sum_{t=1}^{T} \tilde{x}_{it} \tilde{x}'_{it} \right)^{-1} B \left(\sum_{i=1}^{N} \sum_{t=1}^{T} \tilde{x}_{it} \tilde{x}'_{it} \right)^{-1}, \tag{2.85}$$

where $\tilde{x}_{it} = x_{it} - \bar{x}_i$ denotes within-transformed explanatory variables, and where the underlying assumptions determine the form of the "filling" matrix B. Many authors assume that the inclusion of fixed firm effects captures all within-firm correlation over time, so that u_{it} has no serial correlation.[9] One might think that allowing u_{it} to be heteroskedastic only would result in a covariance matrix that is a variant of the White (1980) covariance matrix, where B has the structure

$$B = \frac{T}{T-1} \sum_{t=1}^{T} \sum_{i=1}^{N} \hat{u}_{it}^2 \tilde{x}'_{it} \tilde{x}'_{it},$$

where $\hat{u}_{it} = \tilde{y}_{it} - \tilde{x}'_{it} \hat{\beta}_{FE}$ is the within residual (see Kézdi, 2004) and the adjustment factor $T/(T-1)$ has a similar origin as the devision by $T-1$ rather than T in (2.81). However,

---

8 Accordingly, Stata only reports the F-test when homoskedasticity and no serial correlation are imposed.

9 Note that the within-transformed error term $u_{it} - \bar{u}_i$ is serially correlated (for fixed T) if u_{it} has no serial correlation.

Stock and Watson (2008) show that this covariance matrix estimate is inconsistent for fixed T and $T > 2$. The bias arises because the unit-specific means (hidden in the transformed variables) are not estimated consistently for fixed T, making the usual step of replacing estimated regression coefficients with their probability limits inapplicable.

In general, the inclusion of firm fixed effects in the model does not eliminate all sources of within-firm correlation. Put differently, even with firm-fixed effects, corrections for serial correlation in u_{it} may be required, and ignoring this may lead to standard errors that are seriously misleading. An easy way to accommodate both heteroskedasticity and serial correlation within u_{it}, is by using cluster robust standard errors (CRSE) for the within estimator, where the cluster is the individual firm. This is similar to (2.51), replacing the regressors by their within-transformed counterparts and the OLS residuals by the residuals from the within regression (Arellano, 1987). That is,

$$\hat{V}\{\hat{\beta}_{FE}\} = \left(\sum_{i=1}^{N}\sum_{t=1}^{T}\tilde{x}_{it}\tilde{x}'_{it}\right)^{-1} \sum_{i=1}^{N}\sum_{t=1}^{T}\sum_{s=1}^{T}\hat{u}_{it}\hat{u}_{is}\tilde{x}_{it}\tilde{x}'_{is}\left(\sum_{i=1}^{N}\sum_{t=1}^{T}\tilde{x}_{it}\tilde{x}'_{it}\right)^{-1}. \qquad (2.86)$$

This covariance matrix estimator is also recommended in cases where only heteroskedasticity is present. In Stata, standard errors based on (2.86) are obtained if the option *robust* is used with *xtreg, fe*.

An alternative version imposes homoskedasticity across individuals but allows an unrestricted covariance matrix of $u_{i1}, \ldots, u_{iT}$ and was proposed by Kiefer (1980). Kézdi (2004) provides a Monte Carlo study analysing the properties of these covariance estimators for different N and T and shows that they have reasonably good behaviour in small samples, particularly when T is small and N is large, if the assumptions about homoskedasticity and serial correlation are correct. Importantly, the clustered estimator in (2.86) also works well for large T (when the number of nonzero correlations is high), even with small or moderate N. Pustejovsky and Tipton (2018) analyse a number of small-sample corrections that improve the performance of the above cluster-robust covariance matrix estimates in cases where the number of clusters is small.

A robust Hausman test

In case of heteroskedasticity (of either α_i or u_{it}) or serial correlation in u_{it}, the standard Hausman test comparing the fixed effects and random effects estimators based on (2.83) is no longer appropriate, because these problems invalidate the covariance matrix estimator that is used. Wooldridge (2010, p. 332) has proposed a variant of the Hausman test that can also be applied in the more general case. It is based on the approximation, proposed by Mundlak (1978), that

$$\alpha_i = \beta_0 + \bar{x}'_i\gamma + v_i, \qquad (2.87)$$

where β_0 is an overall intercept term, and v_i a random error term, uncorrelated to $\bar{x}_i$. When x_{it} contains time-invariant variables, these are excluded from the average $\bar{x}_i$.

This assumes that the correlation between the unobserved heterogeneity in α_i and the explanatory variables in the model is fully captured by a linear approximation in $\bar{x}_i$. If we substitute this into our equation of interest, we obtain

$$y_{it} = \beta_0 + x_{it}'\beta + \bar{x}_i'\gamma + \varepsilon_{it}, \tag{2.88}$$

where v_i is embedded in the overall error term (and x_{it} does not include an intercept term). Mundlak (1978) has shown that, estimating this extended model using the random effects approach leads to the within estimator for β. In addition, the estimator for $\beta + \gamma$ corresponds to the between estimator for β. Accordingly, a Wald test for $\gamma = 0$ is equivalent to comparing the within and between estimators and thus provides an alternative way to conduct the Hausman test above. This test can easily be extended to incorporate a more general covariance matrix estimator. If the test rejects the null hypothesis, the fixed effects estimator should be preferred above the random effects and pooled OLS estimators.

Imposing assumption (2.87) and estimating equation (2.88) is sometimes referred to as the **correlated random effects** (CRE) approach (see, e. g., Wooldridge, 2010, Section 10.2). For the linear model, the equivalence of the CRE approach with the fixed effects approach (for β) relies upon linear projections. In dynamic models and nonlinear models, the two approaches are not equivalent, and the correlated random effects approach may provide some leeway when estimation with fixed effects is problematic. See Subsections 6.1.6 and 6.3.3 for examples.

2.9 First-difference estimators

Instead of using the within transformation, the individual effects α_i can also be eliminated by first-differencing (2.74). This results in

$$y_{it} - y_{i,t-1} = (x_{it} - x_{i,t-1})'\beta + (u_{it} - u_{i,t-1})$$

or

$$\Delta y_{it} = \Delta x_{it}'\beta + \Delta u_{it}, \tag{2.89}$$

where Δ is the first-difference (FD) operator, such that $\Delta y_{it} = y_{it} - y_{i,t-1}$. Applying OLS to this equation yields the **first-difference estimator** for β. It is given by

$$\hat{\beta}_{FD} = \left(\sum_{i=1}^{N} \sum_{t=2}^{T} \Delta x_{it} \Delta x_{it}' \right)^{-1} \sum_{i=1}^{N} \sum_{t=2}^{T} \Delta x_{it} \Delta y_{it}. \tag{2.90}$$

The FD estimator is consistent (for $N \to \infty$) under the previous assumption of strict exogeneity of x_{it}. However, it does not require that u_{it} is uncorrelated with $x_{i,t+2}, x_{i,t+3}, \ldots$

This advantage seems mostly of theoretical interest, although there may be empirically relevant cases where there is feedback from y_{it} to one or more of the explanatory variables but with a delay of more than one period. To implement the estimator in Stata, one can use the *regress* command with first-differenced variables and omitting the intercept term. Alternatively, one can use *xtivreg, fd* and ignore the instrumental variables.

Whereas the conditions for consistency of the FD estimator are slightly weaker than those for the within estimator, it is, in general, somewhat less efficient. For $T = 2$, both estimators are identical. If strict exogeneity is violated, the FE and FD estimators are both inconsistent. If the two estimators provide very different results, this may thus indicate violation of the strict exogeneity assumption (that affects both estimators differently) or some other form of model misspecification. Grieser and Hadlock (2019), investigating strict exogeneity in the empirical finance literature, find that the differences between FE and FD estimators are often quite large, often differing by a factor of more than 50%, and recommend a comparison of these two approaches as a simple diagnostic. For models with a lagged dependent variable, in which the strict exogeneity assumption is obviously violated, the FE and FD estimator tend to produce very different results (both of them being inconsistent), see, for example, Verbeek (2017, Section 10.5). We elaborate upon the strict exogeneity assumption in Section 3.6, and we investigate dynamic models in Chapter 5.

The FD estimator is used in Jensen and Murphy (1990), who estimate the relation between CEO cash compensation and firm performance, while including an intercept term in the first-differenced model. This corresponds to the presence of a linear time trend in the model in levels. Another example is Hayes et al. (2012), who use a first-differencing approach to eliminate time-invariant firm-specific heterogeneity in models explaining compensation or incentives of CEOs.

In empirical work, the FE estimator (within estimator) is much more common than the FD estimator. However, first-differencing is often a first step with the use of instrumental variables or the generalised method of moments, for example, in a dynamic model. First-differencing is also popular for the estimation of treatment effects. Consider a situation where we wish to investigate the impact of a certain policy or treatment upon firms. The sample consists of a treatment group, firms which are subject to the treatment in period $t = 2$, and a control group of firms which are not. We also observe the same firms at $t = 1$ before treatment takes place. Denoting treatment by an indicator r_{it}, equal to 1 if the firm was subject to treatment and 0 otherwise, the first-differenced model can be written as

$$\Delta y_{it} = \mu + \gamma r_{it} + \Delta x_{it}'\beta + \Delta u_{it}, \quad t = 2 \tag{2.91}$$

where μ is an overall intercept term (arising from a time dummy in the original model in levels). The intercept captures the population-wide shift in y_{it} from period 1 to 2, irrespective of the treatment (and other variables in x_{it}). This equation can be estimated consistently by OLS, leading to a first-difference estimator, provided both r_{it} and x_{it} are strictly exogenous. Because the first-differencing eliminates any time-invariant element, it is allowed for treatment to be correlated to time-invariant unobserved heterogeneity α_i. When Δx_{it} is not included in the model, the OLS estimator for y in (2.91) corresponds to the sample average of $y_{i2} - y_{i1}$ for the treated minus the average for the non-treated. Defining $\Delta \bar{y}_{i2}^{treated}$ as the average for the treated and $\Delta \bar{y}_{i2}^{non-treated}$ as the average for the non-treated, the OLS estimate is simply

$$\hat{y} = \Delta \bar{y}_{i2}^{treated} - \Delta \bar{y}_{i2}^{nontreated}.$$

This estimator is called the difference-in-differences (DiD) estimator, because one estimates the time difference for the treated and untreated groups and then takes the difference between the two. The first-differencing takes care of unobservable fixed effects and controls for unobservable (time-invariant) differences between firms (e. g., industry, management quality). The second difference compares treated with untreated firms. For example, Derrien and Kecskés (2013) examine the effect of a decrease in analyst coverage on corporate policies, like capital expenditures or share repurchases, by computing the average changes from year −1 to year +1 for treatment firms (which lost an analyst) and control firms (which did not) and the differences between them. The Stata routine *diff* provides treatment effects estimates including their building blocks.

The difference-in-differences approach is commonly used to evaluate the impact of a natural experiment, like an exogenous policy change that affects some firms but not all. For example, Gilje and Taillard (2017) investigate the impact of an exogenous change in basis risk in the oil and gas industry in 2012, which affected Canadian light oil producers but not otherwise similar US oil producers. Gropp et al. (2014) use the fact that government guarantees for savings banks were removed in Germany in 2001, following a law suit, to examine the effect of such guarantees on bank risk-taking. The control group consists of German banks to which the guarantee was not applicable. Agarwal et al. (2018) use a regulatory change in the frequency of mandated portfolio disclosure for mutual funds, to investigate the influence of portfolio transparency on corporate myopia. Treatment firms are those with high ownership by funds affected by the regulation.

In the simplest setting, the effect of the experiment is simply reflected in the average change in y_{it} in the affected subsample (with $r_{i2} = 1$) minus the average change in the control sample. Important for this is that there are no time effects that affect the two subsamples differently. That is, the average change in the control sample should be a good proxy for the average change that would have happened in the treatment group had there be no treatment. This important assumption is typically referred to as the parallel trends assumption. We come back to this assumption in Chapter 7, which deals with difference-in-differences and other approaches to the estimation of (heterogeneous) treatment effects.

2.10 Testing for heteroskedasticity and autocorrelation

In the typical finance application with panel data the presence of heteroskedasticity is taken for granted, and the use of White standard errors or clustered standard errors, which allow for heteroskedasticity, has become the default. Nevertheless, it is possible to test the null hypothesis of homoskedasticity using a variant of the Lagrange Multiplier test of Breusch and Pagan (1980). To test the null hypothesis $V(u_{it}) = \sigma_u^2$ against the alternative

$$V(u_{it}) = \sigma_u^2 h(z_{it}'\gamma),$$

where h is a continuously differentiable function with $h(0) = 1$, and z_{it} is a J-dimensional vector of conditioning variables (often a subset of x_{it}), one can use the fixed effects residuals $\hat{u}_{it}$ and perform an auxiliary regression of the squared within residuals $\hat{u}_{it}^2$ upon a constant and upon the variables z_{it} that are suspected to affect the error variance. A test for the null hypothesis of homoskedasticity corresponds to a test for $\gamma = 0$ and a test statistic can be computed as $N(T-1)$ times the R^2 of the auxiliary regression. Under the null hypothesis, the test statistic has an asymptotic Chi-square distribution with J degrees of freedom.

It is also possible to test for serial correlation in the fixed effects model, using a variant of the Durbin-Watson test proposed by Bhargava et al. (1982). The alternative hypothesis is that

$$u_{it} = \rho u_{i,t-1} + v_{it},$$

where v_{it} is not serially correlated. This allows for autocorrelation over time with the restriction that each firm has the same autocorrelation coefficient. The null hypothesis that $\rho = 0$ is typically tested against the one-sided alternative of positive serial correlation, $\rho > 0$. The test statistic is also based on the residuals from the within regression (or LSDV regression) and is given by

$$dw_\rho = \frac{\sum_{i=1}^{N} \sum_{t=2}^{T} (\hat{u}_{it} - \hat{u}_{i,t-1})^2}{\sum_{i=1}^{N} \sum_{t=1}^{T} \hat{u}_{it}^2}.$$

Using similar derivations as Durbin and Watson, Bhargava et al. (1982) derive lower and upper bounds on the true critical values that depend upon N, T and K only. Unlike the true time-series case, the inconclusive region for the panel data Durbin–Watson test is very small, particularly when the number of firms in the panel is large. Unfortunately, there are no critical values available for unbalanced panels. The test can be obtained in Stata with the *xtregar* command. An alternative test for serial correlation can be derived from the residuals from the FD estimator. If u_{it} is homoskedastic and exhibits no serial correlation, the correlation between Δu_{it} and $\Delta u_{i,t-1}$ is −0.5. Accordingly, a simple test for serial correlation is obtained by regressing the residuals from (2.89) upon their lagged values, and testing whether the coefficient on the lagged residual equals -0.5 using a t-test based on clustered standard errors (see Wooldridge, 2010, Subsection 10.6.3). This test is implemented in Stata in the function *xtserial* (where the option *output* provides the estimation results for the first-differenced model). Despite the clustered standard errors, the test is not robust against time-varying heteroskedasticity (because in this case the correlation between Δu_{it} and $\Delta u_{i,t-1}$ does not equal 0.5 if u_{it} and $u_{i,t-1}$ are uncorrelated.) Several alternative tests for serial correlation in the fixed effects model are discussed in Born and Breitung (2016).

Tests for heteroskedasticity and autocorrelation can be useful to obtain some idea about the structure of these two problems. For example, rather than allowing the error variance to vary across all observations, it may be appropriate to impose homoskedasticity along the firm dimension, but allow heteroskedasticity over time (or vice versa). Imposing more structure on the error covariance matrix of either ε_{it} (in the random effects setting) or u_{it} (in the fixed effects case), can be helpful to determine more efficient estimators. Although using clustered standard errors makes sure inference is robust against heteroskedasticity and within-cluster correlation, this does not affect the precision of the estimator itself.

If one is willing to make specific assumptions about the form of heteroskedasticity or autocorrelation, it is possible to improve upon the efficiency of the OLS, random effects or fixed effects estimators by exploiting the structure of the error covariance matrix using feasible GLS. An overview of a number of such estimators is provided in Baltagi (2013, Chapter 5). Feasible GLS estimators for models where u_{it} is subject to first-order serial correlation (and all other assumptions are maintained) are implemented in Stata in *xtregar*. Kmenta (1986) suggests a relatively simple feasible GLS estimator that allows for first-order autocorrelation in ε_{it} combined with unit-specific heteroskedasticity. Unfortunately, it requires N to be small, relative to T, and it does not allow for a time-invariant component in ε_{it}. Kiefer (1980) proposes a GLS estimator for the fixed effects model that allows for arbitrary covariances between u_{it} and u_{is}; see Hsiao (2014, Section 3.8) for more details. Wooldridge (2010, Subsection 10.4.3) describes a feasible GLS estimator where the $T \times T$ covariance matrix of $\varepsilon_{i1}, \ldots, \varepsilon_{iT}$ is estimated unrestrictedly from the pooled OLS residuals. Consistency of this estimator basically requires the same conditions as required by the random effects estimator, but it does not impose the error components structure. When N is sufficiently large relative to T, this feasible GLS estimator may provide an attractive alternative to the random effects approach.[10]

---

10 A very similar estimator is available in Stata via *xtgee, corr(uns)*.

2.11 Models with fixed time effects

Instead of, or in addition to, the inclusion of firm-specific intercept terms, it is also possible to incorporate fixed time effects. In the simplest case this leads to the model

$$y_{it} = \alpha_t + x'_{it}\beta + \varepsilon_{it}, \tag{2.92}$$

where α_t denote fixed unknown parameters (to be implemented by means of including T time dummies and omitting an overall intercept). The OLS estimator for β in this model, can be written as

$$\hat{\beta}_{FET} = \left(\sum_{i=1}^{N} \sum_{t=1}^{T} (x_{it} - \bar{x}_t)(x_{it} - \bar{x}_t)' \right)^{-1} \sum_{i=1}^{N} \sum_{t=1}^{T} (x_{it} - \bar{x}_t)(y_{it} - \bar{y}_t), \tag{2.93}$$

where $\bar{x}_t = N_t^{-1} \sum_i x_{it}$ is the average value of x_{it} over the entire cross-section of firms in period t (and where N_t denotes the number of firms in period t). This is analogous to the standard fixed effects estimator but with the dimensions i and t switched. The inclusion of fixed time effects in (2.92) is equivalent to transforming all variables in deviations from the period-specific means. This way the analysis controls for aggregate developments in each of the variables and focusses on how individual firms deviate from the period-specific average.

The inclusion of fixed time effects is commonly applied when it is suspected that different observations at the same time are not independent, when the number of time periods is relatively small or when one wishes to control for the impact of aggregate economic developments but is unsure about exactly which factors play a role. The inclusion of fixed time effects eliminates all variables from the model that do not vary across firms. With $N \to \infty$ the time-specific intercepts terms can be estimated consistently as

$$\hat{\alpha}_t = \bar{y}_t - \bar{x}'_t \hat{\beta}_{FET}.$$

Because the cross-section of firms grows asymptotically, the number of observations to estimate α_t grows with the sample size and consistent estimation is possible. When only $T \to \infty$ we cannot estimate α_t consistently, although an unbiased estimator is possible under strict assumptions.

The easiest way in Stata to estimate a model with time fixed effects is to add *i.period* to the equation, where *period* denotes the period identifier. This can be done in the *reg* command, to get a model with fixed time effects only. It can also be done in *xtreg, re* to estimate a random effects model with fixed time effects, or in *xtreg, fe* to estimate a model with both firm and time fixed effects. The function *areg* allows estimation with many dummy variables and suppresses their coefficients in the results. This also allows for other types of group fixed effects. We discuss this in more detail in Section 3.2.

2.12 The Fama-MacBeth approach

An alternative approach to deal with large panel data sets is a **two-step cross-section regression approach**, or two-pass regression approach, typically referred to as Fama-MacBeth regressions (Fama and MacBeth, 1973). It is commonly used in the empirical finance literature. For example, Fama and French (1992) use this approach to show that the CAPM does a poor job in explaining the cross-section of expected stock returns, Sirri and Tufano (1998) use it to estimate the relationship between mutual fund flows and fund performance, while Fama and French (2002) employ it to model firm leverage, so as to test the implications of the trade-off and pecking order theories explaining capital structure.

The Fama-MacBeth approach is a special case of a "sample splitting" approach, where the parameters of interest are estimated over different subsamples, with the average as the final estimate, while the variation across subsamples is used to derive a standard error (see Ibragimov and Müller, 2010). A key assumption, for the latter aspect, is that the different subsamples are independent of other.

2.12.1 Cross-sectional regressions

In the asset pricing literature, the dependent variable typically corresponds to the return (or excess return) on asset i in period t and the explanatory variables are characteristics of stocks (observed before the start of period t) or (estimated) exposures to risk factors. Ignoring estimation error in the latter, let us write the corresponding model as

$$y_{it} = \alpha_t + x_{it}'\beta_t + \varepsilon_{it}, \quad t = 1, \ldots, T, \tag{2.94}$$

where α_t and β_t are unknown coefficients, possibly different across periods. Typically the panel is unbalanced in the sense that the number of assets per period, N_t, varies over time. Because variances of rates of return differ and because asset returns tend to be correlated with each other even after controlling for a common time effect it can typically be expected that ε_{it} is heteroskedastic across assets and correlated cross-sectionally. As a result of this, applying OLS to (2.94) for each period t separately, is inefficient and potentially inconsistent for $N_t \rightarrow \infty$. The inconsistency arises if the cross-sectional correlation in ε_{it} is due to one or more common factors which do not "average out" when the OLS estimator is calculated. In addition, the estimation of a sensible standard error for the OLS estimator is hampered by the fact that the covariance matrix of the error terms cannot be estimated with a single cross-section.

Assuming that $\beta_t = \beta$ for each t, we obtain an estimator for β as the simple average of the T least squares estimates, that is,

$$\hat{\beta}_{FM} = \frac{1}{T} \sum_{t=1}^{T} \hat{\beta}_t, \tag{2.95}$$

where $\hat{\beta}_t$ is the OLS estimator based on cross-section t only. A standard error for $\hat{\beta}_{FM}$ is based on the sample variation of $\hat{\beta}_t$ across the T subsamples and is obtained from the estimated covariance matrix

$$\hat{V}\{\hat{\beta}_{FM}\} = \frac{1}{T} \frac{1}{T-1} \sum_{t=1}^{T} (\hat{\beta}_t - \hat{\beta}_{FM})(\hat{\beta}_t - \hat{\beta}_{FM})', \tag{2.96}$$

where the additional $1/T$ arises because we estimate an average over T observations. The standard errors calculated as the square roots of the diagonal elements in this expression assume that the estimates $\hat{\beta}_t$ are mutually independent, but allow for arbitrary cross-sectional correlation and heteroskedasticity in ε_{it}. This result may seem surprising, as it does not use any of the distributional results of the estimators that are used in calculating $\hat{\beta}_{FM}$. However, it is an intuitively appealing procedure. We simply infer the sample variance of $\hat{\beta}_{FM}$ from how the estimates $\hat{\beta}_t$ vary over different subsamples (one for each t). The asymptotic properties of the Fama–MacBeth procedure were first documented in Shanken (1992), almost 20 years after its first use, and later extended in Jagannathan and Wang (1998).

To see that the sample splitting approach produces correct standard errors under relatively weak assumptions, the first step is to write

$$T\hat{V}\{\hat{\beta}_{FM}\} = \frac{1}{T-1} \sum_{t=1}^{T} (\hat{\beta}_t - \beta)(\hat{\beta}_t - \beta)' - \frac{T}{T-1}(\hat{\beta}_{FM} - \beta)(\hat{\beta}_{FM} - \beta)', \tag{2.97}$$

noting that the expected value of the latter term is exactly equal to the variance we wish to estimate, multiplied by $T/(T-1)$. Accordingly, we need to show that

$$\hat{V}^* = \frac{1}{T} \sum_{t=1}^{T} (\hat{\beta}_t - \beta)(\hat{\beta}_t - \beta)'$$

is a reliable estimator for $TV\{\hat{\beta}_{FM}\}$. Using the definition of the OLS estimator, we can write

$$\hat{\beta}_t - \beta = \left(\sum_{i=1}^{N_t} (x_{it} - \bar{x}_t)(x_{it} - \bar{x}_t)' \right)^{-1} \sum_{i=1}^{N_t} (x_{it} - \bar{x}_t)\varepsilon_{it}, \tag{2.98}$$

where $\bar{x}_t$, as before, denotes the cross-sectional average of x_{it}. Denoting

$$W_t = \sum_{i=1}^{N_t} (x_{it} - \bar{x}_t)(x_{it} - \bar{x}_t)' \tag{2.99}$$

$\hat{V}^*$ can be rewritten as

$$\hat{V}^* = \frac{1}{T}\sum_{t=1}^{T}\left[W_t^{-1}\left(\sum_{i=1}^{N_t}\sum_{j=1}^{N_t}\varepsilon_{it}\varepsilon_{jt}(x_{it} - \bar{x}_t)(x_{jt} - \bar{x}_t)\right)W_t^{-1}\right],$$

which is the average of a typical sandwich formula for the covariance matrix of an OLS estimator. Accordingly, the Fama-MacBeth covariance matrix can be expected to provide a consistent estimator for the covariance matrix of $\hat{\beta}_{FM}$ in case of heteroskedasticity of arbitrary form, as well as within-period correlation of ε_{it}. Importantly, though, the error terms in (2.94) are not allowed to exhibit serial correlation. As stressed by Conley et al. (2018), the sample splitting approach behind the Fama-MacBeth regressions makes similar assumptions about cross-correlations between the error terms as the clustering approach, with the subsamples playing the role of clusters. Thus, the standard Fama-MacBeth regressions allow for arbitrary correlation within each period, as well as heteroskedasticity of unknown form, but do not allow for correlation across periods. The Fama-MacBeth estimator is available in Stata in *xtfmb* and in *asreg*, with the option *fmb*.

2.12.2 Serial correlation and firm effects

What is required for the validity of (2.96) is that the estimation error in $\hat{\beta}_t$ is not correlated across t. From (2.98), we see that we need $\sum_i(x_{it} - \bar{x}_t)\varepsilon_{it}$ to be uncorrelated over time (Petersen, 2009). Given that in a typical application it is very unlikely that x_{it} has no serial correlation, this effectively requires the absence of serial correlation in ε_{it}. Importantly, this excludes the presence of a firm effect in ε_{it}. Instead, the Fama-MacBeth approach allows for time effects in the unobservables, as captured by the time-varying intercepts α_t. More generally, the error terms ε_{it} and ε_{jt} can be arbitrarily correlated, accommodating commonality in shocks to the dependent variables in the same period. Effectively, this makes the Fama-MacBeth approach well-suited to explain asset returns, where – conditional upon observable explanatory variables – the degree of serial correlation is very small, but less suited for corporate finance applications where the dependent variable is, for example, dividend policy, capital structure or firm value. Each of these tend to be characterised by high levels of persistence and a likely presence of a firm effect in the unobservables.

As stressed by Petersen (2009), the fact that the Fama-MacBeth approach does not allow for the presence of serial correlation in the unobservables is often overlooked, or misunderstood (see, e. g., Wu, 2004; Choe et al., 2005). The presence of a firm-specific fixed effect in ε_{it} will make the different estimates for β positively correlated, and, as a result, tends to produce too optimistic standard errors for $\hat{\beta}_{FM}$. Several authors, for example, Christopherson et al. (1998), employ a Newey-West correction to (2.96) to account for the serial correlation in the error term. This way, the covariance matrix estimate for $\hat{\beta}_{FM}$ is extended to

$$\hat{V}\{\hat{\beta}_{FM}\} = \frac{1}{T}\frac{1}{T-1}\sum_{t=1}^{T}(\hat{\beta}_t - \hat{\beta}_{FM})(\hat{\beta}_t - \hat{\beta}_{FM})' \tag{2.100}$$

$$+ \frac{1}{T}\frac{1}{T-1}\sum_{j=1}^{H}\sum_{s=j+1}^{T}w_j[(\hat{\beta}_s - \hat{\beta}_{FM})(\hat{\beta}_{s-j} - \hat{\beta}_{FM})' + (\hat{\beta}_{s-j} - \hat{\beta}_{FM})(\hat{\beta}_s - \hat{\beta}_{FM})']$$

with $w_j = 1 - j/(L + 1)$ denoting the Bartlett weights, as before, and where L is the maximum lag length over which correlation is allowed. Clearly, when consecutive estimates are positively correlated, this adjustment will increase the estimated variance of the Fama-MacBeth estimator. One way to implement this is by performing a simple regression of each element from $\hat{\beta}_t$ upon an intercept term only, and using a (Newey-West) autocorrelation-consistent standard error on the intercept term as the corrected standard error. A variation of this is employed in Pontiff (1996), who models the error terms in the regression of $\hat{\beta}_t$ as a sixth-order autoregressive process (after some initial testing) and determines standard errors accordingly.

As an alternative, Fama and French (2002) and Chakravarty et al. (2004) have proposed a somewhat simpler adjustment based on the estimated serial correlation in $\hat{\beta}_t$. Denoting the first-order serial correlation coefficient in $\hat{\beta}_{tj}$, the j-th element of $\hat{\beta}_t$, by ρ, these authors propose to multiply the standard error of the average derived from (2.96) by a factor[11]

$$\sqrt{\frac{1+\hat{\rho}}{1-\hat{\rho}}}.$$

This is based on the fact that, under homoskedasticity (of $\hat{\beta}_{tj}$), the relevant term in square brackets in (2.100) reduces to $2\rho^j V\{\hat{\beta}_{tj}\}$. Assuming that T is sufficiently large and using that $\rho + \rho^2 + \rho^3 + \cdots = 1/(1 - \rho)$ leads to the above correction factor (see Fama and French, 2002, footnote 1). This pragmatic approach leads to an inflation of the standard errors in the analysis of Fama and French (2002) by a factor of 2.5, thus requiring regular t-statistics around 5.0, rather than the usual, to claim significance. It should work reasonably well if T is not too small, if the serial correlation in $\hat{\beta}_t$ is well described by a first-order autoregressive process and, moreover, if ρ can be estimated with a reasonable degree of precision.

These are critical conditions. In two important cases we can typically not expect this correction to work well. The first one is where T is small and the estimated ρ is imprecise. For example, Petersen (2009) documents poor performance of the correction for $T = 10$, where the confidence interval on the estimated autocorrelation coefficient

---

11 Note that ρ denotes the serial correlation in $\hat{\beta}_t$, not in ε_{it}.

$\hat{\rho}$ is wide. In most cases though, the corrected standard errors are less biased than the uncorrected ones. With a larger number of time periods the adjusted Fama-MacBeth standard errors work quite well. The second case where the correction does not work well is the case where the serial correlation in ε_{it} is characterised by the presence of a firm-specific time-invariant component, a firm fixed effect. In this case the correlations in the unobservables do not die out when they become further apart in time. This is mostly problematic in corporate finance applications, where the dependent variable is characterised by a high degree of persistence. Examples are firm leverage, dividends (Fama and French, 2002) or market-to-book ratios (Pastor and Veronesi, 2003).

Petersen (2009) explains why this is the case. The adjustment, whether based on the pragmatic adjustment factor based on the estimated first-order serial correlation coefficient, or the more elaborate Newey-West correction in (2.100), corrects the estimation of the variance in $\hat{\beta}_t$ around its sample average $\hat{\beta}_{FM}$. However, the true standard error should reflect the variation around the true population parameter β. With a fixed firm effect, the estimated slope coefficient in period t tends to be positively correlated to those in other periods. In other words, the firm effect not only affects all estimated $\hat{\beta}_t$s in the same direction, it also affects the average of the $\hat{\beta}_t$s in a similar way. Thus, the variation around the sample average tends to underestimate the true variation around the population mean β.

2.12.3 Pooled OLS versus Fama-MacBeth

The Fama-MacBeth approach splits the sample into T cross-sections, and estimates the parameters of interest from the average OLS estimates. Its standard errors, based on the variation of the T estimates, allow for within-period correlation in the equation's error term. As an alternative, we could use a pooled OLS estimator, pooling all cross-sections, and adjust the standard errors for within-period clustering. To see how these two estimators are related, let us write the pooled OLS estimator for β, in the model with fixed time effects, as

$$\hat{\beta}_{OLS} = \left(\sum_{t=1}^{T} \sum_{i=1}^{N_t} (x_{it} - \bar{x}_t)(x_{it} - \bar{x}_t)' \right)^{-1} \sum_{t=1}^{T} \sum_{i=1}^{N_t} (x_{it} - \bar{x}_t) y_{it}, \qquad (2.101)$$

where we allow the number of units to differ over time. Note that the subtraction of the cross-sectional averages $\bar{y}_t$ in the final term is redundant, as it cancels out. Using the definition of W_t from (2.99) we can write this as

$$\hat{\beta}_{OLS} = \frac{1}{T} \sum_{t=1}^{T} \left(\frac{1}{T} \sum_{s=1}^{T} W_s \right)^{-1} \sum_{i=1}^{N_t} (x_{it} - \bar{x}_t) y_{it},$$

or

$$\hat{\beta}_{OLS} = \frac{1}{T}\sum_{t=1}^{T}\left(\frac{1}{T}\sum_{s=1}^{T}W_s\right)^{-1}W_t\hat{\beta}_t.$$

This shows that the pooled OLS estimator is a matrix-weighted average of the OLS esti-mators for each period, where the weights are proportional to W_t, a matrix summaris-ing the cross-sectional variation in the regressors. In the special case where W_t does not vary over time ($W_t = W$), the pooled OLS estimator reduces to the Fama-MacBeth estimator. A sufficient condition for this is that both x_{it} does not vary over time and the number of observations per cross-section N_t is the same across periods (Cochrane, 2005, Section 12.3).

When the cross-sectional variation in the explanatory variables is roughly similar across periods, the main difference between $\hat{\beta}_{OLS}$ and $\hat{\beta}_{FM}$ relates to how information from different periods is weighted. With the Fama-MacBeth procedure, each period gets the same weight, irrespective of whether 100 or 10,000 observations are in the cross-section. With pooled OLS, each observation gets the same weight, irrespective of whether it comes from period 1 or period 50. Particularly in cases where there are cross-sections with only a relatively small number of cross-sectional units, or when the number of units differs widely over the different periods, it may be more appro-priate to use a pooled OLS estimator (with time fixed effects), in combination with standard errors clustered by period, rather than the simple average derived from the Fama-MacBeth approach. Apart from the fact that the average in $\hat{\beta}_{FM}$ may be quite sen-sitive to one or a few extreme estimates, the general logic here is one of efficiency. The more efficient estimator will give more weight to those $\hat{\beta}_t$s that are more accurately estimated. The OLS estimator does so, to the extent that the accuracy of $\hat{\beta}_t$ is affected by the sample size N_t and the cross-sectional variation in the regressors. In addition, the variance of ε_{it} and its within-period correlation structure will play a role.

There are some variants of the Fama-MacBeth approach where the first-step re-gressions are based on weighted least squares (e. g., using a stock's market capitali-sation as weight) or generalised least squares (see Skoulakis, 2008; Lewellen et al., 2010; Yoon and Lee, 2019; Hou et al., 2020, for some examples). The generalised least squares approach requires an estimated covariance matrix for the vector $\varepsilon_{1t}, \ldots, \varepsilon_{N_t t}$, which – even in cases where this can be assumed to be time-invariant – is challenging when N_t is large (see Cochrane, 2005, Chapter 12).

Effectively, the conditions for consistency of $\hat{\beta}_{OLS}$ and $\hat{\beta}_{FM}$ are similar and require that x_{it} is uncorrelated to ε_{it} for each t. This requires the explanatory variables to be exogenous in any given period, a requirement that is not always trivial. In the case of a firm-specific effect, where $\varepsilon_{it} = \alpha_i + u_{it}$, this obviously excludes the inclusion of $y_{i,t-1}$ among the explanatory variables. That is, in the presence of time-invariant unobserved heterogeneity, dynamic models cannot be estimated consistently with the Fama-MacBeth approach, nor with any of the other estimation methods discussed so far. Only if there is no serial correlation in ε_{it}, it may be appropriate to assume that $y_{i,t-1}$ is cross-sectionally uncorrelated to ε_{it}. The problem with lagged dependent variables in the Fama-MacBeth approach is also often overlooked. For example, Fama and French (2002) estimate a dynamic model of dividends using standard Fama and MacBeth (1973) methodology (assuming absence of any serial correlation), and Spiegel and Zhang (2013) include lagged flows in a linear model explaining fund flows, and combine this with a Newey-West correction on the standard errors.

Variations and extensions

As mentioned above, the Fama-MacBeth approach is an example of a sample splitting approach: the parameters of interest are estimated over different subsamples, and inference is based on the variation across the different subsamples. The subsamples need not be defined by the time period, as is typically done. For example, Coval and Shumway (2005) employ a variant of the Fama-MacBeth approach in a model explaining afternoon risk-taking by traders from their morning profits using daily data. They conduct trader-by-trader regressions, and then average across traders, as well as day-by-day regressions, and then average across days.

2.12.4 The errors-in-variables problem

In asset pricing tests, some or all of the explanatory variables in (2.94) are often exposures to risk factors, which have to be estimated first. This, effectively, makes the Fama-MacBeth method a three step approach, where in the first step exposures to one or more risk factors ("betas") are estimated from a time-series regression of asset excess returns upon factor excess returns (e. g., the excess return on the market portfolio and the size and value factors, SMB and HML). Chen et al. (1986) use unanticipated changes in a set of macroeconomic variables in the first-step regressions. Several variations on this first-step have been implemented, for example, using a rolling window estimate, or a full-sample one, using OLS or weighted least squares, or using univariate betas (where one factor is included at a time) or multivariate betas (where all factors are included simultaneously). Because a true asset pricing model, where the factors are portfolio excess returns, implies zero intercepts in the time-series regressions, the intercept in the first-stage is often omitted (as recommended by Lewellen et al., 2010, and others).

Given the estimated factor loadings, the second-step involves the estimation of a cross-sectional regression explaining asset returns in period t from the factor loadings. This corresponds to the Fama-MacBeth procedure discussed above. If the factor loadings correspond to the true factor loadings, and the set of factors correctly characterises the asset pricing model, the slope coefficients in the cross-sectional regressions correspond to factor risk premia, and the intercept is the zero-beta return (often the riskfree rate). The cross-sectional regressions can also be done in terms of excess returns, in which case the asset pricing restriction leads to a zero intercept. In reality, however, the estimated factor loadings do not correspond to the true ones. This leads to an errors-in-variables problem in the second step. The errors-in-variables problem has two aspects. First, it leads to a bias in the second-step estimator. As in the standard textbook case of measurement errors in a linear regression model (see Chapter 4), the estimator is typically biased towards zero. This is intuitively obvious. If the regressors in a model are mostly driven by noise, the estimated impact of the regressors tends to be smaller than in reality.

A second problem is due to the noise in the estimated factor loadings itself. Because the regressors in the second-step are not observed, we have a "generated regressor" problem. As a result, standard errors based on the Fama-MacBeth approach tend to be too optimistic. For this latter problem, the correction proposed by Shanken (1992) is commonly employed, which is derived under conditional homoskedasticity.

Fama and French (1992) address this concern by allocating portfolio factor exposures ("betas") to individual stocks. In their words: "we judge that the precision of the full period post-ranking betas, relative to the imprecise beta estimates that would be obtained for individual stocks, more than makes up for the fact that the true betas are not the same for all stocks in a portfolio." (Fama and French, 1992, p. 432). Many recent studies change the level of analysis by aggregating the cross-section of stocks into portfolios in both steps, thus reducing the importance of noise and estimation error. In this case, the cross-sectional units i refer to (cleverly chosen) portfolios of stocks, rather than individual stocks. Diversification reduces the errors-in-variables problem in the estimated factor loadings. However, as stressed by Ang et al. (2020) there is a cost to this: in the cross-sectional regressions the variation in factor betas tends to be smaller, and this reduces precision in the estimated coefficients. The use of more precise factor loadings leads to less precise estimates of the factor risk premia. An alternative solution to the errors-in-variables problem is proposed by Jegadeesh et al. (2019), who use an instrumental variables approach allowing the use of individual assets as test assets.

The small sample properties of the Fama–MacBeth procedure and some alternative approaches (maximum likelihood, GMM) are discussed in Shanken and Zhou (2007); see also Ang et al. (2020, Appendix). The formal derivations in Jagannathan and Wang (1998) support the use of firm characteristics in cross-sectional regressions for detecting factor model misspecifications.

2.13 Goodness-of-fit

In panel data applications it is not routine to report goodness-of-fit measures. There are a few reasons for this. First, the usual R^2, or the adjusted R^2, is only appropriate if the model is estimated by OLS and includes an intercept term. Estimating a model based on transformed data or using any other method than OLS affects the way the R^2 is calculated and may make it inappropriate. Second, because panel data vary over at least two dimensions, say firms and periods, one may attach differential importance to the model's ability to explain variation in y_{it} across these dimensions.

In addition to the above issues, it is important to stress that the R^2 is often not the most important metric or aspect of an econometric model. The value of the R^2 tells us how well the model fits the data, on a scale from 0 to 1. This is often useful. For example, in the context of a time-series factor regression (e. g., Gibbons et al., 1989) the R^2 has an economic interpretation as measuring the proportion of unexplained volatility (idiosyncratic risk) in an asset's return; see Roll (1988). In statistical terms, however, the R^2 does not tell us whether the estimator employed is appropriate or whether any of the assumptions made are correct.

There are alternative mathematical expressions to define the R^2 of a regression model, all of which lead to the same numerical outcome if the model has an intercept term and is estimated by OLS. To introduce goodness-of-fit measures in a panel context, we start from the definition of the R^2 as the squared correlation coefficient between the observed values y_{it} and the fitted values from the model $\hat{y}_{it}$. In mathematical terms

$$R^2 = \text{corr}^2\{y_{it}, \hat{y}_{it}\}, \tag{2.102}$$

where corr^2 denotes the squared (sample) correlation coefficient. The advantage of this definition is that it is easily adjusted when the model is not estimated by OLS (which corresponds to alternative fitted values), can also be used on transformed data, and always leads to an outcome between 0 and 1, where 1 corresponds to a perfect fit. This allows us to define alternative versions of an R^2 measure, depending upon the dimension of the data that we are interested in, and using any estimator for the model coefficients.

For example, the fixed effects estimator $\hat{\beta}_{FE}$ is the OLS estimator in the within-transformed equation. This means, it explains the within variation as well as possible. Accordingly, we can define the within-R^2 as

$$R^2_{\text{within}}(\hat{\beta}_{FE}) = \text{corr}^2\{\hat{y}^{FE}_{it} - \hat{y}^{FE}_i, y_{it} - \bar{y}_i\}, \tag{2.103}$$

where $\hat{y}^{FE}_{it} - \hat{y}^{FE}_i = (x_{it} - \bar{x}_i)'\hat{\beta}_{FE}$ denotes the fitted value in the within-transformed model, based on the fixed effects estimator. We can determine the within-R^2 for any other estimator for β, simply by replacing the fixed effects estimator by an alternative. Because the fixed effects estimator is chosen to maximise the within-R^2, other estimators (e. g., the random effects estimator or first-difference estimator) will produce lower within-R^2s.

The between estimator is usually not reported in empirical work. It is based on OLS applied to the between-transformed model. It thus maximises the between-R^2, which is defined as

$$R^2_{\text{between}}(\hat{\beta}_B) = \text{corr}^2\{\hat{y}_i^B, \bar{y}_i\}, \qquad (2.104)$$

where $\hat{y}_i^B = \bar{x}_i'\hat{\beta}_B$ denotes the fitted value (with the irrelevant intercept term suppressed). The measure captures how well the model explains the variation across units, when all time-variation is averaged out. Again, it can be defined using alternative estimators. Note that, for the fixed effects estimator, fitted values are constructed without the estimated fixed effects.

The above three goodness-of-fit measures are routinely provided by Stata when panel data estimators are chosen. The results will show that the highest within-R^2 is obtained with the fixed effects estimator, the highest between-R^2 by the between estimator, and the highest overall R^2 by the (pooled) OLS estimator. This means that alternative estimators for β, including the random effects estimator, the FD estimator, and the Fama-MacBeth estimator, do not maximise any of these measures. This stresses that goodness-of-fit measures are not adequate to choose between alternative estimators. Instead, they may provide possible criteria for choosing between alternative (potentially non-nested) specifications of a model.

For the Fama-MacBeth estimator it is relatively common to report the average R^2 from the T cross-sectional regressions as a goodness-of-fit measure. This measure is not directly comparable with the three measures above, although, intuitively, it is closest to the between-R^2 in the sense that it reflects the cross-sectional fit. It can be interpreted as the average value of a period-specific overall R^2, but has no easy direct interpretation.

3 Dealing with heterogeneity and endogeneity: fixed effects, IV and GMM

The inclusion of fixed effects in a model is an attractive way to control for unobserved heterogeneity. In this chapter we expand our discussion on fixed effects estimators. In addition, we cover instrumental variables (IV) estimation, extend this to the generalised method of moments (GMM), and we relate this to fixed effects and other panel estimators. We discuss alternative exogeneity assumptions that can be imposed upon a model's explanatory variables, so that consistent estimators can be obtained by appropriately transforming the model and using transformation of explanatory variables as instruments. We pay particular attention to the assumption of strict exogeneity, and how it can be tested, and to the question why it is typically inappropriate to control for unobserved heterogeneity by taking differences from, for example, industry averages, instead of including industry fixed effects.

3.1 Fixed effects and instrumental variables

In many applications, it is hard to impose that the explanatory variables in x_{it} are exogenous. Unobserved heterogeneity is likely to exist that is correlated with both x_{it} and y_{it}, in which case a standard pooled OLS or random effects estimator is inconsistent. Consider the linear model

$$y_{it} = x_{it}'\beta + \varepsilon_{it}, \tag{3.1}$$

where we no longer impose assumption EXO (ols-p) that $E(x_{it}\varepsilon_{it}) = 0$. As an example, think of y_{it} as a measure of firm performance, and one of the elements in x_{it} denoting a measure of corporate governance. Firms with good governance are likely to differ from firms with poor governance on many aspects, and this also results in y_{it} being different (in a way that has nothing to do with governance per se). The traditional approach of dealing with the problem that an explanatory variable in x_{it} may be correlated with the error term ε_{it} is the use of instrumental variables.

For this, we need to assume that a vector z_{it} exists that is correlated with x_{it} but not correlated with ε_{it}. Elements in x_{it} that are exogenous can be copied into the vector z_{it}, whereas for any element in x_{it} that is correlated with ε_{it} we need to find a new variable that satisfies these two conditions. For the moment, we assume that such variables can be found, and we also assume that the dimensions of x_{it} and z_{it} are identical. In this case, the **instrumental variables estimator** for β can be written as

$$\hat{\beta}_{IV} = \left(\sum_{i=1}^{N} \sum_{t=1}^{T} z_{it} x_{it}' \right)^{-1} \sum_{i=1}^{N} \sum_{t=1}^{T} z_{it} y_{it}. \tag{3.2}$$

https://doi.org/10.1515/9783110660739-003

Writing

$$\hat{\beta}_{IV} = \beta + \left(\frac{1}{NT} \sum_{i=1}^{N} \sum_{t=1}^{T} z_{it} x'_{it} \right)^{-1} \frac{1}{NT} \sum_{i=1}^{N} \sum_{t=1}^{T} z_{it} \varepsilon_{it}$$

shows that this instrumental variables (IV) estimator provides a consistent estimator for β if the following two assumptions are satisfied:

$$\textbf{Assumption EXO1 (iv-p)} : E(z_{it}\varepsilon_{it}) = 0 \qquad\qquad (3.3)$$

and

$$\textbf{Assumption RE1 (iv-p)} : E(z_{it}x'_{it}) = \Sigma_{zx} \text{ is of full rank } K. \qquad (3.4)$$

The first of these two conditions says that the instruments should be exogenous, while the second condition requires that the instruments are relevant. A typical requirement for relevance is that an instrument is correlated with the variable in x_{it} it is trying to instrument. If an instrument satisfies both conditions (exogeneity and relevance), we refer to it as a valid instrument.

In Section 3.4, we discuss more general versions of the instrumental variables estimator, including its asymptotic covariance matrix under alternative assumptions. At this stage, we only note that finding valid instruments is often challenging. In the above example, we would need to find a variable that is correlated with the governance measure, but not with firm performance directly. That is, the instrument should only affect firm performance through governance (and potentially one or more of the other regressors), but not directly. When panel data are available, things may be a little bit better because it is possible to use lags or other transformations of the explanatory variables in x_{it} as instruments, and we do not have to find external instruments. The price for this is that we need to impose some restrictions on the relationships between the error term and the explanatory variables. A first example of this is the fixed effects estimator, which can also be interpreted as an instrumental variables estimator, the instruments being within-transformed variables from the original model. This can be seen by writing

$$\hat{\beta}_{FE} = \left(\sum_{i=1}^{N} \sum_{t=1}^{T} (x_{it} - \bar{x}_i)(x_{it} - \bar{x}_i)' \right)^{-1} \sum_{i=1}^{N} \sum_{t=1}^{T} (x_{it} - \bar{x}_i)(y_{it} - \bar{y}_i)$$

$$= \left(\sum_{i=1}^{N} \sum_{t=1}^{T} (x_{it} - \bar{x}_i)x'_{it} \right)^{-1} \sum_{i=1}^{N} \sum_{t=1}^{T} (x_{it} - \bar{x}_i)y_{it}, \qquad (3.5)$$

which has the same structure as the instrumental variables estimator in (3.2) with $z_{it} = x_{it} - \bar{x}_i$ acting as instruments for x_{it}.

To see why this interpretation makes sense, let us start with the equation in levels[1]

$$y_{it} + x'_{it}\beta + \alpha_i + u_{it}, \tag{3.6}$$

where there is an endogeneity problem in the sense that x_{it} and α_i are correlated. This was an important reason to opt for the fixed effects estimator. Now, consider the transformation $x_{it} - \bar{x}_i$. It is obvious that

$$\sum_{t=1}^{T}(x_{it} - \bar{x}_i)\alpha_i = 0$$

by construction. Assuming that $x_{it} - \bar{x}_i$ is also uncorrelated with u_{it} (as implied by the strict exogeneity of x_{it}), this suggests that the within-transformed regressors can act as instruments for x_{it}. The relevance condition requires that these instruments are correlated with the untransformed counterparts, which is trivially satisfied, unless x_{it} has no time-variation.

Indeed, time-invariant variables are eliminated in the fixed effects approach, and the instrumental variables interpretation does not solve this. This is unfortunate, as we may be interested in the effect of time-invariant variables (like gender on the compensation of a CEO). While the pooled OLS and random effects estimators allow for time-invariant explanatory variables, they impose that α_i and x_{it} are uncorrelated, which is a huge drawback. Fortunately, it is possible to derive instrumental variables estimators that can be considered to be in-between a fixed and random effects approach. A simple variant would assume that some elements of x_{it} are exogenous and uncorrelated with α_i. In this case, there is no need to instrument them, or – equivalently – they can be instrumented by themselves. Extending this logic allows us to also estimate the impact of time-invariant variables, even if some variables in x_{it} are correlated with the firm-specific effects α_i, provided we are willing to make some additional assumptions.

The Hausman-Taylor estimator

To extend the fixed and random effects framework, Hausman and Taylor (1981) have proposed an instrumental variables estimator that exploits the panel nature of the data. Consider a general model, where we divide the explanatory variables into four groups

$$y_{it} = x'_{1,it}\beta_1 + x'_{2,it}\beta_2 + w'_{1i}\gamma_1 + w'_{2i}\gamma_2 + \alpha_i + u_{it}, \tag{3.7}$$

where the x variables are time-varying and the w variables are time-invariant. The variables with suffix 1 are assumed to be uncorrelated with both α_i and u_{is}, whereas

---

1 An overall intercept term is omitted, or incorporated in α_i.

the variables $x_{2,it}$ and w_{2i} are correlated with α_i but not with any u_{is}. Under these assumptions, the fixed effects estimator would be consistent for β_1 and β_2, but would not estimate the coefficients for the time-invariant variables. Moreover, it is inefficient because $x_{1,it}$ is instrumented unnecessarily. Hausman and Taylor (1981) suggest that (3.7) be estimated by instrumental variables using $x_{2,it} - \bar{x}_{2,i}$ as instruments for $x_{2,it}$ and $\bar{x}_{1,i}$ as instruments for w_{2i}. The innovative element here is to use the individual-specific averages of the time-varying exogenous regressors $(\bar{x}_{1,i})$ as instruments for the endogenous time-invariant regressors (w_{2i}). Obviously, identification requires that the number of variables in $x_{1,it}$ is at least as large as that in w_{2i}. Further, to prevent weak instrument issues (Bound et al., 1995), the correlation of $\bar{x}_{1,i}$ with w_{2i} should be sufficiently large (after controlling for the other instruments and exogenous regressors).[2] The standard Hausman-Taylor approach exploits the error components structure in (3.7) and thus makes strong assumptions about homoskedasticity of α_i and u_{it}, and absence of serial correlation in u_{it}, similarly to the random effects estimator discussed in Section 2.6. The estimator is available in Stata as *xthtaylor*, which includes the option to combine the random effects assumption exploited in estimation with a robust covariance matrix.

Even though the Hausman-Taylor estimator is not commonly used in applied work, it illustrates one of the advantages of panel data. It is possible to achieve identification in an instrumental variables setting via instruments that are based on transformations of explanatory variables that are already included in the model, like the within transformation. Below, when discussing models with regressors that are not strictly exogenous or models with lagged dependent variables we shall see more examples of this general idea. Before doing so, we delve more into the use of different types of fixed effects to control for group-specific heterogeneity.

3.2 Two-way and interactive fixed effects

Provided the explanatory variables are strictly exogenous, conditional upon the time-invariant heterogeneity α_i, that is, provided

$$E(u_{it} \mid x_{i1}, \ldots, x_{iT}, \alpha_i) = 0,$$

(see assumption EXO3 (fe)), the inclusion of fixed firm effects controls for the endogeneity of one or more of the explanatory variables that is due to a time-invariant component in the error term. In the presence of a time-varying shock that affects all firms equally, potentially correlated with one or more of the explanatory variables, this can be accommodated by extending the standard fixed effects model by also including

---

2 More on weak instruments in Subsection 3.4.2.

fixed time effects. This results in

$$y_{it} = x'_{it}\beta + \alpha_i + \alpha_t + u_{it}. \tag{3.8}$$

This is referred to as a **two-way fixed effects model** (TFE). In principle, it can be estimated using the least squares dummy variable approach where a wide range of dummy variables are included for each firm and time period (with sufficient categories omitted to avoid exact multicollinearity). It is also possible to obtain the TFE estimator for β by applying least squares on transformed data, that is,

$$\hat{\beta}_{TFE} = \left(\sum_{i=1}^{N} \sum_{t=1}^{T} \tilde{x}_{it} \tilde{x}'_{it} \right)^{-1} \sum_{i=1}^{N} \sum_{t=1}^{T} \tilde{x}_{it} \tilde{y}_{it}, \tag{3.9}$$

where

$$\tilde{x}_{it} = x_{it} - \bar{x}_i - \bar{x}_t + \bar{x},$$

with $\bar{x}_t = N^{-1} \sum_i x_{it}$, and $\bar{x} = N^{-1} T^{-1} \sum_i \sum_t x_{it}$. Although this transformation is useful when the number of time periods is large, it cannot directly be used in the typical case where the panel is unbalanced (see Wansbeek and Kapteyn, 1989, for the more general expressions). Instead, for small to moderate T it is typically more attractive to include time dummies in the model and apply a standard (firm-level) fixed effects estimator.

Group fixed effects

Because the inclusion of firm fixed effects eliminates all variables that do not vary within firms, some scholars prefer to include fixed effects for wider groups of observations, for example, industries of firms, investment styles of mutual funds, or states where a company is headquartered. This eliminates variables from the model that do not vary within these larger groups, but allows the inclusion of time-invariant variables, as long as they vary within groups.

To illustrate this, suppose we estimate a model with industry fixed effects only. The model is given by

$$y_{it} = x'_{it}\beta + f_g + u_{it}, \tag{3.10}$$

where g denotes the industry of firm i (for simplicity treated as time-invariant), and f_g is a time-invariant industry effect. Along the lines of the standard fixed effects estimator, the resulting estimator can be written as

$$\hat{\beta}_{FEG} = \left(\sum_i \sum_t (x_{it} - \bar{x}_g)(x_{it} - \bar{x}_g)' \right)^{-1} \sum_i \sum_t (x_{it} - \bar{x}_g)(y_{it} - \bar{y}_g), \tag{3.11}$$

where $\bar{x}_g$ denotes the average of all observations in industry g, averaged across all firms and periods. (Note that the definition of g depends upon i.) Consistency of this estimator requires that

$$E((x_{it} - \bar{x}_g)u_{it}) = 0,$$

which requires that, conditional upon the industry effect, there is no firm-specific heterogeneity left that is correlated with x_{it}. Effectively, the inclusion of industry fixed effects allows for industry-specific time-invariant differences in y_{it} between firms, potentially correlated with one or more of the explanatory variables. Similarly, state or country fixed effects can be added. If the inclusion of such group fixed effects controls for the endogeneity problem, the impact of both time-varying and time-invariant unit-specific variables in x_{it} can be estimated consistently.

The model in (3.10) can easily be extended into a two-way fixed effects model by also including time fixed effects. That is,

$$y_{it} = x'_{it}\beta + f_g + \alpha_t + u_{it}, \tag{3.12}$$

which allows f_g and α_t to be correlated with the explanatory variables in x_{it}, but maintains the assumption that x_{it} is uncorrelated with the idiosyncratic component u_{it}. That is, it allows for industry-specific time-invariant differences between firms, and for period-specific shocks that are common to all industries and all firms, but not for industry-specific shocks. This assumes that all firms within a given industry respond homogeneously to the same time-varying shock α_t.

Groups can be defined on more than one dimension simultaneously. For example, a common choice is to include industry $\times$ period fixed effects, sometimes referred to as interactive fixed effects (IFE). This allows for industry-specific shocks to y_{it}, potentially correlated with x_{it}. Think of changes in the regulatory environment, which may differentially affect different industries. This is more flexible than having both industry and period dummies. The corresponding model is more general than (3.12) and can be written as

$$y_{it} = x'_{it}\beta + f_{gt} + u_{it}. \tag{3.13}$$

An advantage of the use of interactive fixed effects is that one can allow for timevariation in the unobserved heterogeneity, which is not the case with firm fixed effects in (3.8). A disadvantage is that one can only control for heterogeneity at a higher level of aggregation, such as industries. If the heterogeneity in the model captures aspects like managerial quality or investment opportunities, this may be problematic, as these are likely to vary across firms within the same industry, and may also vary over time.

In general, when the model of interest contains fixed effects defined on the basis of two group indicators (TFE), with G_1 and G_2 different outcomes, the model of interest contains up to $G_1 + G_2 + K - 1$ explanatory variables. As stressed by Gormley and

Matsa (2014) this may be computationally challenging if the panel is unbalanced and the group dummies cannot be wiped out by a simple transformation. In such cases, one typically includes explicit dummy variables for the group with the fewest indicators, and applies a within transformation to the equation to eliminate the other group effects, the typical example being the inclusion of time dummies in a model with firm-fixed effects. Even with such partial transformation, estimation may be challenging if both group effects are of high dimension, for example, when one group is defined at the firm level ($G_1 = N$) and the second group is also high-dimensional (e. g., industry $\times$ periods); see Gormley and Matsa (2014) for more discussion. An efficient estimator for models with high-dimensional fixed effects is developed in Guimaraes and Portugal (2010) and Correia (2016) and available in Stata's *reghdfe* procedure.

Interestingly, when two groups are interacted (IFE), the number of variables in the regression (when the dummy variables are explicitly included) can be up to $G_1 \times G_2 + K - 1$, which is much larger. However, because this is effectively a one-dimensional set of fixed effects, estimation is feasible by subtracting the group-by-group specific means from the equation of interest. With one of the groups denoting time, this extends (3.11) into

$$\hat{\beta}_{FEGT} = \left(\sum_i \sum_t (x_{it} - \bar{x}_{gt})(x_{it} - \bar{x}_{gt})'\right)^{-1} \sum_i \sum_t (x_{it} - \bar{x}_{gt})(y_{it} - \bar{y}_{gt}), \tag{3.14}$$

where $\bar{x}_{gt}$ denotes the average across all observations in group g in period t.

Fixed effects can be defined over more than two dimensions. An interesting application of a model with three-way fixed effects is given in Graham et al. (2012), who use a manager-firm matched panel data set from 1992 to 2006, in which the same manager can work at multiple firms (at different points in time). Their main specification includes firm-specific fixed effects, manager fixed effects and year fixed effects. The authors not only wish to control for firm and manager fixed effects in their analysis of the manager's compensation, but they also wish to estimate the magnitudes of each fixed effect separately. Empirically, the separation of manager fixed effects from firm fixed effects is only possible when the firm has at least one manager who switches companies. Another example is provided in Gormley and Matsa (2016), who examine the effect of business combination laws (adopted at different points in time across US states) on risk-taking behaviour, and include firm fixed effects, state-by-year fixed effects and industry-by-year fixed effects. Engelberg and Parsons (2011) investigate the effect of media reporting on the trading volume of stocks trading at 19 different locations, exploring the cross-sectional variation in media coverage. Several of their specifications include industry, newspaper, city and date fixed effects. Alternative specifications include firm $\times$ date fixed effects, firm $\times$ city fixed effects and city $\times$ date fixed effects.

Some concerns and drawbacks

Although the possibility to have multiple and interactive group fixed effects is attractive to achieve robustness against unobserved heterogeneity that biases standard estimators, an important drawback is that the fixed effects remove much of the variation in the data, and may therefore lead to unreliable estimation results. Moreover, it is not possible to estimate the impact of explanatory variables that exhibit no variation within the group structure. An extreme example of this is the inclusion of firm × period fixed effects with firm-level data over time, because there is effectively no variation left after the firm-period fixed effects have been removed. With industry × period fixed effects, the only variation left is within-industry within-period variation, which is what is exploited in (3.14). Another problem is that the impact of measurement errors on the estimates is typically amplified when fixed effects are included. While the transformation to wipe out the fixed effects eliminates much of the genuine variation in the data, it tends to make any noise in the data, due to imprecision and random measurement error, relatively more important; see Gormley and Matsa (2014) and Section 4.4 for more discussion.

Another problem with group × period fixed effects is that it assumes that the groups are defined in such a way that they capture all relevant heterogeneity. That is, conditional on f_{gt} there is no firm-specific time-varying heterogeneity left that is correlated with one or more the explanatory variables. As stressed by Sojli et al. (2021) this is potentially problematic. For example, in many corporate finance applications, the heterogeneity may correspond to the presence of financial constraints, investment opportunities or managerial quality, and it is likely that these affect the outcome variable y_{it} in a time-varying way and heterogeneously across standard groups, such as industries or geographical locations. Put differently, allocating firms in groups based on their industry classification and assuming that all firms within each industry respond in the same way to aggregate shocks is quite arbitrary. Sojli et al. (2021) document how two-way fixed effects and interactive fixed effects estimators may lead to biased results in cases where the true group structure differs from the one employed. They propose an alternative approach where the groups are not pre-specified on the basis of one or more observed variables, but are determined endogenously. Loosely speaking, firms in the same group share similar time paths of residuals. This builds upon Bonhomme and Manresa (2015) who propose a formal "grouped fixed effects" estimator that minimises a least squares criterion with respect to all possible groupings of the cross-sectional units. Recent advances in the clustering literature allow for fast and efficient computation.

A related problem is that the grouping variable could be subject to error. For example, standard industry classifications, such as those based on Standard Industrial Classification (SIC) codes, or the North American Industry Classification System (NAICS) codes may be arbitrary or inappropriate if they are based on incomplete information about a firm. Hoberg and Phillips (2016) argue that fixed classifications like

SIC and NAICS have several shortcomings: they only rarely re-classify firms that move into different industries, they do not allow for the industries themselves to evolve over time, and they impose transitivity even though two firms that are rivals to a third firm may not compete against each other. To remedy this, they propose two new industry text-based classification systems using product similarities in the firms' 10-K descriptions, which are shown to more accurately identify a firm's actual competitors. Accordingly, fixed effects based on industry or industry interacted with time can be based on alternative classification schemes, with potentially different results. The approach of Sojli et al. (2021) may be able to solve this.

Clustered standard errors

It is important to realise that the inclusion of dummy variables for one or more groups has a different role than clustering the standard errors within clusters. The main purpose of a fixed effects approach is to control for unobservable differences between the outcome variable y_{it} that are constant within groups (or within groups interacted with periods) and that are potentially correlated with one or more of the explanatory variables. For example, rather than including a set of industry-specific variables (e. g., industry concentration), country-specific variables (e. g., GDP growth, inflation), one simply includes a set of industry or country dummies, potentially interacted with time, to capture all such variables in a simple way. Typically, this results in a more robust estimator than without the inclusion of such fixed effects. If, within each group, there is no further correlation among the equation's error terms, the use of group fixed effects, in combination with standard OLS, is sufficient to obtain valid inferences. In all cases, the residual error term u_{it} is not allowed to be correlated with x_{it}.

However, if the error terms are correlated within groups, even after controlling for group fixed effects, it is important to adjust the standard errors to reflect this. This can be achieved by combining the fixed effects approach with clustered standard errors where the cluster variable is the same as the group variable. This way, one allows for group-specific heterogeneity that may be correlated with the explanatory variables in the model, and for within group correlation in the error term. This is similar to the cluster-robust covariance matrix for the fixed effects estimator presented in Section 2.8.

Clustering standard errors can be done at other levels than the group level corresponding to the fixed effects in the model. In principle, it is perfectly fine to include industry dummies in the model and to cluster standard errors at the firm level. In this case, one allows the error terms of the same firm to be correlated over time (conditional upon the industry fixed effect), and one allows for industry-specific (time-invariant) heterogeneity correlated with the regressors. However, error terms of firms in the same industry are not allowed to be correlated, and the industry-fixed effects are assumed to capture all commonalities within the industries. Instead, it is more common to have firm-fixed effects while clustering standard errors at the industry level. This allows correlations within and across firms in the same industry. Note that, as stressed in Section 2.5, the number of clusters should be sufficiently large.

When calculating standard errors for a model where a large number of fixed effects are present, the impact of a degrees of freedom correction can be substantial. When combining fixed effects with clustered standard errors defined over the same dimension, or a broader one, adjusting degrees of freedom for the number of fixed effects is not necessary, similar to (2.86). This is because the mechanical correlations that arise in the residuals when the fixed effects are included (or wiped out by a within transformation) are automatically accounted for in the clustering. For example, when estimating a model with firm fixed effects, clustering standard errors at the firm level does not require a large N degrees of freedom adjustment. However, when the fixed effects are not nested within the clusters, this no longer applies and a degrees of freedom correction is appropriate. For example, when industry × year fixed effects are included, and standard errors are clustered at the firm level, it is appropriate to adjust the degrees of freedom downward, to account for the estimation of a large number of fixed effects; see Gormley and Matsa (2014). With this in mind, it appears recommendable to choose a level of clustering that nests the groups of fixed effects in the model. For example, with industry × year fixed effects it appears appropriate to cluster standard errors at the industry level. In Stata, *xtreg, fe* provides the fixed effects estimator (with unit-specific fixed effects) and standard errors can be clustered at the firm level or a broader one (e. g., industries). Alternatively, the *areg* command allows a flexible choice of fixed effects and level of clustering, but routinely adjusts the degrees of freedom in the clustered standard errors downwards. This may lead to standard errors that are too high if the fixed effects are nested within clusters (e. g., industry × year fixed effects with clustering at the industry level).

Singletons
Singletons are fixed effects or combinations of fixed effects that appear in only one observation. Effectively, such observations are not providing any information about the parameters of interest, as their outcome is perfectly predicted, in-sample, by the fixed effects. When combining one or more dimensions of fixed effects with clustered standard errors, including singletons may underestimate the standard errors when the fixed effects are nested within clusters, because the degrees of freedom are not adjusted. For example, in matched CEO-firm regressions many individuals and firms may be short-lived enough in the sample so that singletons abound. It is recommended to eliminate singletons from the estimation sample (in cases where there are many), so as to avoid large biases in clustered standard errors (see Correia, 2015).

Fixed effects that are not fixed
In much of the early panel literature, the time-invariant unobserved heterogeneity is individual-specific and has the connotation of innate ability, intelligence or other per-

sonal characteristics that are arguably constant over longer time periods. When the individual units are firms, the unobserved heterogeneity captures unobservable aspects such as firm culture, managerial quality or investment opportunities, which are less likely to remain constant over time. For example, a firm's management team may change over time, a firm may change its main line of business, or a regulatory change may cause a shift in firm-specific time-invariant heterogeneity. In line with the above, it is possible to allow the fixed firm-specific effects to vary across subperiods in the panel. This possibility is particularly relevant when the number of time periods is large (or, to be more precise, when the time span over which observations are available is large), or when there are economic reasons to suspect the fixed effects to vary across subperiods (e. g., a regulatory change). Grieser and Hadlock (2019) stress that imposing that firm-level unobserved heterogeneity is constant over time is restrictive, and show how much fixed effects estimates vary when estimated over subperiods of 5 or 10 years for typical models estimated in corporate finance.

Investigating the sensitivity of investments to cash flows using firm-level Compustat data from 1967 to 2006, Chen and Chen (2012) allow the fixed effects (as well as the investment-cash flow sensitivity) – somewhat arbitrarily – to vary across subperiods of five years. Hoechle et al. (2012) analyse the diversification discount by relating excess value to diversification and governance variables over the period 1996–2005. They estimate three alternative specifications allowing firm fixed effects to be time-varying. In the first specification, they allow the fixed effects to change before and after 1997, when reporting rules for industry segments changed. In two alternatives, the fixed effects vary between years with positive and negative stock market returns, and between boom and recession periods. Technically, such time-varying fixed effects are easily incorporated by interacting the firm-specific indicators with one or more indicators for the different subperiods.

Another way to alleviate some of the concerns with unit-specific unobserved heterogeneity not being stable over longer time windows, is to include fixed effects over shorter periods corresponding, for example, with the period a CEO or fund manager was in office. For example, Bennedsen et al. (2020), investigating the effect of CEO hospitalisation on firm performance, estimate specifications with firm fixed effects but also with firm-CEO fixed effects. This boils down to the inclusion of fixed effects that are fixed, but over shorter time spans.

3.3 How not to control for unobserved heterogeneity

In this section we discuss two alternative approaches that are commonly employed in the empirical finance literature, particularly when the group is defined broader then the individual unit. For example, in corporate finance studies it is quite common to industry-adjust the dependent variable. In this case, the dependent variable is changed from y_{it} to $y_{it} - \bar{y}_{gt}$, where $\bar{y}_{gt}$ denotes the average value of y_{it} for all firms in industry g. Another approach is to include the industry-specific average as an additional control in the model. Gormley and Matsa (2014) critically review these alternative approaches and show that they rarely provide consistent estimators. Instead, they recommend the use of fixed effects (i. e., the inclusion of industry dummies or industry × period dummies in the model).

Given the abundance of studies using these alternative approaches it is worthwhile to explore further why they are likely to lead to inconsistent estimators. Let us start considering a simple model. Assume the model of interest can be written as

$$y_{it} = x'_{it}\beta + f_{gt} + u_{it},\tag{3.15}$$

where g denotes an unobserved group effect ($g = 1,\ldots,G$), and where each observation i, in any given period t, belongs to one and only one group g. As an example, we can think of i as firms and g denoting the industry of the firm. The industry-specific unobservable component f_{gt} affects all firms in industry g in period t in the same way. If we assume that the observables in x_{it} are conditionally mean independent of both f_{gt} and u_{it} we could estimate (3.15) by means of pooled OLS, with standard errors appropriately clustered. Alternatively, one could explore a feasible generalised least squares approach, making distributional assumptions on the error components. For the moment, we assume that u_{it} and x_{it} are uncorrelated, but we allow correlation between the group-specific component f_{gt} and the explanatory variables. This makes both OLS and GLS inconsistent, and an alternative approach to control for industry-specific heterogeneity is needed.

Group-adjusting the dependent variable

Industry-adjustment implies that we subtract the average of y_{it} within the relevant industry from the dependent variable. For example, the dependent variable could be a firm's leverage ratio in deviation from the average leverage ratio in the firm's industry, typically referred to as industry-adjusted leverage. Defining the group averages (or industry-specific averages) as

$$\bar{y}_{gt} = \frac{1}{N_g} \sum_j y_{jt},$$

where the summation is taken over all observations j in industry g (to which firm i belongs) in period t, and N_g denotes the number of observations in this group (potentially time-varying), we can write a model for the industry-specific average as

$$\bar{y}_{gt} = \bar{x}'_{gt}\beta + f_{gt} + \bar{u}_{gt}.\tag{3.16}$$

Subtracting this from y_{it} results in

$$y_{it}^{adj} = x_{it}^{adj\prime}\beta + u_{it}^{adj},\tag{3.17}$$

where $y_{it}^{adj} = y_{it} - \bar{y}_{gt}$ denotes the industry-adjusted value for y_{it}, and similar for the other variables. Estimating this equation by OLS is fine (and equivalent to estimating (3.15) with dummy variables for each industry in each period) as long as the transformed regressors can be assumed to be uncorrelated with the transformed u_{it}.

However, if we only industry-adjust the dependent variable, we are actually estimating

$$y_{it}^{adj} = x_{it}'\beta + v_{it}, \tag{3.18}$$

where v_{it} is an error term. This equation misses the group average of x_{it}. Because it can be expected that the group averages correlate with the observed values of x_{it} in the group, this leads to an inconsistent estimator for β. This also holds for variants where firm i is excluded from the group average. Why does this happen? As an example, assume that all x_{it} within an industry change due to a common shock. In the absence of any other changes, this will lead to a change in y_{it} but not in y_{it}^{adj}. As a result, there is a change in the explanatory variables of (3.18) but not the dependent variable. In the correct specification (3.17), both the dependent and independent variables change.

Essentially, the bias in the industry-adjusted estimator is due to an omitted variable. The fact that the model does not control for the industry-specific averages in the explanatory variables leads to a biased and inconsistent estimator. Gormley and Matsa (2014) show that predicting the sign and magnitude of the bias is not straightforward, particularly in cases with multiple variables in x_{it}. In general however, biases can be substantial and it is even possible that the sign of an estimate – even in large samples – differs from the sign of the true coefficient. It is important to note that the bias is not due to a small sample problem and also occurs with a large number of observations.

Adding group-specific averages as control variables

A similar problem arises if we keep y_{it} as the dependent variable, but include the industry-specific average as an additional control. This is quite common. For example, models of capital structure often include the industry average (or median) to control for industry characteristics not captured by other explanatory variables (see, e. g., Flannery and Rangan, 2006). Models of mutual fund flows often include category flows or style flows as an additional control (e. g., Sirri and Tufano, 1998). Let us write the resulting model as

$$y_{it} = x_{it}'\beta + \lambda\bar{y}_{gt} + v_{it}, \tag{3.19}$$

where – again – v_{it} denotes an error term. The belief is that, once we control for $\bar{y}_{gt}$, the correlation between x_{it} and the group-specific component in the error term disappears, or even that the entire group-specific component becomes irrelevant. This, however, is unwarranted. The reason is that the group-specific averages

$$\bar{y}_{gt} = \bar{x}_{gt}'\beta + f_{gt} + \bar{u}_{gt}$$

differ from the unobserved group components f_{gt} due to the measurement error

$$-\bar{x}'_{gt}\beta - \bar{u}_{gt}.$$

The measurement error typically covaries with f_{gt} and also with the variables in x_{it}. This results in a nonstandard errors-in-variables problem. Determining the sign and magnitude of the bias in the OLS estimator based on (3.19) is again non-trivial. Gormley and Matsa (2014) argue that the estimator is inconsistent in most applications. They also show that the bias in estimators based on (3.18) or (3.19), that is, industry-adjusting the dependent variable or including the industry-average as an additional control, can be either smaller or larger than the bias in the pooled OLS estimator ignoring the industry effect. As can be expected, the correlation between the group-specific unobserved heterogeneity and the independent variables in x_{it} has a large impact on the relative performance of these estimators. Obviously, if this correlation is zero, the OLS estimator has no bias, whereas the other two estimators do. This illustrates that incorrect attempts to control for unobserved heterogeneity can lead to worse outcomes than simply ignoring it.

Group fixed effects

The solution to these problems is obvious and requires the use of fixed effects estimators. In the example above this means that group-specific dummy variables are included for each group in each period (assuming that the group effects are time-varying). If the group effects are assumed to be time-invariant, we can just include group dummies. As shown in the standard fixed effects case, this is equivalent to running the regression in deviation from group-specific averages. That is,

$$y_{it} - \bar{y}_{gt} = (x_{it} - \bar{x}_{gt})'\beta + \varepsilon_{it} - \bar{\varepsilon}_{gt}, \tag{3.20}$$

where the resulting estimator is given in (3.14). Compared to the alternative approaches above, in this approach both the dependent variable and the explanatory variables are group-adjusted.

When we estimate a model like (3.20) the standard errors are typically adjusted to account for the reduced degrees of freedom (see the previous section). As discussed above, when estimating cluster-robust standard errors, however, the adjustment is not required as long as the fixed effects are nested within the clusters (Gormley and Matsa, 2014; Cameron and Miller, 2015). In Stata, the command *xtreg* restricts attention to the latter types of clustering, while *areg* allows for more general forms of clustering (but reduces the degrees of freedom with the number of fixed effects). This means that *areg* may produce inappropriate standard errors when the group fixed effects are nested within the clusters (e. g., firm fixed effects with standard errors clustered at the firm or industry level).

3.4 More on instrumental variables

The simple instrumental variables estimator discussed in Section 3.1 is based on the model in levels, and assumes that the number of instruments in z_{it} is equal to the number of explanatory variables in x_{it}. In this section we discuss a number of extensions, starting with the case where there are more instruments in z_{it} than variables in x_{it}, in combination with the two-stage least squares (2SLS) interpretation.

3.4.1 Two-stage least squares

The general model of interest is given by

$$y_{it} = x_{it}'\beta + \varepsilon_{it}, \tag{3.21}$$

where there are reasons to believe that one of more of the K variables in x_{it} are correlated with ε_{it}, potentially due to time-invariant unobserved heterogeneity. Assume there is an R-dimensional vector of instruments z_{it}, partly overlapping with x_{it}. Exogeneity of the instruments requires $E(z_{it}\varepsilon_{it}) = 0$ as required by Assumption EXO1 (iv-p), but now the dimension of z_{it} may be larger than that of x_{it}. That is, $R \geq K$. In this case, the simple instrumental variables estimator in (3.2) cannot be calculated unless $R = K$.

A more general instrumental variables estimator, or 2SLS estimator, can be obtained in two steps. In the first step, each of the regressors in x_{it} is regressed upon the instruments in z_{it} (which will typically contain an intercept) using standard OLS. These regression equations are called reduced form equations, and can be written as

$$x_{k,it} = z_{it}'\pi_k + \eta_{k,it}, \quad k = 1,\ldots,K. \tag{3.22}$$

These reduced forms have the interpretation of linear projections of the set of explanatory variable upon the vector of instruments. If $x_{k,it}$ is exogenous and included in z_{it}, the projection is trivial. For the elements of x_{it} that are not exogenous, these reduced forms provide a decomposition in a part that is linearly related to z_{it} and an orthogonal residual. We are particularly interested in the fitted values of these reduced form regressions. They capture exogenous variation in x_{it}. Using the fact that

$$\hat{\pi}_k = \left(\sum_{i,t} z_{it}z_{it}'\right)^{-1} \sum_{i,t} z_{it}x_{k,it},$$

the fitted values can be written as

$$\hat{x}_{k,it} = z_{it}'\left(\sum_{i,t} z_{it}z_{it}'\right)^{-1} \sum_{i,t} z_{it}x_{k,it}.$$

The 2SLS estimator for β in (3.21) is obtained by applying OLS to the equation with x_{it} replaced by $\hat{x}_{it}$. That is,

$$\hat{\beta}_{2SLS} = \left(\sum_{i,t} \hat{x}_{it}\hat{x}'_{it} \right)^{-1} \sum_{i,t} \hat{x}_{it}y_{it}. \tag{3.23}$$

Even though we introduced this estimator as a two-stages estimator, it is normally directly computed from (3.23). In Stata, the 2SLS estimator is obtained with the command *ivregress 2sls*. Interestingly, one can also rewrite (3.23) as

$$\hat{\beta}_{2SLS} = \left(\sum_{i,t} \hat{x}_{it}x'_{it} \right)^{-1} \sum_{i,t} \hat{x}_{it}y_{,it}, \tag{3.24}$$

so that it also possible to give $\hat{x}_{it}$ the interpretation of instruments, in the context of (3.2).

The 2SLS estimator is consistent for β provided the instruments are valid. This means they are exogenous, as specified in Assumption EXO1 (iv-p), as well as relevant. Technically, relevance requires that the $R \times K$ matrix

$$\text{plim} \frac{1}{NT} \sum_i \sum_t z_{it}x'_{it} \quad \text{has rank } K. \tag{3.25}$$

This is the so-called rank condition for identification. It requires that the instruments z_{it} are sufficiently related to x_{it}. In the special case where only one element of x_{it} is instrumented, say $x_{k,it}$, it requires that the instrument is sufficiently correlated with $x_{k,it}$, once the other regressors are controlled for. This means that the instrument should add sufficient explanatory power to the reduced form in (3.22). Under weak regularity conditions, the 2SLS estimator has an asymptotic normal distribution, and its covariance matrix can be obtained depending upon assumptions about heteroskedasticity and serial correlation in ε_{it}; we discuss this in Subsection 3.4.3.

Before continuing with our derivations, let us reflect a bit on why this may work. Consider a key variable that we think is endogenous, that is, correlated with ε_{it}. The problem is that any variation in this variable may correspond with variation in the unobservables and as a result, a standard estimator is unable to estimate the causal impact of this key variable. For example, firms with good governance differ from firms with poor governance in many unobservable aspects, and standard estimators will have a hard time estimating the causal impact of governance quality upon firm performance.[3] The search for valid instruments requires finding one or more other variables that explain variation in governance quality but are unrelated to the unobservables affecting firm performance. The fitted value from the reduced only captures exogenous

---

3 An additional problem is the measurement of governance quality per se; see Section 4.4.

variation. As a result, relating y_{it} to the fitted values is not subject to the endogeneity bias or omitted variable bias, and the 2SLS estimator can be argued to provide a consistent estimator. In addition to the exogeneity of z_{it}, consistent estimation requires that $\hat{x}_{it}$ exhibits sufficient variation and is not collinear. This, in turn, requires that the instruments are "sufficiently important" in the reduced form. (We return to this below.)

Concerns with instrumental variables

The problem for the practitioner is that it is often far from obvious to find variables that could serve as valid instruments, or to establish whether a chosen instrument is indeed exogenous. The requirement that an instrument is relevant is relatively easy. It requires that the instrument is correlated with the endogenous regressor, conditional upon the other regressors in the equation. This correlation should be sufficiently strong to increase statistical power and to avoid a so-called weak instruments problem. If the instrument is only weakly correlated with the endogenous regressor, this means that the R^2 of the reduced form increases only marginally when the instrument is added and the instrumental variables estimator has poor properties. We discuss this in more detail in Subsection 3.4.2.

The requirement that an instrumental variable is exogenous is more complicated. As stressed by Angrist and Pischke (2009, Chapter 4) this actually requires two things. One is that the instrument is as good as randomly assigned and cannot be influenced by the dependent variable y_{it} (conditional upon the other regressors). Second is an "only through" condition and requires that the instrument predicts the dependent variable y_{it} only though the instrumented variable, conditional upon the other regressors, not directly or through a third unobserved variable. This is often called "an exclusion restriction", and it requires that the instrument itself is appropriately excluded from the equation of interest. That is, any variable in z_{it} that is not included in x_{it} must be validly excluded from (3.21).

Unlike the relevance condition, the exclusion or exogeneity condition cannot be tested if $R = K$. This is because ε_{it} is unobserved. Essentially, when using instrumental variables we are replacing one untestable assumption $E(z_{it}\varepsilon_{it}) = 0$ with another untestable assumption $E(x_{it}\varepsilon_{it}) = 0$. When $R > K$, we have more instruments than required for identification and we can test the so-called overidentifying restrictions in $E(z_{it}\varepsilon_{it}) = 0$, without, however, being able to specify which of the instruments is violating the exogeneity condition (see Subsection 3.5.3). The fact that the scope for testing the validity of instruments is very limited indicates that researchers should carefully justify their choice of instruments, paying attention to theoretical arguments or institutional background. The reliability of an instrument relies on argumentation, not on empirical testing.

Because of this concern, instrumental variables approaches are often debated. For example, Larcker and Rusticus (2010) are very critical on the use of instrumental variables in accounting research. After inspecting a number of recently published studies, they conclude that the variables selected as instruments seem largely arbitrary and not justified by any rigorous theoretical discussion. According to them, many IV applications in accounting are likely to produce highly misleading parameter estimates and test statistics. In a similar vein, Roberts and Whited (2013) argue that truly exogenous instruments are extremely difficult to find in corporate finance research and conclude that "many papers in corporate finance discuss only the relevance of the instrument and ignore any exclusion restrictions". Gallen and Raymond (2020) discuss that when instruments sharing significant sources of variation (e. g., weather-related variables) are used to instrument many different explanatory variables across the literature, this increases the likelihood that the exclusion restriction is violated. Atanasov and Black (2016) focus on shock-based instrumental variables in corporate finance and accounting, which rely on an external shock as the basis for causal inference, for example, a change of governance rules imposed by governments. They conclude that only a small minority of the studies they investigated have convincing causal inference strategies. Reiss (2016) stresses the sensitivity of IV estimates to the functional form of the instrument, and document that it can matter much for the resulting estimate whether, for example, levels or logs of an instrumental variable are used.

Another drawback of instrumental variables estimation is that the standard errors of an IV estimator are typically quite high compared to those of the OLS estimator. The most important cause of this is that instrument and regressor have a low correlation; see Wooldridge (2010, Subsection 5.2.6). Jiang (2017) documents that, among published papers in empirical finance, the IV estimates are almost always much larger than the OLS ones, irrespective of the ex ante nature of the endogeneity bias. Because of their lower precision, she suspects that published instrumental variables estimates tend to be larger, in absolute size, than the OLS ones, because larger values are needed to achieve statistical significance. This arises due to the specification search by empirical scholars, and leads to a "publication bias" in published IV results.[4]

Due to the concerns above, some authors argue that under poor conditions instrumental variable estimates are more likely to provide the wrong statistical inference than simple OLS estimates that make no correction for endogeneity (Larcker and Rusticus, 2010).

Finding instruments
The selection and use of instrumental variables estimators requires a careful analysis of the problem at hand. As recommended by Larcker and Rusticus (2010), a good starting point is to describe the economic theories the research questions are based on.

---

[4] A recent study by Brodeur et al. (2020) appears to support this. They find that instrumental variables methods are particularly problematic with respect to p-hacking and publication bias. Moreover, they find some evidence of relatively more p-hacking in finance.

For example, the endogeneity problem could be due to an important control variable that is not available (a confounding variable), the regressor of interest could be the outcome of a choice that individuals or firms are making, partly based upon the costs and benefits of such a choice, the direction of causality could be unclear, or there may be good reason to suspect measurement errors. With a more detailed description of the endogeneity problem, its background and potential alternative theories, a researcher is better equipped to select an empirical approach, and readers are more able to evaluate whether the approach is appropriate. As stated by Roberts and Whited (2013), the only way to find a good instrument is to understand the economics of the question at hand, including the institutional setting, economic mechanisms and restrictions implied by economic theory. An example of this is provided in Nash and Patel (2019), who review instrumental variables used to study the relation between national culture and finance.

It is recommended to investigate and discuss why chosen instruments would be valid, most importantly why they would satisfy the exogeneity requirement. It is rarely the case that instruments are entirely convincing, in the sense that all potential reviewers and discussants would accept them, but that does not imply that one should not try to give convincing arguments. It is also advisable to anticipate the potential reasons why the instrument is not exogenous and demonstrate that these effects are either very small or controlled for by inclusion of other variables in the model (see Larcker and Rusticus, 2010). Occasionally, a reasonably convincing instrument may be available. For example, using a unique data set, Bennedsen et al. (2007) estimate the effect of family succession. As instrument they exploit the fact that family succession is more likely in firms where the first-born is male, which is obviously exogenous. To identify whether a reduction in leverage leads to a subsequent improvement in operating performance of Austrian ski hotels, Giroud et al. (2012) use unexpected snowfall to instrument changes in leverage. More recently, Bernstein et al. (2019) explore the spillover effects of reorganisation and liquidation on geographically proximate firms, addressing the concern that the decision to liquidate (vs. to reorganise) is not exogenous. They exploit the fact that assignment of bankruptcy judges to cases is based on a blind rotation system (and thus random), and instrument liquidation by the heterogeneity in the judge-specific shares of previous cases converted from Chapter 11 reorganisation to Chapter 7 liquidation.

In each of these examples, some kind of randomness is present (first-born gender, snowfall, assignment of a judge), which helps to argue (but not necessarily guarantees) that the instrument is exogenous.[5] Relevance is checked via the reduced forms. Alternatively, instruments can be based on something observed in the distant past, with little or no direct influence on today's outcomes (y_{it}), but still provide exogenous variation in the explanatory variable of interest. A good example of this is Acemoglu

---

5 See Kahn and Whited (2017) for a critical discussion of the assumptions in Bennedsen et al. (2007).

et al. (2001), who estimate the causal impact of institutions upon country GDP and use mortality rates faced by settlers more than 100 years ago, to instrument for the quality of institutions.

In addition to reporting the first-stage regression results, including the F-statistic on the instruments, it is also useful to report results based on OLS or other standard methods ignoring the endogeneity problem. This provides a benchmark and allows comparison, for example, to see whether the difference between the results is consistent with the underlying theory and the hypothesised source of endogeneity. It is typically a bad idea to immediately jump to instrumental variables estimation without having looked at OLS results. For example, Jiang (2017) advocates a comparison of OLS and IV estimates and a discussion of what their relative magnitude says about the nature of the endogeneity or the sign of the correlation between the potentially endogenous regressor and the error term. See also Atanasov and Black (2021). Finding that OLS and IV estimates are very similar does not necessarily indicate that there are no endogeneity concerns. It could also be that the IV approach is done inappropriately, for example, by using an instrument that is highly correlated with the endogenous regressor and is endogenous itself.

The opposite of a weak instrument is a strong instrument. A strong instrument is one that is relatively highly correlated with the variable it is supposed to instrument. Having a strong instrument results in a relatively accurate IV estimator (although having higher standard errors than OLS). Unfortunately, it is often the case that a strong instrument, being highly correlated with the endogenous regressors, is less likely to be entirely exogenous itself. Fortunately, even with a small violation of the exclusion restrictions, the 2SLS estimator often produces estimates that are reasonably close to the true parameter values if the instruments are sufficiently strong (see Conley et al., 2012). Effectively, one may be better off with an estimator that has a lower standard error, but a small bias, than an unbiased one with a large standard error. This is exploited in, for example, Karpoff et al. (2017), who estimate the impact of antitakeover provisions on the likelihood of takeover, and argue that the strength of their instruments mitigates concerns about the exclusion conditions. This argument should not be used lightly, and a careful discussion of the underlying mechanisms is warranted. Conley et al. (2012) present several alternative methods for performing inference while relaxing the exclusion restriction.

Using lagged variables to avoid simultaneity bias

In several applications it is reasonably obvious that the dependent variable and one or more of the explanatory variables are jointly determined, so that the regressors are not exogenous and standard estimators are inconsistent due to a simultaneity bias. This is true even in the absence of time-invariant heterogeneity in ε_{it}. That is, there is a clear case of $E(x_{it}\varepsilon_{it}) \neq 0$. Quite frequently, authors try to avoid the simultaneity bias by including the lagged values of the regressors, rather than the contemporaneous ones, in the regression model. For example, the seminal paper of Dittmar and Mahrt-Smith (2007), on the impact of corporate governance on firm value, in several specifications uses governance in the initial year of observation, rather than the current value. This, of course, is not an instrumental variables approach and doing so will typically not consistently estimate the direct effect of x_{it} on y_{it} (unless strong conditions are satisfied, see Reed, 2015 or Bellemare et al., 2017 for more discussion). In the presence of serial correlation in ε_{it} (e. g., due to an unobserved time-invariant component), lagged values of x_{it} will usually not provide valid instruments either.

Testing for endogeneity

Because instrumental variables estimators tend to be relatively inaccurate compared to standard estimators like OLS, one may be interested in the question whether the instrumentation was necessary in the first place. Using instruments in cases where it is not needed leads to estimators that are unnecessarily imprecise. It is possible to test for endogeneity of the instrumented regressors, under the important conditions that the set of employed instruments is relevant and exogenous. If we can estimate the model coefficients consistently using an IV estimator, irrespective of the question whether the instrumented regressors are endogenous, we can use that to test endogeneity.

Effectively, the test for endogeneity is a Hausman test (Hausman, 1978), which compares the OLS and IV estimators for the same parameters, and tests whether they are significantly different. Under the null hypothesis of exogenous regressors, both the OLS and IV estimators are consistent, where the first is more efficient. In this case, the two estimators should differ by sampling error only. Under the alternative hypothesis, only the IV estimator is consistent. An illustration of the Hausman test is given in, for example, Giroud et al. (2012), who even find different signs for the OLS and IV estimates of their parameter of interest.

The general test statistic is based on a quadratic form, exploiting the differences between the OLS and IV estimators, similar to the one comparing random effects and fixed effects estimators in (2.83). A computationally attractive version of the Hausman test for endogeneity (often referred to as the **Durbin–Wu–Hausman test**) can be based upon a simple auxiliary regression. First, estimate the reduced form equations and save the residuals. Next, add the residuals to the model of interest and estimate

$$y_{it} = x'_{it}\beta + \hat{\eta}'_{it}\gamma + v_{it}, \tag{3.26}$$

where $\hat{\eta}_{it}$ is the set of reduced form residuals for the endogenous regressors. Actually, this procedure reproduces the 2SLS estimator for β, but it also produces an estimate for γ. If $\gamma = 0$, the instrumented regressors are exogenous. Consequently, we can easily test for endogeneity by performing a standard F-test on $\gamma = 0$ in the above regression. This test can be easily made robust against heteroskedasticity and within-cluster correlation by adjusting the covariance matrix in the latter step accordingly. Note that the test assumes that the instruments are valid under both the null and alternative hypothesis. If the instruments are relatively weak, the test may have limited power.

The control function approach

The above test regression illustrates an alternative approach to dealing with endogeneity, that appears particularly useful in nonlinear models and is referred to as the control function approach. The approach involves the estimation of a reduced form for the endogenous regressor(s), including all available instruments and exogenous regressors, and adding the residuals from the reduced form to the main equation, as illustrated in (3.26). Loosely speaking, the reduced form residuals capture the endogenous components in the regressors and controlling for them, controls for the endogeneity in the equation (see Wooldridge, 2010, Section 6.2). In the linear model, we can interpret $\eta'_{it}\gamma$ as the linear projection of the original error term in the equation (ε_{it}) upon the error terms of the reduced form. Because now v_{it} is uncorrelated with both η_{it} and z_{it}, it is also uncorrelated with the endogenous regressors in x_{it}, and applying pooled OLS to (3.26) provides a consistent estimator, with an adjustment in the calculation of the standard errors because $\hat{\eta}_{it}$ are generated rather than observed regressors. As mentioned, in the linear model this is equivalent to 2SLS. However, in nonlinear models the control function approach is often more attractive than 2SLS, albeit that some additional assumptions are needed (as one cannot rely upon linear projections); see Vella and Verbeek (1999a) for more discussion. Subsections 6.1.9 and 6.3.4 provide some examples.

3.4.2 Weak instruments

The problem of weak instruments in instrumental variables estimation has received considerable attention recently; see Andrews et al. (2019) for an overview. The problem is that the properties of the IV estimator can be very poor, and the estimator can be severely biased, if the instruments exhibit only weak correlation with the endogenous regressor(s). In these cases, the normal distribution provides a very poor approximation to the true distribution of the IV estimator, even if the sample size is large. As a result, the standard IV estimator is biased, its standard errors are misleading and hypothesis tests are unreliable.

To illustrate the problem, let us consider the IV estimator for the case of a single regressor, where the overall mean has been eliminated. In this case, the IV estimator can be written as

$$\hat{\beta}_{IV} = \frac{\sum_{i,t} z_{it} y_{it}}{\sum_{i,t} z_{it} x_{it}}.$$

If the instrument is valid (and under weak regularity conditions), the estimator is consistent and converges to

$$\beta = \frac{\text{cov}(z_{it}, y_{it})}{\text{cov}(z_{it}, x_{it})}.$$

However, if the instrument is not correlated with the regressor, the denominator of this expression is zero. In this case, the IV estimator is inconsistent and the asymptotic distribution of $\hat{\beta}_{IV}$ deviates substantially from a normal distribution.

The instrument is weak if there is some correlation between z_{it} and x_{it}, but not enough to make the asymptotic normal distribution provide a good approximation in finite (potentially very large) samples. For example, Bound et al. (1995) show that part of the results of Angrist and Krueger (1991), who use quarter of birth to instrument for schooling in a wage equation, suffer from the weak instruments problem. Even with samples of more than 300,000 individuals, the IV estimator appeared to be unreliable and misleading. To figure out whether you have weak instruments, it is useful to examine the reduced-form regressions and evaluate the explanatory power of the additional instruments that are not included in the equation of interest. The usual rule of thumb is that an instrumental variable should have an F-statistic in the reduced form larger than 10, corresponding to a t-ratio exceeding 3.16 (Stock and Watson, 2007, Chapter 12). This rule of thumb is based on Stock and Yogo (2005) and relies upon homoskedasticity and absence of serial correlation. For cases with heteroskedasticity and within-cluster correlation, both likely to be present with panel data, the "effective" F-statistic developed by Montiel Olea and Pflueger (2013) is attractive, which is a scaled version of the nonrobust first-stage F-statistic. Testing for weak instruments is also more complicated when there are multiple instruments (excluded from the regression of interest) and multiple regressors that are instrumented. For example, when there are two endogenous regressors that require instrumentation, and three instruments, there are six reduced form coefficients that determine the role of the instruments in capturing the variation in the two regressors. In this case it is insufficient that the reduced form coefficients are nonzero, but it should also be the case that the instruments capture different variation in each of the regressors. More technically, this requires that the 2×3 matrix of reduced form coefficients has rank 2. If not, the rank condition for identification in (3.25) will be violated. Kleibergen and Paap (2006) provide a Wald F-test to test for a reduced rank, which has become reasonably popular in this context, typically referred to as a test for underidentification. Stata's *ivreg2* command provides a range of tests for weak instruments.

Andrews et al. (2019) provide more details on tests for weak identification, particularly in the case with nonhomoskedastic error terms, and discuss several alternative procedures for weak-instrument-robust inference on β. The approach by Anderson and Rubin (1949) appears to have reasonable good properties in the presence of weak identification in the case where there is a single endogenous regressor, and allows the construction of confidence intervals for β that are robust to having a weak instrument.

Bazzi and Clements (2013) document the problem of "blunt instruments" in the empirical growth literature, that is, instruments that are invalid or weak, and discuss some alternative approaches to weak-instrument-robust inference. In practice, however, it would be better to try and find a strong instrument instead.

3.4.3 Standard errors

Even though it is possible to obtain the 2SLS estimator as the OLS estimator in a model where the endogenous regressors are replaced by fitted values from the reduced forms, routinely calculated standard errors will be inappropriate (see Maddala and Lahiri, 2009, Section 9.6, for details). This is because the error term in the second-stage model deviates from the original error term in the equation. Instead, standard errors should be calculated that exploit the residuals from (3.21) using the estimator in (3.23).

To derive the correct covariance matrix of the instrumental variables or 2SLS estimator, we need to make assumptions about the error terms ε_{it}, in particular about the presence of heteroskedasticity and within-cluster correlations, conditional upon the instruments z_{it}. Under the earlier assumptions, and weak regularity conditions, the IV estimator is consistent and asymptotically normal, with a covariance matrix that has the typical sandwich structure. In general, it can be written as

$$V(\hat{\beta}_{2SLS}) = \left(\sum_{i,t} \hat{x}_{it}\hat{x}'_{it} \right)^{-1} B \left(\sum_{i,t} \hat{x}_{it}\hat{x}'_{it} \right)^{-1}, \tag{3.27}$$

where B is a matrix that is determined by the variance of $\sum_{i,t} \hat{x}_{it}\varepsilon_{it}$, which depends upon the assumptions about ε_{it}. If we make the standard assumption (unrealistic in a panel context) that the error terms ε_{it} are independently and identically distributed with mean zero and variance σ_ε^2, the middle term is given by

$$B = \sigma_\varepsilon^2 \sum_{i,t} \hat{x}_{it}\hat{x}'_{it} \tag{3.28}$$

and the covariance matrix of $\hat{\beta}_{2SLS}$ can be written as

$$V(\hat{\beta}_{2SLS}) = \sigma_\varepsilon^2 \left(\sum_{i,t} \hat{x}_{it}\hat{x}'_{it} \right)^{-1}. \tag{3.29}$$

Using the definition of $\hat{x}_{it}$, this can also be written as

$$V(\hat{\beta}_{2SLS}) = \sigma_\varepsilon^2 \left(\left(\sum_{i,t} x_{it}z'_{it} \right) \left(\sum_{i,t} z_{it}z'_{it} \right)^{-1} \left(\sum_{i,t} z_{it}x_{it} \right) \right)^{-1}. \tag{3.30}$$

The variance σ_ε^2 can be estimated on the basis of the residuals, for example, as

$$\hat{\sigma}_\varepsilon^2 = \frac{1}{NT} \sum_{i,t} \hat{\varepsilon}_{it}^2,$$

where $\hat{\varepsilon}_{it} = y_{it} - x'_{it}\hat{\beta}_{2SLS}$. It is possible to apply a degrees of freedom correction to this estimator. Note that, with $z_{it} = x_{it}$, the expression in (3.30) reduces to the standard OLS covariance matrix.

A covariance matrix for $\hat{\beta}_{2SLS}$ under more realistic assumptions is easily obtained by adjusting the B matrix appropriately. For example, in the presence of heteroskedasticity, but no correlations between different error terms, we have

$$B = \sum_{i,t} \hat{\varepsilon}_{it}^2 \hat{x}_{it} \hat{x}'_{it}. \tag{3.31}$$

The covariance matrix given by (3.27) with (3.31) provides the White heteroskedasticity-robust covariance matrix for the IV estimator, and is available in Stata's *ivregress* with the *robust* option.

In the presence of both heteroskedasticity and correlation within units, the "filling" matrix can be estimated as

$$B = \sum_{i,s,t} \hat{\varepsilon}_{it} \hat{\varepsilon}_{is} \hat{x}_{it} \hat{x}'_{is}, \tag{3.32}$$

which allows for within-unit clustering. This requires the appropriate *cluster* option with *ivregress*. Obviously, alternative forms of clustering can be accommodated. This is similar to the discussion in Section 2.5, and much of the concerns and recommendations carry over to this case. For example, it is important that the number of clusters G is sufficiently large (at least $G > R$), and asymptotically increases with the sample size. Also, small sample corrections may be useful.

The combination of clustering and instrumental variables, which leads to inflated standard errors anyway, can lead to standard errors that are very high, occasionally making 2SLS estimators almost uninformative. That is, even though the estimator can be argued to be consistent or asymptotically unbiased, its precision can be so low that inference is economically not very meaningful. In the overidentified case, some efficiency gain can be achieved by optimally weighting the different instruments. This is most easily implemented in a generalised methods of moments framework (GMM), which we discuss in Section 3.5.

3.4.4 IV estimators with panel data

A major advantage of the availability of panel data is that one can consider the use of transformations of variables already in the model as instruments, rather than having to resort to "external" instruments. A simple illustration of this is the fixed effects estimator, which can be interpreted as an instrumental variables estimator where the within-transformed regressors are used as instruments. This is appropriate if the endogeneity is due to the time-invariant component of the error term only and if the regressors are strictly exogenous (i. e., x_{it} is uncorrelated to u_{is} for all s, t). Another example is the Hausman and Taylor (1981) estimator discussed in Section 3.1. This idea can be implemented more generally, by transforming the model of interest, for example, by a first-difference or within transformation, and then find instruments for one or more of the transformed regressors. This is often done in the context of dynamic models, as discussed in Chapter 5, but can also be of use in static models.

For the panel case, there are several standard applications of instrumental variables, building upon the variety of estimators discussed in Chapter 2. The pooled IV estimator discussed above is essentially a standard IV estimator, with the panel nature of the data only playing a role in the calculation of the standard errors. In case of a random effects structure of the error term, we have

$$y_{it} = x_{it}'\beta + \alpha_i + u_{it},$$

where x_{it} contains an intercept term. If one or more elements of x_{it} are correlated with the time-invariant component α_i, one can use a fixed effects approach to consistently estimate β (for time-varying regressors). However, if x_{it} is (also) correlated with u_{it} this is no longer appropriate, and an instrumental variables estimator may provide a consistent estimator, on the condition that valid instruments can be found. These instruments should be uncorrelated with both α_i and u_{is}. The random effects IV estimator is obtained by applying the pseudo transformation to both the explanatory variables and the instruments, leading to $x_{it} - \theta \bar{x}_i$ and $z_{it} - \theta \bar{z}_i$, respectively, where θ is given by

$$\theta = 1 - \sqrt{\frac{\sigma_u^2}{\sigma_u^2 + T\sigma_\alpha^2}},$$

as before. The expression for θ is a bit more complicated in the unbalanced panel case, and there are several ways to estimate of the underlying variance components. The random effects IV estimator is more efficient than the pooled IV estimator if the error components assumption is correct, but imposes strict exogeneity of both regressors and instruments (in the sense that z_{it} is uncorrelated to u_{is}).

A more common approach to instrumental variables is based on a fixed effects specification and starts with either the within or first-differenced equation. The transformed equations can then be combined with instrumental variables in levels, within-transformed, first-differenced or otherwise transformed. To illustrate this, consider a model where x_{it} and α_i are likely to be correlated. In addition, it is likely that $x_{k,it}$ is correlated with u_{it}, but not with $u_{i,t-j}$, $j = 1, 2, \ldots$. In this case, one can transform the model using the first-difference transformation

$$\Delta y_{it} = \Delta x_{it}'\beta + \Delta u_{it},$$

and use either the $x_{k,i,t-2}$ or $\Delta x_{k,i,t-2}$ as instrument for $\Delta x_{k,it}$. When the within transformation is used, there is little scope of using internal instruments, because the instruments need to be uncorrelated to $\bar{u}_i$. For large T, however, this problem disappears and the within transformation may be more attractive than the first-difference one (see Wooldridge, 2010, Chapter 11). The Stata command *xtivreg* offers the possibility to apply instrumental variables to the random effects model, the fixed effects model (based on the within transformation) and the model in first-differences, where the option *vce(robust)* provides standard errors clustered at the unit level.

An application of fixed effects in combination with instrumental variables is given in Pérez-González and Yun (2013), who investigate the causal effect of the use of weather derivatives upon firm value. However, hedging decisions are likely to be endogenous, relating, for example, to investment opportunities, and a standard within estimator tends to be inconsistent. As instruments they use the introduction of weather derivatives as an exogenous shock to firms' ability to hedge weather risks, in combination with a measure on how weather-sensitive a firm's cash flows were before this introduction (in 1997).

Both the random effects and fixed effects IV estimators can be combined with clustered standard errors, to make inference robust against heteroskedasticity and within-firm correlation. Note that first-differenced error terms tend to be serially correlated by construction. It is also possible to reformulate the estimators in a GMM setting, with the use of an optimal weighting matrix. This is discussed in the next section.

3.5 Instrumental variables and GMM

The instrumental variables estimators discussed above can be formalised in the framework of the generalised method of moments (GMM). The starting point of GMM is that the model of interest implies a number of moment conditions. Moment conditions state that the expected value of an expression, which depends upon observable data and unknown parameters only, is equal to zero. These population moments can be exploited in estimation by setting the corresponding sample averages to zero, and solving for the unknown parameters, or, more generally, by trying to get the vector of sample averages as close as possible to zero. In this section we introduce the GMM approach starting from the linear regression model with instrumental variables.

3.5.1 Moment conditions

The model of interest is given by

$$y_{it} = x_{it}'\beta + \varepsilon_{it},$$

where it is assumed that $E(z_{it}\varepsilon_{it}) = 0$ for a given vector of instruments z_{it} of dimension $R \geq K$, where K is the number of elements in β. We can write this as a set of population moment conditions as

$$E(z_{it}(y_{it} - x_{it}'\beta)) = 0. \tag{3.33}$$

These R conditions can help us to estimate the K unknown parameters in β. The identifying assumption is that (3.33) is satisfied only for the true parameter values, and nonzero otherwise. That is, if we would solve (3.33) for the unknown β, there would be only one unique solution.

Of course, this procedure does not work in practice, because the expectations in (3.33) are not observed. Instead, we work with sample averages. In the panel context, where we have both a unit and a time dimension, expectations and sample averages can be taken over one dimension only or over both. In general, sample averages should be taken over a dimension that is sufficiently large, because asymptotic theory relies upon the sample averages converging to population means. Taking averages over both N and T, the vector of sample averages, or sample moments, is given by

$$\frac{1}{NT} \sum_{i,t} z_{it}(y_{it} - x'_{it}\beta), \qquad (3.34)$$

where – for convenience – we use the notation for the balanced data case. Note that y_{it}, z_{it} and x_{it} are observed variables, so that the only unknowns in (3.34) are the parameters β. The GMM estimator for β is obtained by minimising a quadratic form in the sample averages. In particular, we solve

$$\min_{\beta}\left(\frac{1}{NT}\sum_{i,t} z_{it}(y_{it} - x'_{it}\beta)\right)' W_{NT}\left(\frac{1}{NT}\sum_{i,t} z_{it}(y_{it} - x'_{it}\beta)\right), \qquad (3.35)$$

where W_{NT} is an $R \times R$ positive definite weighting matrix, which may depend upon the observed sample. Under regularity conditions, this leads to a consistent and asymptotically normal estimator for β, provided that the moment conditions in (3.33) are valid and sufficient to uniquely identify β. The formal conditions and derivations of GMM, in its most general form, are provided in Hansen (1982).

Let us first consider the exactly identified case where $K = R$, that is, the number of moment conditions equals the number of unknown parameters. In this case, the minimisation of (3.35) does not depend upon the weighting matrix and reduces to solving

$$\frac{1}{NT} \sum_{i,t} z_{it}(y_{it} - x'_{it}\hat{\beta}) = 0, \qquad (3.36)$$

with respect to $\hat{\beta}$. The solution of this reproduces the IV estimator presented in (3.2), and is given by

$$\hat{\beta}_{IV} = \left(\sum_{i=1}^{N}\sum_{t=1}^{T} z_{it}x'_{it}\right)^{-1}\sum_{i=1}^{N}\sum_{t=1}^{T} z_{it}y_{it}. \qquad (3.37)$$

More interesting results emerge in the overidentified case, when $R > K$.

3.5.2 The optimal weighting matrix

In the overidentified case, we have more moment conditions (i. e., more instruments) than needed to estimate the unknown parameters. Rather than selecting a subset of the moment conditions, we can use all of them by minimising (3.35). In this case, there exists a wide range of estimators for β, depending upon the choice for the weighting matrix. As long as the weighting matrix is (asymptotically) positive definite, the resulting estimators are all consistent for β. The idea behind the consistency result is that we are minimising a quadratic loss function in a set of sample moments that asymptotically converge to the corresponding population moments, which are equal to zero for the true parameter values. Different weighting matrices lead to different consistent estimators with typically different asymptotic covariance matrices. This allows us to choose an optimal weighting matrix that leads to the most efficient instrumental variables estimator. It can be shown that the optimal weighting matrix is proportional to the inverse of the covariance matrix of the sample moments. Intuitively, this means that sample moments with a small variance, which consequently provide accurate information about the unknown parameters in β, get more weight in estimation than the sample moments with a large variance.

The covariance matrix of the sample moments

$$\frac{1}{NT} \sum_{i,t} z_{it}(y_{it} - x'_{it}\beta) = \frac{1}{NT} \sum_{i,t} z_{it}\varepsilon_{it} \tag{3.38}$$

depends upon the assumptions we impose upon the error distribution (and its relation with the instruments). In the case where ε_{it} is independently and identically distributed (IID), independent of the instruments, the asymptotic covariance matrix of the sample moments is given by

$$\sigma_\varepsilon^2 \operatorname{plim} \frac{1}{NT} \sum_{i,t} z_{it} z'_{it}.$$

Consequently, an empirical optimal weighting matrix is obtained as

$$W_{NT}^{opt} = \left(\frac{1}{NT} \sum_{i,t} z_{it} z'_{it}\right)^{-1},$$

the proportionality factor σ_ε^2 being irrelevant. As a result, the IV-GMM estimator is given by

$$\hat{\beta}_{2SLS} = \left(\sum_{i,t} \hat{x}_{it} \hat{x}'_{it}\right)^{-1} \sum_{i,t} \hat{x}_{it} y_{it}, \tag{3.39}$$

where the optimal weighting matrix is hidden in the definition of $\hat{x}_{it}$. As before

$$\hat{x}_{it} = z'_{it}\left(\sum_{i,t} z_{it} z'_{it}\right)^{-1} \sum_{i,t} z_{it} x_{it}.$$

These results indicate that the 2SLS estimator is (asymptotically) the most efficient estimator for β in the restrictive case where the error terms in the equation of interest are homoskedastic and exhibit no autocorrelation or other cross-correlations. In cases where the distribution of the error term is less restricted, one can adjust the standard errors for $\hat{\beta}_{2SLS}$ to accommodate for heteroskedasticity or within-cluster correlation, as discussed above.

However, in the GMM framework it is potentially more attractive to adjust the weighting matrix to obtain an asymptotically more efficient estimator. For example, if the error term is heteroskedastic, but there is no correlation between different error terms, an empirical optimal weighting matrix is given by

$$W_{NT}^{opt} = \left(\frac{1}{NT} \sum_{i,t} \hat{\varepsilon}_{it}^2 z_{it} z_{it}' \right)^{-1},$$ (3.40)

where $\hat{\varepsilon}_{it}$ is the residual given by $y_{it} - x_{it}' \hat{\beta}_1$, and where $\hat{\beta}_1$ denotes an initial consistent estimator for β, for example, the 2SLS estimator. This makes the optimal GMM estimator a two-step estimator. In the first step, a consistent estimator for β is obtained, which is used to calculate residuals and construct the (estimated) optimal weighting matrix. In the second step, an asymptotically efficient estimator is obtained. From (3.35) and (3.40), the optimal estimator can be written as

$$\hat{\beta}_{GMM} = \left[\left(\sum_{i,t} x_{it} z_{it}' \right) \left(\sum_{i,t} \hat{\varepsilon}_{it}^2 z_{it} z_{it}' \right)^{-1} \left(\sum_{i,t} z_{it} x_{it}' \right) \right]^{-1}$$
$$\times \left(\sum_{i,t} x_{it} z_{it}' \right) \left(\sum_{i,t} \hat{\varepsilon}_{it}^2 z_{it} z_{it}' \right)^{-1} \sum_{i,t} z_{it} y_{it}.$$ (3.41)

A variant of this is the iterated GMM estimator. This estimator has the same asymptotic properties as the two-step one, but may have better small sample properties. It is obtained by computing a new optimal weighting matrix using the two-step estimator, and using this to obtain a new estimator $\hat{\beta}_3$, say, which in turn is used in a weighting matrix to obtain $\hat{\beta}_4$. This procedure is repeated until convergence. These estimators are implemented in Stata in the procedure *ivregress gmm* and *ivregress igmm*, respectively, where the weighting matrix in (3.40) is the default.

In the panel data case, it is unlikely that all error terms are uncorrelated among each other, and within-unit or within-period correlations are likely to be present, depending upon the context. In this case, the optimal weighting matrix is more general and needs to allow for correlation within clusters. As before, this requires that the number of clusters is sufficiently large and increases with the sample size. In practice, it may be recommended to impose more structure on the covariance matrix of (3.38), for example, when the number of time periods is large and within-unit correlation may be an issue; see Cochrane (2005, Chapter 11) for more discussion and recommendations.

Conditional upon having chosen the optimal weighting matrix, the asymptotic covariance matrix of the two-step GMM estimator is given by

$$\hat{V}(\hat{\beta}_{GMM}) = \left(\left(\sum_{i,t} x_{it} z_{it}' \right) W_{NT}^{opt} \left(\sum_{i,t} z_{it} x_{it}' \right) \right)^{-1}$$

(provided the optimal weighting matrix is correctly scaled). It is also possible to perform GMM using a suboptimal weighting matrix (such as the use of 2SLS), and adjust the standard errors for heteroskedasticity and within-cluster correlation. The expressions for the covariance matrix in this more general case are somewhat more complicated (though in principle straightforward). Importantly, the weighting matrix affects the asymptotic efficiency of the GMM estimator, while the estimated covariance matrix only affects our estimates of the standard errors, depending upon the assumptions we are willing to make. One of the most important applications of this IV-GMM approach in finance is the estimation of a model with a lagged dependent variable, that is, a dynamic model where $y_{i,t-1}$ is one of the variables on the right-hand side. We discuss dynamic models in more detail in Chapter 5.

Weak identification

Unfortunately, there is considerable evidence that the asymptotic covariance matrix for the two-step or iterated GMM estimator often provides a poor estimate of the covariance matrix in samples that are typical for empirical work (see, e. g., Hansen et al., 1996). In many cases, the estimated covariance matrix is too optimistic, providing standard errors that are too small. The problem of weak instruments discussed before also extends to the generalised method of moments. To explain the problem more generally, consider the set of moment conditions in (3.33). The parameters of interest β are identified under the assumption that

$$E(z_{it}(y_{it} - x_{it}'\beta_0)) = 0,$$

where β_0 is the true value of β, and that

$$E(z_{it}(y_{it} - x_{it}'\beta)) \neq 0$$

for $\beta \neq \beta_0$. That is, the moment conditions are only satisfied for the true parameter values. The latter condition states that the moment conditions are relevant, and is necessary for identification (and consistency of the GMM estimator). It tells us that it is not sufficient to have enough moment conditions ($R \geq K$), but also that the moment conditions should provide relevant information about the parameters of interest. If $E(z_{it}(y_{it} - x_{it}'\beta))$ is nearly zero for $\beta \neq \beta_0$ then β can be thought of as being weakly identified. As mentioned by Stock et al. (2002), an implication of weak identification is that the GMM estimator can exhibit a variety of pathologies. For example, the two-step estimator and the iterated GMM estimator may lead to quite different estimates and confidence intervals, the GMM estimator may be very sensitive to the addition of one or more instruments, or to changes in the sample. All these features may indicate a weak identification problem.

3.5.3 Tests for overidentifying restrictions

If the model is exactly identified ($R = K$), the validity of the moment conditions, or the validity of the instruments, cannot be tested. This is because all moment conditions are needed to identify the model. As a result, the K sample moments (after estimation) are equal to zero, regardless of whether or not the population moment conditions are true. In case of overidentification ($R > K$), it is possible to test the overidentifying restrictions. In this case, it is typically only possible to set K linear combinations of the sample moments equal to zero. If the population moment conditions are correct, one would expect that the R elements in

$$\frac{1}{NT} \sum_{i,t} z_{it} (y_{it} - x'_{it} \hat{\beta}_{GMM}) \tag{3.42}$$

are all sufficiently close to zero, as they should converge to zero asymptotically. This provides the basis for the overidentifying restrictions test, often referred to as the Sargan test or Sargan–Hansen test. The test statistic is given by the value of the optimand in (3.35) with the optimal weighting matrix, scaled by the number of observations. That is,

$$J = NT \left(\frac{1}{NT} \sum_{i,t} z_{it} (y_{it} - x'_{it} \hat{\beta}_{GMM}) \right)' W_{NT}^{opt} \left(\frac{1}{NT} \sum_{i,t} z_{it} (y_{it} - x'_{it} \hat{\beta}_{GMM}) \right), \tag{3.43}$$

where $\hat{\beta}_{GMM}$ is the optimal GMM estimator. Under the null hypothesis that all moment conditions are valid, the test statistic has an (approximate) Chi-square distribution with $R - K$ the degrees of freedom. Note that $R - K$ is the number of overidentifying restrictions, corresponding to the number of instruments that is not required to consistently estimate β. Only $R - K$ elements in (3.42) are free on account of the K restrictions imposed by the first-order conditions.

If the Sargan test rejects, the specification of the model is rejected in the sense that the sample evidence is inconsistent with the joint validity of all R moment conditions. Without additional information it is not possible to determine which of the moments are valid, that is which instruments are exogenous. Roberts and Whited (2013) are therefore critical on the usefulness of this test because it assumes that a sufficient number of instruments are valid, yet which ones and why is left unspecified. Moreover, the test may lack power if many instruments are used that are uncorrelated with ε_{it} but add little explanatory power to the reduced forms. In a similar spirit, Deaton (2010) stresses that a satisfactory Sargan test does not tell us that all instruments are valid. "Such tests can tell us whether estimates change when we select different subsets from a set of possible instruments. While the test is clearly useful and informative, acceptance is consistent with all of the instruments being invalid, while failure is consistent with a subset being correct. Passing an overidentification test does not validate instrumentation". Only if one is willing to accept the validity of at least K instruments, the overidentifying restrictions test is consistent and optimal to test the validity of the remaining $R - K$ instruments (Newey, 1985).

If a subset of the instruments is known to satisfy the moment conditions, it is possible to test the validity of the remaining instruments or moments provided that the model is identified on the basis of the nonsuspect instruments. Assume that $R_1 \geq K$ moment conditions are nonsuspect and we want to test the validity of the remaining $R - R_1$ moment conditions. To compute the test statistic, estimate the model using all R instruments and compute the overidentifying restrictions test statistic J. Next, estimate the model using only the R_1 nonsuspect instruments. Typically, this will lead to a lower value for the overidentifying restrictions test, J_1, say. The test statistic to test the suspect moment conditions is easily obtained as $J - J_1$, which, under the null hypothesis, has an approximate Chi-square distribution with $R - R_1$ degrees of freedom. In the special case that $R_1 = K$, this test reduces to the overidentifying restrictions test in (3.43), and the test statistic is independent of the choice of the R_1 instruments that are said to be nonsuspect.

3.5.4 Panel estimators

In a panel context, independence across observations is unlikely to be satisfied. As a result, weighting matrices and/or covariance matrices should be used that allow for heteroskedasticity and within-cluster correlation, with an appropriate definition of clusters. In addition, the use of panel data introduces three other aspects that are worth mentioning. First, as we have seen several times already, the equation of interest can be transformed to eliminate unobserved time-invariant heterogeneity, for example, using the first-difference or within transformation. Second, instruments are not necessarily external in the sense that they do not yet play a role in the model somehow, but can be transformations of explanatory variables that are already in the model, for example, lagged values or lagged first-differences. Finally, the moment conditions that were imposed above aggregating over both periods and units, can be imposed per period taking expectations across units only.

To illustrate this, consider the following model

$$y_{it} = x'_{1,it}\beta_1 + x'_{2,it}\beta_2 + \alpha_i + u_{it}, \tag{3.44}$$

where we have separated the set of explanatory variables in two subsets. Both $x_{1,it}$ and $x_{2,it}$ are endogenous in the sense that they are potentially correlated with the time-invariant unobserved heterogeneity in α_i. In addition, the variables in $x_{2,it}$ are potentially correlated with the contemporaneous error term u_{it}, but not with its previous values $u_{i,t-1}, u_{i,t-2}, \ldots$, etcetera. This endogeneity could be due to the presence of measurement error (see Chapter 4), simultaneity or reverse causality. To estimate this model, a first step is to eliminate α_i, which is most conveniently done by the first-difference transformation. This leads to

$$\Delta y_{it} = \Delta x'_{1,it}\beta_1 + \Delta x'_{2,it}\beta_2 + \Delta u_{it}, \tag{3.45}$$

If, conditional upon α_i, $x_{1,it}$ is strictly exogenous, it is uncorrelated with the transformed error Δu_{it} so that no further problems arise. However, if $x_{2,it}$ is correlated with u_{it}, $\Delta x_{2,it}$ is likely to be correlated with Δu_{it} and standard estimation of (3.45) will be inconsistent. However, if $x_{2,it}$ is uncorrelated with $u_{i,t-1}$, it is possible to use $x_{2,i,t-2}$, or $\Delta x_{2,i,t-2}$, as instrument for $\Delta x_{2,it}$. This will require that lagged values of $x_{2,it}$ correlate sufficiently with its future values, so as to make the instruments relevant. Exogeneity relies upon the assumption that $x_{2,it}$ is uncorrelated with lagged idiosyncratic error terms. Whether or not this is appropriate depends upon the source of endogeneity of $x_{2,it}$, as well as on the dynamic properties of u_{it}. The assumption that $E(x_{2,it}u_{i,t-1}) = 0$ is a bit more challenging when both $E(u_{it}u_{i,t-1}) \neq 0$ and $E(x_{2,it}u_{it}) \neq 0$.

Translating the above into moment conditions, we obtain

$$E((\Delta y_{it} - \Delta x'_{1,it}\beta_1 - \Delta x'_{2,it}\beta_2)\Delta x_{1,it}) = 0, \tag{3.46}$$

$$E((\Delta y_{it} - \Delta x'_{1,it}\beta_1 - \Delta x'_{2,it}\beta_2)\Delta x_{2,i,t-2}) = 0. \tag{3.47}$$

If we impose these two sets of moment conditions across all periods, we have an exactly identified model and estimation can be done using a standard IV or 2SLS estimator. However, following Arellano and Bond (1991), it is also possible to impose (3.47) per period, and expand the set of instruments by using longer lags of $x_{2,it}$ as we move later in the panel. That is,

$$E((\Delta y_{it} - \Delta x'_{1,it}\beta_1 - \Delta x'_{2,it}\beta_2)x_{2,i,t-j}) = 0, \quad j = 2, 3, \ldots, t, \tag{3.48}$$

where it is assumed that the first available observation of the instrument is $x_{2,i0}$, for period 0. This way, we expand the number of moment conditions, and the number of instruments. The observations over which we can exploit them differs depending upon where we are in the panel. Note that the error terms in the first-differenced equation are serially correlated by construction.

In addition to using instruments for the first-differenced equation, it is also possible to exploit moment conditions based on the levels equation in (3.44), as proposed by Arellano and Bover (1995) and Blundell and Bond (1998). For example, $\Delta x_{1,it}$, being uncorrelated with α_i and u_{it} (by assumption), can serve as an instrument and we obtain moment conditions as

$$E((y_{it} - \beta_0 - x'_{1,it}\beta_1 - x'_{2,it}\beta_2)\Delta x_{1,it}) = 0, \tag{3.49}$$

where β_0 is an intercept term to accommodate the nonzero unconditional mean of α_i. Depending upon the dynamic properties of $x_{1,it}$, this set of moment conditions may provide additional information about the unknown coefficients. When the optimal weighting matrix is used, the estimation procedure automatically adjusts for moment conditions being highly correlated with each other and thus providing "overlapping" information about β.

An application of this approach can be found in Beck et al. (2000), who estimate a model explaining various measures of growth from a country's financial development, using a sample of 63 countries in a panel with $T = 7$ periods of five years. They assume that $x_{i,t-2}, x_{i,t-3}, \ldots$ are uncorrelated with $\varepsilon_{i,t-1}$, so they can be used as instruments in the first-differenced equation. In addition, they use lagged differences $\Delta x_{i,t-1}$ as instruments for the levels equation. It is assumed that u_{it} has no serial correlation, and all regressors are allowed to be correlated with α_i and u_{it} (simultaneity).

3.6 Strict exogeneity

Many of the panel estimators discussed impose strict exogeneity of the explanatory variables, conditional upon the time-invariant heterogeneity α_i. For example, in the linear model

$$y_{it} = x'_{it}\beta + \alpha_i + u_{it},$$

the standard within estimator imposes that

$$E(u_{it} \mid x_{i1}, \ldots, x_{iT}, \alpha_i) = 0.$$

This says that, conditional upon α_i, the explanatory variables are not allowed to depend upon current error terms, nor upon leads and lags of the error terms. The assumption that $E(u_{it} \mid x_{it}, \alpha_i) = 0$ is a contemporaneous exogeneity assumption. Violations of strict exogeneity where $E(u_{it} \mid x_{is}, \alpha_i) \neq 0$ for $s > t$ are not unlikely in empirical work, and are the focus of Grieser and Hadlock (2019). Think of a situation where y_{it} is a measure of firm performance. If firm performance is higher than expected due to a good realisation of u_{it}, this may have an impact on future values of one or more of the explanatory variables in x_{it}, for example, board structure (Wintoki et al., 2012). Another example is where y_{it} is a measure of performance of a mutual fund. Good performance leads to more investor flows and therefore increases a fund's total net assets (TNA) in later periods. At the same time, we may wish to include fund size (log TNA) in x_{it} to allow for decreasing returns to scale (Pastor et al., 2015). Mechanisms like this are called dynamic feedback mechanisms, which are thus excluded in the standard fixed effects approach. An alternative mechanism is where y_{it} and x_{it} respond to the same underlying shock but with different lags. For example, an industry shock may immediately increase the volatility of a stock, but affect other variables, for example, managerial ownership, with a delay.

When we employ the first-difference (FD) estimator, instead of the within estimator, the exogeneity assumptions are weaker. In particular, the FD estimator requires that $E(u_{it} \mid x_{it}, \alpha_i) = 0$, $E(u_{it} \mid x_{i,t-1}, \alpha_i) = 0$ and $E(u_{it} \mid x_{i,t+1}, \alpha_i) = 0$. Or, briefly, $E(\Delta u_{it} \mid \Delta x_{it}, \alpha_i) = 0$. As a result, a violation of the strict exogeneity assumption is likely to affect the fixed effects (within) and FD estimators in a different way. It may be tempting to think that the FD estimator will suffer from less bias when strict exogeneity is violated, but this is not generally true. Because the within transformation transforms the variables in deviation from averages over time, a violation of strict exogeneity is of the order $1/T$ and disappears with large T when occurring in only one time period. In the FD estimator there is no bias if there is correlation between u_{it} and $x_{i,t+2}$ or later. A simple diagnostic for potential violations of strict exogeneity is therefore a comparison between the within and FD estimators. Recalling that both estimators are numerically identical with $T = 2$, this comparison is only useful with $T > 2$. Grieser and Hadlock (2019) show that the two estimates are often not only quite different but frequently have opposite signs.

Wooldridge (2010, Chapter 10) proposes two simple tests for strict exogeneity (conditional upon imposing contemporaneous exogeneity) that can be obtained from auxiliary regressions. The first test takes the fixed effects model and adds future values of one of more explanatory variables from x_{it} to the righthand side. (Note that it is unlikely to have an economic model that implies that the future value of some characteristic affects today's outcome.) For example,

$$y_{it} = x'_{it}\beta + w'_{i,t+1}\gamma + \alpha_i + u_{it},$$

where $w_{i,t+1}$ is a subset of $x_{i,t+1}$, corresponding to the subset of explanatory variables that is suspected to be not strictly exogenous. Under strict exogeneity the additional variables should be irrelevant and $\gamma = 0$, which can be tested employing a standard (fixed effects) estimator. Alternatively, one starts form the first-differenced equation and adds w_{it} to the righthand side. That is,

$$\Delta y_{it} = \Delta x'_{it}\beta + w'_{it}\gamma + \Delta u_{it},$$

where, again, $\gamma = 0$ is implied by strict exogeneity. The latter test also works for $T = 2$. Grieser and Hadlock (2019) show that the strict exogeneity assumption is largely ignored in empirical work in finance, and tests for strict exogeneity are rare, even though it is a testable assumption.

If instrumental variables are used, strict exogeneity of the instruments may also be required. For example, if we use z_{it} as instruments in a first-differenced of within-transformed equation it is not only required that z_{it} is uncorrelated with both α_i and u_{it}, but z_{it} should also be uncorrelated with $u_{i,t-1}$ for the FD version, and with u_{is} for the within version. A test for strict exogeneity of z_{it} can also be obtained from an auxiliary regression, as discussed in Grieser and Hadlock (2019), who recommend its use.

Long panels

In the case of the within transformation, the violation of the strict exogeneity assumption is often of the order $1/T$, for example, if there is correlation between x_{it} and u_{is}, for one pair s, t only. As a result, the inconsistency in the within estimator tends to be of the order $1/T$ as well (Nickell, 1981). Although this suggests that the within estimator may work well with long panels, Grieser and Hadlock (2019) challenge this and stress that this result depends upon the fixed effects α_i being truly time-invariant over long time periods. If the fixed effects capture aspects as managerial quality, firm culture, investment opportunities, or the skill of a fund manager, this may be not be true. In their words, "as panels get longer, any assumption of constant firm-level heterogeneity becomes highly questionable". In such cases, both the first-difference and within estimators tend to do poorly.

Predictive regressions

The biases discussed in the current section also play a role in predictive regressions using the fixed effects estimator. In a predictive regression, the dependent variable is dated t, whereas the explanatory variables, the predictors, are dated $t - 1$ or before. The panel character arises when data on, for example, multiple countries are pooled together and common slope coefficients are imposed (see, e. g., Hjalmarsson, 2010). This can be written as

$$y_{it} = x'_{i,t-1}\beta + \alpha_i + \varepsilon_{it}, \tag{3.50}$$

where it is assumed that ε_{it} is uncorrelated with $x_{i,t-1}$ (but not necessarily uncorrelated with x_{it}). The typical example here is where y_{it} is the stock return in country i, and $x_{i,t-1}$ is a set of predictor variables, such as the dividend yield. These predictor variables may be contemporaneously correlated with ε_{it}. In combination with the typical high degree of persistence in these predictor variables, this leads to a bias in the estimation of β in the time-series case, as analysed by Stambaugh (1999). This problem carries over to the fixed effects estimator because information after time $t - 1$ is used in the within transformation. Even when T is reasonably large, the bias can be substantial if the persistence in x_{it} is high (see Hjalmarsson, 2008, who also proposes a bias correction for the within estimator).

Estimation without strict exogeneity

As an illustration, consider the relation between the mutual fund performance and fund size (Pastor et al., 2015), that is,

$$y_{it} = \alpha_i + \beta x_{it} + u_{it},$$

where y_{it} is a measure of fund performance (e. g., a benchmark-adjusted return) of fund i during period t, and x_{it} is (the logarithm of) a fund's TNA (fund size) at the beginning of the period. The fund fixed effects α_i capture variation in fund manager skills, as long as skill is constant over time. The coefficient β is of particular interest because it captures decreasing returns to scale (if negative), consistent with the Berk and Green (2004) model. Fund size, however, is not strictly exogenous. First, there is a mechanical relationship between fund size at the end of period t and returns in period t (due to internal growth of the fund). Second, investors respond to past performance when allocating their money, so that fund size depends upon past performance (and past realisations of u_{it}). The good news is that fund size is credibly uncorrelated with future values of u_{it}.

Under the assumption that x_{it} is uncorrelated to $u_{i,t+s}$, $s = 0, 1, \ldots$, it is possible to derive a consistent estimator (for $N \to \infty$ with T fixed) using instrumental variables by appropriately transforming the equation of interest as well as the explanatory variable that serves as an instrument. A simple version would start with first-differencing the equation, that is,

$$\Delta y_{it} = \beta \Delta x_{it} + \Delta u_{it}$$

and employ $x_{i,t-1}$ or $\Delta x_{i,t-1}$ as an instrument. This imposes that $E(u_{it} \mid x_{i,t-s}, \alpha_i) = 0$, $s = 1, 2, \ldots$. Pastor et al. (2015) employ an alternative instrumental variables estimator, inspired by the work of Moon and Phillips (2000). First, the fixed effects are eliminated by forward-demeaning the equation of interest. The forward-demeaned version of a variable x_{it} is defined as

$$\bar{x}_{it} = x_{it} - \frac{1}{T_i - t + 1} \sum_{s=t}^{T_i} x_{is}, \quad t = 1, \ldots, T_i - 1, \tag{3.51}$$

where T_i denotes the number of time periods for which fund i is observed. (This equation allows the panel to be unbalanced due to attrition or late entry, but does not accommodate "gaps"). This transformation takes the average of all future values of x_{it} (including its current value) and subtracts this from the current value. Although it does not eliminate the problem because the transformed regressor and the transformed error will be correlated, it is now relatively easy to find valid instruments. Pastor et al. (2015), inspired by Moon and Phillips (2000), suggest the use of the backward-demeaned version of x_{it}. The backward-demeaned version of a variable is defined as

$$\underline{x}_{it} = x_{it} - \frac{1}{t} \sum_{s=1}^{t} x_{is} \quad t = 2, 3, \ldots T. \tag{3.52}$$

Under the previous assumptions $\text{cov}(\bar{u}_{it}, \underline{x}_{it}) = 0$, while $\text{cov}(\bar{x}_{it}, \underline{x}_{it}) \neq 0$ (because both are derived from x_{it}), so that the corresponding instrumental variables estimator can be argued to be consistent. Because the forward-demeaned error term is heteroskedastic and serially correlated by construction, standard errors that allow for within-unit correlation are needed.

Pastor et al. (2015) determine the estimator using a 2SLS approach, where the fitted values of the reduced form, estimated per individual fund, are included in the model of interest. Neither the forward demeaned equation, nor the reduced form, contain intercept terms. The resulting estimator is referred to as a recursive demeaning (RD) estimator. An alternative estimator is used by Zhu (2018), who advocates the use of $x_{i,t-1}$ (fund size at the beginning of the period) as an instrument for the forward-demeaned equation, as well as the inclusion of an intercept term in the reduced form. Both estimators are expected to be consistent, their precision depending upon the relevance of the employed instruments. Simulation results in Zhu (2018) suggest that her estimator is more accurate than the one employed by Pastor et al. (2015). As noted by Dyakov et al. (2020), given the availability of multiple instruments it is natural to combine them into one estimator, which should be even more precise. Accordingly, they consider a third estimator that includes both the backward-demeaned and the lagged values of fund size as instruments.

4 Outliers, missing values and other data issues

Available data are almost never perfect, and empirical work is hampered by data issues, such as outliers, measurement errors and missing values. In this chapter, we briefly cover these problems. Typically there is no generic or mechanical solution to these challenges and careful inspection may be needed. This may also explain why these issues, with some notable exceptions, receive relatively little attention in the empirical literature.

A common problem in empirical data is the presence of outliers, for example, as the result of large data errors. Outliers are often influential observations in the sense that they have a disproportional or disturbing impact on standard estimates, such as OLS. Section 4.1 discusses the problem of outliers in more detail, including some common remedies, such as winsorisation and the use of more robust estimation methods. Section 4.2 discusses how to deal with missing values, and highlights some inappropriate ways of doing so. In almost all cases, existing panel data sets are unbalanced in the sense that not all units are observed in all periods. Section 4.3 pays attention to the issue how standard estimators are adjusted to deal with this, and reviews some of the problems that arise with nonrandom attrition. Finally, this chapter concludes with a discussion of measurement errors and their impact on different panel estimators in Section 4.4.

4.1 Outliers and influential observations

Loosely speaking, an outlier is an observation that deviates markedly from the rest of the sample. In the context of a linear regression, an outlier is an observation that is far away from the (true) regression line. Outliers may be due to measurement errors in the data, but can also occur by chance in any distribution, particularly if it has fat tails. If outliers correspond to measurement errors, the preferred solution is to discard the corresponding observation from the sample (or correct the measurement error if the problem is obvious). If outliers are correct data points, it is less obvious what to do. Variation in the explanatory variables is a key factor determining the precision of an estimator, so that outlying observations may also be very valuable (and throwing them away is not a good idea).

The problem with outliers is not so much that they deviate from the rest of the sample, but rather that the outcomes of estimation methods, like OLS, can be very sensitive to one or more outliers. In such cases, an outlier becomes an "influential observation". There is, however, no simple mathematical definition of what exactly is an outlier. Nevertheless, it is highly advisable to compute summary statistics of all relevant variables in a sample before performing any estimation. This also provides a quick way to identify potential mistakes or problems in the data. For example, for some units in the sample the value of a variable could be several orders of magnitude

https://doi.org/10.1515/9783110660739-004

too large to be plausibly correct. Data items that by definition cannot be negative are sometimes coded as negative. In addition, missing values may coded as –99 or –999. As an example, Guthrie et al. (2012) inspect a histogram of changes in CEO pay, and use this to identify two outlying firms in their sample. They investigate these outliers in great detail, including the robustness of their key results.

4.1.1 Identifying and eliminating outliers

Outliers are frequently discussed – and somehow dealt with – in empirical finance papers. For example, more than 25% of recent articles in top finance journals mention outliers (Adams et al., 2019). In the context of a linear regression model or OLS, the most common approach is to "winsorise" the data on one of more variables before performing a regression. Winsorising means that the tails of the distribution of each variable are adjusted. For example, a winsorisation at the 1% (and 99%) level would set all data below the 1st percentile equal to the 1st percentile, and all data above the 99th percentile to the 99th percentile. In essence this amounts to saying "I do not believe the data are correct, but I know that the data exist. So instead of completely ignoring the data item, I will replace it with something a bit more reasonable" (Frank and Goyal, 2008). Estimation is done by standard methods, like OLS or fixed effects, treating the winsorised observations as if they are genuine observations. Accordingly, the authors of such papers make statements like "to avoid potential problems with outliers all variables are winsorised", and then continue ignoring the winsorisation. In the context of panel data, it typically makes sense to apply the winsorisation per period, so that one replaces, say, the 1% tails of the distribution in each period rather than across the entire sample.

An alternative to winsorisation is "trimming" (also referred to as truncation). In this case, the extreme values in the tails in the distribution of a variable are simply eliminated from the data set. For example, Ball and Shivakumar (2005) study a trimmed sample that excludes 1% of the accounting variables at each extreme, motivated by the presence of data errors and scaling problems (in financial ratios), and Lemmon and Roberts (2010) trim all financial ratios at 1% to "mitigate the effect of outliers and eradicate errors in the data". As a result, the effective number of observations for any analysis that requires observations for the variables involved will be reduced. This loss of observations may increase if multiple variables are trimmed simultaneously. In Stata, both winsorisation and trimming can be done with the function *winsor2*, where the *by* option allows application per period.

Unfortunately, both winsorisation and trimming are only pragmatic solutions to deal with outliers. There is no statistical argument to motivate their general use, let alone to claim that these are optimal approaches to deal with outliers. The chosen level of winsorisation or trimming, at which to replace or delete the tails of the distributions, is arbitrary. While winsorisation is typically applied at the levels of 1% and

99%, existing studies also use 2.5%, or even 5%. In the latter case, a total of 10% of the observations on a single variable is replaced or dropped from the sample. This means that winsorisation or trimming can seriously affect the univariate distribution of a variable, particular if applied too crudely. An additional problem is that standard winsorisation and trimming approaches are based on the univariate distributions of each variable. As a result, there is no guarantee that influential observations, for example, highly unusual combinations of y_{it} and one or more variables in x_{it}, are eliminated.[1] In a regression context, such observations tend to be very influential. Mitton (2021) investigates the sensitivity of regression results in corporate finance with respect to methodological choices and documents that key results can be highly dependent on how outliers are dealt with. Kothari et al. (2005) illustrate that inappropriate data trimming, especially in skewed distributions, can leads to spurious findings.

Ideally, the treatment of outliers involves identifying observations that have an "extreme" impact on the estimation results. This means that the key estimation results will be very different once such outliers have been removed. For example, Adams et al. (2018) find that outliers caused by data errors and comprising less than 2% of the original sample are responsible for the finding of mutual fund diseconomies of scale in Chen et al. (2004). They also document that the negative relation between industry size and mutual fund performance documented in Pastor et al. (2015) is attributable to extreme observations that comprise less than 0.05% of the sample. Even if the outlying observation is not a data error, but a genuine observation, one would not want the signs and significance of model coefficients to be almost entire driven by only a few observations.[2] If the main findings are due to only a small proportion of extreme observations, further inspection of such influential observations can be insightful too. For example, Knez and Ready (1997) show that the risk premium on size that was estimated by Fama and French (1992) completely disappears when the 1% most extreme observations are trimmed each month. This does not mean that these extreme observations should be ignored in the empirical analysis, but understanding their role helps to better understand the cause of the relation being tested; see Kraft et al. (2006) for a related discussion on the mispricing of accruals and accrual components.

---

1 Adams et al. (2019) give the following example. Consider a panel of employees containing information on natural hair colour, height, weight, eye color, and ethnicity. In this sample, neither a person of 160 centimetre nor an employee with blue eyes or an employee with blond hair would likely register as univariate outliers. Similarly, neither an observation regarding a Chinese male employee nor an employee weighing 100 kilos would appear as outliers. However, if all of these characteristics describe a single employee, then we might suspect this observation is an outlier.

2 Except in cases where one is particularly interested in the effect of rare events, for example, Barro (2006).

The problem with estimation methods like OLS is that they are based on minimising the sum of squared residuals

$$RSS(\beta) = \sum_{i=1}^{N}(y_i - x_i'\beta)^2. \qquad (4.1)$$

Due to the fact that squares are taken, large residuals are penalised more than proportionally. Accordingly, OLS tries to prevent very large residuals. As a result, a few outliers can substantially affect the estimated regression line, and this may make the corresponding residuals look "reasonable" (e. g., within three standard deviation bounds from zero).

It is therefore a better option to investigate the residual of a given observation when the model coefficients are estimated using only the rest of the sample. Denoting the full sample OLS estimate for β by $\hat{\beta}$, the OLS estimate after excluding observation j from the model can be denoted as $\hat{\beta}^{(j)}$. An easy way to calculate $\hat{\beta}^{(j)}$ is to augment the original model with a dummy variable that is equal to one for observation j only and 0 otherwise. This effectively discards observation j. The resulting model is given by

$$y_i = x_i'\beta + \gamma d_{ij} + \varepsilon_i,$$

where $d_{ij} = 1$ if $i = j$ and 0 otherwise. The OLS estimate for β from this regression corresponds to the OLS estimate in the original model when observation j is dropped. The estimated value of γ corresponds to the residual $y_i - x_i'\hat{\beta}^{(j)}$ when the model is estimated excluding observation j. The routinely calculated t-ratio of γ is referred to as the studentised residual. The studentised residuals are approximately standard normally distributed (under the null hypothesis that $\gamma = 0$) and can be used to judge whether an observation is an outlier. Rather than using conventional significance levels (and a critical value of 1.96), one should pay attention to large outliers (t-ratios much larger than 2) and try to understand the cause of them. Are the outliers correctly reported and, if yes, can they be explained by one or more additional explanatory variables? Davidson and MacKinnon (1993, Section 1.6) provide more discussion and background.

Adams et al. (2019) advocate the use of a more advanced multivariate outlier identification approach. A first step is to compare the estimates of robust estimation methods (which are less sensitive to outliers) with those of standard methods (e. g., OLS), in the spirit of a Hausman (1978) test. The next step is to identify potential multivariate outliers, using an "outlier detection plot", to be followed by further inspection of their nature and origin. For example, it is useful to inspect the incidence of outliers across months in a panel, and to inspect the original data for data entry errors and other mistakes (e. g., having an inappropriate sample). After correcting any mistakes, they recommend to examine and discuss the remaining influential outliers, and, when appropriate, the use of an outlier-robust estimation technique to mitigate the influence of outliers. Applications of this are given in Adams et al. (2018, 2019). In contrast to winsorising or trimming, which is quite mechanical, their approach entails a more careful investigation of the outlier problem, requiring consideration of the research question, economic theory, sampling issues and, potentially, some manual inspection of the most influential outliers. The approach of Adams et al. (2019) also provides outlier-robust clustered standard errors and is able to handle large numbers of fixed effects encountered in panel data models.

4.1.2 Robust estimation methods

As mentioned above, OLS can be very sensitive to the presence of one or more extreme observations. This is due to the fact that it is based on minimising the sum of squared residuals, where each observation is weighted equally. As a first step, modelling logs rather than levels often helps to reduce the sensitivity of the estimation results to extreme values. For example, variables like firm size are typically included in natural logarithms in firm-level regression models. Alternatively, empirical models are typically estimated in terms of ratios, such as sales to total assets, leverage, or Tobin's Q.

Alternative estimation methods are available that are less sensitive to outliers. A relatively popular approach is called least absolute deviations (LAD). Its objective function is given by

$$S_{LAD}(\beta) = \sum_{i=1}^{N} |y_i - x_i'\beta|, \qquad (4.2)$$

which replaces the squared terms by their absolute values. There is no closed-form solution to minimising (4.2) and the LAD estimator for β would have to be determined using numerical optimisation. This is a special case of a so-called quantile regression and procedures are readily available, for example, in *qreg* in Stata. In fact, LAD is designed to estimate the conditional median (of y_i given x_i) rather than the conditional mean, and we know medians are less sensitive to outliers than are averages. The statistical properties of the LAD estimator are only available for large samples (see Koenker, 2005, for a comprehensive treatment).

Although the standard LAD estimator can be applied to panel data, the inclusion of either random effects or fixed effects is less straightforward and typically some additional assumptions are required. Some approaches exploit a correlated random effects assumption, which allows α_i to depend upon observed variables in a pre-specified way (see Section 2.8). The inclusion of firm fixed effects is problematic (for short panels) because of the incidental parameters problem (see Section 6.1), and several alternative ways of dealing with this are available; see, for example, Koenker (2004), Canay (2011) and Arellano and Bonhomme (2016). A recent application of the LAD approach in finance is provided in Lee et al. (2019), who explain risk-taking of mutual funds from their performance in the first half of the year, using both pooled OLS with winsorised data, and quantile regression at the median. Given the extreme robustness to outliers of the latter approach, the authors consider the quantile regression results more reliable.

Another alternative is the use of trimmed least squares (TLS). This corresponds to minimising the residual sum of squares, but with the most extreme observations – in terms of their residuals – omitted. More formally, denote the squared residuals as $[\hat{\varepsilon}^2]_{(i)}$ in order of increasing magnitude. That is, $[\hat{\varepsilon}^2]_{(i)} \leq [\hat{\varepsilon}^2]_{(j)}$ for $j > i$. Then the objective function is given by

$$S_{TLS}(\hat{\beta}) = \sum_{i=1}^{q} [\hat{\varepsilon}^2]_{(i)},\qquad(4.3)$$

where q is a trimming constant, to be chosen, with $N/2 < q \leq N$. Effectively, this means that the TLS estimator fits q observations very well, but ignores the rest (those with the largest squared residuals). Because the values of the residuals depend upon the estimated coefficients, the objective function is no longer a quadratic function of β and the estimator should be determined numerically; see Rousseeuw and Leroy (2003, Chapter 3). Note that, unlike standard trimming or winsorising, trimmed least squares will generally not trim the same number of observations from the upper and lower tails of the distribution. It may be sensible to employ TLS for a range of values for h to see how the estimates are affected by the trimming. An application of TLS is provided in Knez and Ready (1997) who investigate the sensitivity of Fama and MacBeth (1973) regressions to extreme observations for the estimation of risk-factor premia, as in Fama and French (1992). Knez and Ready (1997) use TLS to obtain a time series of robust slope coefficients. Rather than discarding them, they argue that the influential observations help shedding light on the question of where risk premia come from. In particular, they relate the differences between TLS and OLS to positive skewness in the return distributions for small young firms. Investors who hold small firms anticipate a few major successes and many minor disappointments. Accordingly, such firms should carry a risk premium.

More advanced robust estimation techniques are available, such as M-estimators, S-estimators and MM-estimators; see Adams et al. (2019) and the references therein. A Stata package including MM-estimators and outlier diagnostics is available by typing "net from http://homepages.ulb.ac.be/~vverardi/stata" from within Stata. In the context of panel data, Baltagi and Bresson (2015) present several robust estimators for static and dynamic panel data models, as well as methods to detect influential observations and outliers.

4.2 Missing values

A frequently encountered problem in empirical work, particularly with micro-level data, is that of missing observations. For example, R&D expenditures are often unobserved for a substantial number of firms (see, e. g., Koh et al., 2021). Abrevaya and

Donald (2017) report that nearly 40% of all papers recently published in four top empirical economics journals have data missingness. In such cases, a first requirement is to make sure that the missing data are properly indicated in the data set. It is not uncommon to have missing values being coded as a large (negative) number, for example, −999, or simply as zero. Obviously, it is incorrect to treat these "numbers" as if they are actual observations. When missing data are properly indicated, most regression software will automatically calculate the required estimators using the complete cases only. Although this involves a loss of efficiency compared to the hypothetical case when there are no missing observations, it is often the best one can do.

Whether or not missing observations are problematic in the sense of causing biased inference, depends upon the question to what extent data missingness is allowed to depend upon observable and unobservable variables. Ideally, missing observations are missing completely at random (MCAR). In this case, the causes of the missing data are completely unrelated to the data (Rubin, 1976). A more realistic situation is where the missing observations are missing at random (MAR). In this case, the probability of a missing observation may depend upon observables (e. g., explanatory variables in the model). This case is also referred to as selection on observables. If the data are not missing at random, standard estimators, like OLS, may be subject to a **sample selection bias**. This is driven by the fact that the probability of an observation to end up in the sample is correlated to the unobservable error term in the model.

To discuss this more formally, let r_{it} be a dummy variable indicating whether unit i has observations for all relevant variables in period t and is thus part of the effective sample available for estimation. Then the key condition for not having a bias in estimating the regression model explaining y_{it} from x_{it} is that the conditional expectation of y_{it} is not affected by conditioning upon the requirement that $r_{it} = 1$. This means that

$$E(y_{it} \mid x_{it}, r_{it} = 1) = E(y_{it} \mid x_{it}). \tag{4.4}$$

What we can estimate from the available sample is the left-hand side of (4.4), whereas we are interested in the right-hand side, and therefore we want the two terms to coincide. The condition in (4.4) is satisfied if the probability distribution of r_{it} given x_{it} does not depend upon y_{it}. This means that selection in the sample is allowed to depend upon the explanatory variables in x_{it}, but not upon the unobservables ε_{it} in the regression model (MAR). Accordingly, for the purpose of estimating a regression model with R&D expenditures as a regressor, missing values for R&D are not a problem if the probability of observing it depend upon observable variables included in the model (but not upon the unobservables). If we estimate a model with fixed effects, the above condition should hold conditional upon α_i. This means that selection bias does not arise in the fixed effects estimator for β if selection depends upon x_{it} or α_i, but not upon u_{it}. See the next section for more discussion.

Suppose we have a sample of 1000 hedge funds, observing their net returns, management and incentive fees and some other characteristics. We also observe the funds'

TNA, but this information is missing for half of the sample. This means that we can estimate a model relating fund performance to the sizes of the incentive and management fees using 1000 observations, but if we wish to control for fund size (TNA) the effective sample reduces to 500. In this case we have to make a trade-off between the ability to control for fund size in the model and the efficiency gain of using twice as many observations (but potentially suffering from an omitted variable bias). In such cases, it is not uncommon to report estimation results for both model specifications using the largest possible sample. The estimation results for the two specifications will be different not only because they are based on a different set of regressor variables, but also because the samples used in estimating them are different. In the ideal case, the difference in estimation samples has no systematic impact. To check this, it makes sense to also estimate the different specifications using the same data sample. This sample will contain the cases that are common across the different subsamples (in this case 500 observations). If the results for the same model are significantly different between the samples of 500 and 1000 funds, this suggests that condition (4.4) is violated, and further investigation into the missing data problem is warranted. The above arguments are even more important when there are missing data for several of the explanatory variables for different subsets of the original sample.

A pragmatic, but inappropriate, solution to deal with missing data is to replace the missing data by some number, for example, zero or the sample average, and augment the regression model with a missing data indicator, equal to one if the original data was missing and zero otherwise. For example, Flannery and Rangan (2006) set R&D expenditures to zero when it is missing, and augment their capital structure model with a dummy variable indicating whether information on R&D expenditures is missing. This pragmatic approach is simple and attractive, as the complete sample of firms can be used. In general, however, it can be shown to produce biased estimates, even if the data are missing at random (Jones, 1996).

Imputation means that missing values are replaced by one or more imputed values. Sometimes, an assumption can be made that may make economic sense. For example, Dittmar (2004) assumes that any firm that does not report R&D expenditures has no R&D expenditures, and replaces missing values with zero. However, Koh et al. (2018) document that firms with confident CEOs are more likely to report their R&D expenditures relative to firms with cautious CEOs, which contradicts the assumption that missing R&D expenditures are effectively zero. In general, simple ad hoc imputation methods are typically not recommended. For example, replacing missing values by the sample average of the available cases will clearly distort the marginal distribution of the variable of interest as well as its covariances with other variables. Hot deck imputation, which means that missing values are replaced by random draws from the available observed values, also destroys the relationships with other variables. Cameron and Trivedi (2005, Chapter 27) provide more discussion of missing data and imputation in a regression context. Koh et al. (2021) compare different imputation techniques to impute R&D expenditures. In general, any statistical analysis that follows after missing data are imputed should take into account the approximation errors made in the imputation process. That is, imputed data cannot be treated simply as if they are genuinely observed data (although this is commonly what happens, particularly if the proportion of imputed values is small). Dardanoni et al. (2011) provide an insightful analysis of this problem.

Nevertheless, when panel data are available, and missing values occur occasionally in the panel, it can make sense to replace the missing values by the most recently available values in the panel. For example, if the TNA of a hedge fund is not observed in quarter t, but it is observed in quarter $t - 1$, one may replace the missing value by the value from quarter $t - 1$. This, again, will induce some bias, but scholars may prefer such small biases while gaining much in terms of the effective sample size. Such imputation is not recommended when TNA is a key variable of interest and one is particularly interested in modelling its dynamics. In some cases, one can assume that economic agents – if a value is missing – respond to the most recently available value, which would give economic content to this simple imputation procedure.

4.3 Incomplete panels

In empirical finance almost all panel data sets are unbalanced in the sense that not all units are observed in all periods. New stocks are listed at exchanges, while others get delisted. New firms emerge, or disappear due to bankruptcy or mergers and acquisitions (M&A), new mutual funds are started, while others are liquidated, etcetera. A consequence is that the resulting panel data set is no longer rectangular. If the total number of units is equal to N, and the number of time periods is T, the total number of observations is substantially smaller than NT. Below, we denote the number of periods unit i is observed by T_i and the number of units in period t by N_t, so that the total number of observations is $\sum_i T_i = \sum_t N_t$. In case the model involves lagged values or changes of variables, the effective number of observations available for estimation may be even less.

A first consequence of working with an incomplete panel is a computational one. Most of the expressions for the estimators in this text are no longer appropriate if observations are missing. A simple "solution" is to discard any unit from the panel that has incomplete information and to work with the completely observed units only. In this approach, estimation uses the balanced subpanel only. This is computationally attractive but potentially highly inefficient: a substantial amount of information may be "thrown away". This loss in efficiency can be prevented by using all observations including those on units that are not observed in all T periods. This way, one uses the unbalanced panel. In principle this is straightforward, but computationally it requires some adjustments to the formulae in the previous sections. We shall discuss some of these adjustments below. Fortunately, most software that can handle panel data also allows for unbalanced data.[3]

Another potential and even more serious consequence of using incomplete panel data is the danger of selection bias. If units are incompletely observed for an endogenous reason, the use of either the balanced subpanel or the unbalanced panel may lead to biased estimators and misleading tests, again due to selection bias. To elaborate upon this, suppose that the model of interest is given by

$$y_{it} = x'_{it}\beta + \alpha_i + u_{it}.$$ (4.5)

Furthermore, define the indicator variable r_{it} as $r_{it} = 1$ if (x_{it}, y_{it}) is observed and 0 otherwise. The observations on (x_{it}, y_{it}) are missing at random (MAR) if r_{it} is independent of α_i and u_{it}. This means that conditioning upon the outcome of the selection process does not affect the conditional distribution of y_{it} given x_{it}. If we want to concentrate upon the balanced subpanel, the conditioning is upon $r_{i1} = \cdots = r_{iT} = 1$ and we require that r_{it} is independent of α_i and $u_{i1}, \ldots, u_{iT}$. In these cases, the usual consistency properties of the estimators are not affected if we restrict attention to the available or complete observations only. If observations are not MAR and selection depends upon the equations' error terms, the OLS, random effects and fixed effects estimators may suffer from selection bias.

4.3.1 Estimation with randomly missing data

The expressions for the (one-way) fixed and random effects estimators are easily extended to the case of unbalanced panel data. The fixed effects estimator can be determined as the least squares dummy variable estimator, as before, where each unit has its own intercept term. Alternatively, it can be determined as OLS in a within-transformed model, where now all variables are in deviation from averages over the available observations for the corresponding unit. As a result, units that are observed only once provide no information about β and should be dropped.

Formally, we define "available means" as

$$\bar{y}_i = \frac{1}{T_i}\sum_{t=1}^{T} r_{it}y_{it}; \quad \bar{x}_i = \frac{1}{T_i}\sum_{t=1}^{T} r_{it}x_{it},$$

where $T_i = \sum_t r_{it}$. With this, the fixed effects estimator can be written as

$$\hat{\beta}_{FE} = \left(\sum_{i=1}^{N}\sum_{t=1}^{T} r_{it}(x_{it} - \bar{x}_i)(x_{it} - \bar{x}_i)'\right)^{-1}\sum_{i=1}^{N}\sum_{t=1}^{T} r_{it}(x_{it} - \bar{x}_i)(y_{it} - \bar{y}_i),$$ (4.6)

---

3 Occasionally, some routines only work in the absence of "gaps" in the data, for example, when a firm leaves the panel and enters again a few periods later.

which is a straightforward generalisation of (2.76), where all sums and averages are now taken over available observations only. For the two-way fixed effects model, with both firm and period fixed effects, the implied transformation is less straightforward and there is no easy generalisation of (3.9). Typically, this is not so much of a problem because the period dummies can be included in the vector x_{it} if their number is not too large, and the estimator in (4.6) can be used.

Clustered standard errors are also easily generalised to the unbalanced panel case. There is some concern, though, that the small sample properties of the clustered covariance matrix may be negatively affected if the number of clusters is relatively small and multiple clusters only have a small number of observations. Recall that, in general, clustered standard errors rely on the number of clusters being sufficiently large. With unbalanced data, the lower bound for what is sufficient (even though there is no clear-cut definition) is likely to be larger (Cameron and Miller, 2015). With typical sample sizes in finance, this does not appear to be a major issue when standard errors are clustered over firms or assets, but when clustering is done at broader levels (e. g., states or industries) this may be of concern in some contexts. Adjustments to the degrees of freedom correction may be appropriate to accommodate the unbalanced nature of the clusters.

For the random effects estimator, the extensions to the unbalanced panel case are also reasonably straightforward. The FGLS estimator, exploiting the error covariance structure, can be written as

$$\hat{\beta}_{RE} = \left(\sum_{i=1}^{N} \sum_{t=1}^{T} r_{it}(x_{it} - \hat{\theta}_i \bar{x}_i)(x_{it} - \hat{\theta}_i \bar{x}_i)' \right)^{-1} \sum_{i=1}^{N} \sum_{t=1}^{T} r_{it}(x_{it} - \hat{\theta}_i \bar{x}_i)(y_{it} - \hat{\theta}_i \bar{y}_i), \qquad (4.7)$$

where $\hat{\theta}_i$ is a consistent estimator for

$$\theta_i = 1 - \sqrt{\frac{\sigma_\alpha^2}{\sigma_u^2 + T_i \sigma_\alpha^2}}.$$

Note that the transformation applied here is firm-specific and depends upon the number of observations for firm i. Consistent estimators for σ_α^2 and σ_u^2 are given by

$$\hat{\sigma}_u^2 = \frac{1}{\sum_{i=1}^{N} T_i - N} \sum_{i=1}^{N} \sum_{t=1}^{T} r_{it}(y_{it} - \bar{y}_i - (x_{it} - \bar{x}_i)'\hat{\beta}_{FE})^2$$

and

$$\hat{\sigma}_\alpha^2 = \frac{1}{N} \sum_{i=1}^{N} \left[(\bar{y}_i - \hat{\beta}_{0B} - \bar{x}_i'\hat{\beta}_B)^2 - \frac{1}{T_i}\hat{\sigma}_u^2 \right],$$

where $\hat{\beta}_B$ is the between estimator for β, and $\hat{\beta}_{0B}$ is the between estimator for the intercept (both based on a regression of averages over periods).

For the pooled OLS and Fama-MacBeth approaches, the adjustments to accommodate unbalanced panels are trivial. In the Fama-MacBeth approach the unbalanced
panel nature implies that the number of observations per period (N_t) varies over time.
Because the standard Fama-MacBeth estimator is an equally weighted average across
all periods, this may imply that some relatively inaccurate estimates, corresponding to
periods with a small number of units, end up getting a relatively high weight in the final estimate. This can be alleviated by using a weighed least squares approach, where,
for example, a weighted average is taken of the period-by-period estimates, where the
weights depend upon the number of observations in each period, or upon some other
measure of the precision of the individual estimates (see Yoon and Lee, 2019, for an
example).

4.3.2 Selection bias and some simple tests

In addition to the usual conditions for consistency, it is assumed above that the data
are missing at random (MAR), so that the response indicator variable r_{it} is independent
of all unobservables in the model. This assumption may be unrealistic. For example,
explaining the performance of hedge funds may suffer from the fact that funds with a
bad performance are less likely to survive (Baquero et al., 2005). In the context of mutual funds and hedge funds, the term "survivorship bias free" is often used to stress
that performance data of the funds are included in the databases, even though funds
no longer exist. Nevertheless, this does not guarantee that the effective sample available for estimation does not suffer from selection bias, for example, if performance
data over multiple consecutive periods are required.

If r_{it} depends upon α_i or u_{it}, selection bias may arise in the standard estimators.
This means that the distribution of y_{it} given x_{it} and conditional upon selection into the
sample is different from the distribution of y_{it} given x_{it} (which is what we are interested
in). For consistency of the fixed effects estimator it is now required that

$$E(u_{it} \mid x_{i1}, \ldots, x_{it}, r_{i1}, \ldots, r_{it}, \alpha_i) = 0,$$

which replaces Assumption EXO3 (fe). This means that selection into the sample is
allowed to depend upon x_{it} and α_i without affecting consistency of the fixed effects
estimator, but it is not allowed to depend upon u_{it} (see Verbeek and Nijman, 1992).

For the random effects estimator, as well as for pooled OLS, the additional assumptions are more severe. For pooled OLS, we need to strengthen Assumption EXO3
(ols-p) to

$$E(x_{it}\varepsilon_{it} \mid r_{it}) = 0,$$

or (somewhat stronger)

$$E(\varepsilon_{it} \mid x_{it}, r_{it}) = 0,$$

which says that selection in the sample should not depend upon the unobservables in ε_{it}, conditional upon the explanatory variables. For the random effects estimator we need that neither α_i nor u_{it} depend upon any of the selection indicators $r_{i1}, \ldots, r_{iT}$. If units with certain values for α_i are less likely to be included in some periods, this will typically bias both the OLS and the random effects estimators. Similarly, if units with certain shocks u_{it} are more likely to leave the panel, the random effects estimator is inconsistent. Note that, because the fixed effects estimator allows selection to depend upon α_i and upon u_{it} in a time-invariant fashion, it tends to be more robust against selection bias than the random effects estimator. Another important observation is that estimators from the unbalanced panel do not necessarily suffer less from selection bias than those from the balanced subpanel. In general, the selection biases in the estimators from the unbalanced and balanced samples need not be the same, and their relative magnitude is not known a priori (Verbeek and Nijman, 1992).

Verbeek and Nijman (1992) suggest a number of simple tests for selection bias based upon the above observations. First, as the conditions for consistency state that the error terms should – in one sense or another – not depend upon the selection indicators, one can test this by simply including some function of $r_{i1}, \ldots, r_{iT}$ in the model and checking its significance. The relevant null hypothesis states that whether a unit was observed in any of the periods 1 to T should not give us any information about its unobservables in the model. For example, the inclusion of $c_i = \prod_t r_{it}$ or $T_i = \sum_t r_{it}$ may provide a reasonable procedure to check for the presence of selection bias when there are no fixed effects in the model. With fixed effects, one could include $r_{i,t-1}$, $T_{it} = \sum_{s=1}^{t} r_{is}$ or $\sum_{s \neq t}^{T} r_{is}$ (Wooldridge, 1995). Under the null hypothesis of no selection bias, any of these simple functions should not matter. Admittedly, the power of the tests may be low, but their simplicity is attractive so as to provide a quick check against possible selection bias in the panel. Another group of tests is based upon the idea that the four different estimators, random effects and fixed effects, using either the balanced subpanel or unbalanced panel, usually all suffer differently from selection bias. A comparison of these estimators may therefore give an indication for the likelihood of selection bias.

Seru et al. (2010) investigate the investment performance of individual investors, and their learning experience, and are concerned that investors may stop trading (and thus leave their sample) endogenously. They apply the Verbeek and Nijman (1992) test by including $r_{i,t-1}$ in their fixed effects regression model and conclude that attrition from the panel is nonrandom. They continue their analysis with a variant of the Heckman (1979) procedure. This procedure, along with some of its extensions, will be discussed in Chapter 6. Unfortunately, the problem of nonrandom sample selection or nonrandom attrition from the panel introduces an identification problem, so that any solution will require additional assumptions (see Verbeek and Nijman, 1996, for an extensive treatment).

4.4 Measurement errors

The final data issue we cover in this chapter is that of measurement errors, also referred to as errors-in-variables. Of course, measurement errors could be the underlying
cause of outliers and influential observations. In this section, we focus on measurement errors that are seemingly random, either because the reporting on a variable is
imprecise and noisy (e. g., TNA of hedge funds), or because the true variables of interest correspond to underlying concepts that are inherently difficult to measure (e. g.,
investment opportunities, quality of governance, tax advantages of debt, or the probability of default). To motivate the discussion, let us start with the standard model,
where the explanatory variable suffers from measurement error. To simplify the pre-
sentation, we focus on the model with one explanatory variable. In panel notation,
the model of interest is given by

$$y_{it} = \beta_0 + \beta_1 x_{it}^* + \varepsilon_{it}, \tag{4.8}$$

where x_{it}^* is a scalar explanatory variable. Initially, we assume that x_{it}^* and ε_{it} are uncorrelated. Instead of observing x_{it}^*, we observe a variable x_{it}, where

$$x_{it} = x_{it}^* + v_{it}. \tag{4.9}$$

In this equation, v_{it} corresponds to the measurement error, typically assumed to have
mean zero. If one estimates a pooled regression model explaining y_{it} from the observed
regressor variable x_{it} and a constant, one is estimating

$$y_{it} = \beta_0 + \beta_1 x_{it} + (\varepsilon_{it} - \beta_1 v_{it}). \tag{4.10}$$

The error term in this regression includes an additional part related to the measure-
ment error in the regressor. If it can be assumed that the composite error term $(\varepsilon_{it} - \beta_1 v_{it})$
is uncorrelated with the regressor x_{it}, the estimation of (4.10) by standard methods,
like OLS, is consistent for β, under the usual regularity conditions. This assumption,
however, is uncommon. A key issue is what is appropriate to assume about the measurement error v_{it} and its correlations with x_{it}, the observed variable, and x_{it}^*, the true
variable.

Classical measurement error
The "classical measurement error" model arises by assuming that the measurement
error v_{it} is random and uncorrelated with the true unobserved variable x_{it}^*. The automatic consequence of this is that v_{it} is correlated with the observed regressor, resulting
in a correlation between regressor and error term in (4.10). As a result, the OLS estimator for β_1 is biased towards zero. To illustrate this, suppose that $\beta_1 > 0$. When the
measurement error in an observation is positive, two things happen: x_{it} has a positive

component v_{it} and the equation's error term has a negative component $-\beta_1 v_{it}$. Consequently, x_{it} and the error term in (4.10) are negatively correlated, and the OLS estimator is biased and inconsistent. If $\beta_1 < 0$, a negative correlation arises and again the OLS estimator is biased. Denoting the variance of v_{it} by σ_v^2 and the variance of x_{it}^* by $\sigma_{x^*}^2$ (assuming homoskedasticity for simplicity), it can be shown that

$$\text{plim}\,\hat{\beta}_1 = \beta_1\left(1 - \frac{\sigma_v^2}{\sigma_{x^*}^2 + \sigma_v^2}\right) = \beta_1\left(1 - \frac{\sigma_v^2}{V(x_{it})}\right) \tag{4.11}$$

under the assumption that v_{it} is uncorrelated with both ε_{it} and x_{it}^*. This means that the OLS estimator is biased towards zero, with a larger attenuation bias if the measurement error is large relative to the variance in the true variable x_{it}^*. The ratio $\sigma_v^2/\sigma_{x^*}^2$ is referred to as a noise-to-signal ratio because it gives the variance of the measurement error (the noise) in relation to the variance of the true values (the signal). If this ratio is small, we have a small bias, if it is large, the bias is also large. The term in parentheses in (4.11) is referred to as the attenuation factor. In general, the OLS estimator underestimates the effect of the true regressor variable if it is subject to measurement error that is unrelated to the true level.

If the slope coefficient of the model is underestimated, the estimator for the intercept term will also be biased (typically overestimated). More generally, when the model of interest contains more than one explanatory variable, the attenuation bias carries over to the other coefficients too, the exact impact depending upon the correlations between the explanatory variables (Roberts and Whited, 2013). If multiple explanatory variables are subject to measurement error, the combined impact is less clear. In most cases, though, a noisy measure of an explanatory variable will imply that its impact is underestimated. In contrast, when the dependent variable y_{it} is subject to random measurement error, the only consequence is an increase in the error variance, and thus less precision of the estimator. However, if the measurement error in y_{it} is not entirely random and correlated with one or more variables in x_{it}, a bias will emerge.

Fixed effects
Now suppose that the model of interest also contains a time-invariant component α_i that is correlated with x_{it}. As before, we may wish to eliminate this heterogeneity by using the first-difference (FD) or within estimator. Following Griliches and Hausman (1986), it can be shown for the FD estimator that

$$\text{plim}\,\hat{\beta}_{1,FD} = \beta_1\left(1 - \frac{V(\Delta v_{it})}{V(\Delta x_{it})}\right). \tag{4.12}$$

Under the typical assumption that the measurement error is random and not serially correlated, $V(\Delta v_{it}) = 2\sigma_v^2$. Because it is commonly the case in economics and finance that explanatory variables exhibit positive serial correlation, $V(\Delta x_{it})$ will usually be smaller than twice the variance, and, as a result, the attenuation bias of the FD estimator is larger than for OLS. In this case, the first-difference transformation magnifies the measurement error and reduces the variation in the signal. Put differently, in first-differenced data there will be more noise and less signal.

There are, however, possible exceptions to this general rule. For example, let us assume that v_{it} is homoskedastic with serial correlation coefficient ρ_v. At the same time, assume x_{it}^* is homoskedastic with variance $\sigma_{x^*}^2$ and first-order serial correlation coefficient ρ_{x^*}. Again assuming independence of the measurement error and the true regressor, we can now rewrite the previous expression as

$$\text{plim}\,\hat{\beta}_{1,FD} = \beta_1 \left(1 - \frac{2\sigma_v^2(1 - \rho_v)}{2\sigma_{x^*}^2(1 - \rho_{x^*}) + 2\sigma_v^2(1 - \rho_v)} \right). \tag{4.13}$$

If the serial correlation in the true explanatory variable is larger than that in the measurement error, the attenuation bias is larger in the first-differencing approach. In the exceptional case where the measurement error is time-invariant ($v_{it} = v_{is}$ for all s, t) the measurement error is eliminated by the first-difference transformation, and the fixed effects approach solves the measurement error problem. In most cases, though, estimation in first-differences will suffer more from measurement error than does OLS, because ρ_{x^*} is much larger than ρ_v.

As noted by Griliches and Hausman (1986), the within estimator typically suffers from a different attenuation bias than does the FD estimator. In general, we can write

$$\text{plim}\,\hat{\beta}_{1,FE} = \beta_1 \left(1 - \frac{V(\tilde{v}_{it})}{V(\tilde{x}_{it})} \right), \tag{4.14}$$

where $\tilde{v}_{it} = v_{it} - \bar{v}_i$, corresponding to the within transformation. In case of serially uncorrelated measurement error ($\rho_v = 0$), this reduces to

$$\text{plim}\,\hat{\beta}_{1,FE} = \beta_1 \left(1 - \frac{T-1}{T} \frac{\sigma_v^2}{V(\tilde{x}_{it})} \right). \tag{4.15}$$

For the typical case where x_{it}^* is positively correlated over time (with decreasing correlogram), the attenuation bias in the within estimator will be smaller than that in the first-difference estimator when $T > 2$. (For $T = 2$, the two estimators are identical.) Griliches and Hausman (1986) exploit this finding to construct an unbiased estimator by combining two biased ones. The use of this approach has not become very common, probably because there may be multiple other reasons why the FD and within estimators produce different results, for example, in cases where the regressors are not strictly exogenous (see Section 3.6). Nevertheless, estimating a model using alternative transformations to eliminate the fixed effects could provide more information on the presence of measurement errors.

Non-classical measurement error

The above results apply to the standard classical measurement error case, where the measurement error is uncorrelated with the true regressor x_{it}^*. If, instead, v_{it} is correlated with x_{it}^*, the key determinant of the bias is the correlation between x_{it} and $\varepsilon_{it} - \beta_1 v_{it}$ in (4.10), or – when ε_{it} and x_{it} are uncorrelated – the correlation between x_{it} and v_{it}. A special case of this arises when the explanatory variable is the optimal predictor, conditional upon some information set. In this case $x_{it} = E(x_{it}^* \mid z_{it})$, where z_{it} are the variables characterising the information set. In this case, we can decompose the true value into two orthogonal components

$$x_{it}^* = x_{it} - v_{it},$$

where v_{it} is the prediction error. By construction, the prediction error, or measurement error, is uncorrelated with the observed x_{it}. This implies that the measurement error, by construction, is correlated with the true unobserved value. Hyslop and Imbens (2001) refer to this case as the "optimal prediction error" model. As long as z_{it} is exogenous, the OLS estimator in this case is unbiased.

In practice it is also possible to have a combination of cases, and a measurement error that is correlated with both x_{it} and x_{it}^*. An example of this arises with a binary explanatory variable. In this case the measurement error cannot be uncorrelated with the true value, nor with the observed value. If the dummy is zero, measurement error can only be positive, and if the dummy is one, it can only be negative. Under realistic assumption, the OLS estimator for β_1 when x_{it} is a mismeasured binary regressor is again biased towards zero (Bollinger, 1996). In the panel data case, it is even more obvious that this may seriously bias the estimators towards zero. For example, a single measurement error in a series of T binary outcomes, will correspond to two incorrect transitions, among $T-1$ first-differences. Again, the desire to control for a bias by using a fixed effects approach magnifies the bias due to measurement error.

Potential solutions

From (4.10), the inconsistency of standard estimators is due to the correlation between the observed regressor x_{it} and the composite error term. A standard solution to obtain a consistent estimator is the use of instrumental variables. If one can find an instrument uncorrelated with the unobservables but correlated with x_{it}, an instrumental variables estimator can provide a consistent estimator (assuming other potential sources of bias are adequately dealt with). Alternatively, it may be possible to identify the parameters of interest once sufficient restrictions are imposed upon the measurement error process, particularly in the case of panel data. For example, the approach of Griliches and Hausman (1986) assumes that the measurement error is not serially correlated. Approaches like these have received much attention in the labour economics literature (see, e. g., Black et al., 2000). It also allows for cases of non-classical measurement error (where the measurement error is correlated over time, or correlated with the true unobserved regressor).

A simple instrumental variables estimator in the panel context is obtained by using the lagged value of x_{it} as instrument for $x_{i,t-1}$. In the absence of a fixed effect, this estimator is given by

$$\hat{\beta}_{1,IV} = \frac{\sum_i \sum_t x_{i,t-1}(x_{it} - \bar{x})}{\sum_i \sum_t x_{i,t-1}(y_{it} - \bar{y})}, \tag{4.16}$$

where $\bar{x}$ denotes the overall sample average. An illustration is this approach (to address the problem of measurement error in beta proxies of firms) is given in Acharya et al. (2013). This estimator is consistent for β_1 if the instrument $x_{i,t-1}$ is uncorrelated with both ε_{it} and v_{it} (the measurement error). The first is a reasonable standard exogeneity assumption. The second condition is satisfied if the measurement error in x_{it} is serially uncorrelated. This shows, again, how internal instruments can help in a panel context, making external instruments unnecessary. This requires, obviously, assumptions. If the measurement error is serially correlated, $x_{i,t-1}$ is likely to correlate with v_{it} and is no longer a valid instrument. In such cases, using longer lags, for example $x_{i,t-2}$, could provide a valid instrument (assuming the autocorrelation in the measurement error is limited to the first lag only). Note that the optimal prediction error case is likely to suffer from positive serial correlation in the measurement error, illustrating that the assumption of no serial correlation in v_{it} may be nontrivial.

In the presence of fixed effects in the equation, they can be eliminated first by a first-difference transformation. The resulting model becomes

$$\Delta y_{it} = \beta_1 \Delta x_{it} + (\Delta u_{it} - \beta_1 \Delta v_{it}).$$

If the measurement error v_{it} is serially uncorrelated, while x_{it} is correlated over time, then $x_{i,t-2}$, $x_{i,t-3}$ or $\Delta x_{i,t-2}$ are valid as instruments for Δx_{it}. An alternative strategy is to keep the equation in levels, but use first-differenced instruments only. Biørn (2000) provides a general exposition of these approaches and potential extensions (combining levels and differences). A further step is to use as many relevant instruments as possible, similar to the dynamic panel data GMM estimator of Arellano and Bond (1991), which we discuss in more detail in the next chapter. This is essentially an instrumental variables estimator based on the first-differenced equation, using as many lags as possible to instrument the mismeasured regressor, and weighting them optimally in a GMM context; see Blundell et al. (1992) for an illustration.

An alternative approach is based on the derivation of moment conditions that provide valid restrictions on the data generating process. Under appropriate conditions, this allows identification of the parameters of interest, as well as (parts of) the measurement error process. Erickson and Whited (2000) apply such an approach to estimate the relationship between investment of a firm and "marginal Q", which corresponds to the expected marginal contribution of new capital goods to future profit. The latter is typically approximated by Tobin's Q, which may be a poor proxy for marginal Q. The authors carefully investigate potential sources of measurement error to defend their "measurement error–consistent" generalised method of moments estimators, which are based on exploiting higher-order moments. Both Almeida et al. (2010) and Erickson and Whited (2012) compare the performance of this estimator with the more traditional approaches: instrumental variables and dynamic panel data GMM, both or which employ lagged mismeasured regressors as instruments. The three estimators differ in their identifying assumptions, related to, among other things, the correlation between the measurement error and the regressor, and the presence or absence of serial correlation and heteroskedasticity. Not surprisingly, estimators using lagged instruments are not robust to serial correlation of the measurement error. Erickson et al. (2014) elaborate upon the framework of Erickson and Whited (2000) and propose a higher-order cumulant estimator, which has better finite-sample properties and a closed-form solution.

5 Linear dynamic models

An important strength of panel data is the ability to model dynamics at the individual level. However, the inclusion of a lagged dependent variable in a model, in combination with unobserved heterogeneity, creates challenges for consistent estimation and testing, particularly so for short T. In the presence of time-invariant unobserved heterogeneity, standard estimators, such as pooled OLS, the Fama and MacBeth (1973) method, as well as fixed effects estimators, are inconsistent for $N \to \infty$. Alternative approaches, relying on instrumental variables or the generalised method of moments are available. Unfortunately, these estimators impose strong conditions, for example, the absence of serial correlation in the idiosyncratic error terms, and often do not perform very well in samples and models typically encountered in empirical finance. In this chapter, we elaborate on the estimation of linear dynamic models, with a particular focus on the linear model with a lagged dependent variable. A discussion of estimation and inference in nonlinear dynamic models is provided in Bazdresch et al. (2018).

5.1 The problem of unobserved heterogeneity

A linear dynamic model can be used to test the predictability of, for example, stock returns (Jegadeesh, 1990) or mutual fund performance (Hendricks et al., 1993). A simple specification is given by

$$y_{it} = \alpha_t + \gamma y_{i,t-1} + \varepsilon_{it}, \tag{5.1}$$

where the autoregressive coefficient γ is assumed to be invariant over units and time, and where y_{it} is the relevant measure to predict. The intercept term α_t may or may not vary over time. When this equation is estimated using pooled OLS or using the Fama and MacBeth (1973) estimator, a bias may arise if there is cross-sectional dispersion in the expected values of y_{it}. For example, when y_{it} denotes the return on a stock, equation (5.1) checks for autocorrelation in returns imposing they are drawings from a distribution with a common (potentially time-varying) mean. That is, it does not only impose that the predictability pattern is the same for all stocks, but also that the expected return on each of the stocks is the same. As argued by Jegadeesh (1990), this may lead to biased estimates for the persistence coefficient, because, relative to the common mean, stock returns do exhibit correlation over time, even if γ is zero. Intuitively, stocks with a high average return are simply more likely to have high returns (relative to the common mean) in all periods. Given that there is variation in expected returns across stocks, estimation by pooled OLS or the Fama-MacBeth estimator will find spurious correlations over time between current and past returns. In general, the estimator for γ tends to overestimate the true predictability, that is, there is a positive bias, which does not disappear for large T.

https://doi.org/10.1515/9783110660739-005

To remedy this problem, it is common to adjust the dependent variable for the cross-sectional variation in expected values. For example, Hendricks et al. (1993), when estimating short-run persistence in mutual fund performance, subtract an estimate for the market equilibrium return from the dependent variable (not from the lagged dependent variable), such as the historical average return over period 1 to T, or the predicted return from a factor model, estimated of the same sample period. The first option replaces the dependent variable in (5.1) by $y_{it} - \bar{y}_i$, where $\bar{y}_i$ is the average of y_{it} over period 1 to T, and estimates

$$y_{it} - \bar{y}_i = \alpha_t + \gamma y_{i,t-1} + \varepsilon_{it}, \tag{5.2}$$

However, as argued by Ter Horst and Verbeek (2000), $\bar{y}_i$ is correlated with $y_{i,t-1}$, even if $\gamma = 0$. This causes a bias, typically of the order $1/T$, which is negative. Although this bias may be small if T is reasonably large, given that the true value of γ is often close to zero (corresponding to no predictability), it may still be of concern with a sample size of 50 to 60 periods, as in Hendricks et al. (1993). A better solution is used by Jegadeesh (1990), when investigating the predictability of security returns, and requires the subtraction of the average return over periods $t + 1$ to $t + S$. (In his case, S is 60 months.) Because these averages are based on future returns they can be argued to be uncorrelated with ε_{it}. Unfortunately, the use of future returns limits the sample over which the model can be estimated.

The key problem with estimating a dynamic model, such as (5.1), is that the lagged dependent variable tends to be correlated with the error term if there is a common component related to differences in the cross-sectional means. This is a cross-sectional correlation, not a time-series correlation. In standard language, this means there is some time-invariant heterogeneity (α_i) in the error term: $\varepsilon_{it} = \alpha_i + u_{it}$. Because α_i is positively correlated with both current and lagged values of y_{it}, standard estimators tend to be biased and inconsistent. Even if there is no time-invariant component in ε_{it}, correlation between $y_{i,t-1}$ and ε_{it} may arise if there is serial correlation in ε_{it}. As a result, consistent estimation of dynamic models with panel data is often relatively complicated when T is finite.

The problem of correlation between a lagged dependent variable and the error term also arises when additional explanatory variables are included. Consider the general model with a lagged dependent variable, given by

$$y_{it} = x'_{it}\beta + \gamma y_{i,t-1} + \varepsilon_{it}, \quad t = 1, \ldots, T. \tag{5.3}$$

Abstracting from potential problems with the explanatory variables in x_{it}, a key issue regarding consistent estimation is whether or not $y_{i,t-1}$ can be assumed to be uncorrelated with ε_{it}. If $E(y_{i,t-1}\varepsilon_{it}) = 0$, as well as $E(x_{it}\varepsilon_{it}) = 0$, for a given t, consistent estimation of (5.3) is possible by pooled OLS or by the Fama and MacBeth (1973) method. However, as illustrated above, the assumption that, in the cross-section, ε_{it} and $y_{i,t-1}$ are uncorrelated is a strong one. Effectively, it requires that, conditional upon the lagged dependent variable (and additional regressors), there is no persistence left in the dependent variable. A clear violation arises if there is an unobserved time-invariant component (α_i) that affects y_{it} in each period, but almost any serial correlation in ε_{it} will cause a nonzero correlation between $y_{i,t-1}$ and ε_{it}, as soon as both are correlated with $\varepsilon_{i,t-1}$.

Despite these concerns, Fama-MacBeth and pooled OLS estimators are commonly used in empirical work. For example, Spiegel and Zhang (2013) estimate a model explaining flows to mutual funds, one of the explanatory variables being lagged flows, using the Fama-MacBeth approach. This can be justified in the absence of serial correlation in the equation's error term only. Adjusting standard errors using the Newey and West (1987) covariance matrix does not remedy this problem, and is inappropriate anyway; see Petersen (2009) and the discussion in Section 2.12. Fama and French (2002) estimate a dynamic model explaining the change in dividends from lagged dividends, and a dynamic model explaining leverage, both by means of the Fama-MacBeth estimator. While this estimator has the advantage of controlling for correlation of the error terms across firms, neither serial correlation in ε_{it} nor unobserved heterogeneity is allowed.

Another application is Brennan et al. (1998), who report several Fama-MacBeth regressions relating (excess or risk-adjusted) stock returns to firm characteristics, such as size and the book-to-market ratio, while also including lagged returns over 2 to 3, 4 to 6 or 7 to 12 months prior to the current month. Similarly, Lewellen (2015), includes lagged returns over months –12 to –2 in Fama-MacBeth regressions explaining current stock returns. In these cases, the bias in the Fama-MacBeth estimator is potentially small, among other reasons because stock returns exhibit very little serial correlation. However, in corporate finance, when the dependent variable is a firm characteristic, such as leverage or Tobin's Q, the assumption of no serial correlation in ε_{it} (and thus no unobserved heterogeneity) is unlikely to be satisfied, and biases can be more substantial. This is particularly worrisome if the dynamics in the model are of particular economic interest (e. g., in the partial adjustment model towards target capital structure of Flannery and Rangan, 2006).

Other studies use pooled OLS, despite the presence of dynamics. For example, Tetlock et al. (2008) estimate a model to predict quarterly firm earnings from the fraction of negative words in firm-specific news stories, controlling for lagged earnings and other firm characteristics. Their defence is that the dependent variable is standardised and therefore has no firm effect. A time effect is important, because firms' earnings are correlated within calendar quarters, and this is reflected in the use of standard errors clustered over time. Because the standardisation of the earnings measures is based on historical data (in most cases the previous 20 quarters), there is no guarantee that a negative bias, similar to the one in (5.2), does not emerge.

5.2 The problem with the fixed effects estimator

Given the discussion in the previous section, it appears to make sense to explicitly incorporate time-invariant unobserved heterogeneity in the model. To do so, consider a linear model with a lagged dependent variable as well as firm-specific heterogeneity α_i, given by

$$y_{it} = x_{it}'\beta + \gamma y_{i,t-1} + \alpha_i + u_{it}, \quad t = 1, \ldots, T. \tag{5.4}$$

If this model is estimated by pooled OLS, the Fama and MacBeth (1973) method, or the random effects estimator, we treat $\alpha_i + u_{it}$ as an error term consisting of two components: a time-invariant one α_i and a time-varying one u_{it} (although estimation may ignore this). Even in the absence of serial correlation in u_{it} this creates a problem due to the fact that, by construction, $y_{i,t-1}$ is correlated with α_i. This is the problem discussed in the previous section. When the true value of y is positive, the OLS and random effects estimators tend to overestimate it (due to the fact that $y_{i,t-1}$ and α_i are positively correlated).

In the linear static model, with strictly exogenous regressors, treating time-invariant heterogeneity as fixed firm effects was able to solve the problem of correlation between unobservables in the equation and the explanatory variables. Therefore, it seems natural in this case to also continue along the fixed effects path. As we know, the fixed effects estimator for β and y is equivalent to an OLS estimator where all variables are expressed in deviations from their firm-specific averages. This can be written as

$$y_{it} - \bar{y}_i = (x_{it} - \bar{x}_i)'\beta + \gamma(y_{i,t-1} - \bar{y}_{i,-1}) + u_{it} - \bar{u}_i, \tag{5.5}$$

where $\bar{y}_i = T^{-1}\sum_{t=1}^{T} y_{it}$ and $\bar{y}_{i,-1} = T^{-1}\sum_{t=1}^{T} y_{i,t-1}$ (assuming we observe y_{i0}), and similarly for the other variables in the model. Consistent estimation of β and y requires that the within-transformed error terms $u_{it} - \bar{u}_i$ are uncorrelated with both the within-transformed regressors in x_{it} and the within-transformed lagged dependent variable $y_{i,t-1} - \bar{y}_{i,-1}$. The first of these is implied by assuming strict exogeneity of x_{it} (see Section 3.6). However, because $y_{i,t-1}$ and $\bar{u}_i$ are negatively correlated by construction (due to $u_{i,t-1}$), OLS applied to (5.4) is asymptotically biased and inconsistent (see Nickell, 1981). Typically, the correlation between $y_{i,t-1} - \bar{y}_{i,-1}$ and $u_{it} - \bar{u}_i$ is of the order $1/T$. This implies that the correlation goes to zero when the number of time periods increases. As a result, the inconsistency in the fixed effects estimator may be small is T is sufficiently large. When y is positive, the fixed effects estimator tends to underestimate it. Nickell (1981) shows that for a model without exogenous variables the asymptotic bias in the fixed effects estimators is still substantial with $T = 10$. For example, when the true value of y equals 0.5, the fixed effects estimators converges to 0.33 for $N \to \infty$. This bias in the fixed effects estimator when a lagged dependent variable is present is popularly referred to as the "Nickell bias".

When T is sufficiently large (e. g., $T > 20$), the Nickell bias may be negligible and standard fixed effects estimators are appropriate. For example, Siriwardane (2019) explains credit default swap (CDS) spreads of firms from capital shocks and other variables, including the lagged change in CDS spread, using weekly data over about 6.5 years. The data are filtered such that each firm has at least 162 observations. The model includes firm fixed effects and industry $\times$ period fixed effects, but given the large number of periods the Nickell bias can be ignored. A similar argument is made in Loutskina (2011), who uses data of banks over 112 quarters, with a minimum of 20 quarters per institution.

Note that, when evaluating the severity of this bias in a given application, one should realise that the typical panel in financial applications is unbalanced. What is relevant for the bias is not the length of the total sample period, but the number of observations that is available to take firm-specific averages. Thus, even with a panel with $T = 25$ years of data, the bias in the fixed effects estimator can still be substantial if the average firm is observed for only 5 or 10 years.

Because the OLS estimator in (5.4) tends to overestimate γ, whereas the within estimator tends to underestimate it, one can argue that these two estimators provide upper and lower bounds to the true autoregressive coefficient, respectively (see Bond, 2002). Flannery and Rangan (2006), estimating a dynamic model for a firm's capital structure, use this argument to discard several estimates that appear to produce unrealistic results.

5.3 Instrumental variables

Eliminating the bias is, in theory, relatively simple, and consists of starting with a first-difference transformation to eliminate the fixed firm effects followed by the use of instrumental variables. Practically, however, this appears quite sensitive and fragile in many cases. The first-difference transformation results in the following equation

$$y_{it} - y_{i,t-1} = (x_{it} - x_{i,t-1})'\beta + \gamma(y_{i,t-1} - y_{i,t-2}) + u_{it} - u_{i,t-1}, \quad t = 2,\dots,T, \tag{5.6}$$

which we can briefly write as

$$\Delta y_{it} = \Delta x_{it}'\beta + \gamma\Delta y_{i,t-1} + \Delta u_{it}, \quad t = 2,\dots,T, \tag{5.7}$$

where Δ is the first-difference operator. Estimating this equation by OLS does not provide a consistent estimator because $\Delta y_{i,t-1}$ and Δu_{it} are negatively correlated (due to $u_{i,t-1}$). The asymptotic bias is quite large and does not disappear for sufficiently large T. Thus, we seem to have made the problem worse by choosing the first-difference transformation rather than the within transformation to eliminate the firm fixed effects. In fact, the first-difference estimator is usually severely biased, even when T is large and even when α_i is relatively unimportant.

It is possible to obtain a consistent estimator for β and γ (for fixed T) provided we can find one or more instruments that are uncorrelated with the first-differenced error term Δu_{it}, but correlated with the explanatory variables in Δx_{it} and $\Delta y_{i,t-1}$. Assuming that Δx_{it} is uncorrelated to Δu_{it} (as implied by strict exogeneity), Anderson and Hsiao (1981) propose two alternative instruments that are both valid if u_{it} exhibits no serial correlation. The first is $y_{i,t-2}$, which is likely to be correlated with $\Delta y_{i,t-1} = y_{i,t-1} - y_{i,t-2}$. The second is $\Delta y_{i,t-2}$. Both of these instruments are uncorrelated with Δu_{it} – in the absence or serial correlation – even though they correlate with $u_{i,t-2}$ and/or $u_{i,t-3}$. These instruments lead to two alternative versions of the Anderson-Hsiao estimator for dynamic panel data: one using the level of the dependent variable, lagged twice, as an instrument, the other using the change in the dependent variable, lagged twice.

To illustrate these estimators, consider the dynamic model without exogenous variables, given by

$$y_{it} = \gamma y_{i,t-1} + \alpha_i + u_{it}, \quad t = 1, \ldots, T, \tag{5.8}$$

where the overall intercept term is subsumed in α_i. In this simplified model, the first Anderson-Hsiao estimator for γ is given by

$$\hat{\gamma}_{IV}^{(1)} = \frac{\sum_{i=1}^{N} \sum_{t=2}^{T} y_{i,t-2}(y_{it} - y_{i,t-1})}{\sum_{i=1}^{N} \sum_{t=2}^{T} y_{i,t-2}(y_{i,t-1} - y_{i,t-2})}, \tag{5.9}$$

where the first available observation is y_{i0}. Consistency of this estimator requires that

$$E((u_{it} - u_{i,t-1})y_{i,t-2}) = 0, \tag{5.10}$$

which says that the instrument is exogenous, and that $y_{i,t-2}$ is "sufficiently" correlated with $y_{it} - y_{i,t-1}$, which says it is relevant. In the absence of serial correlation in u_{it}, there is no reason why $y_{i,t-2}$ would correlate with $u_{i,t-1}$ or later values, and exogeneity is warranted. Ter Horst and Verbeek (2000) use this estimator to estimate short-run persistence in mutual fund performance. The second estimator of Anderson-Hsiao is given by

$$\hat{\gamma}_{IV}^{(2)} = \frac{\sum_{i=1}^{N} \sum_{t=3}^{T} (y_{i,t-2} - y_{i,t-3})(y_{it} - y_{i,t-1})}{\sum_{i=1}^{N} \sum_{t=3}^{T} (y_{i,t-2} - y_{i,t-3})(y_{i,t-1} - y_{i,t-2})}. \tag{5.11}$$

Note that the time-series summation operator starts at $t = 3$. Consistency of this estimator requires that

$$E((u_{it} - u_{i,t-1})(y_{i,t-2} - y_{i,t-3})) = 0, \tag{5.12}$$

which is again implied by the absence of serial correlation in u_{it}. Both versions of the Anderson-Hsiao estimator are reported in Flannery and Rangan (2006, Appendix). They can be obtained in Stata using the *xtivreg, fd* command.

In general, it is not clear whether $y_{i,t-2}$ or $\Delta y_{i,t-2}$ is the better instrument. Both are exogenous under similar assumptions, but their relevance is questionable. In addition, the second instrument can be exploited over a shorter sample, because the change lagged twice requires another lag of the dependent variable. Effectively, this means that only firms with four consecutive observations on y_{it} can contribute to the estimation of the model coefficients. Depending upon the persistence in y_{it} (i. e., the value of y), the correlation between the instrument and $\Delta y_{i,t-1}$ may be small. It is therefore recommended to test the relevance of the instruments by inspecting the reduced form (see Subsection 3.4.2).

Extending the Anderson-Hsiao estimators to the model with additional explanatory variables in (5.4) is straightforward if the variables in x_{it} can be assumed to be strictly exogenous (i. e., uncorrelated with all u_{is} at all leads and lags). If not, we also need to find instruments for Δx_{it} in (5.7). If x_{it} is endogenous (e. g., due to reverse causality or simultaneity) and therefore correlated with u_{it}, lagged regressors $x_{i,t-2}$ or $\Delta x_{i,t-2}$ can serve as instruments, provided that x_{it} is predetermined (uncorrelated with $u_{i,t+1}$ and later).

Arellano (1989) has shown that the estimator that uses the first-differenced instrument, when exogenous variables are added to the model, suffers from large variances over a wide range of values for y. In addition, Monte Carlo evidence by Arellano and Bover (1995) shows that the levels version of the Anderson–Hsiao estimator can have large biases and large standard errors, particularly when y is close to one. A popular alternative builds upon the Anderson-Hsiao approach and tries to exploit as many instruments as possible, while eliminating the disadvantages of reduced sample sizes, using GMM. This is discussed in the next section.

5.4 The Arellano-Bond estimator

A more general estimator starts from the notion that both (5.10) and (5.12) provide a moment condition that is exploited in estimation. It is well known that imposing more moment conditions increases the asymptotic efficiency of the estimators (provided the additional conditions are valid). Holtz-Eakin et al. (1988) and Arellano and Bond (1991) propose to extend the list of instruments by exploiting additional moment conditions and letting their number vary with t, keeping the number of time periods T fixed.

5.4.1 Moment conditions

To introduce the additional moment conditions, consider the case where $T = 4$. In this case, one can impose

$$E((u_{i2} - u_{i1})y_{i0}) = 0$$

as the moment condition for $t = 2$. For $t = 3$, there are two moment conditions

$$E((u_{i3} - u_{i2})y_{i1}) = 0$$

and

$$E((u_{i3} - u_{i2})y_{i0}) = 0.$$

Finally, for $t = 4$, there are three moment conditions, given by

$$E((u_{i4} - u_{i3})y_{i0}) = 0$$
$$E((u_{i4} - u_{i3})y_{i1}) = 0$$
$$E((u_{i4} - u_{i3})y_{i2}) = 0.$$

All these moment conditions can be exploited in a GMM framework. To introduce the GMM estimator, for a given sample size T define the vector of transformed error terms

$$\Delta u_i = \begin{pmatrix} u_{i2} - u_{i1} \\ \cdots \\ u_{i,T} - u_{i,T-1} \end{pmatrix} \tag{5.13}$$

and the matrix of instruments

$$Z_i = \begin{pmatrix} [y_{i0}] & 0 & \cdots & 0 \\ 0 & [y_{i0}, y_{i1}] & & 0 \\ \vdots & & \ddots & 0 \\ 0 & \cdots & 0 & [y_{i0}, \ldots, y_{i,T-2}] \end{pmatrix}. \tag{5.14}$$

Each row in the matrix Z_i contains the instruments that are valid for a given period. Consequently, the set of all moment conditions can be written concisely as

$$E(Z_i'\Delta u_i) = 0,$$

which comprises a total of $1 + 2 + 3 + \cdots + T - 1$. To derive the GMM estimator, write this as

$$E(Z_i'(\Delta y_i - \gamma \Delta y_{i,-1})) = 0. \tag{5.15}$$

Because the number of moment conditions exceeds the number of unknown coefficients, we estimate γ by minimising a quadratic expression in terms of the corresponding sample moments (see Section 3.5). That is,

$$\min_{\gamma} \left[\frac{1}{N} \sum_{i=1}^{N} Z_i'(\Delta y_i - \gamma \Delta y_{i,-1}) \right]' W_N \left[\frac{1}{N} \sum_{i=1}^{N} Z_i'(\Delta y_i - \gamma \Delta y_{i,-1}) \right], \tag{5.16}$$

where W_N is a symmetric positive definite weighting matrix, which may depend upon the sample size N. The GMM estimator for y, with general weighting matrix, is then given by

$$\hat{y}_{GMM} = \left(\left(\sum_{i=1}^{N} \Delta y'_{i,-1} Z_i \right) W_N \left(\sum_{i=1}^{N} Z'_i \Delta y_{i,-1} \right) \right)^{-1}$$
$$\times \left(\sum_{i=1}^{N} \Delta y'_{i,-1} Z_i \right) W_N \left(\sum_{i=1}^{N} Z'_i \Delta y_i \right). \tag{5.17}$$

This estimator is referred to as the first-difference GMM (FD-GMM) estimator and is consistent for y, as long as the weighting matrix is positive definite, under the general conditions that the imposed moment conditions are valid. The asymptotic covariance matrix depends upon the weighting matrix that is chosen.

Weighting matrices

The optimal weighting matrix is the one that provides the most efficient estimator for y and is (asymptotically) proportional to the inverse of the covariance matrix of the sample moments. Accordingly, (in the absence of cross-sectional correlations) the optimal weighting matrix should satisfy

$$\operatorname*{plim}_{N \to \infty} W_N = V(Z'_i \Delta u_i)^{-1} = E(Z'_i \Delta u_i \Delta u'_i Z_i)^{-1}. \tag{5.18}$$

If we do not impose any restrictions on the covariance matrix of the vector u_i, except that there is no correlation across firms, an empirical optimal weighting matrix can be estimated by replacing the expectations operator with a sample average and replacing the unobserved u_{it} with the residuals $\hat{u}_{it}$ from an initial consistent estimator for y. That is,

$$\hat{W}_N^{opt} = \left(\frac{1}{N} \sum_{i=1}^{N} Z'_i \Delta \hat{u}_i \Delta \hat{u}'_i Z_i \right)^{-1}. \tag{5.19}$$

If, instead, one would impose that the error terms u_{it} are homoskedastic and uncorrelated over time, the optimal weighting matrix is much simpler. Note that the absence of serial correlation is required to guarantee the validity of the moment conditions. Under these assumptions, it holds for the $(T - 1)$-dimensional covariance matrix of Δu_i that

$$E\{\Delta u_i \Delta u'_i\} = \sigma_u^2 G = \sigma_u^2 \begin{pmatrix} 2 & -1 & 0 & \cdots \\ -1 & 2 & \ddots & 0 \\ 0 & \ddots & \ddots & -1 \\ \vdots & 0 & -1 & 2 \end{pmatrix}. \tag{5.20}$$

As a result, the optimal weighting matrix is given by

$$W_N^{opt} = \left(\frac{1}{N} \sum_{i=1}^{N} Z_i' G Z_i \right)^{-1}, \tag{5.21}$$

noting that the proportionality factor σ_u^2 is irrelevant. This weighting matrix does not depend upon unknown parameters and is typically used to obtain a consistent first-step GMM estimator. It is optimal under the restrictive condition that u_{it} is homoskedastic across firms and periods.

Properties
Under weak regularity conditions, the FD-GMM estimator for γ, based on the optimal weighting matrix, is consistent and asymptotically normal for $N \to \infty$ and fixed T. Its covariance matrix can be estimated as

$$\hat{V}(\hat{\gamma}_{GMM}) = \frac{1}{N} \left(\left(\frac{1}{N} \sum_{i=1}^{N} \Delta y_{i,-1}' Z_i \right) \hat{W}_N^{opt} \left(\frac{1}{N} \sum_{i=1}^{N} Z_i' \Delta y_{i,-1} \right) \right)^{-1}. \tag{5.22}$$

Because σ_u^2 is not included in the optimal weighting matrix in (5.21), an estimate of it needs to be added to (5.22) based upon the residuals. For an arbitrary weighting matrix, the estimator is still consistent and asymptotically normal, but the expression for the covariance matrix is more complicated. Alvarez and Arellano (2003) show that, in general, the FD-GMM estimator is also consistent when both N and T tend to infinity, despite the fact that the number of moment conditions tends to infinity with the sample size. For large T, however, the FD-GMM estimator will be close to the fixed effects estimator, which provides a more attractive alternative.

Despite its theoretical appeal, the empirical implementation of the FD-GMM estimator quite often suffers from poor small sample properties, mostly attributable to the large number of, potentially weak, instruments. In Subsection 5.4.6 we discuss this issue in more detail, including some ways to control the problem of instrument proliferation.

5.4.2 Models with exogenous variables

The GMM approach extends quite straightforwardly to the model with exogenous variables in (5.4). Depending upon the assumptions made about x_{it}, alternative sets of additional instruments can be chosen and corresponding moment conditions added to the optimisation problem. If x_{it} is strictly exogenous it also holds that

$$E(\Delta x_{it} \Delta u_{it}) = 0 \quad \text{for each } t.$$

Accordingly, we can write the full matrix of instruments as

$$
Z_i = \begin{pmatrix} [y_{i0}, \Delta x'_{i2}] & 0 & \cdots & & 0 \\ 0 & [y_{i0}, y_{i1}, \Delta x'_{i3}] & & & 0 \\ \vdots & & \ddots & & 0 \\ 0 & & \cdots & 0 & [y_{i0}, \ldots, y_{i,T-2}, \Delta x'_{iT}] \end{pmatrix}. \tag{5.23}
$$

If the variables in x_{it} are not strictly exogenous but predetermined, in which case current and lagged x_{it}s are uncorrelated with current error terms, we only have $E(x_{it}u_{is}) = 0$ for $s \geq t$. In this case, only $x_{i,t-1}, \ldots, x_{i1}$ are valid instruments for the first-differenced equation in period t. Thus, the moment conditions that can be imposed are

$$
E(x_{i,t-j}\Delta u_{it}) = 0 \quad j = 1, \ldots, t-1, \text{ for each } t.
$$

In practice, a combination of strictly exogenous and predetermined explanatory variables may occur rather than one of these two extreme cases. The matrix Z_i should then be adjusted accordingly. Baltagi (2013, Chapter 8) provides additional discussion and examples.

5.4.3 System GMM

Arellano and Bover (1995) provide a framework to integrate the above approach with the instrumental variables estimators of Hausman and Taylor (1981) and others. Most importantly, they discuss how information in levels can also be exploited in estimation. That is, in addition to the moment conditions presented above, it is also possible to exploit the presence of valid instruments for the levels equation (5.4), or their averages over time (the between regression). This is of particular importance when the individual series are highly persistent and y is close to one. In this case, the FD-GMM estimator may suffer from severe finite sample biases because the instruments are weak; see Blundell and Bond (1998), and Arellano (2003, Section 6.6). Under certain assumptions, suitably lagged differences of y_{it} can be used to instrument the equation in levels, in addition to the instruments for the first-differenced equation. For example, if $E(\Delta y_{i,t-1}\alpha_i) = 0$, $\Delta y_{i,t-1}$ can be used as instrument for (5.4) or (5.8) in the absence of serial correlation in u_{it}.

Combining instruments for the first-differenced equation with instruments for the levels equation is referred to as system GMM. Lemmon et al. (2008) use both pooled OLS, the fixed effects estimator (based on the within transformation) and the system GMM estimator of Blundell and Bond (1998) to estimate the speed of adjustment (SOA) of a firm towards its target leverage. As expected, the GMM estimate for y is within those obtained from pooled OLS (which would overestimate the true y) and the fixed effects approach (which would underestimate it). The validity of the additional instruments in the system GMM approach depends upon the assumption that changes in y_{it}

are uncorrelated with the fixed effects. This requires firms to be in some kind of steady state, in the sense that deviations from long-term values, conditional upon the exogenous variables, are not systematically related to α_i. Unfortunately, when y is close to one this assumption is the least likely to be satisfied, given that it takes many periods for deviations from the steady state to decay away. As stressed by Roodman (2009a), in situations where system GMM offers the most hope, it may offer the least help. See also Bun and Windmeijer (2010), who document weak instrument problems for the system GMM estimator.

5.4.4 Specification tests

For both the first-difference and system GMM estimators, an important requirement is the absence of serial correlation in u_{it}. If u_{it} is correlated with $u_{i,t-1}$, a correlation will arise between $y_{i,t-2}$ and Δu_{it}, invalidating its use as an instrument for the first-differenced equation. If u_{it} is correlated with $u_{i,t-2}$, this invalidates $y_{i,t-3}$ as instrument. Accordingly, it is good practice to perform and report a test for second-order serial correlation in Δu_{it}, when either the instrumental variables estimator of Anderson and Hsiao (1981) or a dynamic GMM estimator is used. Such tests are developed in Arellano and Bond (1991) and are based on the standardised average covariances of the residuals. Under the null hypothesis of no autocorrelation, the test statistics are asymptotically standard normally distributed. If the test rejects, longer lags, for example, $y_{i,t-3}$ may provide a valid instrument as long as there is no third-order serial correlation in Δu_{it} (which, of course, can be tested as well).

Even if the test for serial correlation in u_{it} does not reject the null hypothesis, this does not mean that the model is correctly specified and that all moment conditions are appropriate. As before, one can test for overidentifying restrictions using the Sargan-Hansen J-test, similar to the one discussed in Subsection 3.5.3. As stressed by Wintoki et al. (2012), these two tests are not specification tests of the empirical specification, but rather tests of the set of instruments under the assumption that the model is correctly specified. If the model is misspecified, for example, due to the presence of an unobserved time-varying variable affecting both the dependent variable and the endogenous explanatory variable, the GMM estimator will be biased. Nevertheless, it is possible that the test for serial correlation and the Sargan-Hansen test "pass" at conventional levels. For example, the Sargan-Hansen test will have low power when the instruments are weak.

5.4.5 When y is close to one

Importantly, the IV and FD-GMM estimators discussed above break down when $y = 1$, a case referred to as a "unit root". This is because the instruments $y_{i,t-2}, y_{i,t-3}, \ldots$ are no longer correlated with the first-differenced regressor $\Delta y_{i,t-1}$. In this case, the estimators are inconsistent and have a nonstandard asymptotic distribution. In the case where y is close to one, the lagged values $y_{i,t-j}$, $j = 2, 3, \ldots$ are weak instruments, and the estimator will perform poorly. The system GMM estimator may work better in these circumstances (Blundell and Bond, 1998).

Hahn et al. (2007) propose an alternative estimator based on "long differences" that appears to perform well when y is close to one. The implementation of this estimator is most easily done when the panel is balanced. Starting point is to not take the first-difference transformation but to take the difference between two observations that are as far as possible apart. In the balanced case, this means

$$y_{iT} - y_{i1} = \gamma(y_{i,T-1} - y_{i0}) + u_{iT} - u_{i1},$$

omitting exogenous variables for convenience. Estimation of this equation by OLS will not be consistent for fixed T, because $y_{i,T-1}$ will depend upon the accumulated history of innovations in $u_{i,T-1}, u_{i,T-2}, \ldots$. However, it can be estimated if one can find instruments not correlated with the long-differenced error terms $u_{iT} - u_{i1}$. Hahn et al. (2007) propose the use of $y_{i0}, y_{i,T-1} - \gamma y_{i,T-2}, \ldots, y_{i2} - \gamma y_{i1}$ as instruments. The latter instruments are exogenous because they only depend upon $u_{i,T-1}, \ldots, u_{i2}$, respectively. These instruments require knowledge of y. An initial consistent estimator for y can be obtained by using only y_{i0} as instrument, after which the remaining instruments can be constructed using an estimated version of y. This process can be made iterative. It is also possible to import all instruments into a set of moment conditions, which are now nonlinear in y.

Unfortunately, the long-difference estimator has some drawbacks. First, including explanatory variables in the equation that are not exogenous complicates estimation. Second, its implementation requires taking differences over longer windows, which is more challenging in unbalanced panels. Therefore, most authors implement the long-difference estimator using a difference of, for example, four or five years, so as not to lose too many firms in estimation. Flannery and Hankins (2013) implement an alternative where for each firm the longest possible difference is taken. A simulation study in Huang and Ritter (2009) shows that, when estimating the speed of adjustment in a dynamic capital structure model, the long-difference estimator has better properties than OLS and the standard fixed effects estimators. Flannery and Hankins (2013), however, find that the long-difference estimator (based on a four-year difference) performs remarkably poorly when the dependent variable is highly persistent ($y = 0.8$).

5.4.6 Too many instruments

When instruments are weak they provide only very little information about the parameters of interest, which leads to poor small sample properties of the GMM estimator. A related problem arises when the number of instruments (moment conditions) is too large relative to the sample size. The estimation of dynamic panel data models is a situation that can easily suffer from having too many instruments. Note, for example, that for both the FD-GMM and system GMM estimators, the number of instruments increases quadratically with T. The consequence is that the GMM estimator has very poor small sample properties, and traditional misspecification tests, like the test for overidentifying restrictions, tend to be misleading. This may be particularly the case for the two-step estimator, which relies upon the estimation of a potentially high-dimensional optimal weighting matrix.

Roodman (2009a) discusses the two main symptoms of instrument proliferation. The first one, which applies to instrumental variable estimators in general, is that numerous instruments can overfit endogenous variables. In finite samples, instruments never have exactly zero correlation with the endogenous components of the instrumented variables, because of sampling variability. Having many instruments therefore results in a small sample bias in the direction of OLS. To illustrate this, consider the extreme case where the number of instruments equals the number of observations. In this case, the first-stage (reduced form) regressions will produce an R^2 of 1, and the instrumental variables estimator reduces to OLS. Accordingly, it is recommendable to reduce the number of instruments, even if they are all theoretically valid and relevant, to reduce the small sample bias in the GMM estimator (see, e. g., Windmeijer, 2005).

The second problem is specific for the two-step GMM estimator that employs an optimal weighting matrix, which needs to be estimated. The number of elements in this matrix is quadratic in the number of instruments, and therefore extremely large when the number of instruments is large. As a result, estimates for the optimal weighting matrix tend to be very imprecise when there are many instruments (Roodman, 2009a). This has two consequences. First, the standard errors for two-step GMM estimators tend to be severely downward biased. Second, the overidentifying restrictions test, as discussed in Subsection 3.5.3, is far too optimistic in the sense that it rejects the null hypothesis in far too few cases. When the number of instruments is large, the overidentifying restrictions test may therefore fail to indicate any misspecification or invalid instrumentation. Windmeijer (2005) derives a correction to improve the estimator for the GMM covariance matrix.

From this it follows that it is recommendable to reduce the instrument count in the estimation of dynamic panel data models. An obvious way of doing so is to use only certain lags instead of all available lags of the instruments. This way the number of columns in (5.14) can be substantially reduced. An alternative approach is presented in Roodman (2009a), who suggests to combine instruments through addition into smaller sets. This has the potential advantage of retaining more information, as no instruments are dropped. Instead of imposing

$$E((u_{it} - u_{i,t-1})y_{i,t-s}) = 0, \quad t = 2, 3, \ldots, T, \quad s = 2, 3, \ldots$$

we impose

$$E((u_{it} - u_{i,t-1})y_{i,t-s}) = 0, \quad s = 2, 3, \ldots$$

The new moment conditions embody the same belief about the orthogonality of $u_{it} - u_{i,t-1}$ and $y_{i,t-s}$, but we do not separate the sample moments for each time period. The matrix of instruments then collapses to

$$Z_i^* = \begin{pmatrix} y_{i0} & 0 & 0 & \cdots & 0 \\ y_{i0} & y_{i1} & 0 & \cdots & 0 \\ y_{i0} & y_{i1} & y_{i2} & \cdots & 0 \\ \vdots & \vdots & \vdots & \ddots & \vdots \\ y_{i0} & y_{i1} & \cdots & y_{i,T-3} & y_{i,T-2} \end{pmatrix} \tag{5.24}$$

These ways of reducing the number of instruments provide some relevant robustness checks for the coefficient estimates, standard errors and misspecification tests. Roodman (2009a) presents Monte Carlo evidence showing that reducing and/or collapsing instruments helps to reduce the bias in first-difference and system GMM estimators and to increase the ability of the overidentifying restrictions tests to detect misspecification. In general, he recommends that "results should be aggressively tested for sensitivity to reductions in the number of instruments".

Stata has a number of routines to obtain the Arellano-Bond and system GMM estimators in dynamic panel models. The easiest one to use is *xtabond2* (an improved version of the built-in *xtabond*), which provides the Arellano and Bond (1991) estimator and the system GMM estimators of Arellano and Bover (1995) and Blundell and Bond (1998). Related routines are *xtdpd* and *xtdpdsys*. Implementation of these estimators is relatively complicated and can easily generate invalid estimates. A useful guide to the use of these commands is given in Roodman (2009b).

5.5 Applications

As stressed at several places already, the estimation of a dynamic panel model with short T tends to be challenging, and the performance of the more advanced estimators, like FD-GMM, system GMM or the long-differencing estimator, depends crucially upon some assumptions and their performance may differ substantially across applications. A particular application that has received much attention in the financial literature is the estimation of a dynamic model for a firm's capital structure (e. g., Flannery and Rangan, 2006). The model assumes that firms adjust their leverage towards some target, optimal level. The target leverage of firm i in period i is denoted by y_{it}^* and is assumed to depend upon firm characteristics, known at time $t - 1$ and related to the costs and benefits of operating with various leverage ratios. These characteristics are collected in a vector x_{it} (where, for simplicity, we keep the time suffix t, even though variables may actually refer to earlier periods). Accordingly, the target debt ratio is assumed to satisfy

$$y_{it}^* = x_{it}'\delta + \eta_{it},$$

where η_{it} is a mean zero error term accounting for unobserved heterogeneity.

Adjustment costs may prevent firms from choosing their target leverage at each point in time. To accommodate this, we specify a target adjustment model as

$$y_{it} - y_{i,t-1} = (1 - \gamma)(y_{it}^* - y_{i,t-1}),$$

where $1 - \gamma$ ($0 \le \gamma \le 1$) measures the speed of adjustment (SOA), which is assumed to be identical across firms. If $\gamma = 0$, firms adjust immediately and completely to their target debt ratio (SOA = 100%). Combining the previous two equations, we can write

$$y_{it} = x_{it}'\beta + \gamma y_{i,t-1} + \alpha_i + u_{it},$$

where we have introduced time-invariant unobserved heterogeneity (α_i), and where $\beta = \delta(1 - \gamma)$. The financial literature has presented a variety of estimates for the speed of adjustment (see, for example, Huang and Ritter, 2009), with estimated γ's varying between 0.9 and 0.65, depending upon the econometric method, the sample, and whether book leverage or market leverage is used. The half-life is the number of years it takes for a firm to move halfway toward its target leverage, and can be calculated as $\ln(0.5)/\ln(\gamma)$. It is particularly sensitive to γ for values of γ close to one.

Flannery and Rangan (2006) report a variety of estimates for γ and the other model coefficients, where y_{it} is a firm's market debt ratio (MDR). The pooled OLS and Fama-MacBeth estimator ignore the presence of unobserved heterogeneity (α_i) in the equation, are biased in the same direction, and produce quite similar results, with an estimated γ of around 0.86 (SOA = 14%). The fixed effects estimator eliminates α_i through the within transformation, and is biased towards zero, with an estimated γ of 0.62 (SOA = 38%). The Anderson and Hsiao (1981) estimator (using $y_{i,t-2}$ as an instrument for $\Delta y_{i,t-1}$) produces an estimate for γ that is even smaller than the fixed effects estimate, which is not what one would expect. As mentioned above, the validity of these instrumental variables estimators relies on the absence of first-order serial correlation in u_{it} (which implies no second-order serial correlation in the first-differenced error Δu_{it}). Zero serial correlation of u_{it} is rejected, casting serious doubts on the validity of the instruments. This problem also extends to the Arellano and Bond (1991) estimator, which also produces an estimated γ that is suspiciously low (implying a very high SOA), and outside the boundaries implied by the OLS and FE estimates. Because the Sargan test of overidentifying restrictions also rejects, the authors decide to discard this estimator, despite its theoretical appeal, from their main set of results. For their preferred specification, they resort to the use of an external instrument for $y_{i,t-1}$ (lagged book leverage), resulting in an estimated γ that is slightly higher than the

FE one. Because book leverage and market leverage are correlated by construction, it is not obvious that this instrument satisfies the exogeneity condition. As argued by Huang and Ritter (2009), at least some shocks are likely to affect both book leverage and market leverage.

Several alternative estimators have been used in this context. For example, Lemmon et al. (2008) use a system GMM estimator, and Huang and Ritter (2009) use the long-differencing estimator of Hahn et al. (2007). Elsas and Florysiak (2015) stress that leverage is a fractional variable, bounded by 0 and 1, and propose an alternative estimator taking this into account. Their proposed maximum likelihood estimator is based on an extension of the dynamic random effects tobit model, which we discuss in Chapter 6. Because in many cases, the fixed effects estimator appears to perform reasonably well, despite being biased for fixed T, another alternative is to approximate the bias in this estimator and apply a bias-adjusted version of the fixed effects estimator, based on the work of Kiviet (1995) and Bruno (2005). Zhou et al. (2014) provide a further investigation into bias-correction methods in dynamic models for capital structure, and propose a bias-corrected global minimum variance combined estimation procedure. Recent theoretical developments in this area are summarised in Bun and Sarafidis (2015).

Flannery and Hankins (2013) provide an evaluation of the performance of a wide range of alternative estimators under conditions that are likely to apply to corporate finance, with particular attention to a firm's capital structure choice. They note that complications, like second-order serial correlation or endogenous regressors in x_{it}, can seriously compromise many of the estimation methodologies, consistent with the theoretical literature. "Perhaps surprisingly, these complications can be large enough that there are occasions when the much maligned fixed effects estimator performs best". A similar study is Dang et al. (2015), who spend more attention to bias-corrected estimators and estimators taking into account the fractional nature of the dependent variable. They caution against the use of system GMM and IV/GMM estimators, especially in the presence of autocorrelation, and recommend the more robust bias-corrected estimators.

Another area in corporate finance where the GMM estimator is used is in models explaining the diversification discount, as in Hoechle et al. (2012). Among other specifications, they estimate a dynamic model explaining excess firm value based on sales from a dummy variable for whether the firm is diversified, excess firm value with one and two lags, and a set of controls related to firm governance. The estimation results, based on the system GMM estimator as proposed by Arellano and Bover (1995) and Blundell and Bond (1998), show economically and statistically significant persistence in the dependent variable. In estimation, they do not impose that the explanatory variables are strictly exogenous, and employ the governance variables with three or more lags as instruments. Importantly, the test for second order collection (in Δu_{it}) does not reject, nor does the Sargan overidentifying restrictions test. This way, the estimation accounts for the dynamic endogeneity, unobservable heterogeneity, as well as the simultaneity.

Similar to the previous study, Wintoki et al. (2012) use the dynamic GMM estimator to estimate the effect of board structure on firm performance. Unobserved heterogeneity is important here as it captures, among other aspects, managerial quality, which is likely to correlate with both firm performance and board structure. Their equation of interest can be written as

$$y_{it} = x_{it}'\beta + \gamma_1 y_{i,t-1} + \gamma_2 y_{i,t-2} + \alpha_i + u_{it}, \tag{5.25}$$

where y_{it} is a measure of fund performance, in their case either return on assets (ROA) or return on sales (ROS), and x_{it} includes three board structure variables: board size, board composition, and board leadership. An important reason to include two lags of firm performance in the model is to make the equation dynamically complete, in the sense that any residual serial correlation in u_{it} is controlled for. Control variables include the firm's market-to-book ratio, firm age, and the standard deviation of its stock returns (over the previous 12 months). In their empirical application, the authors sample at two-year intervals instead of every year, using governance data from 1991, 1993, . . . , 2013 (so that T is effectively very small). As a result, $t-1$ refers to an observation two years before t. On the one hand, this is because board structure is highly persistent. On the other hand, this alleviates the concerns with second order serial correlation in the equation's idiosyncratic error term, as required for the dynamic panel GMM estimators.

For the first-differenced equation, lagged values $y_{i,t-p}$ and $x_{i,t-p}$ are used as instruments, where $p > 2$ (because of the second lag in the equation). For these instruments to be valid they must be relevant, that is, capture variation in current governance, as well as exogenous. This means they should be uncorrelated to u_{it}. According to Wintoki et al. (2012), theory provides a motivation for this. If the board structure today is one that trades off the expected costs and benefits of alternative board structures, then current shocks to performance must have been unanticipated when the boards were chosen. The inclusion of two lags of firm performance helps to achieve this. The final estimator uses the system GMM estimator employing (appropriately) lagged levels as instruments for the first-differenced equation and using lagged differences as instruments for the levels equation. The maintained assumption is that there is no serial correlation in u_{it}, and thus no second order serial correlation in Δu_{it}. Wintoki et al. (2012) provide an elaborate discussion of considerations, concerns and caveats with the implication of the system GMM estimator, including a Monte Carlo study to show how powerful the test for no serial correlation and the overidentifying restrictions test are to detect misspecification. They also explain why other commonly used estimators that ignore the dynamic relationship between current governance and past firm performance may be biased.

Another interesting application is provided in Massa (2003), who investigates how product differentiation by mutual fund families affects performance and fund proliferation. Most models not only contain a lagged dependent variable, but also suffer from simultaneity or reverse causality in the sense that x_{it} may be correlated with u_{it}. In addition to the first-difference transformation, he also employ an orthogonal deviations transformation. It constructs, for each observation, the deviation from the average of all future observations of the same unit (Arellano and Bover, 1995). That is,

$$x_{it}^* = \left(x_{it} - \frac{x_{i,t+1} + \cdots + x_{i,T}}{T-t} \right) \left(\frac{T-t}{T-t-1} \right)^{1/2}, \tag{5.26}$$

where the second term in parentheses serves the purpose to produce homoskedastic errors u_{it}^*, in the situation where u_{it} is homoskedastic. Unlike first differencing, which introduces a moving average structure in the error term, orthogonal deviations preserve lack of correlation among the transformed errors if the original ones are not autocorrelated. The advantage of this transformation is that u_{it}^* is uncorrelated with lagged values of x_{it} if the explanatory variables are predetermined, so that they can serve as instruments. Apart from some minor details, this approach is similar to the recursive demeaning approach discussed in Section 3.6 (fixed effects without strict exogeneity). The empirical results in Massa (2003) based on first-difference GMM or orthogonal deviations GMM are surprisingly similar.

As a final example, we discuss Ellul and Yerramilli (2013). Among other models, they estimate a dynamic model as specified in equation (5.25), where y_{it} is a measure of tail risk, and the key variable of interest in x_{it} is a risk management index (RMI). Their sample contains data of 72 bank holding companies (BHCs) over the period 1994-2009, and is unbalanced. The model is estimated using the FD-GMM estimator of Arellano and Bond (1991). Given the presence of two lags of the dependent variable, the variables in x_{it} are lagged three periods or more for use as instruments. The Sargan test for overidentifying restrictions does not reject, but a test for serial correlation is not presented.

6 Models with limited dependent variables

In practical applications it occurs quite frequently that the phenomena of interest are of a discrete or mixed discrete-continuous nature. For example, one could be interested in the question whether or not a firm pays dividends, whether or not a firm hedges its currency risks, or what the share of risky assets is in a household's portfolio. If these type of variables are modelled, a linear regression model is generally inappropriate (although it may provide reasonable approximations in some cases). In this chapter we consider alternative models that are developed to explain discrete or discrete/continuous variables. This includes, among others, logit and probit models, tobit models and models with sample selection.

Other situations that may require special models are counts, where the dependent variable is a discrete number, for example, the number of takeover bids received by a target firm, duration data, where the dependent variable is a duration, for example, the duration of a firm-bank relationship, or models with qualitative outcomes, for example, the credit rating of a bond. In all such cases, it is common to employ nonlinear models to accommodate the specific nature of the dependent variable.

In empirical finance, many authors tend to more or less ignore the panel nature of the data and specify a standard cross-sectional model, where the panel nature is taken care of by allowing clustering over one or more dimensions when calculating standard errors. This is often appropriate, but it imposes some important restrictions. Fully exploiting the panel nature of the data is often more challenging, for example, because it requires making assumptions about the joint distribution of a series of outcomes (and their interdependence). This may be overly restrictive or make model estimation difficult. Nevertheless, fully specified panel data models with limited dependent variables can provide more insight, for example, into the dynamics of a process.

Most of the models in this chapter are highly parametric in the sense that specific distributional assumptions, such as normality and homoskedasticity, are imposed, which are often necessary for consistent estimation. Unfortunately, empirical results tend to be more sensitive to violations of these assumptions than in linear models. A common issue is that the inclusion of firm fixed effects, to control for a time-invariant source of endogeneity, is nontrivial. To be precise, the firm fixed effects often cannot be eliminated and leaving them in the model as in the least squares dummy variable approach suffers from an incidental parameters problem: the number of coefficients increases with the sample size N and consistent estimation for fixed T is not possible. Only in specific cases this can be solved. Another issue is that the inclusion of a lagged dependent variable creates estimation problems in the presence of serial dependence or time-invariant firm-specific heterogeneity in the unobservables. This is reflected in an initial conditions problem (which disappears with large T).

In this chapter we provide an overview of different models with limited dependent variables, count data and duration data, and their use in finance. Section 6.1 starts with a discussion of binary choice models, including the random effects probit

https://doi.org/10.1515/9783110660739-006

model and the fixed effects logit model. Subsection 6.1.2 elaborates on the methods of maximum likelihood and quasi-maximum likelihood, which are typically employed for the models in this chapter. Models for multiple discrete outcomes, for example, a credit rating, are discussed in Section 6.2. Models with censoring or truncation are typically referred to as tobit models and are presented in Section 6.3. Section 6.4 discusses the estimation of dynamic models and introduces the problem of initial conditions. Count data models are covered in Section 6.5. The chapter concludes with a discussion of duration models in Section 6.6. More information on the models in this chapter is provided in Maddala (1983), Cameron and Trivedi (2005) and Wooldridge (2010). Maddala (1987) provides an excellent overview of limited dependent variable models using panel data. Regression models for count data are covered extensively in Cameron and Trivedi (2013, 2015).

6.1 Binary choice models

In many applications the dependent variable is not continuous, but of a discrete nature. For example, we may wish to have a model to predict bankruptcy of a firm (e. g., Ohlson, 1980), to predict a firm going public (e. g., Pagano et al., 1998) or to explain whether or not a firm issues dividends (e. g., Fama and French, 2001). In this situation, the dependent variable is binary, where it is the convention to label a positive outcome by 1 and a negative outcome by 0. Thus, the dependent variable can be denoted as $y_{it} = 1$ or $y_{it} = 0$. Essentially, a binary choice model describes the probability that $y_{it} = 1$ as a function of a set of variables collected in x_{it}. In general, we can write this as $Pr(y_{it} = 1) = F(x'_{it}\beta)$, where $F(\cdot)$ is a monotonically increasing function over the interval $[0, 1]$. This imposes the "single index" assumption meaning that the probability of observing y_{it} equal to 1 depends upon the explanatory variables in x_{it} only through the single index $x'_{it}\beta$. Of course, this may contain nonlinear functions of explanatory variables as well as interaction terms.

With panel data the different outcomes of the same firm are often not independent and we may wish to consider the joint probability of observing a range of outcomes $y_{i1}, y_{i2}, \ldots, y_{iT}$. Alternatively, we may be interested in the probability of $y_{it} = 1$ conditional upon the previous value $y_{i,t-1}$. These aspects require modelling the joint distribution of multiple outcomes and a more complex (and complete) econometric specification is required. A similar remark holds if we wish to take into account that the probabilities of $y_{it} = 1$, for example, the probabilities of bankruptcy, are not independent across firms in the same period.

In this section we discuss the estimation of binary choice models when panel data are available. We will start with simple pooled estimation where the panel nature of the data only plays a role when estimating standard errors. Accordingly, estimation is similar to that in cross-sectional contexts.

6.1.1 Specification and interpretation

Before moving to nonlinear models, let us consider the case where we would employ a standard regression model to explain a binary variable. That is, we specify and estimate

$$y_{it} = x'_{it}\beta + \varepsilon_{it}, \tag{6.1}$$

where $y_{it} = 0, 1$. Imposing the assumption that the error term is conditionally mean independent of the explanatory variables in x_{it}, this implies that

$$E(y_{it} \mid x_{it}) = x'_{it}\beta.$$

However, at the same time

$$E(y_{it} \mid x_{it}) = Pr(y_{it} = 1 \mid x_{it})$$

due to the discrete $(0, 1)$ nature of y_{it}. Accordingly, the linear model imposes that

$$Pr(y_{it} = 1 \mid x_{it}) = x'_{it}\beta, \tag{6.2}$$

which says that the probability of observing $y_{it} = 1$ is a linear function of the set of variables collected in x_{it}. This result is problematic for several reasons. First, it does not restrict probabilities to lie in the $[0, 1]$ interval. Second, and related to the previous, it imposes that the marginal effect of a change in one of the explanatory variables in x_{it} is constant, irrespective of the characteristics of the firm. This means that, with every increase in x_{it}, the implied probability increases proportionally. For example, if $\beta_2 = 0.1$ the probability of observing $y_{it} = 1$ increases by 10 percentage points with every unit increase in the corresponding variable $x_{2,it}$ (other things equal). This is undesirable when the probability is already close to 100% (and logically cannot increase much further). Another issue with the linear model is that, conditional upon x_{it}, the error term ε_{it} can only have two outcomes (depending on whether $y_{it} = 0$ or $y_{it} = 1$), the probabilities of which depend upon $x'_{it}\beta$. This means that, even if we ignore the first two problems, the error term in (6.1) is heteroskedastic, and standard errors should take this into account.

Even though the linear model is not logically correct when the dependent variable is binary, it is still surprisingly popular in finance. The model, referred to as the **linear probability model**, is attractive because it avoids much of the complications that arise with nonlinear binary choice models, as we shall see below. For example, Brown et al. (2007) use a linear model explaining whether a firm increases dividends after a dividend tax cut, and Ouimet and Tate (2020) use the linear probability model to explain whether an employee participates in an employee stock purchase plan, including both firm-month and location-month fixed effects.

To overcome the problems with the linear model, binary choice models are designed to explain discrete outcomes. A standard binary choice model imposes that

$$Pr(y_{it} = 1 \mid x_{it}) = F(x'_{it}\beta),$$

where $F(\cdot)$ is a known function (without unknown parameters). A natural choice is to choose F to be a distribution function (cumulative density function), such that it is monotonically increasing and bounded between 0 and 1. Two choices are very common. The first is to choose F to be the standard logistic distribution function, given by

$$F(w) = \Lambda(w) = \frac{e^w}{1 + e^w}. \tag{6.3}$$

This allows us to write the probability of observing $y_{it} = 1$ as

$$Pr(y_{it} = 1 \mid x_{it}) = \Lambda(x'_{it}\beta) = \frac{\exp(x'_{it}\beta)}{1 + \exp(x'_{it}\beta)}. \tag{6.4}$$

This model is referred to as the **logit model** or logistic regression model. It is easily seen that the probability that $y_{it} = 1$ is bounded between 0 and 1 and monotonically increases with $x'_{it}\beta$.

An alternative choice is to let F be the standard normal distribution function, that is,

$$F(w) = \Phi(w) = \int_{-\infty}^{w} \frac{1}{\sqrt{2\pi}} \exp\left(-\frac{1}{2}t^2\right) dt, \tag{6.5}$$

which results in the **probit model**. For the latter distribution function no closed-form expression exists. We will typically write this as

$$Pr(y_{it} = 1 \mid x_{it}) = \Phi(x'_{it}\beta), \tag{6.6}$$

with Φ defined in (6.5).

In fact, the functions Φ and Λ are reasonably similar in shape, although their scaling is different. In both cases $F(0) = 0.5$, indicating that $y_{it} = 1$ is more likely than $y_{it} = 0$ if $x'_{it}\beta > 0$ in both the logit and probit model. Because the logistic distribution has a variance of $\pi^2/3$ whereas the standard normal distribution has variance of 1, the absolute size of the slope coefficients in β is larger in the logit model. The difference between the logit and probit specifications is somewhat larger in the tails, that is, when probabilities get close to zero or one. Nevertheless, the probit and logit models typically produce quite similar results in empirical work. Despite its limitations, the linear probability model also tends to produce reasonably similar results, particularly when the implied probabilities are reasonably close to 0.5.

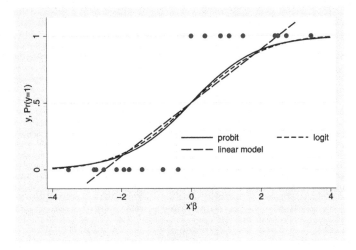

Figure 6.1: Logit and probit functions, linear model.

The differences between the functional form assumptions of the logit and probit models, as well as the linear probability model, are visualised in Figure 6.1. The horizontal axis depicts values of the single index $x'_{it}\beta$ (appropriately scaled), while the vertical axis reflects the probability that $y_{it} = 1$ as a function of the single index. The logit and probit functions transform the linear index nonlinearly, to guarantee probabilities between 0 and 1, and imply smaller marginal effects when the probabilities get further away from 0.5. The linear probability model does not do this, and leads to (logically impossible) probabilities less than 0 or larger than 1 for small or large values of the single index. For many values of $x'_{it}\beta$, the slopes of the three curves are reasonably similar.

The choice between alternative models is typically based on the convention in a particular segment of the literature, or on personal preferences.[1] For example, the logit model is very popular in the literature predicting bankruptcy or financial failure (Ohlson, 1980). The probit specification is more common in multivariate contexts, for example, when two outcomes are jointly modelled, or when the binary choice model is part of a larger set of equations. This is because the use of a multivariate normal distribution is attractive and flexible (unlike a multivariate logistic distribution). The linear probability model is often used when one or more high-dimensional fixed effects are included, when instrumental variables estimation is required, or simply because of its simplicity.

In a binary choice model, a positive coefficient, $\beta_k > 0$, say, implies that the probability that $y_{it} = 1$ increases if $x_{k,it}$ increases, keeping the other variables in x_{it} fixed. Because the function F is nonlinear, the exact size of the effect is not constant and

---

1 One advantage of a logit specification is that F has a closed-form expression.

depends upon the shape of F and the values of all explanatory variables. This is reflected in Figure 6.1 by a slope that varies with $x'_{it}\beta$. To help interpretation of binary
choice models, it is possible to calculate so-called **marginal effects**. For a continuous
explanatory variable, the marginal effect is the partial derivative of $P(y_{it} = 1 \mid x_{it}) = F(x'_{it}\beta)$ with respect to $x_{k,it}$. That is,

$$\frac{\partial Pr(y_{it} = 1 \mid x_{it})}{\partial x_{k,it}} = F'(x'_{it}\beta)\beta_k, \tag{6.7}$$

where $F'(w) = \partial F(w)/\partial w = f(w)$ denotes the derivative of $F(w)$.[2] These marginal effects
not only depend upon the choice for the function F but, importantly, also upon the
values of the explanatory variables in x_{it}. The means that marginal effects vary across
the sample. In contrast, marginal effects in the linear probability model are constant
and equal to the model coefficients.[3]

For logit and probit models, marginal effects can either be computed for the average observation in the sample, replacing x_{it} by a sample average, or as the average of
all individual marginal effects, as calculated for each observation in the sample. These
alternatives are often referred to as the marginal effect at the mean (MEM) and the
average marginal effect (AME), respectively. The latter metric avoids calculating the
marginal effect for a hypothetical average firm with, say, a 0.8 male CEO and a board
size of 6.31. Greene (2011, Section 17.3) provides a discussion on the difference between
the average marginal effect and the marginal effects at the average, and on how to calculate standard errors for marginal effects. In Stata, marginal effects for binary choice
models can easily be obtained after estimation using the command *margins, dydx(x2
x3)*, where *x2* and *x3* denote the explanatory variables of interest. The default is that
average marginal effects are estimated; to determine the marginal effect at the average
one should add the option *atmeans*.[4] Because $F'(x'_{it}\beta) > 0$, the sign of the marginal effect corresponds to the sign of β_k, so one can quickly infer the sign of a marginal effect
from the corresponding coefficient. For a discrete explanatory variable, for example,
an $(0, 1)$-indicator, it is common to determine the "marginal" effect as the change in
predicted probability from $x_{k,it} = 0$ to $x_{k,it} = 1$, again keeping all other variables in x_{it}
fixed.

Using (6.4), we can write for the logit model that

$$\frac{p}{1 - p} = \exp(x'_{it}\beta),$$

---

2 When $F(\cdot)$ is the standard normal distribution function, $f(\cdot)$ is the standard normal density, denoted
$\phi(\cdot)$.
3 Of course, these marginal effects loose their interpretation if the probabilities are not within the
$[0, 1]$ interval.
4 The *margins* command is very flexible and a wide range of other options is available.

or

$$\ln \frac{p}{1-p} = x'_{it}\beta, \tag{6.8}$$

where $p = Pr(y_{it} = 1 \mid x_{it})$ is the probability of observing $y_{it} = 1$, conditional on x_{it}. The lefthand side of (6.8) is referred to as the log odds ratio and for the logit model it is linear in the coefficients. An odds ratio of 2 means that the odds of $y_i = 1$ are twice those of $y_i = 0$. Using this expression, the model coefficients can be interpreted as describing the effect on (the natural logarithm of) the odds ratio. For example, if $\beta_k = 0.05$, a one-unit increase in $x_{k,it}$ increase the odds ratio by about 5% (keeping all other variables fixed). For larger coefficients, for example, $\beta_k = 0.5$, the difference in the odds ratio is $\exp(0.5) - 1 = 0.65$ or 65%. Thus we can write that the odds of $y_{it} = 1$ for a firm with $x_{k,it} = 1$ are 65% of the corresponding odds for a firm with $x_{k,it} = 0$. Several papers interpret the estimation results of logit models in terms of odds ratios rather than marginal effects (and rather than model coefficients); see, for example, Dittmar and Thakor (2007), who model the decision of a firm to issue equity ($y_{it} = 1$) or debt ($y_{it} = 0$).

Marginal effects and interaction terms
The condition to keep all other variables in x_{it} fixed is not realistic if the model contains additional functions of the relevant variable, for example, a square or an interaction term. When the model of interest contains interaction terms, a subtle issue emerges. To illustrate this, consider the case where the model contains $\beta_2 x_{2,it} + \beta_3 x_{3,it} + \beta_4 x_{2,it} x_{3,it}$. When both β_2 and β_4 are positive, this seems to suggest that $P(y_{it} = 1 \mid x_{it})$ increases with $x_{2,it}$, the marginal effect being larger when $x_{3,it}$ is bigger. This latter conclusion is not necessarily correct. To see this, note that the marginal effect of a change in $x_{2,it}$ is now given by

$$\frac{\partial F(x'_{it}\beta)}{\partial x_{k,it}} = f(x'_{it}\beta)(\beta_2 + \beta_4 x_{3,it}), \tag{6.9}$$

where $f(\cdot)$ denotes the derivative of $F(\cdot)$. Because $x_{3,it}$ is correlated with $f(x'_{it}\beta)$, it is possible for the marginal effect to decrease if $x_{3,it}$ gets larger, also when $\beta_4 > 0$ (see Ai and Norton, 2003). In general, evaluating the sign and significance of the coefficient β_4 of the interaction term is inappropriate to argue that the likelihood that $y_{it} = 1$ is more sensitive to $x_{2,it}$ when $x_{3,it}$ is either larger or smaller. The true interaction effect equals the cross derivative of the conditional probability that $y_{it} = 1$ with respect to $x_{2,it}$ and $x_{3,it}$. That is,

$$\frac{\partial^2 F(x'_{it}\beta)}{\partial x_{2,it}\partial x_{3,it}} = f(x'_{it}\beta)\beta_4 + f'(x'_{it}\beta)(\beta_3 + \beta_4 x_{2,it})(\beta_2 + \beta_4 x_{3,it}),$$

where $f'(\cdot)$ denotes the derivative of $f(\cdot)$. In general, the sign of this interaction effect may differ from the sign of β_4, and its magnitude and sign will depend upon x_{it}. Moreover, the statistical significance of the interaction effect does not equal the statistical significance of β_4.

An illustration of the above issue is given by Powers (2005) in the context of the management turnover literature. Here, the dependent variable y_{it} denotes managerial turnover (the departure of a key executive), with $y_{it} = 1$ indicating that a manager departs, and $y_{it} = 0$ if the manager remains with the firm during year t. Logit models are commonly applied when trying to show that the likelihood of turnover is more sensitive to changes in performance for one type of firm than for another. In the previous notation, this means that $x_{2,it}$ is a measure of firm performance (e. g., an industry-adjusted return), and $x_{3,it}$ is an indicator defining the type of firm (e. g., whether the firm is foreign-owned, or whether the CEO is the founder of the firm). Many earlier studies appear to ignore this problem with marginal effects in nonlinear models with interaction terms, although it is by now well understood. The preferred solution is to calculate the estimated magnitude of the interaction effect for given values of the explanatory variables, similar to the calculation of (average) marginal effects. Ai and Norton (2003) describe how standard errors should be calculated in this case; see Lel and Miller (2008) for a more recent application on management turnover. The *margins* command in Stata will calculate correct marginal effects provided the factor variables and interactions are properly defined.

A latent variable framework

Economists often formulate a binary choice model in terms of an underlying latent variable model. In this case, the starting point is a linear model, similar to a standard linear regression model, with the exception that the dependent variable is not fully observed. In the binary case, we only observe the sign of the dependent variable. More formally, we write

$$y_{it}^* = x_{it}'\beta + \varepsilon_{it}, \qquad (6.10)$$

where y_{it}^* is a latent, unobserved, variable. Instead, we observe

$$y_{it} = 1 \text{ if } y_{it}^* > 0$$
$$= 0 \text{ otherwise.}$$

Occasionally, the latent variable is given a more formal interpretation, for example, the utility difference between alternative 1 and 0, or the willingness or propensity to choose option 1 rather than 0. For example, Billett and Xue (2007) and Edmans et al. (2012) define a latent variable to describe the takeover process of a firm, with the binary outcome y_{it} reflecting whether firm i receives a bid in year t or not; Barber et al.

(2021) interpret the latent variable as the utility of an investor investing in a particular venture capital fund. The model coefficients β describe the impact of a change in one of the explanatory variables (ceteris paribus) upon the latent variable y_{it}^*. Starting from (6.10) the probability of observing $y_{it} = 1$, conditional upon x_{it}, is given by[5]

$$Pr(y_{it} = 1) = Pr(y_{it}^* > 0) = Pr(-\varepsilon_{it} < x_{it}'\beta) = F(x_{it}'\beta), \tag{6.11}$$

where $F(\cdot)$ denotes the distribution function of $-\varepsilon_{it}$, or, in the common case of a symmetric distribution, the distribution function of ε_{it}. The functional form assumption about $F(\cdot)$ in the binary choice models leading to logit or probit, is now an assumption about the error term in a latent variable equation.[6]

Because the scale of the latent variable is not identified, a normalisation on the distribution of ε_{it} is required, for example, imposing a standard normal distribution with a variance of one. Similarly, the location of the latent variable is fixed by setting the mean of the error distribution to zero. A standard probit model is obtained if we complement the above model with the assumption that ε_{it} is IID standard normal, independent of x_{it}. A logit model is obtained when imposing a logistic distribution upon ε_{it}. To illustrate the normalisation issue, suppose we assume that ε_{it} has a normal distribution with mean zero and variance σ^2. In that case,

$$Pr(y_{it} = 1) = Pr(y_{it}^* > 0) = Pr\left(-\frac{\varepsilon_{it}}{\sigma} < \frac{x_{it}'\beta}{\sigma}\right) = \Phi\left(\frac{x_{it}'\beta}{\sigma}\right).$$

This shows that, empirically, only the ratio β/σ is identified, and there is no harm in imposing that $\sigma^2 = 1$.

The latent variable framework is not necessary for a standard binary choice model, but it helps to interpret specification issues in terms of assumptions about the error term ε_{it} (e. g., heteroskedasticity, or exogeneity of x_{it}). A more important advantage of the latent variable framework, typically in combination with the normal distribution, is that it is easily extended to other forms of censoring (e. g., y_{it}^* being observed only if it is positive), to models with multinomial outcomes, and, most importantly, to multivariate frameworks where multiple outcomes are investigated simultaneously. The latter is important in the context of panel data, for example, if we wish to model the probability of a sequence of outcomes $y_{i1}, y_{i2}, \ldots, y_{iT}$.

---

5 For notational convenience, we drop the conditioning set from the probabilities.

6 Occasionally, articles (even in top journals) inappropriately mix up notations and present $y_{it} = x_{it}'\beta + \varepsilon_{it}$ as representing a probit or logit model. This is incorrect. Some authors include ε_{it} within the function F and write $Pr(y_{it} = 1) = F(x_{it}'\beta + \varepsilon_{it})$. This is also incorrect.

6.1.2 Estimation: maximum likelihood

Nonlinear models, such as probit and logit, are usually estimated using maximum likelihood. This section briefly discuss some theoretical results on this method, in a general notation. We illustrate this with the linear model, and then move to binary choice models in Subsection 6.1.3.

Maximum likelihood estimation is based on maximising the (log) likelihood function with respect to the unknown parameters. Let us, in general, denote the K-dimensional unknown parameter vector by θ, and let the probability mass function or density function of y_i, conditional on X_i, be denoted as $f(y_i \mid X_i; \theta)$, where y_i could be a multidimensional vector. If the observations in the sample are independent over i, the loglikelihood function is given by

$$\ln L(\theta) = \sum_{i=1}^{N} \ln L_i(\theta) = \sum_{i=1}^{N} \ln f(y_i \mid X_i; \theta). \tag{6.12}$$

The term $\ln L_i(\theta)$ is referred to as the loglikelihood contribution of observation i. The maximum likelihood estimator $\hat{\theta}_{ML}$ maximises (6.12) and is the solution to the first-order conditions

$$\frac{\partial \ln L(\theta)}{\partial \theta} = \sum_{i=1}^{N} \frac{\partial \ln L_i(\theta)}{\partial \theta} = 0. \tag{6.13}$$

If the loglikelihood function is globally concave, there is a unique global maximum, and the maximum likelihood estimator is uniquely defined by the first-order conditions. For many standard models efficient algorithms are available to numerically optimise (6.12).

Provided that the likelihood function is correctly specified, it can be shown under weak regularity conditions that the ML estimator $\hat{\theta}_{ML}$ is consistent for θ, asymptotically efficient and asymptotically normally distributed. The covariance matrix is determined by the shape of the loglikelihood function. To describe it in the general case, define the information in observation i as

$$I_i(\theta) = E\left\{\frac{\partial^2 \ln L_i(\theta)}{\partial \theta \partial \theta'}\right\},$$

which is a symmetric $K \times K$ matrix. Loosely speaking, this matrix summarises the expected amount of information about θ contained in observation i. The average information matrix (IM) for a sample of size N is defined as

$$\bar{I}_N(\theta) \equiv \frac{1}{N} \sum_{i=1}^{N} I_i(\theta) = -E\left\{\frac{1}{N} \frac{\partial^2 \ln L(\theta)}{\partial \theta \partial \theta'}\right\}, \tag{6.14}$$

while the limiting information matrix is defined as $I(\theta) = \lim_{N \to \infty} I_N(\theta)$. In the special case where the observations are independently and identically distributed, it follows that

$$I_i(\theta) = \bar{I}_N(\theta) = I(\theta).$$

Under appropriate regularity conditions, the asymptotic covariance matrix of the maximum likelihood estimator can be shown to equal the inverse of the information matrix, that is,

$$\sqrt{N}(\hat{\theta}_{ML} - \theta) \to N(0, V), \tag{6.15}$$

where $V = I(\theta)^{-1}$.

The term on the right-hand side of (6.14) is the expected value of the matrix of second-order derivatives, scaled by the number of observations and reflects the curvature of the loglikelihood function. Clearly, if the loglikelihood function is highly curved around its maximum, the second derivative is large, the variance is small and the maximum likelihood estimator is relatively accurate. If the function is less curved, the variance will be larger. Given the asymptotic efficiency of the maximum likelihood estimator, the inverse of the information matrix $I(\theta)^{-1}$ provides a lower bound on the asymptotic covariance matrix for any consistent asymptotically normal estimator for θ. The ML estimator is asymptotically efficient because it attains this bound, often referred to as the Cramèr–Rao lower bound.

To estimate the asymptotic covariance matrix of the maximum likelihood estimator in (6.15), different choices can be made. The standard approach is to start from (6.14) and replace the expectations operator by a sample average and the unknown coefficients by their maximum likelihood estimates. This leads to

$$\hat{V}_H = \left(-\frac{1}{N} \sum_{i=1}^{N} \frac{\partial^2 \ln L_i(\theta)}{\partial\theta\partial\theta'} \bigg|_{\hat{\theta}_{ML}} \right)^{-1}, \tag{6.16}$$

where the derivatives are evaluated at the point $\theta = \hat{\theta}_{ML}$. The suffix H refers to the fact that this estimator for V is based on the Hessian matrix, the matrix of second derivatives.

An alternative expression for the information matrix can be obtained from the result that the matrix

$$J_i(\theta) \equiv E\{s_i(\theta)s_i(\theta)'\}, \tag{6.17}$$

is identical to $I_i(\theta)$, provided that the likelihood function is correctly specified, where

$$s_i(\theta) = \frac{\partial \ln L_i(\theta)}{\partial\theta} \tag{6.18}$$

is the vector of first derivatives of the loglikelihood contribution, also known as the score contribution. This indicates that V can also be estimated from the first-order derivatives of the loglikelihood function as

$$\hat{V}_G = \left(\frac{1}{N} \sum_{i=1}^{N} s_i(\hat{\theta}_{ML}) s_i(\hat{\theta}_{ML})' \right)^{-1}, \tag{6.19}$$

where the suffix G reflects that the estimator employs the outer product of the gradients (first derivatives). This estimator for V was suggested by Berndt et al. (1974) and is sometimes referred to as the BHHH estimator. Computation of $\hat{V}_G$ is simpler than $\hat{V}_H$ because only first-order derivatives are needed.

In general, consistency of the maximum likelihood estimator requires that the likelihood is correctly specified. This requires that the joint density or probability mass function of the observed data is correctly chosen. This is, obviously, a fairly strong requirement, partly responsible for the shift away from maximum likelihood in favour of more robust alternatives in empirical work. Alternative estimators are not available for all relevant situations. Fortunately, there are cases where the maximum likelihood estimator is still consistent even when the likelihood function is misspecified. Intuitively, this means that the chosen loglikelihood has, asymptotically, the same maximum as the true loglikelihood. When the likelihood function is misspecified, the resulting estimator is referred to as a **quasi-maximum likelihood** (QML) estimator.

An alternative starting point to argue that a QML estimator can be consistent, even with a misspecified likelihood, is that the true model satisfies the following set of, potentially nonlinear, moment conditions

$$E(s_i(\theta)) = 0, \tag{6.20}$$

with s_i defined in (6.18). This is naturally satisfied for a correct likelihood, but can be more generally valid. The QML estimator satisfies the sample equivalent of this given by

$$\frac{1}{N} \sum_{I=1}^{N} s_i(\theta) = 0,$$

which corresponds to the first-order conditions given in (6.13). Let us, in general, denote the resulting estimator as $\hat{\theta}_{QML}$. Even in cases where this estimator is consistent for θ, its asymptotic distribution will differ from that of the true maximum likelihood estimator. Fortunately, the appropriate asymptotic covariance matrix can easily be derived. In general, it holds that

$$\sqrt{N}(\hat{\theta}_{QML} - \theta) \rightarrow N(0, V), \tag{6.21}$$

where

$$V = I(\theta)^{-1} J(\theta) I(\theta)^{-1}, \tag{6.22}$$

with

$$I(\theta) \equiv \lim_{N \to \infty} \frac{1}{N} \sum_{i=1}^{N} I_i(\theta)$$

and

$$J(\theta) \equiv \lim_{N \to \infty} \frac{1}{N} \sum_{i=1}^{N} J_i(\theta),$$

with $I_i(\theta)$ and $J_i(\theta)$ defined above. This covariance matrix generalises the one in (6.15) and its expression resembles the typical "sandwich formula". Many software packages have the option to estimate robust standard errors based on the sandwich formula for estimators based on maximising a quasi-loglikelihood function. In Stata, these are typically obtained with the option *vce(robust)*. Importantly, whereas such standard errors do allow for some misspecification in the assumed model, for consistency it remains necessary that (6.20) is satisfied for the true parameter vector θ.

The information matrix test (IM test) suggested by White (1982) tests the equality of the two $K \times K$ matrices $I(\theta)$ and $J(\theta)$ by comparing their sample counterparts. Because of the symmetry, a maximum of $K(K+1)/2$ elements have to be compared, so that the number of degrees of freedom for the IM test is potentially very large. Depending on the shape of the likelihood function, the IM test checks for misspecification in a number of directions simultaneously (like functional form, heteroskedasticity, skewness and kurtosis). For additional discussion and computational issues, see Davidson and MacKinnon (2004, Section 15.2).

Panel data

The previous approach can be applied to panel data in different ways. The first and simplest way is to assume that, despite the panel nature of the data, the sample is independent over both i and t. In this case, the loglikelihood function becomes

$$\ln L(\theta) = \sum_{i=1}^{N} \sum_{t=1}^{T} \ln f(y_{it} \mid x_{i1}, \dots, x_{iT}; \theta), \tag{6.23}$$

and estimation proceeds as in the cross-sectional case in (6.12), where all summations are over both firms and periods, and no new issues arise. However, independence of the observations across both the cross-section as well as the time-series is quite restrictive and in many applications unlikely to be satisfied. As an alternative, one can opt for a quasi-maximum likelihood approach and maximise the quasi-loglikelihood function in (6.23) assuming that the first-order conditions lead to a consistent estimator for θ, and estimate its covariance matrix using the more general sandwich expression in (6.22). This is similar to using pooled OLS in a linear model, and using heteroskedasticity or cluster-robust standard errors. We illustrate this pooled approach for binary choice models in Subsection 6.1.3.

A third way to build upon the previous formulae is to choose a full maximum likelihood approach and extend the definition of y_i to a T-dimensional vector $(y_{i1}, \ldots, y_{iT})'$. In this case $f(\cdot)$ refers to the joint density or probability mass function. In case of independence across i, we can use the previous expressions provided N is sufficiently large to justify the use of asymptotic approximations for $N \to \infty$. Unfortunately, specifying the joint distribution of $y_{i1}, \ldots, y_{iT}$ (conditional upon the explanatory variables) is typically more challenging than to specify the distribution of a single y_{it}. Most importantly, it requires us to specify the dependence across different observations for the same firm. A variant of this is to combine the multivariate likelihood approach with a robust covariance matrix, assuming that conditions for consistency are still satisfied. We illustrate these latter two approaches with the linear model with random firm effects from Section 2.6.

The linear model with random effects

Consider the linear random effects model given by

$$y_{it} = x_{it}'\beta + \alpha_i + u_{it}.$$

To be able to derive the likelihood function we need to impose distributional assumptions upon α_i and u_{it}, in addition to the usual random effects assumptions. Assuming normality, we impose that

$$\alpha_i \sim NID(0, \sigma_\alpha^2)$$

and

$$u_{it} \sim NID(0, \sigma_u^2),$$

both independent of all explanatory variables in x_{it}. Under these assumptions, the vector of error terms ε_i, with typical element $\varepsilon_{it} = \alpha_i + u_{it}$, is normally distributed with mean zero and covariance matrix

$$\Sigma_\varepsilon = \sigma_u^2 I_T + \sigma_\alpha^2 \iota_T \iota_T',$$

where ι_T is a T-dimensional vector of ones, and I_T is the $T \times T$ identity matrix. Accordingly, the loglikelihood function under cross-sectional independence can be written as

$$\ln L(\beta, \sigma_u^2, \sigma_\alpha^2) = -\frac{TN}{2}\ln(2\pi) - \frac{N}{2}\ln|\Sigma_\varepsilon| - \frac{1}{2\sigma_u^2}\sum_{i=1}^{N}(y_i - X_i'\beta)'\Sigma_\varepsilon^{-1}(y_i - X_i'\beta), \qquad (6.24)$$

where $\sigma_\varepsilon^2 = \sigma_u^2 + \sigma_\alpha^2$ denotes the total error variance, and where $|\Sigma_\varepsilon|$ denotes the determinant of the covariance matrix of the vector ε_i. The random effects assumptions lead to

$$|\Sigma_\varepsilon| = \sigma_u^{2(T-1)}(\sigma_u^2 + T\sigma_\alpha^2).$$

The error components structure simplifies the loglikelihood function, as Σ_ε^{-1} can de de-termined analytically, and the first-order conditions can also be written in analytical form (see Hsiao, 2014, Chapter 3). The resulting expression for the ML estimator $\hat{\beta}_{ML}$ is similar to (2.66). The difference is that the loglikelihood function is optimised simulta-neously with respect to β and the two variance components σ_u^2 and σ_α^2. This means that the ML estimator for β and the RE (FGLS) estimator of Section 2.6 are asymptotically equivalent, irrespective of whether the error components have a normal distribution. In Stata, the ML version of the random effects estimator is obtained with *xtreg, mle,* which can be combined with cluster-robust standard errors.

It is possible to specify more general forms of Σ_ε, for example, to allow for het-eroskedasticity or arbitrary correlations over time within a given firm, at the expense of complicating the likelihood function and making numerical optimisation more chal-lenging. For example, it may occur that the loglikelihood function is not globally con-cave. The additional drawback of these approaches is that any misspecification in Σ_ε may also lead to an inconsistent estimator for β. In practice, researchers therefore tend to prefer more standard estimators (in this context: quasi-maximum likelihood esti-mators) in combination with standard errors that allow for clustering or heteroskedas-ticity. While this is relatively straightforward in linear models, this may not always work in nonlinear ones.

6.1.3 Pooled estimation approaches

In a standard cross-sectional case, a logit or probit model is typically estimated by maximum likelihood, assuming that the sample is IID. As a first step, we can extend this to the panel data case, by assuming independence over i and t (even though this is often unrealistic). The probability of observing a given outcome y_{it} is given by

$$f(y_{it} \mid x_{it}) = F(x_{it}'\beta)^{y_{it}}(1 - F(x_{it}'\beta))^{1-y_{it}},$$

where $f(\cdot)$ is generic notation for a probability mass function. Accordingly, the loglike-lihood function can be written as

$$\ln L(\beta) = \sum_i \sum_t [y_{it} \ln F(x_{it}'\beta) + (1 - y_{it})(1 - F(x_{it}'\beta))], \tag{6.25}$$

where the double summation follows from the independence assumption. The maxi-mum likelihood estimator for β is obtained by maximising this expression with respect to β, after an appropriate choice for F is made. The first-order conditions of this prob-lem are given by

$$\frac{\partial \ln L(\beta)}{\partial \beta} = \sum_i \sum_t \left[\frac{y_{it} - F(x_{it}'\beta)}{F(x_{it}'\beta)(1 - F(x_{it}'\beta))} f(x_i'\beta) \right] x_{it} = 0, \tag{6.26}$$

where f denotes the derivative of F. The term in square brackets is often referred to as the generalised residual of the binary choice model (Gourieroux et al., 1987), so that the first-order conditions state that the regressors should be orthogonal to the generalised residuals, within the sample.

The first-order conditions are nonlinear in β and cannot be solved analytically. The maximum likelihood estimator for β is therefore determined by numerically maximising the loglikelihood function, for which efficient algorithms are available. In Stata, one can estimate these models with the *probit* or *logit* command. The asymptotic distribution of the resulting estimator $\hat{\beta}_{ML}$ is derived from the general theory of maximum likelihood. When F is the logistic distribution function, we can rewrite the first-order conditions as

$$\frac{\partial \ln L(\beta)}{\partial \beta} = \sum_i \sum_t \left[y_{it} - \frac{\exp(x_{it}'\beta)}{1 + \exp(x_{it}'\beta)} \right] x_{it} = 0 \tag{6.27}$$

or

$$\frac{\partial \ln L(\beta)}{\partial \beta} = \sum_i \sum_t [y_{it} - \Lambda(x_{it}'\beta)] x_{it} = 0.$$

It can be shown that the maximum likelihood estimator for the binary choice model are consistent even in cases where there is dependence across i or t (Robinson, 1982). This is a special case of the quasi-maximum likelihood approach discussed before. As result, it is quite common in panel data applications of binary choice models in finance to more or less ignore the panel nature of the data by applying a standard probit or logit estimator, but combining this with clustered standard errors to allow for correlations within a cluster (either firms or periods). Importantly, though, this is only appropriate if the error terms in the latent variable equation are homoskedastic. The presence of heteroskedasticity in the latent variable equation affects the scaling and functional form of the model probabilities and this cannot be fixed by calculating clustered standard errors.

A probit model with heteroskedasticity

To illustrate the problem of heteroskedasticity in a probit model, assume that

$$y_{it}^* = x_{it}'\beta + \varepsilon_{it},$$

where ε_{it} is assumed to follow a normal distribution with variance

$$\sigma_{it}^2 = (\exp\{z_{it}'\alpha\})^2, \tag{6.28}$$

where z_{it} is a vector of covariates, excluding an intercept, which may overlap with x_{it}. For $\alpha = 0$, this reduces to the standard case with $\sigma_{it}^2 = 1$. Now, the probability of observing $y_{it} = 1$, conditional upon x_{it} and z_{it}, is given by

$$Pr(y_{it} = 1) = \Phi\left(\frac{x_{it}'\beta}{\exp\{z_{it}'\alpha\}}\right). \tag{6.29}$$

If this is the correct model specification, the standard probabilities given in (6.6) are misspecified and estimation of a standard probit model using QML will be inconsistent. Effectively, introducing heteroskedasticity changes the functional form of the model probabilities. This also affects the marginal effects, particularly so in cases where elements of x_{it} are included in z_{it}. In Stata, the command *hetprobit* estimates this model, where the user has to specify both the variables in x_{it} and z_{it}. Convergence of the numerical optimisation routine may be slow or problematic. A test for heteroskedasticity of the form in (6.28) against homoskedasticity ($\alpha = 0$) can be obtained using a likelihood ratio test.

6.1.4 Clustered standard errors

Even when there is dependence across i or t, it is possible to obtain consistent estimators for β by maximising the pooled loglikelihood function in (6.25), ignoring the dependence, which corresponds to quasi-maximum likelihood. Wooldridge (2010, Chapter 13) refers to this as pooled maximum likelihood or partial maximum likelihood. Cameron et al. (2011) refer to this as an m-estimator because the estimator is obtained by optimising a function that is not necessarily the full likelihood function.

The key in this approach is that, in expectation, the maximum of the pooled likelihood function is the same as that of the full likelihood function. An intuitive way to understand this, is to see that the first-order conditions of the pooled maximum likelihood approach also correspond to moment conditions that are valid in the presence of dependence over i or t. For example, the first-order conditions for the pooled binary choice model follow from $E(y_{it} \mid x_{it}) = F(x_{it}'\beta)$ or

$$E(y_{it} - F(x_{it}'\beta) \mid x_{it}) = 0. \tag{6.30}$$

This is a conditional moment condition, which implies unconditional moment conditions of the form

$$E([y_{it} - F(x_{it}'\beta)]w(x_{it})) = 0,$$

where w is a function of the explanatory variables in the conditioning set. For the logit model, we obtain the population version of the first-order conditions in (6.27) for $w(x_{it}) = x_{it}$ (and $F = \Lambda$). For the probit model, we need

$$w(x_{it}) = \left[\frac{\phi(x_{it}'\beta)}{\Phi(x_{it}'\beta)(1 - \Phi(x_{it}'\beta))}\right]x_{it}.$$

Even though this expression is a bit more complex than the one for the logit case, the term in square brackets only affects the efficiency of the resulting GMM estimator, not its consistency. With $w(x_{it})$ being of dimension K, the number of parameters in β, the GMM estimator is based on a set of exactly identified moment conditions. As long as (6.30) is valid, setting the unconditional sample moments to zero, as in (6.26), will, under regularity conditions, provide a consistent estimator for β.

For the pooled estimation approaches to work there are two important conditions. First, the conditional mean of the binary indicator, $F(x_{it}'\beta)$, should be correctly specified. Second, the dependence over i and t is somehow limited (see Robinson, 1982). In these cases we can consistently estimate β from a pooled maximum likelihood approach and employ standard errors that are clustered along one or more dimensions to account for the dependence. As with the linear model, we require the number of clusters to grow with the sample size, which limits the dependence structure.

To see how this works, let us denote the moment conditions (or first-order conditions) as

$$\frac{1}{NT} \sum_i \sum_t s_{it}(\theta) = 0, \tag{6.31}$$

where we denote the parameter vector as θ, to stress generality. For notational convenience, the panel is assumed to be balanced, extensions to the unbalanced case being reasonably straightforward. The pooled estimator is the solution to this set of restrictions and denoted by $\hat{\theta}$. Following Cameron et al. (2011), $\hat{\theta}$ is asymptotically normal under standard regularity conditions, and the asymptotic covariance matrix of $\hat{\theta}$ can be estimated as

$$\hat{V}(\hat{\theta}) = \hat{A}^{-1}\hat{B}\hat{A}'^{-1},$$

where

$$\hat{A} = \sum_i \sum_t \frac{\partial s_{it}(\theta)}{\partial \theta'}\bigg|_{\hat{\theta}},$$

and where $\hat{B}$ is an estimate for

$$V\left(\sum_i \sum_t s_{it}(\theta)\right).$$

The covariance matrix thus has the usual sandwich structure, where the matrix $\hat{B}$ in the middle depends upon the clustering chosen. How we estimate this depends upon the correlations we allow between the different s_{it}s. In the case of clustering over firms only, we can use

$$\hat{B} = \sum_i \left(\sum_t s_{it}(\hat{\theta})\right)\left(\sum_t s_{it}(\hat{\theta})\right)'.$$

For clustering over time we reverse the role of i and t in the above expression. It is also possible to cluster over both firms and time; see Cameron et al. (2011) for the general expressions. Clustering over firms and time allows observations for the same firm to be correlated over time, and allows observations in the same period to be correlated as well. Importantly, the moment conditions in (6.31) need to remain valid in the presence of clustering.

Pooled probit and pooled logit approaches, in combination with clustered standard errors, have become quite common in empirical work in finance. Often standard errors are clustered at the firm-level, and fixed time effects are included in the model to accommodate aggregate shifts in the probabilities over time. Unfortunately, it seems that much of the older literature employs pooled probit or logit (referred to as "maximum likelihood") and simply ignores the possibility of dependence over time, or – if not – does not mention anything on this issue in the text (see, for example, Pagano et al., 1998). This has changed since the publication of Petersen (2009). For example, Offenberg and Pirinsky (2015) use a pooled probit model to explain the probability for a takeover deal to be structured as a tender offer, with standard errors clustered at the year and industry level; Sun and Teo (2019) estimate pooled probit regressions to model the probability of launching new funds for listed and unlisted hedge fund management companies, with standard errors clustered at the firm level, and Boyson et al. (2017) use a pooled logit model, with standard errors clustered by year and firm, to explain the probability of receiving a takeover bid.

Note that, even though the clustered standard errors adjust for correlation within a cluster, they do not address the problem of heteroskedasticity. Heteroskedasticity in a binary choice model, in the sense that ε_{it} in (6.10) does not have constant variance, implies that the conditional expectation of y_{it} is misspecified, and thus makes the pooled maximum likelihood estimator inconsistent. Accordingly, it does not make sense to write that probit or logit standard errors are robust against heteroskedasticity.

6.1.5 Fama-MacBeth estimation

An alternative approach that attempts to control for the panel nature of the data is inspired by the cross-sectional regression approach of Fama and MacBeth (1973), as discussed in Section 2.12. In this case, a standard binary choice model is estimated across different subsets of the sample, after which the estimates of interest are determined as the average over all subsamples, with a standard error based on the variation across the subsamples. The typical approach in finance is to estimate a cross-sectional logit or probit model for each period in the panel, and then to average the estimates over the periods. For example, Fama and French (2001) and DeAngelo et al. (2006) estimate logit regressions explaining which firms pay dividend, separately for each year in their sample, and use the time-series standard deviations of the annual coefficient estimates to derive standard errors for the average coefficients.

This approach is potentially attractive. As in the linear case, the Fama and Mac-Beth (1973) approach accommodates within-period correlations across all firms. Importantly, it does not allow for serial dependence, for example, attributable to firm-specific time-invariant heterogeneity. Standard errors based on Newey and West (1987) or similar corrections based on the serial correlation in the estimated coefficients do not help here either (see Petersen, 2009, for more discussion). An important condition for the Fama-MacBeth approach to deliver a consistent estimator in nonlinear models is that the estimation error in each period averages out when taking averages across periods.

6.1.6 Binary choice models with random effects

The pooled probit approach may be able to consistently estimate the probability that y_{it} is equal to one, as a function of a set of characteristics x_{it}, but it does not provide information on how the binary outcomes y_{it} evolve dynamically or how the probability that $y_{i2} = 1$ depends upon, for example, y_{i1}. Whereas the use of clustered standard errors allows for dependence across observations (within clusters), this dependence is not modelled explicitly, because the likelihood function does not specify the joint distribution of all outcomes. A random effects specification may remedy this.

Let us start considering the joint distribution of a set of binary outcomes for a given firm, that is, $y_{i1}, \ldots, y_{iT}$. In general, it is nontrivial to specify an attractive and flexible form of dependence across a sequence of binary outcomes. To see this, let us start from the latent variable specification

$$y_{it}^* = x_{it}'\beta + \varepsilon_{it},$$

with, as before, $y_{it} = 1$ if $y_{it}^* > 0$ and 0 otherwise. Assuming independence over i, the joint distribution of $y_{i1}, \ldots, y_{iT}$ is determined by the joint distribution of the set of disturbances $\varepsilon_{i1}, \ldots, \varepsilon_{iT}$. Because the logistic distribution has no flexible multivariate form, it is common to impose a joint normal distribution upon the disturbances. To determine the joint probability of a sequence $y_{i1}, \ldots, y_{iT}$, we need to integrate the joint density of $y_{i1}^*, \ldots, y_{iT}^*$ over the appropriate regions. Unfortunately, this is only feasible if either the number of time periods is very small, or if a specific structure is imposed upon the covariance matrix of $\varepsilon_{i1}, \ldots, \varepsilon_{iT}$.

To illustrate this, let us consider the case of $T = 3$, and we impose that

$$\begin{pmatrix} \varepsilon_{i1} \\ \varepsilon_{i2} \\ \varepsilon_{i3} \end{pmatrix} \sim NID \left(\begin{pmatrix} 0 \\ 0 \\ 0 \end{pmatrix}, \begin{pmatrix} 1 & \rho_{12} & \rho_{13} \\ \rho_{21} & 1 & \rho_{23} \\ \rho_{31} & \rho_{32} & 1 \end{pmatrix} \right),$$

independent of all explanatory variables, where $\rho_{ts} = \rho_{st}$ denotes the correlation coefficient between ε_{is} and ε_{it}. From this, the joint probability of observing a sequence, say, $y_{i1} = 1$, $y_{i2} = 0$, $y_{i3} = 1$ is given by

$$\int_0^\infty \int_{-\infty}^0 \int_0^\infty f(y_{i1}^*, y_{i2}^*, y_{i3}^*) dy_{i1}^* dy_{i2}^* dy_{i3}^*,$$

where $f(\cdot)$ denotes the joint density of the latent variables, conditional upon the explanatory variables. This can be written as

$$\int_{-x_{i1}'\beta}^\infty \int_{-\infty}^{-x_{i2}'\beta} \int_{-x_{i3}'\beta}^\infty f(\varepsilon_{i1}, \varepsilon_{i2}, \varepsilon_{i3}) d\varepsilon_{i1} d\varepsilon_{i2} d\varepsilon_{i3},$$

which tells us that the probability to observe a sequence of binary outcomes is given by the joint density of ε_{i1}, ε_{i2}, ε_{i3} integrated over the relevant segments along three dimensions. Unfortunately, this three-dimensional integral cannot be simplified or determined analytically. With $T = 3$ numerical integration is feasible, but with $T = 4$ or more, calculation of these joint probabilities, and thus estimation based on the full likelihood function, becomes unfeasible due to the "curse of dimensionality". Although it is possible to circumvent this problem using estimators based on simulation, see, for example, Keane (1993) or Liesenfeld and Richard (2010), this has not become very popular in finance.

Rather than ignoring any potential dependence (and work with a pooled probit approach), it is possible to impose some structure on the covariance matrix of the disturbances in the latent variable equation. An obvious choice to do so is to specify the typical error components structure,

$$\varepsilon_{it} = \alpha_i + u_{it}.$$

With this restriction, the probabilities of observing the outcomes y_{it} are independent conditional upon α_i. The joint probability of observing a sequence $y_{i1} = 1$, $y_{i2} = 0$, $y_{i3} = 1$ can then be written as

$$\int_{-\infty}^\infty \left[F(x_{i1}'\beta + \alpha_i)[1 - F(x_{i2}'\beta + \alpha_i)]F(x_{i3}'\beta + \alpha_i) \right] f(\alpha_i) d\alpha_i, \qquad (6.32)$$

where $f(\alpha_i)$ denotes the marginal distribution of α_i, and where $F(\cdot)$ is the cumulative distribution function of $-u_{it}$. The three terms involving $F(\cdot)$ denote the marginal probabilities of observing either $y_{it} = 0$ or $y_{it} = 1$, conditional upon the firm-specific time-invariant heterogeneity in α_i. The integral over the density of α_i will have to be determined numerically (for which efficient algorithms are available).

The error components assumption allows dependence between the different outcomes for the same firm, but only in a restricted way. All outcomes are driven by the same unobserved firm-specific heterogeneity, and conditional upon this element and the explanatory variables, different outcomes are assumed to be independent. In principle, arbitrary assumptions can be made about the parametric distributions of u_{it} and α_i (which determine the form of the functions F and f in (6.32)). A standard random effects probit model is obtained if it is assumed that $u_{it} \sim NID(0,1)$, that is, standard normal, and α_i also has a normal distribution (with mean 0 and variance σ_α^2). This is consistent with ε_{it} having a normal distribution with mean 0 and variance $1 + \sigma_\alpha^2$. Accordingly, the full loglikelihood function for the **random effects probit model** for arbitrary T is given by

$$\ln L(\beta, \sigma_\alpha^2) = \sum_{i=1}^{N} \ln \int_{-\infty}^{\infty} \left[\prod_{t=1}^{T} \Phi(x'_{it}\beta + \alpha_i)^{y_{it}} [1 - \Phi(x'_{it}\beta + \alpha_i)]^{(1-y_{it})} \right] f(\alpha_i) d\alpha_i, \qquad (6.33)$$

where Φ denotes the standard normal cumulative density function, and f denotes the normal density of α_i, given by

$$f(\alpha_i) = \frac{1}{\sqrt{2\pi\sigma_\alpha^2}} \exp\left\{ -\frac{1}{2} \frac{\alpha_i^2}{\sigma_\alpha^2} \right\}. \qquad (6.34)$$

Importantly, the distribution of α_i is assumed to be independent of any of the variables in x_{it}. As always in binary choice models, a normalisation constraint needs to be imposed upon the distribution of the unobservable error terms in the latent variable equation. In this case, the normalisation chosen is that the variance of u_{it} is equal to one, so that σ_α^2 becomes a free parameter to estimate. It is also quite common to impose that the variance of ε_{it} is 1. This is irrelevant for the implied probabilities, as well as the marginal effects, but it does affect the scaling of the β coefficients in the model. In Stata, the random effects probit model can be estimated with the command *xtprobit, re*.

To illustrate the role of the scaling issue, note that the random effects probit model implies that

$$Pr(y_{it} = 1) = Pr(-\varepsilon_{it} < x'_{it}\beta) = F\left(x'_{it}\beta / \sqrt{1 + \sigma_\alpha^2} \right),$$

which is different from the expression estimated with a pooled probit approach. Accordingly, depending upon the normalisation chosen, a random effects probit model will yield different coefficient estimates for β than a pooled probit model, owing to the difference in the scaling of the latent variable distribution.

Strictly speaking, a random effects logit model is not feasible. This is because there is no multivariate logistic distribution for $\varepsilon_{i1}, \ldots, \varepsilon_{iT}$ that allows an arbitrary correlation between the different time periods. Assuming that both α_i and u_{it} have a logistic distribution does not imply that ε_{it} also has a logistic distribution. An alternative, often referred to as a random effects logit model is to assume that u_{it} has a logistic distribution, whereas α_i has a normal distribution (with free variance). The loglikelihood function is similar to the one for the random effects probit, except that the functional form of F is different. It should be noted, though that these assumptions are inconsistent with a cross-sectional logit function, so that pooled estimation will not provide a consistent estimator under the same assumptions. This random effects logit model is estimated in Stata with the command *xtlogit, re*.

Similar to the fact that generalised least squares is more efficient that OLS (under assumptions), so will random effects maximum likelihood estimation of the probit model, when properly specified, be more efficient than a pooled probit approach. This is because the first exploits the dependence among the observations in estimation. In addition, the random effects probit model provides explicit insight in the persistence of the process determining the discrete outcomes y_{it}. The variance of σ_a^2, or rescaled to a correlation coefficient, $\rho = \sigma_a^2/(1 + \sigma_a^2)$, is an additional parameter of interest estimated in the random effects model. It tells us how important time-invariant unobserved heterogeneity is to describe the randomness in the binary outcomes.

Malmendier and Tate (2005) use a random effects probit model to explain whether a CEO exercises a five-year old option that reaches at least 67% in-the-money; Hertzberg et al. (2010) use it to model the probability of firm i entering default in one year. A logit model with random firm effects, in combination with standard errors clustered at the industry-year level, is employed in Maksimovic et al. (2013), who model the probabilities that a firm buys (or sells) a plant in the next period. Unfortunately, it is rarely the case that published papers present information about the magnitude of the random effects, for example, by presenting the estimated value of σ_a^2 or the implied correlation coefficient. An exception is Christiansen et al. (2007) who model the probability of stock market participation of individual investors.

Marginal effects
When determining the marginal effects, the firm-specific random component α_i should not be ignored. If you would set $\alpha_i = 0$ and then calculate the marginal effects, they would be over- or underestimated, because the firm-specific heterogeneity, unrelated to the explanatory variables, is ignored. To be more precise, if we set $\alpha_i = 0$ we effectively estimate the median marginal effect. The appropriate approach is to integrate α_i out, in which case we estimate the average marginal effect. Because the probabilities are nonlinear functions of x_{it} and α_i, the mean and median can be quite different (depending upon the variance of α_i); see Bland and Cook (2019) for more details and discussion.

For a continuous variable, the mean marginal effect, for a given firm i and period t, is given by

$$\frac{\partial Pr(y_{it} = 1 \mid x_{it})}{\partial x_{k,it}} = \int_{-\infty}^{\infty} F'(x_{it}'\beta + \alpha_i)\beta_k f(\alpha_i)d\alpha_i.$$

In the random effects probit case, with $F = \Phi$ the standard normal distribution function, this can be simplified to

$$\frac{\partial Pr(y_{it} = 1 \mid x_{it})}{\partial x_{k,it}} = \frac{\beta_k}{\sqrt{1 + \sigma_\alpha^2}} \phi\left(\frac{x_{it}'\beta}{\sqrt{1 + \sigma_\alpha^2}}\right). \tag{6.35}$$

This reduces to the standard expression if $\sigma_\alpha^2 = 0$. For a random effects logit specification, such simplification does not exist.

Correlated random effects

Even though the random effects binary choice models allow for unobserved heterogeneity α_i in the latent variable equation, an important assumption is that this heterogeneity does not depend upon the explanatory variables in x_{it}. This is similar to the linear random effects model. To allow α_i to depend upon x_{it}, two routes can be chosen. One is to explicitly model the dependence and extend the model to incorporate this. For example, if we assume that

$$\alpha_i = \beta_0 + \bar{x}_i'\gamma + v_i,$$

we can include $\bar{x}_i$ (and an overal intercept term) in the probit equation, and include v_i as a new unobserved component in the disturbances, independent of the explanatory variables. This approach is chosen by Chamberlain (1980). In empirical work it is not used very commonly. One reason is that, in financial data sets, the panel is typically unbalanced so that the number of observations that can be used to calculate the average $\bar{x}_i$ varies across firms. When determining marginal effects, it is appropriate to keep the part relating to $\bar{x}_i$ fixed, because this is only meant to control for the endogeneity of x_{it} that is attributable to α_i. That is, when we interpret the model, a change in x_{it} is assumed to not affect α_i. Wooldridge (2010, Section 15.8) provides more details and conditions under which quantities of interest, such as average marginal effects, can be identified. Extensions to unbalanced panels are discussed in Wooldridge (2019).

Alternatively, in some special cases it is possible to treat α_i as fixed firm-specific parameters and work with a fixed effects binary choice model. We discuss this in the next subsection.

6.1.7 Binary choice models with fixed effects

When the terms α_i are treated as fixed unknown parameters, there is no need to impose any distributional assumption upon them. More importantly, it allows α_i to vary over the cross-section in a way related to the observables in x_{it}. To introduce the binary choice model in this case, consider the latent variable equation

$$y_{it}^* = \alpha_i + x_{it}'\beta + u_{it},$$

where we have moved α_i to the front to stress that it is a firm-specific intercept term. An overall intercept is omitted from x_{it}. Assuming that the idiosyncratic error term u_{it} has a symmetric distribution with distribution function F, IID across both firms and time, independent of the explanatory variables in x_{it}, the loglikelihood function is given by

$$\ln L(\beta, \alpha_1, \ldots, \alpha_N) = \sum_i \sum_t y_{it} \ln F(\alpha_i + x_{it}'\beta)$$
$$+ \sum_i \sum_t \ln[1 - F(\alpha_i + x_{it}'\beta)]. \tag{6.36}$$

Unfortunately, maximising this function with respect to β and α_i $(i = 1, \ldots, N)$, does not result in a consistent estimator for either β or α_i for fixed T and $N \to \infty$. This is caused by the fact that the number of parameters we are estimating increases with the sample size, a problem known as the **incidental parameters problem** (Lancaster, 2000). With every new firm, there is a new intercept to estimate, and with fixed T we only have a limited number of observations to estimate each of these intercept terms. Because of the nonlinear nature of the model, the inconsistency carries over to the estimator for β. Greene (2004b) provides a Monte Carlo study examining the small sample properties of fixed effects maximum likelihood estimators in a variety of nonlinear models and shows that the bias in estimating β is often quite substantial. In addition to the bias in estimating the parameters of interest, the numerical optimisation of the loglikelihood function above may be challenging if the number of firms, and thus the number of parameters, is large (e. g., several thousands).

In the linear model with fixed effects discussed in Chapter 2, it is also impossible to consistently estimate α_i for fixed T. However, there the problem does not carry over to the estimation of β. This can be understood by noting that the within transformation eliminates α_i from the model, but leaves enough variation in the data to estimate the slope coefficients (at least for the time-varying variables). In nonlinear models, such as binary choice models, this trick does not work.

A feasible solution, at least in some cases, is to work with a **conditional maximum likelihood** approach (Chamberlain, 1980). Instead of working with the usual likelihood function, this requires us to specify the conditional likelihood of observing $y_{i1}, \ldots, y_{iT}$, conditional upon a "sufficient statistic" t_i. The trick is that, once we condition upon t_i, in some specific cases the incidental parameters α_i drop out. As a result, we can maximise the conditional likelihood function with respect to β only, and this provides a consistent estimator. For the binary choice case, the question whether or not such a sufficient statistic t_i exists, depends upon the function we choose for F. This allows us to estimate a fixed effects logit model, but not a fixed effects probit model.

The **fixed effects logit model** is estimated using $t_i = \bar{y}_i$ as a sufficient statistic. To derive the conditional likelihood function, one needs to derive the probability of a sequence $y_{i1}, \ldots, y_{iT}$ (as a function of α_i and $x_{it}'\beta$), conditional upon the average $\bar{y}_i$. In general, this is cumbersome to do (although reasonably straightforward). Let us consider the simplest case with $T = 2$. First, note that conditional upon $\bar{y}_i = 0$, the only possible outcomes are $y_{i1} = 0$ and $y_{i2} = 0$, so that these observations do not help in estimating β. Similarly, conditional upon $\bar{y}_i = 1$, the only possible outcomes are $y_{i1} = 1$ and $y_{i2} = 1$. Again, these observations do not contribute anything to the conditional likelihood function. This implies that, similar to the linear fixed effects model, time-variation is essential to identify the role of explanatory variables. Another way to see this is to note that, if a firm does not change status over the sample period, we can estimate α_i as being plus or minus infinity, leaving no role for $x'_{it}\beta$. Identification in the fixed effects logit model rests upon firms that change status over time within the sample period. This requirement may substantially reduce the effective sample size in applications.

Given that the only relevant observations are those that change over time, we focus on $\bar{y}_i = 1/2$ and $T = 2$. Conditional upon $\bar{y}_i = 1/2$, the only possible sequences of outcomes are $(0, 1)$ and $(1, 0)$. The conditional probability of observing a sequence $(0, 1)$ is given by

$$Pr(y_{i1} = 0, y_{i2} = 1 \mid \bar{y}_i = 1/2) = \frac{Pr(y_{i1} = 0, y_{i2} = 1)}{Pr(y_{i1} = 0, y_{i2} = 1) + Pr(y_{i1} = 1, y_{i2} = 0)}.$$

The bivariate probabilities in the expression are given by the standard logit expressions, noting that (conditional on the fixed effects α_i) the two outcomes are independent. That is,

$$Pr(y_{i1} = 0, y_{i2} = 1) = Pr(y_{i1} = 0)Pr(y_{i2} = 1)$$

with

$$Pr(y_{i2} = 0) = \frac{1}{1 + \exp(\alpha_i + x'_{i1}\beta)}$$

and

$$Pr(y_{i2} = 1) = \frac{\exp(\alpha_i + x'_{i2}\beta)}{1 + \exp(\alpha_i + x'_{i2}\beta)}.$$

Combining all this, and after some rewriting, it follows that

$$Pr(y_{i1} = 0, y_{i2} = 1 \mid \bar{y}_i = 1/2) = \frac{\exp((x_{i2} - x_{i1})'\beta)}{1 + \exp((x_{i2} - x_{i1})'\beta)}. \tag{6.37}$$

The important finding here is that the resulting expression does not depend upon α_i anymore, as they cancel out in the derivations. Unfortunately, this result is specific to the logit model; if we replace the distributional assumption by a normal one (i. e., $F = \Phi$), α_i does not cancel out and $\bar{y}_i$ cannot play the role of a sufficient statistic.

According to the above results, we can estimate a fixed effects logit model using the conditional maximum likelihood approach. For $T = 2$ this reduces to modelling the event of observing $(0, 1)$ versus that of observing $(1, 0)$ and the explanatory variables correspond to the change in x_{it} from period 1 to 2. In this sense, conditioning upon $\bar{y}_i$ has the same effect as first-differencing or within transforming the data in a linear model. Clearly, time-invariant variables will be dropped from the model (as their role cannot be separated from α_i). For the case with larger T, it is quite cumbersome to derive all relevant conditional probabilities, but it in principe it is a straightforward extension of the above case (see Chamberlain, 1980; Maddala, 1987). Interestingly, this way of estimating a fixed effects logit model is not equivalent to maximising the log-likelihood function for the logit model with N intercepts in (6.36). The latter approach remains inconsistent (see Hsiao, 2014, Section 7.3.1, for an example with $T = 2$, where plim $\hat{\beta} = 2\beta$).

To determine the asymptotic covariance matrix of the conditional maximum likelihood estimator, we can simply use the general theory for estimation by maximum likelihood, while replacing the likelihood contributions with conditional likelihood contributions in all expressions. Put differently, we can ignore the fact that we work with a *conditional* likelihood function. The inclusion of fixed time effects is not problematic as long as the cross-section is sufficiently large. Accordingly, the inclusion of time dummies does not cause any problems and captures the role of aggregate market-wide changes in the average probability of observing $y_{it} = 1$. The fixed effects logit model, estimated by conditional maximum likelihood, is available in Stata with the *xtlogit, fe* command. Clearly, *xtprobit, fe* is not supported.

An example of the fixed effects logit model in finance is given in Hsu (2004), who estimates the probability that an offer from a venture capitalist is accepted by a start-up. In his case, the panel nature is obtained by considering multiple offers for the same start-ups (so that the offer is the unit of analysis). His model is estimated using the conditional maximum likelihood approach including start-up fixed effects. This way, it is possible to control for unobservable differences in start-ups (most importantly their quality) that may also correlate with offer characteristics. Another example is Ma (2019), who models the probability of simultaneous issuance and repurchases by firms (e. g., issuing additional debt, while also repurchasing equity) as a function of variables reflecting the costs of debt and equity. Controlling for firm fixed effects allows the author to focus on how a given firm's action changes over time in light of the relative pricing of its debt and equity.

An extension to three-dimensional data is provided in Granja et al. (2017), who model the probability that a potential acquirer j acquires a failed bank i in quarter t, as a function of the financial and asset characteristics of the potential acquirer (adding up to more than 3 million observations). They estimate alternative logit models with quarter fixed effects, with failed bank fixed effects, potential acquirer fixed effects or potential acquirer-quarter fixed effects. Several of these specifications are estimated using the conditional maximum likelihood approach discussed above (with substantial reductions in the number of observations). In all cases, standard errors are clustered at the failed bank's state headquarters. This implies that the number of clusters is relatively small (in relation to the sample size), and it allows for many potential cross-correlations. The small-sample performance of such clustered standard errors may be suboptimal (see the discussion in Section 2.5 and Cameron and Miller, 2015).

A drawback of the fixed effects logit model is that, in the absence of knowledge about α_i, it does not specify the full distribution of the outcomes. Accordingly, interpretation of the resulting estimates in terms of marginal effects is not possible. The fixed effects model simply does not allow calculation of probabilities for $y_{it} = 1$ in the absence of knowledge of α_i. Unfortunately, the magnitude of the marginal effects depends upon α_i. This is intuitive: a firm with a very large value for α_i will have probabilities of observing $y_{it} = 1$ very close to one, so that the marginal effect of a change in one of the explanatory variables can only be very small. It is possible, however, to calculate marginal effects for the probability of a change from, for example, $y_{i1} = 0$ to $y_{i2} = 1$, similar to the conditional probabilities derived above. Another approach is to interpret the model in terms of the log odds ratio, which is not affected by the incidental parameters. Many papers also report estimates for a linear probability model with fixed effects, in companion with a fixed effects logit, to ease the interpretation in terms of marginal effects; see, for example, Marin and Olivier (2008), who predict the probability of a crash for stock i in period t, as a function of measures of insider trading.

6.1.8 Goodness-of-fit

A goodness-of-fit measure is a summary statistic indicating the accuracy with which a model approximates the observed data, like the R^2 measure in the linear regression model. When the dependent variable is qualitative, there is no single measure for the goodness-of-fit and a variety of measures exists; see Cameron and Trivedi (2005, Section 8.7) for a general discussion of alternative goodness-of-fit measures in nonlinear models. In a linear model, the R^2 has multiple interpretations. First, it is the squared correlation coefficient between fitted values and observed values, second, it is the explained variance in the dependent variable as a proportion of the total variance, and third, it measures the increase in fit (in terms of sums of squares) of the model relative to a model without any explanatory variables.

The most popular approach in limited dependent variable models is based on the latter idea and compares the estimated model with a simpler version that only includes an intercept term. To formalise this, let $\ln L_1$ denote the maximum loglikelihood value of the model of interest and let $\ln L_0$ denote the maximum value of the loglikelihood function when all parameters, except the intercept, are set to zero. The larger the difference between the two loglikelihood values, the more the extended model adds to the very restrictive model. The most popular measure based on this comparison is proposed by McFadden (1974) and is given by

$$\text{pseudo-}R^2 = 1 - \frac{\ln L_1}{\ln L_0}. \tag{6.38}$$

Because the loglikelihood is the sum of log probabilities, it follows that $\ln L_0 \leq \ln L_1 < 0$, so that the pseudo-R^2 takes on values in the $[0, 1]$ interval only. The upper bound of 1 is only attained if all estimated probabilities in the loglikelihood function are equal to 1, which is unrealistic. In practice, goodness-of-fit measures in binary choice models are usually well below unity.

The above goodness-of-fit measure can be reported in case the model is estimated using a pooled maximum likelihood approach, although it completely ignores potential serial correlation, or – more generally – within-cluster correlation. It can also be reported as the average goodness-of-fit measure over all periods in a Fama-MacBeth version of the estimator. In either case, interpretation is relatively loose and, at best, the goodness-of-fit is used to compare alternative specifications of the model (based on the same estimation method), not as an absolute measure of the quality of the model. In principle, the above measure can also be used to calculate a pseudo-R^2 for a random effects probit model, using the appropriate loglikelihood function. Note that a perfect fit in a random effects model also needs the random effects to be zero, so an R^2 of one becomes even more unrealistic. In practice, goodness-of-fit measures for panel binary choice models are rarely reported.

Another perspective on goodness-of-fit is provided by comparing observed outcomes, y_{it}, with predicted outcomes, $\hat{y}_{it}$, say. One can generate predictions by translating the estimated probabilities implied by the model into a 0-1 outcome. For example, in the pooled case, the probability of observing $y_{it} = 1$ is estimated as $F(x'_{it}\hat{\beta})$, with the appropriate choice for F. A natural prediction is then $\hat{y}_{it} = 1$ if $F(x'_{it}\hat{\beta}) > 0.5$ or $x'_{it}\hat{\beta} > 0$, and 0 otherwise. Based on a cross-tabulation of actual and predicted outcomes, several goodness-of-fit measures can be developed. For example, Henricksson and Merton (1981) focus on the proportions of correctly predicted 0's and correctly predicted 1's and show that their sum should exceed 1 for a good model. This approach can also be applied to the panel case, provided we can determine univariate probabilities. For the random effects models, this requires integrating out the random effects. Whereas this does not directly lead to a measure in the interval $[0, 1]$, it provides an easy way to compare across models. Lahiri and Yang (2013) provide a survey on forecasting binary outcomes and how to evaluate them, and also discuss extensions to panel data.

6.1.9 Binary choice models and instrumental variables

The standard binary choice model assumes that the explanatory variables are exogenous, and one estimates the conditional probability that $y_{it} = 1$ given x_{it}. These probabilities do not reflect causal effects if an explanatory variable is endogenous. For example, Edmans et al. (2012) are interested in estimating effect of a firm's discount on the likelihood of a takeover bid. Discount is the discount at which a firm trades relative to its maximum potential value absent managerial inefficiency and mispricing, for example, the difference between the net asset value (NAV) of a closed-end fund and its market price. The magnitude of the discount is likely to depend upon the extent to which the market anticipates the probability of takeover, and is therefore endogenous. A low discount is more likely when the market anticipates a takeover. It is possible to address this concern using an instrumental variable approach, although it requires a few more assumptions than in the linear case.

To see how this works, consider the latent variable specification,

$$y_{1,it}^* = x_{it}'\beta_1 + \beta_2 y_{2,it} + \varepsilon_{it}, \tag{6.39}$$

where $y_{2,it}$ is the endogenous explanatory variable, and we observe $y_{1,it} = 1$ if $y_{1,it}^* > 0$ and 0 otherwise. We complement this with a reduced form equation for $y_{2,it}$ as

$$y_{2,it} = x_{it}'\gamma_1 + z_{it}'\gamma_2 + \eta_{it}, \tag{6.40}$$

where z_{it} is a vector of one or more instruments. The two error terms, ε_{it} and η_{it}, are assumed to be jointly normally distributed with zero mean, independent of x_{it} and z_{it}, and covariance matrix

$$\Sigma = \begin{pmatrix} 1 & \sigma_{\varepsilon\eta} \\ \sigma_{\varepsilon\eta} & \sigma_\eta^2 \end{pmatrix},$$

where the variance of ε_{it} is normalised to 1, as is usual for a probit model. The variable $y_{2,it}$ is endogenous in equation (6.39) if the covariance between the two error terms, $\sigma_{\varepsilon\eta}$, is nonzero. If $\sigma_{\varepsilon\eta} = 0$, (6.39) can be estimated with standard probit methods.

The model in equations (6.39)–(6.40) can be estimated by pooled maximum likelihood, where – as usual – the panel nature is ignored except in the calculation of the standard errors. The expression of the pooled loglikelihood function is reasonably straightforward. This is employed in Edmans et al. (2012), using mutual fund investor flows as an instrument in z_{it}, assuming this is sufficiently exogenous. Despite the fact that their standard errors are adjusted for heteroskedasticity and correlation clustered at the firm level, heteroskedasticity will typically lead to an inconsistent estimator here. The validity of the instrument in Edmans et al. (2012) (and many related studies) is recently challenged (e. g., Wardlaw, 2020), because it would not properly identify liquidity needs of mutual fund investors that are truly exogenous to firm fundamentals.

As an alternative to the bivariate maximum likelihood approach, the model can be estimated with a two-step estimator, also known as the control function approach (Rivers and Vuong, 1988). In this approach, equation (6.40) is estimated by pooled OLS and the residuals of this equation are added to the equation of interest in (6.39).

This is appropriate, because the conditional distribution of ε_{it}, given $y_{2,it}$ (and x_{it} and z_{it}) is also normal, with a nonzero mean given by

$$E(\varepsilon_{it} \mid y_{2,it}, x_{it}, z_{it}) = \frac{\sigma_{\varepsilon\eta}}{\sigma_\eta^2} \eta_{it}.$$

This allows us to rewrite (6.39) as

$$y_{1,it}^* = x_{it}'\beta_1 + \beta_2 y_{2,it} + \beta_3 \eta_{it} + \varepsilon_{it}^*, \qquad (6.41)$$

where $\beta_3 = \sigma_{\varepsilon\eta}/\sigma_\eta^2$, and ε_{it}^* is a mean zero normal error term with variance

$$1 - \rho_{\varepsilon\eta}^2,$$

where $\rho_{\varepsilon\eta} = \sigma_{\varepsilon\eta}/\sigma_\eta$, the correlation coefficient between ε_{it} and η_{it}. These expressions follow from those of a conditional normal distribution. Estimation can be done by applying standard probit ML to (6.41), replacing the unobserved error term η_{it} by the residual $\hat{\eta}_{it}$. Taking into account the different normalisation constraints, this provides consistent estimators for the parameters in (6.39), while controlling for the endogeneity of $y_{2,it}$. A test for $\beta_3 = 0$ is a test for endogeneity. Identification requires that $y_2 \neq 0$, so that the instruments are relevant. Because of the normality assumption, this approach only makes sense if the endogenous explanatory variable $y_{2,it}$ is continuous. An application of this can be found in Bradley et al. (2010), where $y_{1,it}$ indicates an attempt to open-end a closed-end fund, $y_{2,it}$ is the discount, and z_{it} includes three different instruments.

The maximum likelihood estimator is typically more efficient in large samples than the two-step approach, but computationally more demanding. For the two-step approach, the standard errors in the second step need to be adjusted to take into account the fact that η_{it} is estimated rather than observed. Both the maximum likelihood estimator and the two-step estimator are available in Stata using *ivprobit*. Extensions of the two-step approach to panel data, with random effects in both equations, are presented in Vella and Verbeek (1999b).

In case the endogenous explanatory variable $y_{2,it}$ is binary (e. g., Sun and Teo, 2019), the two-step approach typically does not lead to consistent estimators, even if the first-step model is replaced by probit, and the residual by a generalised residual. In these cases, a bivariate probit model would make more sense; see Wooldridge (2010, Section 17.7.3).

6.2 Multiple outcomes

As the name indicates, binary response models are developed to explain a binary outcome only. Several extensions are available to explain multiple different outcomes. For example, we may be interested in explaining the credit rating of a bond (Blume et al., 1998), or the likelihood of a firm using different types of currency derivatives (or non at all) (Gézky et al., 1997). An important distinction exists between ordered response models and unordered models. An ordered response model is generally more parsimonious but is only appropriate if there exists a logical ordering of the alternatives. The reason is that it assumes there is one underlying latent variable that drives the choice between the alternatives. Consequently, empirical results will be sensitive to the ordering of the alternatives. Unordered models are insensitive to the way in which the alternatives are numbered. In either case, the ambition is to model the probabilities of each of the different outcomes in a relatively parsimonious way, as well as logically consistent. For example, all probabilities should be in the $[0, 1]$ interval and add up to one across all alternatives.

6.2.1 Ordered probit and ordered logit

Let us consider a situation with M different outcomes, numbered from 1 to M. For example, Blume et al. (1998) explain the bond rating of a panel of firms where the dependent variable is assigned the value of 4 if bond i at time t has a rating by S&P of AAA, 3 if AA, 2 if A, and 1 if BBB. Similarly, Ashbaugh-Skaife et al. (2006) explain a firm's credit rating in seven categories. Because there is a natural ordering in these outcomes, an ordered response model can be used. The model is based on the assumption of a single underlying latent variable, with a mapping from the latent variable y_{it}^* to the observable outcomes y_{it}. In particular, it is as assumed that

$$y_{it}^* = x_{it}'\beta + \varepsilon_{it} \tag{6.42}$$
$$y_{it} = j \text{ if } y_{j-1} < y_{it}^* \le y_j,$$

for unknown y_j, with $y_0 = -\infty$, $y_1 = 0$ and $y_M = \infty$. Consequently, the probability that outcome j is observed is the probability that the latent variable y_{it}^* is between the two boundaries y_{j-1} and y_j. Assuming that ε_{it} is IID standard normally distributed, independent of the explanatory variables in x_{it}, leads to the ordered probit model, imposing a logistic distribution produces the ordered logit model. When there are only two alternatives ($M = 2$), we obtain the binary choice model. One of the earliest implementations in finance of the ordered probit model is provided in Hausman et al. (1992), who use it to model the conditional distribution of trade-to-trade price changes.

The pooled loglikelihood function is determined by the probabilities of observing each of the outcomes $1, 2, \ldots, M$. These probabilities are also important ingredients for the interpretation of the model and its coefficients. If, as an example, we focus on the model with four alternatives, there are two unknown boundaries y_1 and y_2 that need to be estimated, along with β. The relevant probabilities are

$$Pr(y_{it} = 1 \mid x_{it}) = Pr(y_{it}^* \le 0 \mid x_{it}) = F(-x_{it}'\beta)$$

$$Pr(y_{it} = 2 \mid x_{it}) = Pr(0 < y_{it}^* \leq \gamma_1 \mid x_{it}) = F(\gamma_1 - x_{it}'\beta) - F(-x_{it}'\beta)$$
$$Pr(y_{it} = 3 \mid x_{it}) = Pr(\gamma_1 < y_{it}^* \leq \gamma_2 \mid x_{it}) = F(\gamma_2 - x_{it}'\beta) - F(\gamma_1 - x_{it}'\beta)$$
$$Pr(y_{it} = 4 \mid x_{it}) = Pr(y_{it}^* > \gamma_2 \mid x_{it}) = 1 - F(\gamma_2 - x_{it}'\beta),$$

where F is the appropriate distribution function. The interpretation of the coefficients in β is readily done in the latent variable framework. With a positive coefficient, we can interpret the corresponding explanatory variable as increasing the expected latent outcome, other things equal. The precise impact on the different probabilities is a bit more subtle. If $\beta_k > 0$, an increase in $x_{k,it}$ increases the probability of $j = 4$, and decreases the probability of $j = 1$. However, the effect for the intermediate probabilities (for $j = 2$ and $j = 3$) may be either positive or negative. If the focus is on $Pr(y_{it} \leq m \mid x_{it})$ for a given m, the signs of the marginal effects are unambiguously determined by those of β. (This is because these are effectively binary probit or logit expressions.) In general, marginal effects can be estimated in a straightforward way following the logic discussed for binary models.

For the case with $M = 4$ alternatives, Figure 6.2 shows the (normal) distribution of the latent variable y_{it}^*, with a mean of $x_{it}'\beta$ and a variance of 1. A shift in the single index $x_{it}'\beta$ moves the curve to the left or the right, while the boundaries 0, γ_1 and γ_2 stay fixed. The probability mass within two boundaries determines the probability of observing a given outcome y_{it}. With the curve shifting horizontally, the probabilities of the two intermediate outcomes may either increase or decrease, depending upon its initial position.

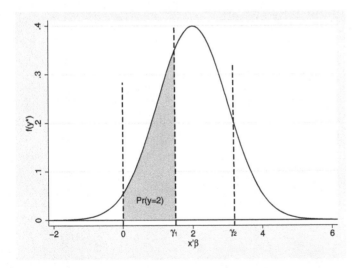

Figure 6.2: The ordered probit model.

Much of the discussion for the standard probit and logit models extends to the current case. The estimation by a pooled maximum likelihood approach is reasonably straightforward, where the probabilities listed above enter the loglikelihood function. The unknown boundaries γ_1 and γ_2 are estimated simultaneously with β. It is possible to include fixed time effects (provided T is small relative to N) and to use standard errors clusters over firms and/or time. Blume et al. (1998) employ standard errors based on the Newey-West approach to accommodate serial correlation in the unobservables in ε_{it}. The ordered probit model can be estimated in Stata with the *oprobit* command, albeit that it imposes a different normalisation constraint. Rather than setting the boundary γ_1 to zero, it excludes the intercept term from x_{it}. This is entirely equivalent, and the model probabilities (and estimated β coefficients) are not affected.

As in the binary case, heteroskedasticity of ε_{it} violates the functional forms of the probabilities and therefore cannot be addressed using clustered standard errors. Blume et al. (1998) extend the model above by allowing the variance of ε_{it} to depend upon an explanatory variable as[7]

$$\sigma_{it}^2 = V(\varepsilon_{it}) = \left[\exp(z_{it}'\alpha)\right]^2,$$

similar to the heteroskedastic probit model discussed in Subsection 6.1.3. Its incorporation requires a straightforward adjustment of the model probabilities and the parameters in α can be estimated jointly with the other parameters.[8] For example, Goergen et al. (2005) use an ordered probit model to explain whether firms decide to cut, maintain, or increase their dividends, allowing for heteroskedasticity. However, the marginal effects will be affected, particularly if the variables in z_{it} are functions of those in x_{it}. To illustrate this, note that the probability of observing $y_{it} = 1$, conditional upon x_{it} and z_{it}, is given by

$$Pr(y_{it} = 1 \mid x_{it}, z_{it}) = Pr(y_{it}^* \leq 0 \mid x_{it}, z_{it}) = F\left(-\frac{x_{it}'\beta}{\exp(z_{it}'\alpha)}\right).$$

When $z_{it} = x_{it}$, or if some elements overlap, it is clear that a change in one of the explanatory variables affects the probability through $x_{it}'\beta$ and $z_{it}'\alpha$. This makes the marginal effects different from the standard expressions. Further, it does not make sense to present estimates for β without reporting those for α. This is because the β vector cannot be interpreted in isolation. The heteroskedastic ordered probit model can be estimated by pooled maximum likelihood, available in the Stata command *het-oprobit*.

---

7 To allow this, the conditioning set of the model must include z_{it}.

8 As a normalisation constraint, Blume et al. (1998) set the intercept term in the latent variable equation (in one period) to zero; this allows them to estimate α without restrictions. If not, a normalisation constraint has to be imposed upon α.

It is also possible to specify a random effects ordered probit model. This allows the presence of serial correlation in ε_{it} driven by a time-invariant unit specific component, which is exploited in estimation. For example, Afonso et al. (2009) use a random effects ordered probit model to estimate the determinants of sovereign credit ratings, in 17 different levels. It is possible to combine the random effects probit approach with cluster-robust standard errors, provided the panel variable is nested within the cluster variable. This is available in the Stata command *xtoprobit*.

6.2.2 Multinomial models

In several cases, there is no natural ordering in the alternatives, and it is not realistic to assume that there is a monotonic relationship between one underlying latent variable and the observed outcomes. Suppose, as before, that there are M alternatives, denoted $j = 1, 2, \ldots, M$. Different from the models above, the order and numbering of the alternatives is arbitrary. For example, to test the pecking order theory, Helwege and Liang (1996) try to explain whether a firm issues public bonds, private debt or public equity, given that the firm has chosen to obtain external financing.

In the absence of a natural ordering, it is not possible to define the probabilities of each of the outcomes, conditional upon a set of explanatory variables, as a function of a single latent variable. Instead, we start with defining a set of M latent variables, and assume that

$$y_{j,it}^* = x_{j,it}'\beta + \varepsilon_{j,it}, \quad j = 1, 2, \ldots, M,$$

where $x_{j,it}$ is a set of characteristics that depend upon the alternative. We can loosely interpret $y_{j,it}^*$ as the utility of firm i in period t of choosing alternative j. The terms $\varepsilon_{j,it}$ contain factors, unobservable to the econometrician, affecting these utility levels, and are assumed to be random. Firms are assumed to choose the alternative providing the highest utility level. Under appropriate distributional assumptions about the unobservables, this structure implies that

$$Pr(y_{it} = j) = \frac{\exp(x_{j,it}'\beta)}{\sum_{h=1}^{M} \exp(x_{h,it}'\beta)}, \tag{6.43}$$

where, for notational convenience, the explanatory variables are omitted from the conditioning set. It is easily seen that these M probabilities add up to one by construction. Moreover, all probabilities are necessarily bounded between 0 and 1. Because utility levels are not observed, it is common to normalise the deterministic part for one of the alternatives to zero, for example, by setting $x_{1,it}'\beta = 0$. Equivalently, one can rewrite (6.43) by dividing both numerator and denominator by $\exp(x_{1,it}'\beta)$. This effectively means that the alternative-specific characteristics are measured relative to those of the first alternative ($j = 1$).

The above model is known as the **conditional logit model**, attributable to McFadden (1974). A positive coefficient means that the utility of an alternative improves if the corresponding characteristic increases, other things equal. It is possible to derive the marginal effects, quite similar to a standard binary logit model. These marginal effects are specific to each alternative, so they assume that the characteristics of the other alternatives are fixed.

A closely related model is the **multinomial logit model**. The difference is that in this model the explanatory variables do not vary across alternatives, but only over firms and periods. Instead, the coefficients are alternative-specific. We can write the relevant probabilities as

$$Pr(y_{it} = j \mid x_{it}) = \frac{\exp(x_{it}'\beta_j)}{1 + \sum_{h=2}^{M} \exp(x_{it}'\beta_h)}, \quad j = 2, \ldots, M, \tag{6.44}$$

where we have chosen alternative 1 as the base case (i. e., we have imposed that $\beta_1 = 0$). The model coefficients are therefore relative to the omitted outcome (which has no coefficients to report). In the multinomial logit model we thus estimate a set of slope coefficients and an intercept for each of the $M - 1$ alternatives. It is possible to combine firm-specific and alternative-specific variables in the model, leading to a mixed logit model. All these models can be estimated in Stata, using pooled maximum likelihood, with the *cmclogit* command.

Despite the attractiveness of the analytical expressions given in (6.43) and (6.44), these models have one big drawback, which is most easily seen from the odds ratio between two alternatives. For example, the conditional logit model implies

$$\frac{Pr(y_{it} = 2)}{Pr(y_{it} = 1)} = \exp(x_{2,it}'\beta),$$

irrespective of the number of other alternatives or their nature. This means that the relative odds of alternative 2 versus alternative 1 do not depend upon any of the other alternatives. This is particularly problematic if two alternatives are similar in nature. McFadden (1974) calls this the assumption of **independence of irrelevant alternatives** (IIA), with an illustrative example of choosing a mode of transportation, and two of the alternatives being "blue bus" and "red bus" (rather than "bus"). The crucial reason for this restriction is that, in the random utility framework, the different $\varepsilon_{j,it}$s are assumed to be independent across alternatives. Hausman and McFadden (1984) propose a test for the IIA restriction based on the result that the model parameters can be estimated consistently by applying a multinomial logit model to any subset of alternatives. The test compares the estimates from the model with all alternatives to estimates using a subset of alternatives. This way, the IIA property can also be exploited and become an advantage, in the sense that part of the model can be estimated without specifying (and observing) detailed alternatives (see Ljungqvist and Wilhelm, 2005, for an example explaining the choice of the SEO lead manager).

As an alternative, it is possible to impose a multivariate normal distribution upon the $\varepsilon_{j,it}$s, leading to a multinomial probit model (or conditional probit model), see Hausman and Wise (1978). This model is not very popular among empirical scholars, partly because its estimation involves a difficult maximum likelihood optimisation problem that sometimes fails to converge, even with cross-sectional data.

With panel data, the conditional logit model and the multinomial logit model can be estimated by a pooled maximum likelihood approach, where the probabilities of the observed outcomes enter the loglikelihood function. As with other models, it is possible to allow for some dependence across observations by clustering the standard errors. For example, Puri and Zarutskie (2012) track firms from their year of entry and model the probability of an IPO, acquisition or shut down, relative to the probability of no exit, to investigate the role of financing by venture capitalists, and estimate a multinomial logit model with standard errors clustered at the firm-level. Controlling for heteroskedasticity does not appear to make much sense here. If the unobservables in the latent variable equations are heteroskedastic, this means that the scaling of the latent variables is different across observations (or across alternatives), and the model probabilities no longer correspond to the attractive expressions given above.

To some extent, it is also possible to add random effects to the model. In the multinomial case, this would involve the inclusion of a firm-specific time-invariant component for each of the alternatives, except the base one, and impose distributional assumptions upon them, for example, normality. The probabilities are first determined conditional upon the random effects, which are subsequently integrated out. This is similar to the random effects binary logit model. Because the integration over the random effects has to be done numerically, estimation may take a bit more time and the number of alternatives should be limited. Implementation in Stata would require the *gsem* command. It is also possible to estimate a fixed effects multinomial logit model, using a variant of the conditional maximum likelihood approach discussed for the binary case (Chamberlain, 1980). Neither of these two approaches appears very common in financial applications.

6.3 Tobit models

6.3.1 Introduction to censoring

Occasionally, we wish to explain variables that are a mixture of a discrete outcome and a wide range of continuous outcomes. For example, y_{it} may denote the amount of share repurchases of a firm (e. g., Dittmar, 2000), the fraction of a household's wealth invested in risky assets (e. g., Angerer and Lam, 2009), or the proportion of foreign sales that a firm hedges against currency risk (e. g., Huang et al., 2019). In each of these cases, the variable of interest is likely to have a substantial proportion of observations equal to zero. An appropriate model for such variable should explicitly take into account the probability mass at zero.

It is useful to think of the outcomes y_{it} as potentially the result of two different decisions. First, the participation decision, which describes whether we observe a zero or not. Second, the outcome decision resulting in a wide range of non-zero values for y_{it}. These two decisions may be captured by the same process, for example, if the optimal or desired outcome for a firm would be negative, the actual outcome being censored at zero. The two decisions should be modelled separately (but not independently) if the decision to participate is affected by other factors than the (potential) outcomes. There is a variety of tobit or censored regression models that can be used in these cases.

A first approach is to use a censored regression model, typically referred to as a tobit model (Tobin, 1958). It consists of a latent variable equation and an observation rule that tells us when the latent variable is observed, and when a discrete outcome is observed. The standard model, in panel notation, is given by

$$y_{it}^* = x_{it}'\beta + \varepsilon_{it},\tag{6.45}$$

where we observe

$$y_{it} = y_{it}^* \quad \text{if } y_{it}^* > 0,$$
$$y_{it} = 0 \quad \text{otherwise.}$$

The usual assumption, consistent with the cross-sectional case, is that ε_{it} is independently and identically normally distributed with mean zero and variance σ_ε^2, independent of the explanatory variables in x_{it}. Note that this model is similar to a probit model, except that the latent variable is partially observed (as a result of which no normalisation constraint is required). Figure 6.3 depicts the regression line corresponding to the latent variable equation (in the bivariate case), where all values for y_{it}^* below 0 are set to zero. Clearly, fitting a straight line to all observations y_{it} and x_{it}, as done by OLS ignoring the censoring, results in a biased estimator for the intercept and slope of the model. The model in (6.45) is a censored regression model: it is a linear regression model where the dependent variable is censored at zero. That is, negative values are mapped to zeros. Often, we can interpret $y_{it} = 0$ as a corner solution.

A tobit model thus describes two elements of the distribution of y_{it}. First, it gives the probability of observing a zero outcome, similar to that of a binary choice model. In this case

$$Pr(y_{it} = 0 \mid x_{it}) = Pr(y_{it}^* < 0 \mid x_{it}) = Pr\left(\frac{\varepsilon_{it}}{\sigma_\varepsilon} \leq -\frac{x_{it}'\beta}{\sigma_\varepsilon}\right) = 1 - \Phi\left(\frac{x_{it}'\beta}{\sigma_\varepsilon}\right),\tag{6.46}$$

where Φ, as before, denotes the standard normal distribution function. Second, it provides the distribution of y_{it}, conditional on being positive. This is a truncated normal

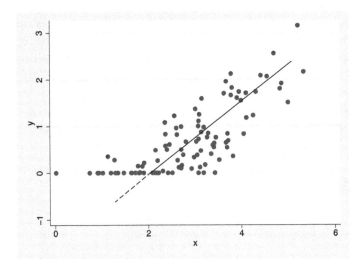

Figure 6.3: The tobit model with censoring at 0.

distribution with expectation

$$E(y_{it} \mid x_{it}, y_{it} > 0) = x'_{it}\beta + E(\varepsilon_i \mid \varepsilon_{it} > -x'_{it}\beta) = x'_{it}\beta + \sigma_\varepsilon \frac{\phi(x'_{it}\beta/\sigma_\varepsilon)}{\Phi(x'_{it}\beta/\sigma_\varepsilon)}, \qquad (6.47)$$

where ϕ is the standard normal density. The last term in this expression is positive and denotes the conditional expectation of a mean-zero normally distributed variable, conditional on the fact that it exceeds $-x'_{it}\beta$. The result in (6.47) explains why it is inappropriate to restrict attention to the positive observations only and estimate a linear model from this subsample: the conditional expectation of y_{it} differs from $x'_{it}\beta$ and is actually nonlinear in x_{it}.

Marginal effects
The coefficients in the tobit model can be interpreted in several different ways, depending on what is the question of interest. Similarly, several different marginal effects can be distinguished. In case the latent variable has a relevant economic interpretation (e. g., desired level of the outcome variable), we can interpret the β coefficients as describing the marginal effects on the expected value of y^*_{it}. Typically, we would be more interested in the marginal effect of a variable on the probability of having a zero outcome, in the marginal effect on y_{it} for the subpopulation for which y_{it} is nonzero, or in the marginal effect on the expected value of y_{it}. While these marginal effects are all determined by the same equation with the same coefficients, their magnitudes are different. Importantly, the key parameter in the marginal effect is β_k and, in general, the sign of the marginal effect of $x_{k,it}$, on both the probability of observing a non-zero

value and the level of y_{it}, will correspond to the sign of β_k. This is an important restriction of the standard tobit model: a variable that has a positive impact on participation (say, the decision of a household to hold risky assets) well also have a positive impact on the expected value of the outcome (say, the fraction of household wealth invested in risky assets). Extensions discussed below are able to relax this.

The marginal effect of a change in $x_{k,it}$ on the probability of observing a zero outcome is derived along the same lines as in the probit model. From (6.47) it follows that the expected value of y_{it} is given by

$$E(y_{it} \mid x_{it}) = x'_{it}\beta\Phi(x'_{it}\beta/\sigma_\varepsilon) + \sigma_\varepsilon\phi(x'_{it}\beta/\sigma_\varepsilon),$$

from which it follows that the marginal effect of a change in $x_{k,it}$, other things equal, is given by (Greene, 2011, Section 19.9)

$$\frac{\partial E(y_{it} \mid x_{it})}{\partial x_{k,it}} = \beta_k\Phi(x'_{it}\beta/\sigma_\varepsilon)$$

(where several terms cancel out). Thus, the marginal effect of a change in an explanatory variable upon the expected outcome y_{it} is equal to the variable's coefficient β_k, multiplied by the probability of having a positive outcome. If this probability is close to one for a particular unit, the marginal effect is very close to β_k, as in the linear model. The marginal effect on $E(y_{it} \mid x_{it}, y_{it} > 0)$ can be derived from (6.47). In all cases, the marginal effects vary within the sample and depend upon x_{it}. An appropriate approach is to calculate the average marginal effects, averaged across all observations in the panel (or subsamples of interest).

After estimation, the *margins* command in Stata produces marginal effects for the probability of a positive observation with the options *dydx(*) predict(p(0,.))*. The marginal effects on y^*_{it} are obtained with *dydx(*)* and reproduce the slope coefficients (in the absence of interaction terms). The marginal effects on $E(y_{it} \mid x_{it}, y_{it} > 0)$ are obtained with *dydx(*) predict(e(0,.))*. Finally, the marginal effects on $E(y_{it} \mid x_{it})$ are obtained with the options *dydx(*) predict(ystar(0,.))*. In each case, it is assumed that the censoring is from below at 0.

Empirical studies often simply state that "marginal effects" are reported, without being explicit which alternative version of the marginal effects is meant. Because the numbers can be quite different, particularly if there are many zeroes in the sample, this is not recommended. The marginal effect on $E(y_{it} \mid x_{it})$ is most commonly reported, even though it is probably not the most interesting one. This is because it effectively discards the additional insights one could get from a tobit model. For example, if we increase $x_{k,it}$ what is the expected increase in the proportion of firms reporting a positive value for y_{it}? And second, by how much does the expected value of y_{it} increase for those firms that already report a positive value?

The truncated regression model

In some cases observations are completely missing if $y_{it}^* \leq 0$. For example, our sample may be restricted to firms that do hedge against currency risk. In this case, we only have positive observations on the proportion of foreign sales hedged against currency risk, and no information on firms that do not hedge. The difference with the previous case is that we do not know exactly how many cases there are with non-positive outcomes and what their characteristics are. In this case, we can still assume that the same underlying latent variable structure applies, but with a different observation rule. This leads to a so-called **truncated regression model**, given by

$$y_{it}^* = x_{it}'\beta + \varepsilon_{it}, \tag{6.48}$$

where we observe

$$y_{it} = y_{it}^* \quad \text{if } y_{it}^* > 0,$$
$$(y_{it}, x_{it}) \text{ not observed, otherwise.}$$

As before, the typical assumption is that ε_{it} is normally distributed with mean 0 and variance σ_ε^2, independent of x_{it}. In this case, the sample we observe is no longer a random sample, because the probability of observing y_{it} depends upon the drivers of y_{it}^* and is therefore endogenous. The truncated regression model makes the simple, but restrictive, assumption that observations on y_{it} are solely missing because $y_{it}^* \leq 0$.

Alternative forms of censoring

The standard tobit model assumes that observations are censored from below at zero. The model is easily adjusted to allow for censoring at any other given value. In fact, it is even possible to allow the censoring points to differ across observations (as long as they are known). Similarly, one can allow for censoring from above, for example, if a non-ignorable proportion of the data is unavailable when the underlying true value exceeds a certain limit. A two-sided tobit is obtained if there is censoring from both below and above, for example, when the dependent variable is a proportion with probability masses at 0 and 100. For example, Chen et al. (2008) model the proportion of directors in a mutual fund family that hold more than $100,000 in total in the family, which is bounded to be between 0% and 100%. Adjustments to the model (and resulting likelihood function) to accommodate these alternative forms of censoring are reasonably straightforward.

6.3.2 Pooled estimation

The tobit model fully specifies the distribution of y_{it} as a function of x_{it}. As a result, we can estimate the unknown parameters by maximum likelihood. The contribution of an observation to the likelihood function is either the probability mass (at the observed point $y_{it} = 0$), or the conditional density of y_{it}, given that it is positive, multiplied by the probability of observing $y_{it} > 0$. Accordingly, the loglikelihood function, in general, can be written as

$$\ln L(\beta, \sigma_\varepsilon^2) = \sum_{i,t \in I_0} \ln Pr(y_{it} = 0 \mid x_{it}) \tag{6.49}$$

$$+ \sum_{i,t \in I_1} [\ln f(y_{it} \mid x_{it}, y_{it} > 0) + \ln Pr(y_{it} > 0 \mid x_{it})],$$

where $f(\cdot)$ is generic notation for a density function, and where I_0 and I_1 are defined as the sets of indices corresponding to the zero and positive observations, respectively. For example, $I_0 = \{(i, t); y_{it} = 0\}$. Using the appropriate expressions for a normal distribution, we can write the loglikelihood function as

$$\ln L(\beta, \sigma_\varepsilon^2) = \sum_{i,t \in I_0} \ln \left[1 - \Phi \left(\frac{x_{it}'\beta}{\sigma_\varepsilon} \right) \right] \tag{6.50}$$

$$+ \sum_{i,t \in I_1} \ln \left[\frac{1}{\sqrt{2\pi\sigma_\varepsilon^2}} \exp \left\{ -\frac{1}{2} \frac{(y_{it} - x_{it}'\beta)^2}{\sigma_\varepsilon^2} \right\} \right].$$

If the loglikelihood function is correctly specified, maximising it with respect to the unknown parameters provides consistent estimators for β and σ_ε^2 under mild regularity conditions. Note, however, that some crucial assumptions were made. First, it is assumed that the error terms have a normal distribution. This is less innocent than in a linear model because the normality assumption affects the expected value of the observed outcomes (as in (6.47)). Second, the error term is assumed to be homoskedastic. Again, this is less innocent than in a linear model because heteroskedasticity affects the functional form of the probabilities and conditional expectations too. The results in Hurd (1979) suggest that the asymptotic bias can be considerable if the errors in a tobit model are not homoskedastic. Because these two assumptions are problematic, Billett and Xue (2007) discard the tobit model to explain open market repurchases. Third, the loglikelihood function in (6.50) also assumes independence of the error terms across i and t, which is highly restrictive in the panel data case.

Fortunately, it is again possible to address the latter concern using a pooled maximum likelihood approach in combination with clustered standard errors (Cameron and Miller, 2015). That is, we can apply a pooled tobit estimation and cluster the standard errors within firms, within periods or both. For example, Colla et al. (2013) use pooled probit and tobit approaches, clustering their standard errors at the firm level, to explain to what extent firms specialise in their debt structure. Similarly, Brockman and Unlu (2009) use a pooled tobit model, with year and industry fixed effects, to relate the amount of dividends paid by a firm (scaled by sales) to creditor rights and other firm-level variables.

The tobit model, with flexible censoring thresholds, can be estimated (using pooled maximum likelihood) in Stata using the *tobit* command. The truncated regression model, which has a different loglikelihood function, is estimated using *truncreg*. With panel data, standard errors would typically be clustered at the firm level. As in the probit case, the use of clustered standard errors does not solve the problem of heteroskedasticity. This is because the pooled tobit model is misspecified, and maximum likelihood based on (6.50) becomes inconsistent if the variance of ε_{it} is not constant.

To illustrate this problem, assume that we have two periods where the variance of ε_{it} in period 2 is twice as large as the one in period 1. Due to the bigger dispersion, the censoring affects the outcomes differently, and the probabilities of observing a non-zero outcome in period 2 are different from those in period 1. This is because a bigger segment of the distribution is affected by the censoring if the dispersion in the latent variable increases.

Allowing for heteroskedasticity in the tobit model is possible if we are willing to impose a specific parametric form on the error variance. It requires to specify how $V(\varepsilon_{it})$ varies over the observations. If the error variance varies over time only, one could easily let $V(\varepsilon_{it}) = \sigma_t^2$ and estimate a separate variance for each period. More generally, it can be assumed that

$$V(\varepsilon_{it}) = \sigma_{it}^2 = \left[\exp(z_{it}'\alpha)\right]^2,$$

where z_{it} is a set of observed variables (including an intercept), potentially identical to x_{it}, and α is a vector of unknown coefficients. Replacing σ_ε^2 by this expression in the loglikelihood function would result in a tobit model with heteroskedasticity. This approach can also be used to test for homoskedasticity, against a specific alternative, by testing whether all elements in α, except the intercept term, are equal to zero.

6.3.3 A tobit model with random effects

As in the binary case, allowing arbitrary forms of serial correlation in ε_{it} is challenging, because the full likelihood function will require numerical integration over T dimensions. Even a simple first-order serial correlation structure, such as $\varepsilon_{it} = \rho\varepsilon_{i,t-1} + v_{it}$, is hard to accommodate explicitly. A popular approach is to allow the serial correlation in the unobservables to be driven by the existence of a time-invariant firm-specific component. Accordingly, we specify a latent variable equation with the usual error components structure

$$y_{it}^* = x_{it}'\beta + \alpha_i + u_{it},$$

and the same observation rule as before. The terms α_i and u_{it} are assumed to be IID normally distributed with zero means and variances σ_α^2 and σ_u^2, respectively, independent of $x_{i1}, \ldots, x_{iT}$. The loglikelihood function for this model has a similar structure as the one for the random effects probit model, and involves a numerical integral over the distribution of α_i. We can write it as

$$\ln L(\beta, \sigma_\alpha^2, \sigma_u^2) = \sum_{i=1}^{N} \ln \int_{-\infty}^{\infty} \prod_t f(y_{it} \mid x_{it}, \alpha_i) f(\alpha_i) d\alpha_i,$$

where $f(\cdot)$ is generic notation for a density or probability mass function. Because conditional upon α_i, observations are independent over time, the numerical challenge is limited to a one dimensional integral. The terms in the loglikelihood function are given by

$$f(y_{it} \mid x_{it}, \alpha_i) = \frac{1}{\sqrt{2\pi\sigma_u^2}} \exp\left\{-\frac{1}{2} \frac{(y_{it} - x_{it}'\beta - \alpha_i)^2}{\sigma_u^2}\right\} \quad \text{if } y_{it} > 0$$

$$= 1 - \Phi\left(\frac{x_{it}'\beta + \alpha_i}{\sigma_u}\right) \quad \text{if } y_{it} = 0, \quad (6.51)$$

and where $f(\alpha_i)$ is given in (6.34). This maximum likelihood estimator can be obtained in Stata using *xttobit*, which also provides a test for $\sigma_\alpha^2 = 0$.

A random effects tobit model is employed in Angerer and Lam (2009), who estimate a model explaining the risky asset share of a panel of households over six different years. The latent variable is interpreted as the desired risky asset share, but – because a household cannot go short on risky assets – the observed risky asset share is nonnegative. More than 60% of their observations correspond to $y_{it} = 0$. Similarly, Love (2010) uses a random effects tobit to investigate the role of marital transitions on a household's risky asset share.

Importantly, the random effects model assumes that the time-invariant individual-specific heterogeneity α_i is not correlated with any of the observed characteristics in x_{it}. This is a key assumption, which is also implicit in the pooled tobit approaches. Unfortunately, a tobit model with fixed effects is nontrivial, due to the incidental parameters problem discussed before. Greene (2004a), using a Monte Carlo study, documents that the bias in estimating β due to the incidental parameters problem tends to be fairly limited, although the estimation of the error variance is heavily biased. This has its impact on the estimation of marginal effects. Clearly, the problem does not arise when the number of fixed effects is limited and not increasing with the sample size, for example, when including fixed time effects and using asymptotics for $N \to \infty$.

An alternative to the fixed effects approach is to allow the random effects to be correlated with $\bar{x}_i$ in a parametric way, as discussed in Subsection 6.1.6 for the probit model. This correlated random effects approach imposes that

$$\alpha_i = \beta_0 + \bar{x}_i'\gamma + v_i,$$

where v_i is assumed to follow a normal distribution with mean 0 and constant variance, independent of the explanatory variables. Estimation is then simply done with a pooled or random effects tobit procedure, including the averages of x_{it} as additional regressors. (The intercept term appears only once.) See Wooldridge (2010, Section 17.8) for more discussion and the estimation of marginal effects. Estimation with unbalanced panels is a bit more complicated (Wooldridge, 2019).

Semiparametric alternatives

The binary choice and censored regression models discussed above suffer from two important drawbacks. First, the distribution of u_{it} conditional upon x_{it} and α_{it} needs to be specified, and second, with the exception of the fixed effects logit model, there is no simple way to estimate the models treating α_i as fixed unknown parameters. Several semiparametric approaches have been suggested for these models that do not impose strong distributional assumptions on u_{it} and somehow allow α_i to be eliminated before estimation. In the binary choice model, it is possible to obtain semi-parametric estimators for β that are consistent up to a scaling factor whether or not α_i is treated as fixed or random. For example, Manski (1987) suggests a maximum score estimator, while Lee (1999) provides root N-consistent estimator for the static binary choice model; see Hsiao (2014, Section 7.4) for more details. A tobit model as well as a truncated regression model with fixed effects can be estimated consistently using the trimmed least absolute deviations or trimmed least squares estimators in Honoré (1992). The essential trick of these estimators is that a first-difference transformation, for appropriate subsets of the observations, no longer involves the incidental parameters α_i; see Hsiao (2014, Section 8.4) for more discussion. The censored least absolute deviation estimator of Powell (1984) and censored least squares estimator of Powell (1986) do not incorporate fixed effects, but allow for nonnormality and heteroskedasticity, while assuming symmetry. Applications of these estimators are provided in Falkenstein (1996), who explains ownership of stock outstanding held by mutual funds, and Billett and Xue (2007), who model open market repurchases.

6.3.4 Extensions

The standard tobit model imposes a structure that is often too restrictive: exactly the same variables affecting the probability of a nonzero observation determine the level of a positive observation and, moreover, with the same sign. This is reflected in the fact that all different marginal effects in the tobit model discussed above tend to have the same sign and are determined by the same coefficients and characteristics. This imposes, for example, that households with characteristics that make them more likely to own stocks are also those who tend to hold more stocks relative to their total wealth. A different way to formulate this is to state that the zero observations correspond corner solutions. In this section, we shall discuss models that relax this restriction. This allows the decision to participate to be different from the decision how large the outcome variable is. The resulting model is referred to as the **tobit II model** (Amemiya, 1984) or the **sample selection model** (Heckman, 1979), and popularly coined "heckit" or the "Heckman model".[9]

Assume we wish to explain what the share of stocks is in a household's portfolio. Typically, only a limited number of households participate in the stock market (e. g., Bonaparte et al., 2014). We assume that the share of stocks can be described by a linear latent variable equation

$$y_{it}^* = x_{it}'\beta_1 + \varepsilon_{1,it},\tag{6.52}$$

where the observed share y_{it} is zero for households that do not participate in the stock market, and $y_{it} = y_{it}^*$ for those that do. The decision of the household to participate or not is indicated by $d_{it} = 1$ versus $d_{it} = 0$, and is explained by a second equation, given by

$$d_{it}^* = z_{it}'\beta_2 + \varepsilon_{2,it},\tag{6.53}$$

with $d_{it} = 1$ if $d_{it}^* > 0$ and zero otherwise. (The standard tobit model imposes that these two equations are identical.) The vectors z_{it} and x_{it} typically overlap to a large extent, where it is recommended to have at least one variable in z_{it} that is not included in x_{it}. We return to this below.

The model is complemented with distributional assumptions on the two error terms. The standard assumption is that $(\varepsilon_{1,it}, \varepsilon_{2,it})$ are independent of all variables in x_{it} and z_{it}, and follow a bivariate normal distribution with expectations zero, variances σ_1^2 and 1, respectively, and covariance σ_{12}. As a result, the model in (6.53) is a standard probit model, describing the choice between participation or not. Therefore, a normalisation restriction is required, and the variance of $\varepsilon_{2,it}$ is set to one.

The expected share of stocks of a household, given that it participates in the stock market, is given by

$$\begin{aligned}
E(y_{it} \mid d_{it} = 1) &= x_{it}'\beta_1 + E(\varepsilon_{1,it} \mid \varepsilon_{2,it} > -z_{it}'\beta_2) \\
&= x_{it}'\beta_1 + \sigma_{12} E(\varepsilon_{2,it} \mid \varepsilon_{2,it} > -z_{it}'\beta_2) \\
&= x_{it}'\beta_1 + \sigma_{12} \frac{\phi(z_{it}'\beta_2)}{\Phi(z_{it}'\beta_2)},
\end{aligned}\tag{6.54}$$

where the last equality uses the expression for the expectation of a truncated standard normal distribution, similar to the one in (6.47). This expression shows that the expected value of y_{it} given that it is positive differs from $x_{it}'\beta_1$ unless the error terms in the two equations are uncorrelated ($\sigma_{12} = 0$). The term $\phi(z_{it}'\beta_2)/\Phi(z_{it}'\beta_2)$ is known as

---

9 It appears inappropriate to narrow down the very many contributions to econometrics by James J. Heckman to this popular model or the associated estimation method.

the inverse Mills ratio (IMR). Because it is denoted $\lambda(z'_{it}\beta_2)$ by Heckman (1979) it is also referred to as Heckman's lambda.

In the empirical banking and corporate finance literature, tobit models are often used to identify the presence of private information, corresponding to $\sigma_{12} \neq 0$ (see Li and Prabhala, 2007). As an example, consider a sample of bank loans and assume that y_{it} denotes the interest rate that a bank charges for a loan. We only observe the interest rate paid on a loan for individuals who are granted a loan, not for those whose loan application is denied. The decision to grant a loan ($d_{it} = 1$) is taken by a bank on the basis of observable information about the applicant (z_{it}), but also on the basis of private information that is not observed by the econometrician. When private information is related to the creditworthiness of an individual, it is likely to affect both the probability that a loan is granted and the interest rate charged on the loan. In this case, $\sigma_{12} \neq 0$ is an indication of the presence of such private information.

If $\sigma_{12} = 0$, the error terms in the two equations are uncorrelated and we can consistently estimate (6.52) by OLS (with clustered standard errors to accommodate for the panel nature of the data). Ignoring any potential complications from the panel nature, we can estimate (6.53) by a standard probit maximum likelihood approach. If $\sigma_{12} \neq 0$, the probability of observing (a positive) y_{it} depends upon the unobservables in the equation and OLS in (6.52) suffers from a sample selection bias.

Estimation
The tobit II model can be estimated by pooled maximum likelihood, similar to pooled probit or pooled tobit, with the use of clustered standard errors. This requires to write down the joint distribution of y_{it} and d_{it}, conditional upon both x_{it} and z_{it} (assuming independence across observations). The pooled loglikelihood function can be written as

$$\ln L(\beta_1, \beta_2, \sigma_1^2, \sigma_{12}) = \sum_{i,t \in I_0} \ln[1 - \Phi(z'_{it}\beta_2)]$$

$$+ \sum_{i,t \in I_1} \left[\ln \frac{1}{\sqrt{2\pi\sigma_1^2}} \exp\left\{ -\frac{1}{2} \frac{(y_{it} - x'_{it}\beta_1)^2}{\sigma_1^2} \right\} + \ln \Phi\left(\frac{z'_{it}\beta_2 + (\sigma_{12}/\sigma_1^2)(y_{it} - x'_{it}\beta_1)}{\sqrt{1 - \sigma_{12}^2/\sigma_1^2}} \right) \right],$$

where I_0 denotes the set of observations with $d_{it} = 0$, and I_1 the set with $d_{it} = 1$. The second term within square brackets is the probability of $d_{it} = 1$, conditional upon y_{it} (and the exogenous variables). Consistency of the pooled ML estimator requires that the distributional assumptions imposed upon $(\varepsilon_{1,it}, \varepsilon_{2,it})$, such as normality and homoskedasticity, are correct. It also requires that the disturbance terms are independent of the explanatory variables in both x_{it} and z_{it}.

In empirical work, the sample selection model is often estimated in a two-step way. This is computationally simpler, and it will also provide good starting values for the maximum likelihood procedure. The two-step procedure is due to Heckman (1979) and exploits the conditional expectation in equation (6.54) to estimate

$$y_{it} = x'_{it}\beta_1 + \sigma_{12}\lambda_{it} + \eta_{it}, \tag{6.55}$$

over the subsample with $d_{it} = 1$, where

$$\lambda_{it} = \frac{\phi(z'_{it}\beta_2)}{\Phi(z'_{it}\beta_2)}.$$

This means that one can estimate β_1 and σ_{12} by running a least squares regression of y_{it} upon the original regressors x_{it} and the inverse Mills ratio λ_{it}. The fact that λ_{it} is not observed is not a real problem because the only unknown element in λ_{it} is β_2, which can be estimated consistently by a pooled probit maximum likelihood applied to the participation equation. This means that in the regression (6.55) we replace λ_{it} with its estimate $\hat{\lambda}_{it}$ and OLS will still produce consistent estimators of β_1 and σ_{12}. This two-step estimator will not be efficient, but it is computationally simple and consistent.

A minor problem with the two-step estimator is that routinely computed OLS standard errors are incorrect, unless $\sigma_{12} = 0$. This problem is often ignored because it is still possible to validly test the null hypothesis of no sample selection bias using a standard t-test on $\sigma_{12} = 0$. In general, however, standard errors will have to be adjusted because η_{it} (6.55) is heteroskedastic and because λ_{it} is estimated. In Stata, both the pooled maximum likelihood estimator and the two-step estimator can be obtained with the *heckman* command, which also allows standard errors to be clustered over units (or time).

Some words of warning
Although the two-step estimator is frequently used in empirical work,[10] its validity can often be challenged. There appears to be a strong belief that the inclusion of the IMR in a model eliminates all problems of selection bias. This is not generally true, and the sample selection model should be employed with extreme care. The presence of nonrandom selection induces a fundamental identification problem (Manski, 1989), and consequently the validity of any solution will depend upon the validity of the assumptions that are made, which can only be partly tested. Much of the concerns raised with instrumental variables estimation (see Chapter 3) translate directly to the sample selection model. If there are no exclusion restrictions in x_{it}, that is, if all variables in z_{it} from the participation equation are included in the equation of interest, the two-step estimator is solely identified through the joint normality assumption (leading to the particular functional form of the IMR λ_{it}). Even if this assumption would be correct, the two-step estimator is very likely to suffer from multicollinearity. This is the subject

---

10 Heckman (1979) is one of the most highly cited papers in econometrics.

of many Monte Carlo studies; see Puhani (2000) for a short overview. One implication of this is that insignificance of the IMR is not a reliable guide as to the absence of selection bias. It is therefore highly recommended to include additional exogenous variables in z_{it} that do not appear in x_{it}. This requires a valid exclusion restriction, just as in the case of instrumental variables.

The importance of this is often neglected, frequently resulting in studies that either have no exclusion restrictions, or where the specification of the first stage is not reported and thus unclear; see Lennox et al. (2012) for a critical survey on the use of the Heckman two-step procedure in the accounting literature. Because identification rests critically upon the exclusion restriction(s), estimation results tend to be very sensitivity to the choices made, and a small difference in the specification of (6.53) can yield wildly different estimates for (6.52). Therefore, exclusion restrictions should be well documented and well motivated, similar to the argumentation required for choosing instrumental variables (see Section 3.4). Moreover, a careful sensitivity analysis with respect to robustness and multicollinearity is desirable. Because the sample selection model easily suffers from misspecification problems, a simple first check is to investigate the implied correlated coefficient from the estimate for $\sigma_{12} = \rho_{12}\sigma_1$ to see whether it is within the $[-1, 1]$ interval.

Applications in finance

The sample selection model is commonly used in financial applications. An example is given in Ramadorai (2012), who explains the premium (in excess of NAV) at which a hedge fund is traded on Hedgebay from its past performance, liquidity and a number of other variables. Because being traded on Hedgebay is not exogenous, a selection bias arises. This bias is dealt with using the Heckman two-step approach, where the first stage is a probit model explaining if a trade occurs on Hedgebay. An offshore indicator is included in the first-stage, but excluded from the main stage. This exclusion restriction is motivated from the assumption that the domicile of a fund affects the propensity of a fund to be traded on Hedgebay, but does not affect the premium at which the fund changes hands. Estimation in the second stage is done by pooled OLS, including the IMR, while adjusting standard errors for (some forms of) heteroskedasticity and cross-correlations.

Dass and Massa (2011), among other things, investigate the impact of the strength of a bank-firm relationship on the liquidity of a stock. Because the decision of a firm to borrow from a bank is potentially endogenous, they control for selection bias using the model outlined above, where $d_{it} = 1$ indicates that firm i initiates a loan in year t and y_{it} is a measure of stock illiquidity or information asymmetry. In both steps of the analysis, standard errors are clustered at the firm level. At the same time, the second stage regressions include a lagged dependent variable, which does not allow for the presence of firm-specific heterogeneity. Interestingly, in their implementation y_{it} is observed irrespective of d_{it}, but the key explanatory variable (the strength of the borrower-lender relationship) is not available when $d_{it} = 0$. Accordingly, the second stage can only be estimated over a subsample, and a selection bias arises.

Zmijewski (1984) stresses the potential of sample selection bias when estimating the probability of bankruptcy of firms. Complete data for financially distressed firms are often not available. When the bankruptcy prediction model is only estimated over firms with complete data, a bias may arise. The sample selection model discussed above can be extended to cover the case where the variable of interest y_{it} is binary (in which case (6.52) corresponds to the latent variable equation of a probit model). In this case, the complete model corresponds to a bivariate probit model. The two-step approach of Heckman (1979) would be inappropriate because the distribution of $\varepsilon_{1,it}$, conditional upon selection, is no longer normal. This issue is often neglected in the expectation that a probit model with λ_{it} included provides a reasonable approximation. Estimation based on the full likelihood function does not suffer from this problem and is recommended.

Further extensions

Early applications of tobit II models in finance (in a panel context) are provided in Acharya (1988, 1993). In one of his models, the indicator $d_{it} = 1$ indicates the observation of a specific event (e. g., the announcement of a takeover bid). The decision process leading to such an event may be based on information that is not widely available to the market, making the event potentially endogenous. (In this case, the latent variable d_{it}^{*} may be interpreted as the net present value of the firm i announcing the event minus the net present value of not doing so, at time t.) In a second stage, one can analyse the abnormal returns conditional upon the event taking place. The author relates σ_{12} to the quality of the relevant information released by the event.

An extension is to also consider the outcomes in case the event announcement is skipped ($d_{it} = 0$). Conditional upon this, the expected outcome y_{it} is given by

$$E(y_{it} \mid d_{it} = 0) = x_{it}'\beta_1 - \sigma_{12}\frac{\phi(z_{it}'\beta_2)}{1 - \Phi(z_{it}'\beta_2)}.$$

Acharya (1988) uses such a structure to investigate the response to two possible signals a firm can decide to give ($d_{it} = 1$ vs. $d_{it} = 0$). In the empirical illustration, d_{it} denotes whether the firms calls or does not call (postpones) an outstanding convertible bond in period t, and y_{it} is a measure of the stock performance of the firm.

A further extension allows estimating the impact of an endogenous dummy variable in the model, or, more generally, the estimation of treatment effects based upon two potential outcomes. We discuss this in Chapter 7.

Incorporating the panel nature

The tobit II model and its extensions can be estimated by either pooled maximum likelihood methods or pooled two-step methods, and standard errors can be adjusted to allow for clustering within firms or within periods. Note that the presence of het-eroskedasticity invalidates the expressions used in estimation, just as in the pooled probit case. Thus, heteroskedasticity results in a misspecified model and standard es-timation approaches tend to be inconsistent. In the two-step approach, one can allow for heteroskedasticity in η_{it}, provided σ_{12} is constant, in which case (6.55) is correctly specified.

None of these approaches allows for the presence of a lagged dependent variable in one of the equations, in combination with serial correlation. More generally, the panel nature is not exploited in estimation. It is possible to consider a random effects version of the tobit II model. In this case, both error terms in the participation equation and the outcome equation are decomposed into a firm-specific time-invariant compo-nent and a remainder term that is not correlated over time. We can write this as

$$y_{it}^* = x_{it}'\beta_1 + \alpha_{1i} + u_{1,it}, \qquad (6.56)$$
$$d_{it}^* = z_{it}'\beta_2 + \alpha_{2i} + u_{2,it}, \qquad (6.57)$$

with $d_{it} = 1$ and $y_{it} = y_{it}^*$ if $d_{it}^* > 0$, and $d_{it} = 0$ otherwise. (If $d_{it} = 0$, the outcome y_{it} may either zero (or some other fixed number), or unobserved.) If we assume that all error components have a joint normal distribution, independent of all explanatory variables, with nonzero covariances between α_{1i} and α_{2i} and between $u_{1,it}$ and $u_{2,it}$, the full loglikelihood function can be derived. Estimation is somewhat cumbersome, because it requires numerical integration over two dimensions to integrate out the two firm-specific effects). It is available in Stata in *xtheckman*.

An attractive two-step approach, building upon Heckman (1979), is presented in Verbeek and Nijman (1992). Interestingly, the required additional terms are time-invariant if $u_{1,it}$ and $u_{2,it}$ are uncorrelated, or if $z_{it}'\beta_2 = 0$ is time-invariant. This restrictive case provides an attractive opportunity to estimate (6.56) using the sub-sample with $d_{it} = 1$, while including firm-level fixed effects to (also) control for a time-invariant selection effect. The decision to participate or not ($d_{it} = 0, 1$) in this case solely affects the time-invariant part of the outcome equation, and its effects can be wiped out by using a fixed effects estimator (Campa and Kedia, 2002; Li and Prab-hala, 2007). Of course, the estimated fixed effects, when of interest, will be affected by the selection bias. Several alternative approaches, based on conditional mean in-dependence assumptions, are proposed in Wooldridge (1995); see Seru et al. (2010) for an application.

Campa and Kedia (2002) and Hoechle et al. (2012) use the Heckman selection model with panel data to control for the endogeneity of the decision of a firm to di-versify. The key outcome variable is a measure of relative firm value, and the decision to diversify or not is modelled by means of a probit model. Sun et al. (2012) employ a "Heckman correction" to control for the fact that their sample of surviving hedge funds may be nonrandom, where the first stage is a probit modelling fund survival over the next 12 months. An alternative specification is the two-part model, as employed in

Chen et al. (2008). In this case, the first stage remains a probit equation, while the second stage involves a standard regression model, which is assumed to apply to the positive observations only. This allows the same regressors to appear in both equations. The two-part model allows selection only to depend upon the observables in z_{it} and is otherwise random, while the Heckman sample selection model permits selection on both observables and unobservables; see Cameron and Trivedi (2005, Chapter 16) for more discussion.

6.4 Dynamic models

An important advantage of panel data is that unit-specific histories are available and can be exploited in a model. A typical case of this is the inclusion of a lagged dependent variable in a model. Unfortunately, when the number of time periods is relatively short, the modelling of individual dynamics is not without challenges. In Chapter 5, we discussed the estimation of linear dynamic models for short T, and noted that many standard estimators, like pooled OLS and fixed effects estimators, are biased and inconsistent. In this section we discuss dynamic models with limited dependent variables.

6.4.1 State dependence versus unobserved heterogeneity

We start with the binary choice model, so we observe $y_{it} = 0$ or $y_{it} = 1$. Before discussing a dynamic model in this context, it is instructive to consider a simple example, which will allow us to understand the subtleties, or complexities, when estimating dynamics. First, consider a situation where we have two types of firms: firms that are likely to pay dividends in any given year and those that are unlikely to do so. Assume that likely firms have a probability of 75% of paying dividends, while unlikely firms do so with a probability of 25%. Although part of this difference may be attributable to observable characteristics, such as industry, another part is assumed to be attributable to unobserved heterogeneity. If, in this case, we estimate a dynamic binary choice model, and relate $y_{i,t}$ to $y_{i,t-1}$ we can expect to find a positive relationship, even though the lagged status of the firm is not directly relevant, and differences in the probability of paying dividends are completely attributable to time-invariant firm-specific heterogeneity. Heckman (1978b) refers to this as spurious state dependence.

Now, consider an alternative data generating process. In some initial period, which may be before the start of our sample period, firms make a random choice to either pay dividends or not. After this, a firm that pays dividend in year $t-1$ will also pay dividends in year t with a probability of, say 75%, whereas firms that do not will continue to do so with a probability of 75%. This is a simple first-order Markov chain. An interpretation of this may be that firms do not want to deviate from their previous choice, due to a signalling effect. When we relate $y_{i,t}$ to $y_{i,t-1}$ we can also expect to find a positive relationship, which reflects true state dependence.

In reality a mixture of these two processes may apply, where both unobserved heterogeneity and a lagged dependent variable matter. Empirically, it is challenging to separate the two. At the same time, their implications may differ. In the case of true state dependence, there is a causal effect of a firm experiencing $y_{it} = 1$ that alters, for example, preferences, costs, or constraints relevant to future choices. In this case, past choices have a genuine behavioural effect: otherwise identical firms that did not pay dividends would behave differently in the future relative to those who did. Potential explanations are habit persistence, adjustment costs or slow adjustment towards a desired or optimal outcome (see, e. g., the discussion in the capital structure literature in Lemmon et al., 2008). The alternative explanation, unobserved heterogeneity, states that there are firms that have a preference for paying dividends, while others do not. Previous choices seem to affect current choices, leading to spurious state dependence, because they proxy for heterogeneity that is not properly controlled for.

6.4.2 A dynamic probit model with unobserved heterogeneity

We consider the random effects probit model with a lagged dependent variable, noting that the discussion for a random effects tobit model is very similar. The latent variable equation is now given by

$$y_{it}^* = x_{it}'\beta + \gamma y_{i,t-1} + \alpha_i + u_{it}, \tag{6.58}$$

where we observe $y_{it} = 1$ if $y_{it}^* > 0$ and 0 otherwise, and where we assume that u_{it} has an IID standard normal distribution, independent of x_{it} and $y_{i,t-1}$. In this model, $\gamma > 0$ indicates positive state dependence: ceteris paribus the probability of observing $y_{it} = 1$ is larger if $y_{i,t-1} = 1$. Effectively, this model implies that

$$Pr(y_{it} = 1 \mid x_{it}, y_{i,t-1}, \alpha_i) = \Phi(x_{it}'\beta + \gamma y_{i,t-1} + \alpha_i).$$

To estimate it, we can follow the estimation approach of a static random effects model, with some adjustments. The full loglikelihood function for the dynamic model is given by

$$\ln L(\beta, \gamma, \sigma_\alpha^2) = \sum_{i=1}^{N} \ln \int_{-\infty}^{\infty} \left[\prod_{t=2}^{T} \Phi(x_{it}'\beta + \gamma y_{i,t-1} + \alpha_i)^{y_{it}} \left[1 - \Phi(x_{it}'\beta + \gamma y_{i,t-1} + \alpha_i) \right]^{(1-y_{it})} \right.$$

$$\left. \times Pr(y_{i1} = 1 \mid x_{i1}, \alpha_i)^{y_{i1}} \left[1 - Pr(y_{i1} = 1 \mid x_{i1}, \alpha_i) \right]^{(1-y_{i1})} \right] f(\alpha_i) d\alpha_i,$$

where f denotes the normal density of α_i as given in (6.34), which is assumed to be independent of $x_{i1}, \ldots, x_{iT}$ (justifying the choice for random effects rather than fixed effects).

The term $Pr(y_{i1} = 1 \mid x_{i1}, \alpha_i)$ in the loglikelihood function is left unspecified. It describes the probability of observing $y_{it} = 1$ in the first year of observation for firm i, conditional upon the explanatory variables x_{i1} and – importantly – conditional upon the unobserved heterogeneity α_i. It is not conditional upon a lagged value of y_{it} because this is not available. The specification of this initial probability is problematic and it does not follow from the specified model. What makes it complicated is that it depends upon α_i and is therefore placed inside the integral.

If the initial value is exogenous in the sense that its distribution does not depend upon α_i, we can put the terms involving $Pr(y_{i1} = 1 \mid x_{i1}, \alpha_i) = Pr(y_{i1} = 1 \mid x_{i1})$ outside the integral. In this case, we can simply consider the likelihood function conditional upon y_{i1} and ignore the term related to y_{i1} in estimation. This approach would be appropriate if the initial state is the same for all firms or if it is randomly assigned to firms.

However, it may be hard to argue in many applications that the initial value y_{i1} is exogenous and does not depend upon a firm's unobserved heterogeneity. After all, any of the other y_{it}s depend upon α_i by construction. In such a case we need an expression for $Pr(y_{i1} = 1 \mid x_{i1}, \alpha_i)$ and this is problematic. If the process we are estimating has been going on for a number of periods before the current sample period, $Pr(y_{i1} = 1 \mid x_{i1}, \alpha_i)$ is a complicated function that depends upon firm i's unobserved history. This means that it is typically impossible to derive an expression for the marginal probability that is consistent with the rest of the model. Heckman (1981) suggests an approximate solution to this initial conditions problem that appears to work reasonably well in practice. It requires an approximation for the marginal probability of the initial state by a probit function, using as much pre-sample information as available, without imposing restrictions between its coefficients and the structural β and y. Wooldridge (2005) proposes an alternative approach where the likelihood contributions are employed conditional upon y_{i1}. This implies that the expressions $Pr(y_{i1} = 1 \mid x_{i1}, \alpha_i)$ disappear from the likelihood function, but instead that the density of α_i is made conditional upon y_{i1} and other explanatory variables. This estimator is available in Stata in the (user-written) procedure *xtpdyn*. Christiansen et al. (2007) employ this approach in a model to explain stock market participation of individual investors. The impact of the initial conditions diminishes if the number of sample periods T increases, so one may decide to ignore the problem when T is fairly large; see Hsiao (2014, Subsection 7.5.2) for more discussion.

Pooled approaches

Without fully specifying the role of unobserved heterogeneity and the lagged dependent variable, it is nontrivial to separate the causal role of the lagged dependent variable from time-invariant unobserved components. One may be tempted to specify a dynamic binary model of the form

$$Pr(y_{it} = 1 \mid x_{it}, y_{i,t-1}) = \Phi(x_{it}'\beta + yy_{i,t-1}).$$

This expression does not follow from the dynamic probit model discussed above (except in the trivial case where $\alpha_i = 0$). Although we can interpret this as (an approximation of) the conditional probability of y_{it} given both x_{it} and $y_{i,t-1}$, the role of the lagged dependent variable will be determined via the two channels discussed above. Estimating this expression using a pooled likelihood approach or the Fama and MacBeth (1973) sample splitting approach does not provide consistent estimators for the coefficients in (6.58), except when there is no serial correlation in ε_{it} (and thus also $\alpha_i = 0$).

Fixed effects

The conditional maximum likelihood approach to estimate a logit model with fixed effects, unfortunately, does not remain valid in the presence of a lagged dependent variable. This is because $\bar{y}_i$ no longer works as a sufficient statistic in this case. See Honoré and Weidner (2020) for a recent discussion of this problem and some potential solutions. Some pragmatic scholars may prefer to revert to the linear probability model with fixed effects in these cases, in combination with instrumental variables or GMM to address the Nickell (1981) bias for small T.

6.5 Count data

In some applications we would like to explain the number of times a given event occurs, for example, the number of patents obtained by a given firm (e. g., Bena et al., 2017) or the number of takeover bids received by a target firm (e. g., Jaggia and Thosar, 1993). In these cases, the outcome variable y_{it} is a count, and can take the values $0, 1, 2, \ldots$ Count data models are developed to explain the distribution of y_{it}, or the expected value of y_{it}, given a set of characteristics x_{it}.

A common assumption with count data is that the expected value of y_{it} given x_{it} can be written as

$$E(y_{it} \mid x_{it}) = \exp(x_{it}'\beta), \tag{6.59}$$

where β is a vector of unknown parameters. This specification guarantees that the conditional mean is nonnegative. It is also monotonically increasing in $x_{it}'\beta$. Although it is useful to know how the conditional mean varies across observations, this is insufficient to determine the probability of any given outcome. For example, we may be interested in the probability that y_{it} is two or more, as a function of x_{it}. To derive this, we need to specify the full distribution.

A distributional assumption in count data models consistent with (6.59), is that, for given x_{it}, the count variable y_{it} has a Poisson distribution with expectation $\lambda_{it} = \exp(x_{it}'\beta)$. This implies that the probability mass function of y_{it} conditional upon x_{it} is given by

$$Pr(y_{it} = y \mid x_{it}) = \frac{\exp(-\lambda_{it})\lambda_{it}^y}{y!}, \quad y = 0, 1, 2, 3, \ldots, \tag{6.60}$$

where $y!$ is short-hand notation for $y \times (y - 1) \times \cdots \times 2 \times 1$ (referred to as "y factorial"), with $0! = 1$. Substituting the appropriate functional form for λ_{it} produces expressions for the probabilities that can be used to construct the loglikelihood function for this model, referred to as the **Poisson regression model**. Assuming that observations are independent across i and t, estimation of β by means of maximum likelihood is therefore reasonably simple: the loglikelihood function is the sum of the appropriate log probabilities, interpreted as a function of β. An application of the Poisson model using a panel of firms is found in Yermack (1996), who explains the number of directors leaving a company's board, and the number of directors joining, from company performance and several other variables. Standard errors are "robust", but appear to ignore the panel nature of the data.

An important drawback of the Poisson distribution is that it automatically implies that the conditional variance of y_{it} is also equal to λ_{it}. That is, in addition to (6.59), the assumption in (6.60) implies that

$$V(y_{it} \mid x_{it}) = \exp(x_{it}'\beta).$$

This condition is referred to as **equidispersion** and illustrates the restrictive nature of the Poisson distribution. In many applications, the equality of the conditional mean and variance of the distribution has been rejected. A typical finding is overdispersion, meaning that the conditional variance is larger than implied by the Poisson distribution. A wide range of alternative count distributions have been proposed that do not impose (6.60). A popular group of models is based on the negative binomial distribution; see Cameron and Trivedi (2013) for an overview. Occasionally, or as a robustness check, authors estimate a linear model explaining $\ln y_{it}$ (while dropping the zeroes) or $\ln(1 + y_{it})$ from x_{it}; see, for example, Aghion et al. (2013), who explain the number of patents of a firm.

There are, however, good reasons to prefer the Poisson regression model. This is because the (quasi) maximum likelihood estimator is consistent as long as the conditional mean is correctly specified. This can be seen from the first-order conditions, which are given by

$$\sum_i \sum_t [y_{it} - \exp(x_{it}'\beta)]x_{it} = 0. \tag{6.61}$$

By using the robust sandwich formula for the covariance matrix, we obtain valid standard errors even if the Poisson distribution is invalid. From this, we can easily extend to the panel data case by clustering the standard errors over firms and/or periods.

These clustered standard errors not only allow for arbitrary correlations within a cluster, but also adjust for a misspecified conditional variance. In Stata, the *poisson* command estimates the Poisson regression model. The option *vce(robust)* produces the quasi-maximum likelihood estimator assuming independence across observations. The option *vce(cluster firmid)* produces the pooled quasi-maximum likelihood estimator for panel data allowing for within-firm correlation.

Random effects and fixed effects models

The Poisson model can be extended to include fixed or random firm-specific effects, often written as

$$E(y_{it} \mid x_{it}, \alpha_i) = \exp(x'_{it}\beta + \alpha_i) = \exp(\alpha_i)\exp(x'_{it}\beta). \tag{6.62}$$

The typical random effects assumption is that α_i is independent of x_{it} and $E(\exp(\alpha_i)) = 1$. In this case, (6.62) implies (6.59), after averaging out the firm-specific effects, which shows that a Poisson regression model with random effects can be estimated consistently using the pooled maximum likelihood approach. More efficient estimation is possible by exploiting the random effects structure. This leads to a likelihood function where the random effects have to be integrated out numerically, as in the random effects probit case. The Stata command *xtpoisson* estimates this model assuming either that $\exp(\alpha_i)$ has a gamma distribution with mean 1, or α_i has a normal distribution with mean 0.

To allow the firm-specific heterogeneity α_i to depend upon the explanatory variables in x_{it}, one can treat α_i as fixed unknown parameters, resulting in a fixed effects Poisson regression model. In this model it is possible to eliminate α_i by quasi-differencing, which results in a set of moment conditions that can be exploited to estimate β. This appears equivalent to maximising the Poisson loglikelihood with respect to both β and all α_i, showing that the fixed effects Poisson model does not suffer from the incidental parameters problem discussed above. The model with firm fixed effects can be combined with robust standard errors clustered at the firm level. An example of this is provided by Aghion et al. (2013) who employ a fixed effects Poisson regression model to relate the number of patents, as a measure of innovation, to institutional ownership of a firm. More details on models for count data in a panel context are given in Cameron and Trivedi (2015), who also discuss some extensions to dynamic models.

6.6 Duration models

In some applications we are interested in the duration of a certain event. For example, we may be interested in the duration of a firm's bank relationships (Ongena and Smith, 2001), the time it takes for an open-ending attempt in a closed-end fund to be successful (Bradley et al., 2010), or the time it takes for a loan to default (Ioannidou et al., 2015). The data we have contain duration spells, that is, we observe the time elapsed until a certain event occurs. Usually, duration data are censored in the sense that, at the time the data are analysed, the event of interest has not occurred for a number of units in the sample. Detailed discussions of duration models are provided in Lancaster (1990), Cameron and Trivedi (2005, Chapters 17–19) and Wooldridge (2010, Chapter 22).

6.6.1 Hazard rates and survival functions

Before describing empirical models that can explain a duration, we first discuss some general concepts and formulas. Let y denote the time spent in the initial state, for example, the number of months before a loan is downgraded to the default status. It is most convenient to treat y as a continuous variable, although is also possible to formulate all concepts in discrete time (see, e. g., Shumway, 2001, who advocates the use of hazard models to predict bankruptcy). The distribution of y is characterised by the cumulative density function

$$F(t) = Pr(y \leq t),$$

which denotes the probability that the event has occurred by time t. Conversely, $S(t) = 1 - F(t)$, the survivor function, denotes the probability of surviving past t, for example, the probability that a loan has not defaulted after t months. Effectively, a duration model provides a convenient way to characterise the distribution of y as a function of characteristics of the units of interest. We assume that the distribution function $F(t)$ is differentiable, so that the density of y can be written as $f(t) = F'(t)$.

The conditional probability of leaving the initial state within the time interval t until $t + h$, given survival up to time t, can be written as

$$Pr(t \leq y < t + h \mid y \geq t).$$

Dividing this probability by h (the length of the interval), we obtain the average probability of leaving per unit time period over the interval t until $t+h$. The **hazard function** is formally defined as

$$\lambda(t) = \lim_{h \downarrow 0} \frac{Pr(t \leq y < t + h \mid y \geq t)}{h}. \tag{6.63}$$

At each time t, the hazard function is the instantaneous rate of leaving the initial state per unit of time. For example, if y is the number of months it takes for a loan to default, $\lambda(10)$ is roughly the probability that the loan defaults in month 11, conditional on not having defaulted in the first 10 months. The hazard function can be expressed as a function of the (cumulative) density function of y, and vice versa. In particular, it holds that

$$F(t) = 1 - \exp\left(-\int_0^t \lambda(s)ds\right).$$

Most duration models start with a specification for the hazard function, the cumulative density function being important for constructing the likelihood function of the model.

A constant hazard rate, that is, $\lambda(t) = \lambda$, implies that the probability of leaving during the next time interval does not depend upon the duration spent in the initial state. In this case, $F(t)$ simplifies to

$$F(t) = 1 - \exp(-\lambda t),$$

corresponding to the exponential distribution. In most cases, researchers work with a convenient, more flexible, specification for the hazard function, for example, one that leads to closed-form expressions for $F(t)$. Moreover, the hazard function is typically allowed to depend upon unit-specific characteristics, x_i, say. Let us, in general, denote the hazard function for unit i with characteristics x_i as $\lambda(t, x_i)$. For the moment, we assume that these characteristics do not vary with survival or calendar time. A popular class of models are the so-called proportional hazard models (Cox, 1972), in which the hazard function can be written as the product of a baseline hazard function independent of x_i and a unit-specific nonnegative function that describes the effect of the characteristics x_i. In particular,

$$\lambda(t, x_i) = \lambda_0(t) \exp(x_i'\beta). \tag{6.64}$$

In this model, $\lambda_0(t)$ is a baseline hazard function that describes the risk of leaving the initial state for (hypothetical) units with $x_i = 0$, which serve as a reference group, and $\exp(x_i'\beta)$ is an adjustment factor that depends upon x_i. Note that the adjustment is the same at all durations t. To identify the baseline hazard, x_i should not include an intercept term. If $\lambda_0(t)$ is not constant, the model exhibits **duration dependence**. There is positive duration dependence if the hazard rate increases with the duration. In this case, the probability of leaving the initial state increases (ceteris paribus) the longer a unit is in the initial state.

There are roughly three different approaches to estimating a proportional hazard model. The first is to assume a specific functional form for the baseline hazard $\lambda_0(t)$. This is reasonably straightforward, and one can use maximum likelihood to estimate the model. The second is to approximate $\lambda_0(t)$ in a flexible way, for example, by a step function. The final approach is to focus on the estimation of β and make no assumptions about the baseline hazard. This builds upon the partial likelihood function, as discussed in Cox (1972), and is implemented in Stata in the *stcox* command.

A wide range of possible functional forms can be chosen for the baseline hazard $\lambda_0(t)$. Some of them impose either positive or negative duration dependence at all durations, whereas others allow the baseline hazard to increase for short durations and to decrease for longer durations. A relatively simple specification is the Weibull model, which states that

$$\lambda_0(t) = \gamma \alpha t^{\alpha-1},$$

where $\alpha > 0$ and $\gamma > 0$ are unknown parameters. For $\alpha = 1$, this simplifies to the exponential distribution. If $\alpha > 1$, the hazard rate is monotonically increasing, whereas for $\alpha < 1$ it is monotonically decreasing. The log-logistic hazard function is given by

$$\lambda_0(t) = \frac{\gamma \alpha t^{\alpha-1}}{1 + \gamma t^{\alpha}}.$$

When $\alpha \leq 1$, the hazard rate is monotonically decreasing to zero as t increases. If $\alpha > 1$, the hazard is increasing until $t = [(\alpha - 1)/\gamma]^{1-\alpha}$ and then it decreases to zero. With a log-logistic hazard function, it can be shown that the log duration, $\ln(y)$, has a logistic distribution.

6.6.2 Estimation

Duration data are typically obtained from longitudinal data, where the same units are tracked over a longer time window. Two types of samples may be available. With stock sampling, we consider all units who are in the initial state at a given time t_0. For example, we collect information on all loans that have not defaulted on 1 January 2010. We then analyse how long it takes for these loans to default. With flow sampling, we collect information on all units that enter the initial state between 0 and time t_0. For example, we collect information on all bank-firm relationships that started in the period 2008-2010. In both cases, we record the length of time each unit is in the initial state. Because after a certain amount of time we stop following units in the sample (and start analysing our data), both types of data are typically right-censored. That is, for those units who are still in the initial state we only know that the duration lasted at least as long as the tracking period. With stock sampling, the data may also be left-censored if some or all of the starting times in the initial state are not observed. Moreover, stock sampling introduces a sample selection problem. Both censoring and the sample selection problem require adjustments in the likelihood function.

Let our sample be given by a set of durations y_i, $i = 1, 2, \ldots, N$, where we observe a single duration per unit. Assume we have a random sample of loans that are issued between time 0 and t_0. Denote the time at which loan i is issued by a_i, and the total duration until default by y_i^*. For many loans y_i^* is not directly observed because of right-censoring: the loan has not defaulted yet, or the loan has reached maturity. If c_i denotes the censoring time of loan i, we observe

$$y_i = \min\{y_i^*, c_i\}.$$

That is, for some loans we observe the exact time to default, whereas for others we only know it exceeds c_i.

The contribution to the likelihood function of unit i is given by the conditional density of y_i if the observation is not censored, or the conditional probability that $y_i^* > c_i$ (i.e., $y_i = c_i$) in the case of censoring, both conditional upon the observed characteristics x_i. We make the (strong) assumption that the distribution of y_i, given x_i, does not depend upon the starting time a_i. This implies, for example, that loans issued in January 2010 have the same expected time to default as those that are issued in January 2011. If there are seasonal effects, we may capture them by including calendar dummies in x_i corresponding to different values of a_i (see Wooldridge, 2010, Chapter 22). Thus, the likelihood contribution of unit i is given by

$$f(y_i \mid x_i; \theta), \tag{6.65}$$

if the duration is uncensored, where θ denotes the vector of unknown parameters that characterise the distribution. For right-censored observations, the likelihood contribution is

$$Pr(y_i = c_i \mid x_i; \theta) = P\{y_i^* > c_i \mid x_i; \theta\} = 1 - F(c_i \mid x_i; \theta). \tag{6.66}$$

The likelihood function is easily constructed from these expressions, after substituting the appropriate functional forms for f and F.

With stock sampling, the loglikelihood function is slightly more complicated because of the sample selection problem. Suppose we are interested in defaults of loans issued in 2009, but we only have a sample of loans still outstanding on 1 January 2010. In this case, any loans that have defaulted before the end of 2009 will not be included in the sample. This sample selection problem is similar to the one in the truncated regression model that was discussed in Section 6.3, and we can correct for it in a similar fashion. The likelihood contribution for unit i in the absence of censoring is changed into

$$f(y_i \mid x_i, y_i \geq t_0 - a_i; \theta) = \frac{f(y_i \mid x_i; \theta)}{1 - F(t_0 - a_i \mid x_i; \theta)}, \tag{6.67}$$

where t_0 corresponds to 1 January 2010. With right-censoring, the likelihood contribution is the conditional probability that y_i^* exceeds c_i, given by

$$Pr(y_i^* > c_i \mid x_i, y_i \geq t_0 - a_i; \theta) = \frac{1 - F(c_i \mid x_i; \theta)}{1 - F(t_0 - a_i \mid x_i; \theta)}. \tag{6.68}$$

Unlike in the case of flow sampling, both the starting dates a_i and the length of the interval $t_0 - a_i$ appear in the likelihood contributions. The exact functional form of the loglikelihood function depends upon the assumptions that we are making about the distribution of the duration variable. As mentioned earlier, these assumptions are typically stated by specifying a functional form for the hazard function.

When the explanatory variables are time-varying, things are a bit more complicated, because it does not make sense to study the distribution of a duration conditional upon the values of the explanatory variables at one point in time. This leads to

$$\lambda(t, x_{it}) = \lambda_0(t) \exp(x'_{it}\beta). \tag{6.69}$$

Because both the baseline hazard and the variables in x_{it} can vary with the duration, separating the effects of time and the covariates is challenging. Another extension is the inclusion of unobserved heterogeneity in the model, because the explanatory variables that are included in the model may be insufficient to capture all heterogeneity across individuals. In the proportional hazards model, this implies that the specification for the hazard rate is extended to (Meyer, 1990)

$$\lambda(t, x_i, v_i) = \alpha_i \lambda_0(t) \exp(x'_{it}\beta), \tag{6.70}$$

where α_i is an unobservable positive random variable with $E(\alpha_i) = 1$. The expression in (6.70) describes the hazard rate given the characteristics x_{it} and given the unobserved heterogeneity α_i. The latter is integrated out of the likelihood function after imposing an appropriate parametric distribution, similar to the random effects probit model. See Wooldridge (2010, Chapter 22) for more details on these extensions. Stata provides several routines to estimate duration models. The command *streg* estimates a variety of parametric duration models (after the data are appropriate defined using *stset*). A useful introduction to duration analysis with Stata is Cleves et al. (2016).

Using hazard models has become a preferred approach for the prediction of bankruptcies. One advantage is that duration models take into account each firm's period at risk, as well the potential unfavourable indicators a firm may have had during multiple periods before going into bankruptcy (Shumway, 2001). In comparison with the traditional logit model, the hazard model is based on information from bankrupt and non-bankrupt firms for years prior to the final year before bankruptcy (see also Beaver et al., 2005, who explore the stability of the model coefficients over time for the prediction of bankruptcy). Both of these papers allow for time-varying covariates in x_{it}, and assume all firm-specific heterogeneity is captured by the covariates (so that $\alpha_i = 1$ for all i).

Another example of duration analysis in finance is provided in Ongena and Smith (2001), who examine the duration of firm-bank relationships and investigate the presence of positive or negative duration dependence. They also relate the duration to firm-specific characteristics, such as age, size and Tobin's Q. They estimate their model assuming either an exponential or Weibull baseline hazard function, accounting for right-censoring. Whited (2006) uses a hazard model to study the frequency of large investments (spikes), and the spells between spikes. She estimates the baseline hazard semi-nonparametrically using a step function of discrete spell lengths, based on the techniques of Meyer (1990).

An extension of the standard hazard rate function is provided in a competing risks model. In this case, there are multiple hazard rates corresponding to different exit reasons, where the observed duration corresponds to the shortest one (whichever happens first). For example, Hollifield et al. (2006) use this to model the time an order remains in the limit-order book, with cancellation and execution as two crucially different reasons. More technical details of duration models can be found in Lancaster (1990, Chapter 5) and Van den Berg (2001).

7 Estimating average treatment effects

A substantial part of the empirical literature attempts to identify causal effects, and the topic of causal inference has been receiving increasing amounts of attention in recent years. Much of this literature is framed as the estimation of treatment effects (or as "programme evaluation"). A treatment effect refers to the causal impact of a certain treatment (policy, event, decision) upon a given outcome. Because the effect of a treatment may differ across firms and selection into treatment may be nonrandom, the estimation of treatment effects is nontrivial. In the simplest case, the treatment effect is simply the coefficient for a treatment indicator in a linear regression model. Because we are interested in the causal effect of treatment, we need to worry about endogeneity of the treatment dummy. That is, we need to worry about the question how units are selected, or select themselves, into treatment. When the effect of a treatment differs across units, additional issues emerge, including the question which (average) treatment effect we wish to estimate.

In this chapter, we provide a brief review of the literature on the estimation of average treatment effects, with particular attention to its use in finance. The advantage of having panel data is that multiple observations on the same units are available, which ideally include observations before and after treatment has occurred. This way, a comparison before and after can be combined with a comparison with firms that are not treated (the control group). Such difference-in-differences approaches are very popular in empirical work. Section 7.1 discusses the potential outcomes framework, which underlies much of the recent literature. It provides a convenient way to illustrate the identification challenge (the fact that counterfactual outcomes are not observed), and helps introducing several solutions. Section 7.2 considers possible solutions if it can be assumed that treatment is independent of the potential outcomes, conditional upon a set of covariates. This includes inverse probability weighting (IPW), regression-adjustment and matching. Section 7.3 introduces regression discontinuity design (RDD). We then move to more challenging cases where treatment is potentially endogenous, conditional upon a set of covariates. Section 7.4 relates the alternative outcomes framework to the more traditional switching regression model. In Section 7.5, we come back to the role of instrumental variables estimation in the presence of heterogeneous treatment effects, and discuss the concept of a local average treatment effect (LATE).

All approaches are implicitly or explicitly based on a comparison of outcomes for units that treated with those of one or more (potentially hypothetical) units that are not treated. The panel nature of the data is reflected in the calculation of the corresponding standard errors, or in the use of lagged variables as conditioning variables or instruments. In Section 7.6, we conclude this chapter with a discussion of the difference-in-differences approach, which compares outcomes before and after treatment, and between groups of units that receive treatment and does that do not. This can be combined with some of the earlier approaches, such as matching. However,

https://doi.org/10.1515/9783110660739-007

the panel nature of the data may also complicate the identification and estimation of treatment effects, for example, when treatment can take place a different points in time and the effect of treatment varies across periods. We also discuss some of these concerns in Section 7.6.

The literature on causal inference is extensive and expanding rapidly. More detailed coverage is provided in Lee (2005), Angrist and Pischke (2009), Angrist and Pischke (2015), Cerulli (2015), Imbens and Rubin (2015), Abadie and Cattaneo (2018), Hernán and Robins (2020) and Cunningham (2021). The problem of endogeneity in corporate finance, with a discussion of potential solutions, is covered very well in Roberts and Whited (2013). An account of the diffusion of techniques to identify causal relationships in corporate finance research since the mid-1990s is provided in Bowen et al. (2017).

7.1 Potential outcomes

A common starting point is to define two potential outcomes for a given firm, denoted y_{0i} and y_{1i}, where – for simplicity – we ignore any time variation in these outcomes (Rubin, 1974). The outcome y_{0i} denotes the outcome in a situation without treatment, whereas y_{1i} is the outcome with treatment. The firm-specific gains to treatment are given by $\delta_i = y_{1i} - y_{0i}$, which is the difference between an actual outcome and a counterfactual one. Only one of these outcomes is observed, depending upon the decision of the firm, or some other allocation mechanism, to participate in treatment. In general, we are interested in making statements about the expected or average gains of treatment for particular subsets of the population, or the entire population of firms. Let us denote treatment by the indicator r_i. That is, $r_i = 1$ denotes that a firm is subject to treatment, and $r_i = 0$ otherwise. This means that we observe

$$y_i = r_i y_{1i} + (1 - r_i) y_{0i},$$

but never both y_{0i} and y_{1i}.

The term "treatment effect" originates from the medical literature, where scholars investigate, for example, the effect on patients of being treated by a new drug. Here, we use it denote any (binary) variable that we wish to estimate the causal impact of. There are many examples in corporate finance and corporate governance that involve the identification and estimation of the effects of a binary outcome. For example, Bertrand and Mullainathan (2003) investigate the impact of the passing of an antitakeover law at the state level upon outcomes such as production worker wages and capital expenditures at the plant level, Adams et al. (2005) investigate the impact of powerful CEOs (proxied by several alternative indicators) on firm performance, and Bennedsen et al. (2007) compare the changes in the operating performance of firms that choose a family member as the new CEO to that of firms that appoint an external

CEO. From these examples it is clear that treatment can refer to something that is externally imposed, such as the passage of a law or a new regulation, or some (more or less voluntary) choice made by a firm or an individual. A key issue is to what extent firms receiving treatment are otherwise similar to those that do not.

7.1.1 Average treatment effects

In many cases we can expect that the gains to treatment vary across firms or individuals. For example, if treatment refers to a financial literacy training, it can be argued that this may have greater effects on individuals who are less educated and less financially literate (see, e. g., Cole et al., 2011). Several alternative population parameters exist to summarise the effect of treatment for a particular group of units. The **average treatment effect** (ATE) is defined as

$$ATE = E(y_{1i} - y_{0i}), \tag{7.1}$$

which describes the expected effect of treatment for an arbitrary firm or individual. That is, it measures the effect of randomly assigning a unit in the population to receive treatment. An important alternative measure is the **average treatment effect on the treated** (ATT), defined as

$$ATT = E(y_{1i} - y_{0i} \mid r_i = 1), \tag{7.2}$$

also denoted as ATET. This measures the mean effect of treatment for those firms or individuals that are in the treatment group. As argued by Imbens and Wooldridge (2009), in many cases ATT is the more interesting estimand than the overall average effect. For example, it does not appear very interesting to determine the effect of a financial literary training for finance professors. Note that we can write ATT as

$$ATT = E(y_{1i} \mid r_i = 1) - E(y_{0i} \mid r_i = 1). \tag{7.3}$$

The first term is potentially observed and denotes the average outcome, conditional upon treatment, for those units that are treated. The second term is the counterfactual one and denotes the outcomes for treated units, had they not chosen treatment. Because counterfactual outcomes are not observed, identification of measures of causal treatment effects, like ATE and ATT, is only possible if some identifying – and partly untestable – assumptions are imposed.

One can also define the average treatment effect for the untreated as

$$ATU = E(y_{1i} - y_{0i} \mid r_i = 0). \tag{7.4}$$

Untreated units are also known as control units, or the control group. ATU measures the expected gains from treatment for units in the control group, in the counterfactual situation where they would have chosen treatment (or would have been assigned to treatment). It is easily verified that

$$\text{ATE} = Pr(r_i = 1)\text{ATT} + Pr(r_i = 0)\text{ATU},$$

that is, the average treatment effect in the population is the weighted average of the average treatment effects on the treated and untreated units, where the weights correspond to the probability of treatment (or no treatment). The three concepts are identical if there is no heterogeneity in the treatment effect ($\delta_i = \delta$). With heterogeneous treatment effects, the potential estimands, ATE, ATT and ATU are typically different. In general, it can be thought that firms or households that would benefit most from treatment, other things equal, are more likely to choose treatment.

7.1.2 Randomised experiments

In the ideal situation, firms are randomly selected for treatment, that is, the decision for treatment is exogenous. This is referred to as a **randomised experiment** or a randomised clinical trial (RCT). For example, in 2004 the Securities and Exchange Commission (SEC) initiated a controlled experiment in which one-third of the stocks in the Russell 3000 index were arbitrarily chosen as pilot stocks and exempted from short-sale price tests (see Fang et al., 2016, for an illustration). In some cases, randomised field experiments are used to identify the impact of an intervention. For example, Duflo and Saez (2003) sent letters to a random selection of university employees, encouraging them to attend an employee benefits fair, so as to try to increase the enrolment in retirement plans. Cole et al. (2011) conduct a field experiment in Indonesia offering a financial education programme on bank accounts to a random selection of unbanked households.

If selection into treatment is completely random, it is independent of the potential outcomes. This is summarised in

Assumption (random assignment) : r_i is independent of y_{1i}, y_{0i}.

Under random assignment, there is no difference between ATE, ATT and ATU and an obvious estimator is the difference of the sample averages of y_{1i} and y_{0i}, that is,

$$\hat{\delta}_{ATE} = \bar{y}_1 - \bar{y}_0 = \frac{1}{N_1}\sum r_i y_{1i} - \frac{1}{N_0}\sum(1 - r_i)y_{0i}, \tag{7.5}$$

where $N_1 = \sum_i r_i$ and $N_0 = \sum(1 - r_i)$ denote the number of treated and untreated firms, respectively. In general, this estimator is a consistent estimator for

$$E(y_{1i} \mid r_i = 1) - E(y_{0i} \mid r_i = 0), \tag{7.6}$$

which coincides with any of the average treatment effects under random assignment. Biases may arise when information correlated with the potential outcomes is used to assign treatment or when firms self-select into treatment based on a trade-off between potential gains and losses. This makes identification and estimation more challenging.

Natural experiments

In a natural experiment, history (or nature) provides random assignment of treatment. In finance, this typically means that some policy or regulatory measure is taken, affecting a subset of units in the population, leaving another group unaffected. Because most "experiments" in finance are not natural, Atanasov and Black (2016) refer to these cases as "shocks". If assignment is truly random, the treatment and control groups should not be systematically different, and a comparison of outcomes provides an easy estimate of the average treatment effect. Experiments in which firms are randomly selected into treatment are rare. Often, natural experiments imply that some policy or measure is imposed upon a group of firms in a particular region, whereas firms in another region are not affected, or are subject to a similar policy at a later point in time. For example, Becker and Strömberg (2012) examine the effect of managerial fiduciary duties on equity-debt conflicts, using a legal ruling which only affected directors of Delaware corporations, but not of firms incorporated elsewhere. Bertrand and Mullainathan (2003) investigate the impact of antitakeover laws, which are passed by many US states at different points in time. This way, the control group of firms evolves over time, consisting of the firms in states where the antitakeover law has not (yet) been passed.

7.1.3 Biases

In most cases, treated firms and control firms tend to differ in observable and unobservable characteristics, owing to the selection process into treatment. As a result of this, the naive estimator in (7.5), comparing the average outcome of the treated group with the average outcome for the control group, tends to be a biased estimator for both ATE and ATT. This is due to selection bias (i. e., the endogeneity of the treatment decision). For example, firms with particular characteristics of their governance (e. g., board composition) may differ in many ways from those with other characteristics. As a result, relating firm performance to governance may capture unobservable differences between firms with different governance, rather than the causal effect of having certain governance characteristics (see, e. g., Adams et al., 2010). This problem arises even if there is no heterogeneity in treatment effects.

In general, the naive estimator $\hat{\delta}_{ATE} = \bar{y}_1 - \bar{y}_0$ is estimating (Cunningham, 2021, Chapter 4)

$$E(y_{1i} \mid r_i = 1) - E(y_{0i} \mid r_i = 0) = \text{ATE}$$
$$+ \left[E(y_{0i} \mid r_i = 1) - E(y_{0i} \mid r_i = 0) \right]$$
$$+ \left[1 - Pr(r_i = 1) \right](\text{ATT} - \text{ATU}). \qquad (7.7)$$

The term in the second line of this equation corresponds to the **selection bias**. It reflects the (unobserved) differences between the treatment and the control groups, even in the absence of treatment. The final term is the **heterogeneous treatment effect bias**. It captures the average difference in the treatment effects on the treated and untreated groups, multiplied by the proportion of firms that do not receive treatment. If the treatment effect is homogenous (i. e., $y_{1i} - y_{0i}$ does not vary with i), ATT = ATU, and the final term disappears, but the selection bias term remains. For example, even if the gains to treatment are identical, if firms with low values of y_{i0} are more likely to choose treatment, comparing the average outcomes of treated and untreated groups may underestimate the average treatment effect due to selection bias. It is also possible to rewrite (7.7) as (Angrist and Pischke, 2009)

$$E(y_{1i} \mid r_i = 1) - E(y_{0i} \mid r_i = 0) = \text{ATT}$$
$$+ \left[E(y_{0i} \mid r_i = 1) - E(y_{0i} \mid r_i = 0) \right],$$

leaving only the selection bias term if one is interested in the average treatment effect on the treated. Because of this, the estimation of ATT is often somewhat less challenging than that of ATE.

Independence of r_i from both y_{1i} and y_{0i} (random assignment) is sufficient to eliminate these biases. Unfortunately, in many cases this is unlikely to hold. If the effect of treatment varies and firms have some freedom to choose whether or not to go for treatment they are likely to optimise their decisions taking into account the potential costs and benefits of treatment. As a result, r_i is likely to depend upon the potential outcomes y_{0i} and y_{1i}. This makes the identification of the different treatment parameters much more challenging.

SUTVA

In addition to the independence assumption, there is one additional assumption that needs to be imposed, although it is often ignored in empirical work. This is the **stable unit treatment value assumption** (SUTVA). It requires that the assignment of a firm to treatment does not affect the treatment effects or potential outcomes of any other firm. In general terms, Hernán and Robins (2020) refer to this as the absence of interference. In certain contexts this may be violated. For example, if firms are competing in the same market, a treatment that benefits one firm may also have an impact on other firms. In addition to such competition effects, there may be spillover effects: if some firms are choosing treatment, other firms may benefit or suffer from it, for example, firms in the supply chain of the treated firms. Third, there may be agglomeration effects or spatial spillovers. Firms in the same area may suffer or benefit from each other's treatment. This also relates to the issue of general equilibrium. For example, if many firms choose to appoint a female CEO, this may affect the renumeration of female CEOs and thus affect the supply and demand of female CEO candidates. Even with random treatment assignment, spillovers lead to a bias in estimating treatment effects.

Atanasov and Black (2016) discuss why it is important to worry about SUTVA in the context of estimating the impact of corporate governance on firm performance. For example, consider the case where the dependent variable is profitability. If an improvement in corporate governance leads to an increase in efficiency, this may increase profitability of the firm. However, if many firms experience a similar improvement, these additional profits tend to be competed away. As another example, suppose that some regulation makes firms improve their disclosure. This may have a negative impact on other firms that do not do so, because of a signalling effect. The literature on how to deal with violations of the SUTVA assumption in economics and finance is slowly emerging; see Berg et al. (2021) for a recent contribution. In general, there are no easy solutions here, and further modelling of the spillover effects is required, often in the context of a structural model that helps understanding the interactions between economic agents. Below, we shall assume that SUTVA is satisfied.

About identification

Because the estimation of treatment effects relies upon a comparison of actual and counterfactual outcomes, consistent estimation of the different average treatment effects relies upon imposing identifying assumptions, which – by definition – are partially not testable. This means we cannot rely on statistical techniques only, and need to investigate and discuss the economic mechanisms underlying the problem of interest. We made this point before in the context of the use of instrumental variables (see Chapter 3), but it applies more generally to any identification strategy to estimate causal effects.

Kahn and Whited (2017) stress the difference between identification and establishing causality. Identification is, in principle, an econometric condition to make sure that we can consistently estimate some unknown parameter from observed data. There are many interesting and important papers in finance that do not establish causality. In the words of Kahn and Whited (2017), "not all interesting questions are causal in nature, and not all identification issues revolve around establishing causality". Some papers that establish causality, even those that do so convincingly, may not estimate something that is economically of great interest (but just happen to estimate a causal effect that is well identified). Structural models, which carefully articulate economic behaviour, can provide an attractive alternative; see, for example, Keane (2010), Heckman and Urzúa (2010) or Strebulaev and Whited (2011) for more discussion.

7.2 Conditional independence

A common assumption in the estimation of treatment effects is the conditional independence assumption (CIA):

Assumption (conditional independence) : r_i is independent of

$$y_{0i}, y_{1i}, \text{ conditional upon } x_i,$$

It says that, conditional upon x_i, r_i is independent of the potential outcomes (y_{0i}, y_{1i}). This assumption is also referred to as (conditional) unconfoundedness or "selection on observables". It requires that a sufficient number of predictors for the treatment indicator is available, such that, conditional upon these predictors in x_i, allocation to treatment is random. This condition is importantly weaker than complete randomisation because it allows the treatment allocation to depend upon observed characteristics in x_i. For example, it allows that firms in certain industries are more likely to be treated than in other industries, as long as, within an industry, treatment is random.

Under conditional independence, it holds that $E(y_{0i} \mid x_i, r_i) = E(y_{0i} \mid x_i)$ and $E(y_{1i} \mid x_i, r_i) = E(y_{1i} \mid x_i)$. Let $\mu_0(x_i) = E(y_{0i} \mid x_i)$ and $\mu_1(x_i) = E(y_{0i} \mid x_i)$, denote the expected potential outcomes conditional upon the covariates in x_i. With this we can write

$$y_{0i} = \mu_0(x_i) + \varepsilon_{0i}$$
$$y_{1i} = \mu_1(x_i) + \varepsilon_{1i},$$

where conditional independence implies that r_i is independent of the unobservables in ε_{0i} and ε_{1i}. The conditional probability of assignment to treatment given a vector of variables x_i is formally written as

$$p(x_i) = Pr(r_i = 1 \mid x_i), \tag{7.8}$$

where it is assumed that

Assumption (overlap) : $0 < p(x_i) < 1$ for all x_i.

This condition, typically referred to as the overlap assumption (or common support assumption), ensures that for each value of x_i there is a positive probability to observe units in both the treatment and the control group. If, for example, there is no chance of observing a firm in the treatment group with negative earnings, we will never be able to estimate the average treatment effect over the population that also includes firms with negative earnings. The probability $p(x_i)$ is known as the **propensity score** (Rosenbaum and Rubin, 1983). It can be estimated parametrically using one of the binary choice models from Section 6.1, but it is also possible to use semi-parametric alternatives.

An important result is that, under conditional independence, r_i is independent of y_{0i} and y_{1i} conditional upon the propensity score $p(x_i)$ (Rosenbaum and Rubin, 1983). This implies, for example, that

$$E(y_i \mid r_i = 1, p(x_i)) = E(y_{1i} \mid p(x_i)).$$

Conditioning upon the propensity score is thus sufficient to make r_i exogenous.

Under conditional independence, several alternative approaches are available to estimate ATE and ATT.

7.2.1 Weighting

Assuming conditional independence, consistent estimators for ATE and ATT can be derived based upon weighting using the propensity score. To see how this works, consider

$$E\left\{\frac{r_i y_i}{p(x_i)}\right\} = E\left\{\frac{r_i y_{1i}}{p(x_i)}\right\} = E\left\{E\left\{\frac{r_i y_{1i}}{p(x_i)} \mid x_i\right\}\right\} = E\left\{\frac{p(x_i)E\{y_{1i} \mid x_i\}}{p(x_i)}\right\} = E\{y_{1i}\},$$

which is the unconditional expected outcome under treatment. The third equality holds by virtue of the conditional independence assumption. Similarly, it can be shown that

$$E\left\{\frac{(1 - r_i)y_i}{1 - p(x_i)}\right\} = E\{y_{0i}\}.$$

Combined, these two expressions suggest an obvious estimator for ATE as

$$\hat{\delta}_{ATE,ipw} = \frac{1}{N} \sum_{i=1}^{N} \left(\frac{r_i y_i}{\hat{p}(x_i)} - \frac{(1 - r_i)y_i}{1 - \hat{p}(x_i)} \right), \tag{7.9}$$

where $\hat{p}(x_i)$ is the estimated propensity score. This estimator is known as the inverse probability weighting (IPW) estimator. To estimate ATT, the estimator is changed into

$$\hat{\delta}_{ATT,ipw} = \frac{1}{N_1} \sum_{i=1}^{N} \left(r_i y_i - \frac{\hat{p}(x_i)(1 - r_i)y_i}{1 - \hat{p}(x_i)} \right), \tag{7.10}$$

where N_1 is the number of treated units, $N_1 = \sum_i r_i$. In this case, the weights only adjust the average for the control group. The key input for the calculation of these estimators is the estimated propensity score, and alternative approaches have been proposed for its specification and estimation. Rosenbaum and Rubin (1983) suggest that the propensity score be estimated using a flexible logit model, where squares and interactions of x_i are included. An implementation of the IPW estimator, based on a logit model, is given in Black et al. (2017). In Stata, *teffects ipw* can estimate ATE and ATT using propensity scores based on logit, probit or heteroskedastic probit models. Hirano et al. (2003) improve upon the efficiency of the estimator using a more flexible logit model where the number of functions of the covariates increases with the sample size. If the estimated propensity scores are very close to zero or one, the weighting estimators for ATE may not be very accurate (and this will be reflected in their standard errors). This is because some observations will end up having an extremely high weight. For ATT, we need to make sure that $\hat{p}(x_i)$ is not too close to 1.

7.2.2 Regression-adjustment

An alternative approach is to use regression-adjustment, making assumptions about the functional form of $\mu_0(x_i)$ and $\mu_1(x_1)$. Assuming that the conditional mean functions are linear in x_i, we can write

$$y_{0i} = \alpha_0 + x_i'\beta_0 + \varepsilon_{0i} \tag{7.11}$$
$$y_{1i} = \alpha_1 + x_i'\beta_1 + \varepsilon_{1i}, \tag{7.12}$$

where the regressor vector x_i does not contain an intercept, and where ε_{0i} and ε_{1i} are zero mean error terms, satisfying

$$E(\varepsilon_{0i} \mid x_i) = 0, \quad E(\varepsilon_{1i} \mid x_i) = 0.$$

The assumption of linearity in x_i is not crucial, and some exclusion restrictions may be imposed upon the covariate vectors in the two equations. In fact, both (7.11) and (7.12) are pretty standard regression models, describing conditional expectations, except for the fact that the dependent variables are not observed for all i.

As before, we observe y_{1i} if $r_i = 1$ and y_{0i} otherwise. Accordingly, the observed outcome is given by

$$y_i = \alpha_0 + x_i'\beta_0 + r_i[(\alpha_1 - \alpha_0) + x_i'(\beta_1 - \beta_0) + (\varepsilon_{1i} - \varepsilon_{0i})], \tag{7.13}$$

where the term in square brackets denotes the gain from treatment, that is, the treatment effect for unit i. The unit-specific gain from treatment consists of three components: a constant, a component related to observable characteristics and an idiosyncratic component related to unobservables, that is,

$$\delta_i = y_{1i} - y_{0i} = (\alpha_1 - \alpha_0) + x_i'(\beta_1 - \beta_0) + (\varepsilon_{1i} - \varepsilon_{0i}). \tag{7.14}$$

To determine average treatment effects, possibly for subgroups defined by x_i, the final term in this expression is irrelevant in two important cases. The first arises if there are no unobservable components in the gain from treatment, that is, if $\varepsilon_{1i} = \varepsilon_{i0}$. The second case arises if the allocation to treatment does not depend upon the unobservables, which is implied by conditional independence.

It is possible to rewrite (7.13) as

$$y_i = \alpha_0 + x_i'\beta_0 + \delta r_i + r_i x_i'\gamma + \varepsilon_i, \tag{7.15}$$

where $\delta = \alpha_1 - \alpha_0$, $\gamma = \beta_1 - \beta_0$ and $\varepsilon_i = \varepsilon_{1i} - \varepsilon_{i0}$. This is a regression model that includes the covariates x_i, the treatment indicator r_i and their interactions. Under conditional independence, the average treatment effect for a firm with characteristics x_i is given by

$$\text{CATE}(x_i) = \delta + x_i'\gamma,$$

If the treatment effect depends upon one or more characteristics in x_i, the conditional average treatment effect (CATE) will vary across subgroups with different values of x_i, and will thus not equal ATE or ATT. To obtain the unconditional average treatment effect, one would need to take expectations over x_i across the relevant population. To obtain estimates for ATE and ATT, we can exploit that fact that – under conditional independence – equations (7.11) and (7.12) can be estimated consistently by OLS over the relevant subsamples. This way, we can easily predict actual and counterfactual outcomes.

Writing

$$\hat{y}_{0i} = \hat{\alpha}_0 + x_i'\hat{\beta}_0, \tag{7.16}$$

and

$$\hat{y}_{1i} = \hat{\alpha}_1 + x_i'\hat{\beta}_1 \tag{7.17}$$

where $\hat{\alpha}_0, \hat{\beta}_0$ are the OLS estimates from (7.11) using the control sample, and $\hat{\alpha}_1, \hat{\beta}_1$ are those from (7.12) using the treatment sample, we can estimate ATE as

$$\hat{\delta}_{\text{ATE,ra}} = \frac{1}{N} \sum_{i=1}^{N} (\hat{y}_{1i} - \hat{y}_{0i}), \tag{7.18}$$

where the average is taken over the entire sample. Using the definition of the OLS estimator for the intercept, this can be written as

$$\hat{\delta}_{\text{ATE,ra}} = \bar{y}_1 - \bar{y}_0 - (\bar{x}_1 - \bar{x}_0)'\left(\frac{N_0}{N}\hat{\beta}_1 + \frac{N_1}{N}\hat{\beta}_0\right). \tag{7.19}$$

To adjust for the differences in covariates, the simple difference in average outcomes in (7.5) is adjusted by the difference in average covariates multiplied by the weighted average of the regression coefficients. If the average values of the covariates are very different across the subsamples, the adjustment to the sample mean is typically large. Similar to (7.18) and (7.19), ATT can be estimated as

$$\hat{\delta}_{\text{ATT,ra}} = \frac{1}{N_1} \sum_{i=1}^{N} r_i(\hat{y}_{1i} - \hat{y}_{0i}) = \bar{y}_1 - \bar{y}_0 - (\bar{x}_1 - \bar{x}_0)'\hat{\beta}_0. \tag{7.20}$$

Both ATE and ATT using this regression-adjustment can directly be obtained in Stata using *teffects ra*.

It is important to note that the adjustment strongly depends upon the linear regression models being accurate over the entire range of covariate values. If the models are used to predict outcomes far away from where the regression parameters were estimated, the results can be quite sensitive to minor changes in the specification (Imbens and Wooldridge, 2009). To be more precise, we need to assume that the regression functions provide a good approximation to the counterfactual outcomes, even though the control and treatment groups may have quite different values of x_i. For ATT, the requirement is a bit weaker, because we only need to predict y_{i0} for the treatment group. Because regression methods are fundamentally not robust to substantial differences between the treatment and control groups (see Imbens, 2015), recent empirical work on the estimation of treatment effects has moved away from pure regression-based approaches.

Nevertheless, the possibility to include covariates in the two regression equations is an attractive option to attempt to control for the endogeneity of the treatment indicator. This is because the conditional independence assumption tends to get weaker once more controls are added, that is, when x_i contains more variables. However, it is inappropriate to assume that adding more controls in all cases increases the likelihood of the regression estimates having a causal interpretation. In general, it is recommended to control for the pre-treatment covariates, variables that matter for y_i and r_i, but are not affected by r_i. Some variables you may wish to include are so-called **bad controls** (Angrist and Pischke, 2009, Section 3.2). These are variables that are likely to be affected by the treatment. A typical example is firm size in a regression explaining firm performance (e. g., Tobin's Q), because firm size may itself also be an outcome of a particular treatment chosen by a firm. With panel data, this issue requires even more attention because the controls can correspond to different points in time. Firm size before the decision of treatment is taken, would be a good control, whereas firm size after the decision is taken might be a bad control. In general, good controls are variables that can be interpreted as fixed when the treatment was chosen (whether by the firm or someone else). As an example, Ahern and Dittmar (2012) estimate the effect of gender quota on firm value in Norway, and exclude R&D expenditures and several other firm characteristics as controls, because R&D expenditures may also change as a result of the quota. Their most parsimonious specification only includes firm fixed effects as controls.

Lee (2005, Chapter 3) provides a more detailed discussion regarding the choice of variables to control for. For example, a variable that only affects the outcomes y_{0i}, y_{1i}, but not r_i, is not necessarily included in x_i. Similarly, a variable that only affects r_i, but not the outcomes, is not necessarily included in x_i. Having too many variables in x_i may lead to a dimension problem, where conditioning on a given value for x_i can result in too few observations for each subpopulation characterised by x_i. Moreover, there may be a support problem (or overlap problem): the values of x_i observed for the treatment group may not overlap much with those observed for the control group. On the other hand, having too few variables in x_i (or the wrong ones), may violate the conditional independence assumption.

7.2.3 Regression with a treatment indicator

If conditional independence holds and the slope coefficients do not depend upon treatment ($\beta_0 = \beta_1 = \beta$), the average treatment effect reduces to a constant and can be estimated from OLS in

$$y_i = \alpha_0 + x_i'\beta + \delta r_i + \varepsilon_i, \tag{7.21}$$

where δ denotes the average treatment effect. This error term satisfies $E(\varepsilon_i \mid x_i, r_i) = 0$ by virtue of the conditional independence assumption. In fact, the conditional independence assumption guarantees that the regression equation can be interpreted as a conditional expectation, or a linear projection, and we do not have to worry about possible correlation between x_i and the error term ε_i. In a sense, (7.21) is a reduced form, where the only purpose of x_i is to adjust the estimate for δ to make it reflect a causal effect. This is an important result and tells us that we can estimate the causal effect of a treatment by choosing a set of controls x_i that makes the conditional independence assumption valid. For example, in their investigation of the causal effect of media reporting on trading volume (across stocks traded at 19 cities), Engelberg and Parsons (2011) include a wide set of control variables in an attempt to control for any simultaneous determinants of local media coverage and local trading. Effectively, this assumes that "after the inclusion of these controls, a media's decision to report an earnings announcement is unrelated to local trading".

The linearity assumption of the regression model in (7.21) is for convenience and can easily be relaxed (e. g., by including polynomials of x_i, or sets of dummies corresponding to different ranges of the control variables, etcetera). If we put in some control variables that are uncorrelated to r_i, they can still serve the purpose of reducing the residual variance and improving the precision of our estimate for δ.

However, if the treatment effect is heterogeneous, the OLS estimator in (7.21) can be severely biased for estimating ATE or ATT. Recently, Słoczyński (2021) shows that, under certain conditions, the OLS estimand is a convex combination of ATT and ATU where the weights – surprisingly – are inversely related to the proportion of observations in each group. To estimate ATE, this is particularly problematic if the proportion of treated cases is very different from 50%. On the other hand, to accurately estimate ATT, the proportion of treated units needs to be small. If conditional independence is satisfied, but $\beta_0 \neq \beta_1$, one can estimate the treatment effects from a single regression as in (7.15), that is, by including interactions between the treatment indicator and the control variables.

7.2.4 Matching

With matching, the counterfactual outcomes are taken to be the actual outcomes of a matched unit of the other group. For example, to estimate the average treatment effect on the treated (ATT), each member of the treatment group is matched with a "similar" counterfactual member of the control group, or the average over a number of members of the control group. The idea is that, by choosing a control firm with similar characteristics x_i, one can find a sensible counterfactual outcome for any given firm in the treatment group. As a result, a matching estimator for ATT can be written as

$$\hat{\delta}_{\text{ATT,m}} = \frac{1}{N_1} \sum_{i=1}^{N} \left(r_i y_i - \sum_{j=1}^{N} w_{ij}(1 - r_j) y_j \right),$$

where w_{ij} represents a set of scaled weights that measure the distance between each control case j and the target treatment case i. Typically, $\sum_i w_{ij}(1-r_j) = 1$ for each i. Under the assumptions of conditional independence and overlap, we can use the matched observation as a sensible counterfactual observation. Averaging across all treated observations, and their corresponding matched counterfactuals, provides an estimate of ATT. The overlap assumption makes sure that there are no values for x_i for which, in the population, no counterfactual firm can be found. That is, one needs to be able to find counterfactual units with similar characteristics at any value of x_i observed in the treatment group. For example, if the treatment firm is in a given industry, there need to be control firms in the same industry that can be used as a match. Accordingly, a matching estimator for ATT can work well if there is a sufficiently large reservoir of control firms to select a match from. When estimating ATE, both the treatment and control groups are matched with members from the alternative group (see Imbens, 2004, Roberts and Whited, 2013, and Imbens, 2015 for more details).

Discrete covariates in x_i with a small number of support points (e. g., industry indicators of firms, investment styles of mutual funds), can be easily dealt with by matching on the basis of their exact values. When the covariates in x_i are continuous (or when the sample is small relative to the number of discrete outcomes), exact matching is typically not possible. Instead, matching can be based on choosing a firm from the control sample with values of each element in x_j that are "as close as possible" to the observed values x_i of the treatment firm i. It is also possible to match using an average of M counterfactuals that are close. In this case, the M nearest matches have $\omega_{ij} = 1/M$ (and 0 otherwise). A first approach is to base the matching upon the Euclidian distance between x_i (in the treatment group) and x_j (in the control group), defined as

$$\|x_i - x_j\| = \sqrt{(x_i - x_j)'(x_i - x_j)}.$$

Alternatively, the norm $\| \cdot \|$ can be generalised to include a positive definite weighting matrix (e. g., based on inverse of the covariance matrix of x_i). This makes sense, as it adjust for the scaling and variation in the covariates. The most popular variant of this corresponds to the Mahalanobis distance and is given by

$$\|x_i - x_j\| = \sqrt{(x_i - x_j)'\Sigma_x^{-1}(x_i - x_j)},$$

where Σ_x is the variance-covariance matrix of x_i. An alternative uses only the diagonal elements of Σ_x (leading to the normalised Euclidian distance). Below, we use $\| \cdot \|$ to denote either of these norms.

Let $j_m(i)$ denote the index j that solves $r_j = 1 - r_i$ and

$$\sum_{\{\ell : r_\ell = 1 - r_i\}} I(\|x_i - x_j\| \leq \|x_i - x_\ell\|) = m, \tag{7.22}$$

where $I(\cdot)$ is the indicator function. In other words, $j_m(i)$ is the index of the unit in the control group that is the mth closest to unit i in the treatment group (Imbens, 2004; Abadie and Imbens, 2006), where closest is defined in terms of the norm $\| \cdot \|$. Matching can be done without replacement, which means that each unit is used as a match at most once.[1] To improve the quality of the matching process, matching is often done with replacement, allowing units to serve as a match more than once. The set of indices corresponding to the first M matches is denoted as $J_M(i)$, and contains the M nearest neighbours (in terms of the distance metric chosen). The matched counterfactual for treatment observation i is simply

$$\hat{y}_{0i} = \frac{1}{M} \sum_{j \in J_M(i)} y_j.$$

so that the estimator for ATT can be written as

$$\hat{\delta}_{ATT,m} = \frac{1}{N_1} \sum_{i=1}^{N} r_i(y_i - \hat{y}_{0i}).$$

---

[1] When matching without replacement, the order in which you match can affect the estimates, because a unit that is used as a match is not available as a potential match for later observations (Roberts and Whited, 2013).

It is not a priori clear what the best choice for M is. For example, if $M = 1$, the counterfactual is based on the single best match, and will be least biased. However, the estimator tends to be less precise compared to the case where multiple matches are used. However, larger M tends to increase the bias in the matching process. In other words, there is a trade-off between bias and precision. Asymptotic properties of matching estimators are somewhat complicated. In particular, Abadie and Imbens (2006) show that the matching estimators are not root-N-consistent, but converge to the true treatment effects at a lower rate than usual, among other things depending upon the number of covariates used in the matching process. A bias-correction is proposed in Abadie and Imbens (2011), which exploits the quality of the matches; see Cunningham (2021, Chapter 5) for an intuitive discussion.

Propensity score matching (Rosenbaum and Rubin, 1983) is a common alternative to matching upon the full vector of covariates (see also Dehejia and Wahba, 2002). It reduces the dimensionality of the matching problem, and avoids the need of a bias correction. It can be defended by the earlier result that r_i is independent of the potential outcomes, conditional upon the propensity score $p(x_i)$. Units for the treatment group are now matched with one or more units from the control group with a similar propensity score, that is, with a similar conditional probability of treatment (but not having been exposed to treatment). In this case, the matching is based on $j_m(i)$, the index j that solves $r_j = 1 - r_i$ and

$$\sum_{\{\ell : r_\ell = 1 - r_i\}} I\left(\left| \hat{p}(x_i) - \hat{p}(x_j) \right| \leq \left| \hat{p}(x_i) - \hat{p}(x_\ell) \right| \right) = m, \tag{7.23}$$

where $\hat{p}(x_i)$ is an estimate for $p(x_i)$. This facilitates the matching process because units with dissimilar covariate values may nevertheless have similar values for their propensity score. The rest of the implementation follows the previous steps.

Matching adjusts for the potential endogeneity of the treatment only to the extent that treatment depends upon the covariates. This is implied by the assumption of conditional independence (unconfoundedness). In the same spirit, adding control variables in a regression model adjusts for omitted variable bias that may drive the endogeneity of the treatment indicator (Imbens, 2004). Matching is often combined with other approaches, such as weighting or the difference-in-differences analysis discussed below (see Gormley and Matsa, 2016, for an example). Matching will never be able to fix an endogeneity problem that is due to unobserved variables (because you cannot match on something that is not observed). It also does not solve problems of simultaneity bias (where r_i and y_i are jointly determined) or bias due to measurement error (in r_i).

One drawback of propensity score matching approach is that the propensity score needs to be estimated. This is typically done by means of a standard logit or probit function, occasionally by a linear regression. Hirano et al. (2003) propose to use a nonparametric series estimator. Results may be sensitive to the choice of model in this step. Similarly, results may be sensitive to the choice of covariates and the choice of matching method. Importantly, the covariates should be exogenous and not be affected by the treatment. For example, Smith and Todd (2005) stress that selecting too many variables in x_i may violate the conditional independence assumption, and may also challenge the common support condition. In general, it is recommended to perform some robustness checks making alternative choices.

An implementation of the matching estimator based on the Mahalanobis distance (with $M = 1$) is given in Almeida et al. (2017). Their treatment group has only 73 firm-year observations, with a group of more than 21,000 firm-years acting as a pool of candidate matches, where matching is based upon about a dozen covariates. Similar to many studies using matching, they provide a comparison of descriptive statistics of the covariates across treated observations and matched control observations. Comparing the distribution of covariates between the treatment group and control group sheds some light on the assumption of overlap. An example of matching on the propensity score is provided in Cooper et al. (2005), who investigate the effect of mutual fund name changes on inflows to the funds. They create a control sample of funds to calculate the "abnormal flows" to funds that change their name (typically toward a hot style). The control sample (based on $M = 1$) is taken from the larger pool of funds that do not change their name and is chosen on the basis of their estimated probability to change their name, as a function of characteristics as past returns, past flows and fees. This is estimated using a logit model for each event date, where the dependent variable is an indicator equal to 1 for a name-change fund, and 0 for all other funds in the sample. Another example of matching on the propensity score is Malmendier and Tate (2009), who evaluate the impact of CEOs achieving superstar status on firm performance, where superstar status refers to being conferred a prestigious business award by a major media organisation. They estimate a logit model to explain that the CEO of a firm was given an award, and use the propensity score from this model to match, in each award month, a winning CEO to a nonwinning CEO with the closest propensity score. They also employ the bias-correction of Abadie and Imbens (2011). Lemmon and Roberts (2010) employ propensity score matching with $M = 4$ matches, because their control group is more than 14 times larger than the treatment group.

Stata offers the command *teffects nnmatch* to estimate ATE and ATT using nearest neighbour matching. The covariates on which to match should be listed, the number of matches can be larger than one ($M \geq 1$) and alternative distance measures can be chosen. For categorical variables, exact matching can be required (e. g., a treatment firm should only be matched with a control firm in the same industry). Alternatively, *teffects psmatch* implements matching based on the propensity score. As with the IPW estimator, different parametric models can be chosen to estimate the propensity score.

Synthetic controls

A related approach is the synthetic control method; see Abadie (2021) for an overview. Originally developed for comparative case studies where one aggregate unit is exposed to treatment (e. g., a state), treatments effects are estimated as the differences between the outcome for the treated unit and that of a synthetic control unit, which is a weighted average of units from the donor pool of untreated units. This counterfactual is assumed to capture what would have happened to the treated unit in case the treatment had never occurred. The matching process in this case is not solely based on covariates but also on pre-treatment values of the outcome variable. This controls for the effect of unobservable factors that have an impact on the common time trend in the treatment and control groups (Abadie et al., 2010). To enable this, implementation of the synthetic control approach requires information for a large pre-treatment window. The user-written Stata package *synth* implements this method.

An application of synthetic controls in finance is given in Acemoglu et al. (2016), who extend the application to cases where there are multiple treated firms. They investigate the role of political connections in relation to the stock market response to the announcement of Timothy Geithner as nominee for Treasury Secretary in November 2008.

7.3 Regression discontinuity

In recent years, a growing number of studies in economics and finance have relied on regression discontinuity designs (RDD) to estimate the causal impact of a treatment; see Imbens and Lemieux (2008), Lee and Lemieux (2010) and Cattaneo et al. (2020) for detailed overviews and guidelines for practitioners; see Cook (2008) for an interesting account of the history of regression discontinuity. RDD does not rely upon the availability of panel data, although applications often use multidimensional data (e. g., covenant violations of firms over a period of 10 years, as in Chava and Roberts, 2008, or loan applications over a period of 3.5 years, as in Berg, 2015). The crucial starting point of RDD is that the assignment of treatment is related to an observable continuous variable x_i, say, with a discontinuity at a known value, c, say. Following Roberts and Whited (2013), we refer to x_i as the forcing variable (also known to as the running variable), and c as the threshold (also known as the cutoff). The threshold will often be constant, but it is allowed to vary over the observations, as long as it is known (ex ante) and observed. The relationship between the outcome variable y_i and the forcing variable x_i is assumed to be continuous (for both the treated and untreated units). Because the treatment and control group in this case are characterised by different values of x_i, propensity score weighting cannot be used (the no overlap assumption is violated). Similarly, regression adjustment is not attractive because the regression functions would need to be extrapolated substantially.

7.3.1 Sharp RDD

In the **sharp regression discontinuity design**, the treatment indicator r_i is simply based on whether x_i is above or below the threshold c. That is,

$$r_i = I(x_i \geq c), \tag{7.24}$$

where I is the indicator function, equal to 1 if its argument is true (and 0 otherwise). In this case, the assignment to treatment is completely determined by x_i being on either side of a known threshold, c. The outcome variable y_i is assumed to be continuously related to x_i, and an estimate of the treatment effect is the difference in expected values of y_i just below and just above the threshold. A graphical illustration of this is given in Figure 7.1. There are observations of x_i on both side of the threshold c. The straight lines give the theoretical relationships around which the observations are scattered. The jump at $x_i = c$ is the discontinuity and its height is the treatment effect.

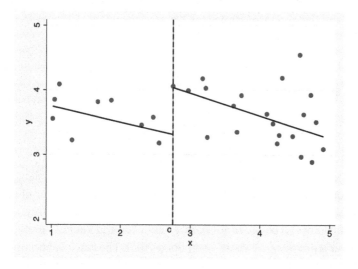

Figure 7.1: Regression discontinuity design.

As an example, suppose we are interested in determining how institutional owner-ship of a stock is affected if it is included in the Russell 1000 index, rather than the Russell 2000 index (Appel et al., 2021). The Russell 1000 is a value-weighted index of the largest 1000 US listed firms; the Russell 2000, very popular as a benchmark for fund managers, contains the next 2000 firms. Average institutional ownership will vary across stocks in these two indices, because firm sizes differ considerably. How-ever, inclusion in either index can also matter, because institutional investors have in-centives to minimise tracking error relative to their benchmark, and the relative weight of a stock in an index varies significantly depending on the index. For example, a firm that just made it into the Russell 1000 (e. g., a firm with rank 995) will have a low weight in that index, while a firm that just made it into the Russell 2000 (e. g., firm with rank 1005) will have a very high weight. Institutional investors who wish to mimic an index, tend to not hold the firms with very little weight (Boone and White, 2015). As a result, institutional ownership may increase considerably if the marginal firm moves from the Russell 1000 to the Russell 2000 index. This creates a discontinuity around the 1000/2000 threshold.

Assume the relevant total market cap rankings in year t used by Russell are observed, and denote these by x_{it}. Then a firm is included in the Russell 1000 index if $x_{it} \leq 1000$, which defines the treatment indicator r_{it}. The treatment effect we are interested in is the change in institutional ownership y_{it}. Because firms in the Russell 1000 index are substantially larger than those in the Russell 2000 index, a simple comparison of average institutional ownership between the two groups of firms would not give an accurate representation of the treatment effect. Regression discontinuity exploits the discontinuity at the threshold and assumes that firms just above and just below the threshold are roughly the same. Accordingly, the treatment effect is estimated by comparing the outcomes y_{it} of firms with x_{it} just below and just above the threshold. This is then the estimated treatment effect for the firms at the margin of receiving treatment (x_{it} close to c). That is, it estimates $E(y_{1it} - y_{0it} \mid x_{it} = c)$. A simple estimator is the difference between the average outcome y_{it} for firms just below the threshold and those just above. For example, Boone and White (2015) compare average institutional ownership during the period 1996-2006 using a set of three fixed bandwidths, where bandwidth is the number of firms on either side of Russell 1000/2000 threshold.

In the application of Chava and Roberts (2008) treatment refers to the violation of a debt covenant by a firm, which arises if either the current ratio or the net worth falls below the corresponding threshold value specified in the covenant. Accordingly, x_i denotes a firm's observed current ratio, or net worth, and c is the threshold, which will be contract-specific.[2] The outcome variable is investments of the firm, and the challenge in the estimation of the treatment effect is that we wish to compare y_i for firms with and without treatment (covenant violation) that are as similar as possible. This allows one to isolate the effect of treatment from other effects.

Comparing average outcomes in a small range around the threshold may be problematic because the number of effective observations is small, and increasing the bandwidth challenges the requirement that firms on both sides are as similar as possible. Therefore, it is more common to exploit a wider sample in estimation and mitigate the bias by the inclusion of functions of the forcing variable. To illustrate this, assume that both actual and counterfactual outcomes are linearly related to x_i,

---

2 The sign of the inequality in (7.24) is arbitrary.

that is,

$$y_{0i} = \alpha_0 + \beta_0(x_i - c) + \varepsilon_{0i},$$

and

$$y_{1i} = \alpha_1 + \beta_1(x_i - c) + \varepsilon_{1i}.$$

The linearity assumption is made for convenience and can easily be relaxed, as long as the relation between y_{ji} and x_i is continuous (in the neighbourhood of c). The treatment effect is simply the difference between the two intercepts α_1 and α_0. We can write this in one equation as

$$y_i = \alpha_0 + \delta r_i + \beta_0(x_i - c) + (\beta_1 - \beta_0)r_i(x_i - c) + \varepsilon_i, \tag{7.25}$$

where $\delta = \alpha_1 - \alpha_0$, and $\varepsilon_i = r_i\varepsilon_{1i} + (1 - r_i)\varepsilon_{0i}$. Because, conditional upon x_i, r_i is deterministic, the unconfoundedness requirement is trivially satisfied. The estimate of the treatment effect δ is just the jump in the linear function around c. If we are convinced that the functional form assumption is correct (over the entire support of x_i), we can easily estimate this by standard methods, such as (pooled) OLS using the entire sample. Allowing the slope coefficients β_0 and β_1 to differ across the two sides of the threshold is a useful flexibility, although authors often impose the functional forms to be the same.

Effectively, (7.25) is an illustration of "selection upon observables". Conditional upon the observables (in this case x_i), assignment to treatment does not depend upon unobservables, such as ε_i. This makes RDD a local randomised experiment.[3] Because r_i is a deterministic function of x_i, identification of the treatment effect relies on the ability to separate the discontinuous function, $I(x_i \geq c)$, from the smooth (and in this case linear) functions of x_i. The key identifying assumption of regression discontinuity is

Assumption (continuity) : $E(y_{1i} \mid x_i = c)$ and $E(y_{0i} \mid x_i = c)$ are continuous

in x_i in the neighbourhood of c.

Absence the treatment, the expected potential outcomes would not jump around c. An alternative way of formulating this is that $E(\varepsilon_i \mid x_i)$ is continuous in x_i at c. If there is an omitted variable that would make the outcome jump at c, even if there was no treatment at all, the continuity assumption is violated and identification via RDD would fail. The continuity assumption is required because the no overlap assumption fails in this case.

---

3 An additional assumption that is required is that units are not able to perfectly manipulate their x_i to make them end up at the desired side of the threshold; see Subsection 7.3.2.

A regression like (7.25) is used in several papers using the Russell 1000/2000 index assignments (e. g., Crane et al., 2014). Recently, these approaches are criticised, one of the key issues being that the exact market cap rankings used by Russell (i. e., the true x_i) are not observed; see Appel et al. (2021) and Wei and Young (2021) for different perspectives on this issue.

Whereas (7.25) imposes linearity in x_i, this may provide a poor approximation to the true conditional means just above and below the threshold. Therefore, researchers often include polynomial functions of x_i in the equation, up to orders as large as 5 or 6. However, as explained by Gelman and Imbens (2019) this is not recommended. Effectively – as with all estimators for average treatment effects – the estimated treatment effect is the difference between two weighted averages, one for the treated units and one for the control units. Using higher order polynomials implicitly leads to weights in these averages that are very noisy, which in turn produces noisy estimates. By extrapolating the polynomials, such polynomial regression models use data relatively far away from the threshold to predict the value of y_i at the threshold, and this is not very appealing. Estimates are very sensitive to the degree of the polynomial, while confidence intervals are often misleading. Therefore, Gelman and Imbens (2019) recommend to not use higher-order polynomials, but instead to control for local linear or quadratic polynomials, or other smooth functions, and focus on a smaller bandwidth of observations around the threshold. In this case, researchers do not use data on units that are more than some bandwidth h away from the threshold, that is, observations with $|x_i - c| > h$ are discarded. Procedures to choose an optimal bandwidth are available (Imbens and Kalyanaraman, 2012; Calonico et al., 2014), which are based on a trade-off between bias, due to errors in the linear approximation, and variance, due to the number of observations that is used. This approach can be combined with the use of kernel weights, to give higher weights to observations where the forcing variable x_i is close to the threshold c; see Lee and Lemieux (2010) for more discussion.

The model in Chava and Roberts (2008), relating firm investments to debt covenant violations, is estimated using the complete sample as well as a subsample of firm-quarter observations that are close to the point of discontinuity (which reduces their sample by more than 60%). Boone and White (2015) examine the sensitivity of the selected bandwidth by re-estimating the treatment effect for different bandwidths around the threshold. Another robustness check is to include additional covariates or fixed effects in the equation. If the regression discontinuity design is valid, these controls are not needed to obtain a consistent estimator of the treatment effect, and they effectively serve the purpose of reducing noise in the outcome variable, that is, of improving precision.

Cuñat et al. (2012) use the discontinuity that arises around the outcomes of shareholder-sponsored governance proposals in annual meetings. Their analysis compares the stock market's reaction to proposals that pass by a small margin to those that fail by a small margin. Intuitively, the average characteristics of firms on both sides of the 50/50 threshold can be expected to be very similar. However, a small difference in the vote share, around the threshold, leads to a discrete change in the probability of implementing a proposal, and a discontinuity in abnormal returns around the election. Flammer (2015) uses a similar design to study the effect of corporate social responsibility (CSR) on financial performance.[4]

Another illustration of the use of RDD is given in Berg (2015), who investigates the role of risk-management involvement on the default rates of mortgage loans. In most cases, mortgage loans are approved by loan officers of the bank, but applications exceeding specified risk thresholds must be evaluated by the risk department. These thresholds are derived from a personal credit score (based on income and credit history) and a loan-to-value (LTV) percentage. It is clear that loan applications with and without risk management approval are not directly comparable: applications that do not require risk-management approval have better ratings and lower LTVs. The regression discontinuity estimator is derived from a specification that extends (7.25) by including polynomials in the difference to cutoff, $x_i - c$, and adding a set of controls. such as loan and customer characteristics.

The Stata package *rdrobust* of Calonico et al. (2017) provides a wide array of estimation, inference, and falsification methods for the analysis and interpretation of regression-discontinuity designs.

7.3.2 Challenges to identification

The use of RDD is limited to cases where there is a clear, clean and observed threshold x_i. If x_i is not observed, the regression discontinuity design simply does not apply (Lee and Lemieux, 2010). A clean threshold requires that there are no other programmes that use the same threshold that may interfere with the one under investigation. That is, the threshold must be exogenous. As mentioned above, the most important assumption underlying identification is that $E(y_{1i} \mid x_i = c)$ and $E(y_{0i} \mid x_i = c)$ are continuous in x_i in the neighbourhood of c. If units can manipulate their value of the forcing variable x_i, or if the agents who allocate units to treatment can manipulate x_i or its threshold c, the continuity assumption may be violated (Roberts and Whited, 2013). Some manipulation is allowed, as long as agents are not able to *precisely* manipulate the forcing variable to push them over the threshold. This requires an inspection of the institutional settings, the ability of agents to manipulate, and their incentives to do so.

Berg (2015) carefully discusses the two key assumptions underlying the RDD design. First, there should be no "contaminating" thresholds, which means that loans

---

4 A recent paper by Bach and Metzger (2019) documents that close votes on shareholder proposals are disproportionately more likely to be won by management than by shareholder activists, challenging the internal validity of RDD approaches that exploit this discontinuity.

just below and above the threshold are treated differently, apart from risk management involvement. Whether or not this assumption is reasonable depends upon the context, and in this case relies upon information provided by the bank. Second, the continuity assumption requires that loan applications just below and just above the threshold are otherwise comparable. Because there is some evidence that the final rating and final LTV are manipulated (e. g., customers may be incentivised to bring in more equity so as to reduce their LTV and avoid the involvement of the risk-management department), the author uses the initial rating and initial LTV (available from the bank's internal systems) as instruments. Similarly, Chava and Roberts (2008) go to great lengths to discuss the validity of the key assumptions in their context. Institutional knowledge is required to evaluate to what extent borrowers and administrators are able to manipulate either the forcing variable or the threshold.

A **manipulation test** is a statistical test that tries to determine whether there is evidence of a discontinuity in the density of the forcing variable around the threshold. Essentially, such tests are based on estimating the density of x_i and testing a discontinuity at $x_i = c$. Because the tests typically test for a discontinuity at a fixed value, it makes sense to transform the key variable into $x_i - c$ and test for a discontinuity at 0. A simple version is proposed by McCrary (2008), often called the McCrary density test. In the first step, the forcing variable is partitioned into equally spaced bins and the numbers of observations within each bin are counted (where no bin contains points on both side of the threshold). In the second step, the frequency counts are used as the dependent variable in two local linear regressions with $x_i - c$ as the regressor. The test is based on the difference between the estimated intercepts. Several other tests for manipulation are available, including graphical procedures; see Cattaneo et al. (2018) for more details (and the accompanying Stata package *rddensity*). As stressed by Roberts and Whited (2013), even if a test does not reveal any clear discontinuity, a solid understanding and discussion of the relevant institutional details and incentives is still required. Recently, Gerard et al. (2020) have proposed an approach to derive bounds on the causal treatment effect in the presence of manipulation of the running variable. Their method exploits the McCrary test to estimate the share of cases just below the threshold that is not randomly assigned, and then considers two extreme scenarios (with these cases having either the highest or the lowest outcomes); see Bach and Metzger (2019) for an application of this method to RDD based on shareholder votes.

The local continuity assumption also requires that units close to either side of the threshold are comparable in terms of observable and unobservable characteristics. For example, should an observed characteristic of a firm display a jump in its values around the threshold, any difference in y_i at the threshold could be attributable to this (pre-assignment) characteristic, rather than the treatment itself. It therefore makes sense to test for similarities in the observable characteristics. One way to test this is to redo the RDD analysis but replace the initial outcome variable y_i by an observed characteristic. Alternatively, one can do a test similar to McCrary (2008)'s and determine averages for the characteristic within bins based on the forcing variable. These averages should not display a discontinuity and thus be similar on both sides of the threshold. This is a placebo test, in the sense that one is looking for a discontinuity where there should not be one. For example, Boone and White (2015) check that firm characteristics prior to the reconstitution of the Russell indices are similar on each side of the threshold.

Another robustness check (Roberts and Whited, 2013) is to include observed co-variates in (7.25). If continuity is satisfied, the inclusion of additional covariates should not systematically influence the estimated treatment effect. For example, Chava and Roberts (2008) include a wide range of controls in the equation, including firm fixed effects and year-quarter fixed effects, and estimate the model using pooled OLS with standard errors clustered at the firm level. Their estimated treatment effects are largely unaffected by the inclusion of the additional control variables. Finally, one can also perform a placebo test using alternative values for the threshold for which no discontinuity should be present (Imbens and Lemieux, 2008).

As stressed by Imbens and Lemieux (2008), the regression discontinuity design, at best, provides estimates for a subpopulation only (firms with x_i very close to the threshold), which can only be extrapolated under strong assumptions (e. g., homogeneity of the treatment effect). Accordingly, regression discontinuity methods do not necessarily identify causal effects for larger and perhaps more representative groups of subjects.

7.3.3 Extensions and variations

In the **fuzzy regression discontinuity** design, it is assumed that there is a discrete jump in the probability of receiving treatment, again at the point $x_i = c$. That is,

$$Pr(r_i = 1 \mid x_i) = g_1(x_i) \quad \text{if } x_i \geq c, \quad g_0(x_i) \quad \text{otherwise,} \tag{7.26}$$

where the continuous functions g_0 and g_1 must differ discretely at $x_i = c$. In this situation, the estimation approaches discussed above are inappropriate. The problem is that r_i and ε_i in (7.25) are likely to be correlated, unless assignment to treatment is random, conditional upon x_i. The good news is that one can estimate the parameters of interest using an instrumental variables approach (estimated in a small neighbourhood around the discontinuity), using $d_i = I(x_i \geq c)$, possibly interacted with powers of x_i, as instruments; see Angrist and Pischke (2009, Chapter 6).

Under the assumption of linearity, we can write

$$E(r_i \mid x_i) = \gamma_0 + \gamma_1 d_i + \gamma_2 (x_i - c),$$

or

$$r_i = \gamma_0 + \gamma_1 d_i + \gamma_2 (x_i - c) + v_i, \tag{7.27}$$

where v_i is a mean zero error term, with $E(v_i \mid x_i) = 0$. Note that, for a given threshold, d_i is a deterministic function of x_i. We combine this with the equation of interest

$$y_i = \alpha_0 + \delta r_i + \beta(x_i - c) + \varepsilon_i, \tag{7.28}$$

which is a variant of (7.25). Estimation of (7.28) by least squares requires that treatment r_i is exogenous, which is unlikely to be true. However, we can estimate the two equations by means of 2SLS, where we instrument r_i in the outcome equation on the basis of (7.27). This leads to

$$y_i = \alpha_0 + \delta \hat{r}_i + \beta(x_i - c) + \varepsilon_i, \tag{7.29}$$

where $\hat{r}_i$ is the fitted value from (7.27). Identification is achieved because d_i is only relevant for the outcome y_i via its effect on r_i. Thus, d_i should not appear in (7.28).

Estimation of the system is usually done using a selected bandwidth of observations for each equation, allowing flexible polynomials in $x_i - c$ to improve the approximation to the unknown functional forms. As in the case of sharp RDD, one can allow the polynomials to differ on both sides of the threshold. Usually, these are chosen the same for the two equations. The relevance of the instrument can be tested in the usual way by exploring the role of d_i in (7.27); see the weak instruments test in Section 3.4.2.

This approach easily extends to cases where the treatment variable is continuous, and this is perhaps the most common variant in empirical work. Scholars are interested in the causal effect of a variable, w_{it}, say, upon the outcome y_{it} and they identify a discontinuity in the distribution of w_{it} around a well-defined threshold, driven by an underlying forcing variable x_{it}. This discontinuity is exploited to create exogenous variation in w_{it}. In panel notation, the system of equations is given by

$$w_{it} = \gamma_0 + \gamma_1 d_{it} + \gamma_2(x_{it} - c) + v_{it}, \tag{7.30}$$
$$y_{it} = \alpha_0 + \delta w_{it} + \beta(x_{it} - c) + \varepsilon_{it}, \tag{7.31}$$

where the threshold c is assumed to be time-invariant. For example, Boone and White (2015) estimate a variant of (7.30) explaining institutional ownership (w_{it}), exploiting the discontinuity around the Russell index assignment. In the second stage, where they explain proxies for a firm's information environment (y_{it}), they use the fitted value from (7.30), estimated using a subset of firms close to the threshold, to replace observed institutional ownership in equation (7.31), following the usual 2SLS logic. Note that the validity of the fuzzy regression discontinuity approach requires that the first step is a "proper" sharp regression discontinuity; see Appel et al. (2021) for a critical discussion of the use of Russell 1000/2000 index assignments in this context. Other applications of the fuzzy RDD approach in financial economics are widespread; see Kerr et al. (2014), Malenko and Shen (2016), Almeida et al. (2016) or Meling (2021) for some examples.

7.4 A switching regression model

We now return to the alternative outcomes framework, where each of the potential outcomes can be described by a linear model. That is,

$$y_{0i} = \alpha_0 + x_i'\beta_0 + \varepsilon_{0i} \tag{7.32}$$
$$y_{1i} = \alpha_1 + x_i'\beta_1 + \varepsilon_{1i}, \tag{7.33}$$

but we no longer assume conditional independence. The traditional econometric literature has treated this as a switching regression model (e. g., Heckman, 1976), which is complemented by a model that explains the decision to take treatment. The most common choice is to specify a probit model, as

$$r_i^* = x_i'\beta_2 + \eta_i, \tag{7.34}$$

with $r_i = 1$ if $r_i^* > 0$ and 0 otherwise, and where η_i has a standard normal distribution, independent of x_i. For notational convenience, the intercept term in (7.34) is not included explicitly. As before, we observe y_{1i} if $r_i = 1$ and y_{0i} if $r_i = 0$. Exclusion restrictions are typically present.

In this framework, conditional independence implies that η_i is independent of ε_{0i} and ε_{1i}. Instead, we now assume that both ε_{0i} and ε_{1i} have a normal distribution, with variances σ_0^2 and σ_1^2, and covariances σ_{02} and σ_{12} with η_i, respectively. This is a special case of what is referred to as "selection upon unobservables". With these assumptions, we can write

$$E\{\varepsilon_{0i} \mid x_i, r_i = 0\} = \sigma_{02} E\{\eta_i \mid x_i, \eta_i \leq -x_i'\beta_2\} = \sigma_{02}\lambda_i(x_i'\beta_2) \tag{7.35}$$
$$E\{\varepsilon_{1i} \mid x_i, r_i = 1\} = \sigma_{12} E\{\eta_i \mid x_i, \eta_i > -x_i'\beta_2\} = \sigma_{12}\lambda_i(x_i'\beta_2), \tag{7.36}$$

where

$$\lambda_i(x_i'\beta_2) = E\{\eta_i \mid x_i, r_i\} = \frac{r_i - \Phi(x_i'\beta_2)}{\Phi(x_i'\beta_2)(1 - \Phi(x_i'\beta_2))}\phi(x_i'\beta_2) \tag{7.37}$$

denotes the generalised residual of the probit model, and where ϕ and Φ denote the standard normal density and distribution function, respectively. It extends the definition of the inverse Mills ratio of Subsection 6.3.4 to cases with $r_i = 0$. Note that $\lambda(\cdot) < 0$ if $r_i = 0$ and $\lambda(\cdot) > 0$ if $r_i = 1$. In the general case where σ_{02} and σ_{12} may be nonzero, these results indicate that the parameters in (7.11) and (7.12) can be estimated consistently by full maximum likelihood or by using a variant of the two-step control function approach discussed for the sample selection model, including the inverse Mills ratio as additional variable in each of the two equations.[5] See Li and Prabhala (2007) for more discussion.

---

5 Switching regression models can also be used in cases where the regime r_i is not observed. In this case, estimation by full maximum likelihood is required; see Hovakimian and Titman (2006) and Almeida and Campello (2007) for examples (with panel data).

An example of the above model is given in Madhavan and Cheng (1997), who investigate the price impact of a block trade, where traders choose between two market mechanisms based on a comparison of the (expected) execution costs. As a result, the trading venue is endogenous, and the price-impact equations are estimated controlling for the endogenous choice of the venue as described above. Another example is Fang (2005), where r_i denotes whether if a bond issue is underwritten by a reputable bank, and y_{1i} and y_{0i} denote the yield for reputable and less-reputable banks, respectively. The switching regression model takes into account the endogenous nature of the matching between issuers and underwriters.

If the slope coefficients in the two equations are identical, we can simplify the model to

$$E\{y_i \mid x_i, r_i\} = \alpha_0 + x_i'\beta + \delta r_i + E\{\varepsilon_i \mid x_i, r_i\}$$
$$= \alpha_0 + x_i'\beta + \delta r_i + \sigma_{12} r_i \lambda_i(x_i'\beta_2) + \sigma_{02}(1 - r_i)\lambda_i(x_i'\beta_2),$$

which extends the model in (7.21) by allowing selection into treatment to depend upon the unobservables in a particular way. The treatment parameter δ can be estimated from a single regression provided we include the generalised residual of the probit model explaining the probability of treatment interacted with the treatment indicator. If $\sigma_{12} > 0$, this means that firms that choose treatment have higher expected outcomes for y_{1i} than a random firm would have had. If $\sigma_{02} < 0$, this means that firms that do not choose treatment, have higher expected outcomes for y_{0i} than a random firm would have had. If $\sigma_{12} = \sigma_{02} < 0$, firms with higher values of y_i are relatively less likely to choose treatment.

Note that identification strongly rests upon distributional and functional form assumptions and it is strongly advisable to have exclusion restrictions in (7.11) and (7.12). If not, the model is identified only through the nonlinearity of the function λ_i. Effectively this means that one needs to be able to find one or more instruments that affect the decision for treatment, but are not related to the potential outcomes.

If it can be assumed that $\sigma_{02} = \sigma_{12}$, simpler alternative estimation techniques are available. For example, the two-step approach reduces to the standard approach described in Subsection 6.3.4, provided we extend the definition of λ_i to the $r_i = 0$ cases. This is the dummy endogenous variable model of Heckman (1978a). Alternatively, the model parameters can also be estimated consistently by instrumental variables techniques, as discussed in Chapter 3 and the next section, provided there is a valid exclusion restriction in (7.21). In this case, the omitted variable in (7.21) serves as an instrument, and a standard instrumental variables estimator can be applied. Heckman (1997) and Vella and Verbeek (1999a), among others, stress the behavioural assumptions that are implicitly made in an instrumental variables context.

The pooled maximum likelihood estimator and two-step estimator are available in Stata using the *etregress* command, which allows the inclusion of interactions between the treatment indicator and one or more variables in x_i. Two separate equations can be estimated with the user-written routine *movestay*, or *ivtreatreg* with the option *heckit* (see Cerulli, 2014).[6]

An example of this model, with panel data, is given in Campa and Kedia (2002). In their model, r_{it} denotes the decision of a firm to diversify and y_{it} is a measure of relative firm value. Because firms that choose to diversify are not a random sample of firms, r_{it} is endogenous, and potentially correlated with unobservables that also affect firm value. To estimate the magnitude of the diversification discount, they estimate the model using several alternative approaches, including a standard fixed effects estimator (which assumes that any selection effects are time-invariant), an instrumental variables approach, and the two-step approach described above, assuming $\sigma_{02} = \sigma_{12}$ (referred to as the "self-selection model").

7.5 Instrumental variables

In Chapter 3, we covered the use of instrumental variables to estimate the effect of one or more explanatory variables that were correlated with the unobservables in the outcome equation. Finding instruments that are both exogenous and relevant is often challenging (see, e. g., Larcker and Rusticus, 2010; Roberts and Whited, 2013; Atanasov and Black, 2016, for more discussion). Many of the instruments in the literature are poorly motivated. Even in cases where the authors carefully discuss the identification conditions of one or more instruments, the validity of instruments is often debated. Papers like Deaton (2010) and Heckman and Urzúa (2010) question the increased use of instrumental variables. Nevertheless, instrumental variables estimators are an important technique in empirical finance. In this section, we briefly return to the instrumental variables estimator, but now with the alternative outcomes framework in mind. In particular, we discuss the role of instrumental variables when unconfoundedness is violated and the treatment effect is heterogeneous. If so, what is an instrumental variables estimator actually estimating?

Starting from the alternative outcomes framework, the treatment effect of a given unit is theoretically defined as $\delta_i = y_{1i} - y_{0i}$. As before, treatment is indicated by $r_i = 1$. Because treatment is not assumed to be independent of the potential outcomes, y_{1i} and y_{0i}, let us explore the use of instrumental variables. In the simplest case, the instrument is a binary indicator z_i. Loosely speaking, the instrument should affect the probability of treatment, but not the potential outcomes directly. Sometimes, z_i is referred to as "treatment assignment". Atanasov and Black (2016) refer to this as shock-based instrumental variables, where a shock is a discrete, external event that causes some firms to be treated. Shocks are often of a legal nature, such as the adoption of the

---

6 A different control function estimator is available in *eteffects*, where the difference $r_i - \Phi(x_i'\hat{\beta}_2)$ is included to control for the endogeneity of treatment instead of the probit generalised residual. This makes slightly different assumptions (see Wooldridge, 2014).

Sarbanes-Oxley Act (SOX), new reporting requirements by the SEC, or the introduction of antitakeover laws, but can also refer to other outcomes, such as the sudden death of a CEO or an election outcome. If a firm is assigned to treatment, it may or may not choose to go for treatment, depending upon the particular setting. What is important is that assignment to treatment affects the likelihood of a firm to choose treatment.

To introduce the local average treatment effect (LATE), as defined by Imbens and Angrist (1994), we need one more additional concept, which is the actual and counterfactual treatment indicators. That is, we define r_{1i} the treatment indicator of unit i if it would have $z_i = 1$ and r_{0i} the treatment indicator if $z_i = 0$. We thus observe

$$r_i = z_i r_{1i} + (1 - z_i) r_{0i} = r_{0i} + z_i (r_{1i} - r_{0i}). \tag{7.38}$$

Combining this with the observed outcome, we can write

$$y_i = y_{0i} + r_i (y_{1i} - y_{0i}) = y_{0i} + r_{0i} (y_{1i} - y_{0i}) + z_i (r_{1i} - r_{0i})(y_{1i} - y_{0i}). \tag{7.39}$$

The independence assumption requires that the instrument z_i is independent of the potential outcomes and the potential treatment indicators. That is,

Assumption (independence) : z_i is independent of $(y_{1i}, y_{0i}, r_{1i}, r_{0i})$. $\quad$ (7.40)

This is similar to the exogeneity assumption in Chapter 3, combined with the assumption that the instrument is as good as randomised. Note that z_i determines whether we observe r_{1i}, or r_{0i}, but it must not contain information about the distribution of either.

Under this assumption, consider the expected outcomes based on (7.39), conditional upon the instrument

$$E(y_i \mid z_i = 1) = E(y_{0i}) + E(r_{0i}(y_{1i} - y_{0i})) + E((r_{1i} - r_{0i})(y_{1i} - y_{0i}))$$

and

$$E(y_i \mid z_i = 0) = E(y_{0i}) + E(r_{0i}(y_{1i} - y_{0i})),$$

so that the difference between these two expected outcomes is given by

$$E(y_i \mid z_i = 1) - E(y_i \mid z_i = 0) = E((r_{1i} - r_{0i})(y_{1i} - y_{0i})). \tag{7.41}$$

Because r_{0i} and r_{1i} are binary, $r_{1i} - r_{0i}$ can take three different outcomes: $-1, 0, 1$. With this, we can write the previous term as

$$E(y_{1i} - y_{0i} \mid r_{1i} - r_{0i} = 1)Pr(r_{1i} - r_{0i} = 1)$$
$$- E(y_{1i} - y_{0i} \mid r_{1i} - r_{0i} = -1)Pr(r_{1i} - r_{0i} = -1), \tag{7.42}$$

the term with $r_{1i} - r_{0i} = 0$ being irrelevant. To eliminate the second term in this expression, we need an important additional assumption, which is

Assumption (monotonicity) : $r_{1i} \geq r_{0i}$ for all i.

This requires that the instrument operates in the same direction for all units.[7] Any firm that would be up for treatment in the case of $z_i = 0$ would also be up for treatment if $z_i = 1$. For example, a firm that would adopt an audit committee in the absence of some regulation, would also do so in case such regulation were imposed. A firm that would not adopt an audit committee in the absence of a regulation, but would do it in case regulation imposed it, a called a **complier** (Imbens and Angrist, 1994). A firm that would adopt an audit committee in the absence of regulation, but would *not* do it in case regulation was implemented, is called a **defier**. The monotonicity assumption states that there are no defiers, which is often a reasonable assumption. Typically, not all firms are compliers, and not all firms are sensitive to the instrument. Some firms may be "never-takers" and will never take the treatment, regardless of the instrument; other firms may be "always-takers" and will always take the treatment, regardless of z_i.

Under the monotonicity assumption, the latter term in (7.42) disappears, and we obtain

$$E(y_i \mid z_i = 1) - E(y_i \mid z_i = 0) = E(y_{1i} - y_{0i} \mid r_{1i} - r_{0i} = 1)Pr(r_{1i} - r_{0i} = 1). \quad (7.43)$$

Now, the **local average treatment effect** is defined as

$$LATE(z) = E(y_{1i} - y_{0i} \mid r_{1i} - r_{0i} = 1), \quad (7.44)$$

which is the average causal effect for those firms that would be induced to go for treatment if the instrument (z_i) changes from 0 to 1. Importantly, it depends upon the chosen instrument. If we use a different instrument, the definition of LATE changes. Accordingly, a local average treatment effect can only be defined with reference to a given instrument, although in special cases it coincides with other concepts such as ATT or ATU. For example, if $r_{0i} = 0$ for every firm, there are no always-takers (because the control group does not have access to the treatment), and LATE coincides with ATT. To stress the dependence on the instrument, z is included in the expression on the lefthand side of (7.44).

To estimate LATE, we divide an estimate of (7.43) by an estimate of $Pr(r_{1i} - r_{0i} = 1)$, the estimated probability that a unit is a complier. Both $E(y_i \mid z_i = 1)$ and $E(y_i \mid z_i = 0)$ are easily estimated using a random sample of observations on y_i and z_i. These are simply the average y_i in the sample for firms with $z_i = 1$, and the average y_i for firms with $z_i = 0$. Further, we need to estimate $Pr(r_{1i} - r_{0i} = 1)$. Recall, that we only observe r_i, not both r_{1i} and r_{0i}. We again need the instrument to estimate it. To do so, we write

$$Pr(r_{1i} - r_{0i} = 1) = E(r_{1i} - r_{0i}) = E(r_i \mid z_i = 1) - E(r_i \mid z_i = 0), \quad (7.45)$$

---

7 The inequality sign can be reversed to obtain $r_{1i} \leq r_{0i}$, in which case the first term in (7.42) disappears.

which is the difference in probabilities of treatment between firms with $z_i = 1$ and those with $z_i = 0$. Empirically, we can estimate (7.45) as the sample average of r_i for firms with $z_i = 1$ minus the average of r_i for firms with $z_i = 0$. The resulting estimator is sometimes called a Wald estimator, because it appeared in an early paper on errors-in-variables (Wald, 1940). It is actually identical to the instrumental variables (2SLS) estimator for δ in a model that relates y_i to r_i, where z_i is a binary instrument.

Importantly, in order to be able to identify LATE, we need to impose that (7.45) is positive, that is,

$$\textbf{Assumption (first-stage)} : E(r_{1i} - r_{0i}) > 0.$$

This condition reflects the **relevance** of the instrument z_i, and is often formulated as "the existence of a first-stage". It requires the instrument z_i to have some effect on the probability of treatment.[8]

The local average treatment effect is the average treatment effect for those whose behaviour is affected by the instrument. Each instrumental variables estimator of a treatment effect estimates the average effect for a different subgroup of the population, namely for those who change treatment status because they comply with the assignment-to-treatment mechanism implied by the instrument. A critical discussion of what question LATE is answering is given in Heckman (2010). For example, there is no reason to believe that the estimated LATE is capturing a relevant policy effect, unless the policy affects the instrument in exactly the same way as is used in constructing the estimate itself. As stressed by Cunningham (2021, Chapter 7), as soon as treatment effects are heterogeneous, the concepts of internal validity and external validity start to diverge. It may be possible to perfectly estimate the causal impact within a given sample, for example, via LATE, but this does not necessarily mean that one is also estimating a concept relevant for the larger population (external validity). For policy purposes, we may be interested in how a particular treatment or intervention affects the population of interest, and this is not necessarily what LATE is estimating.

The fact that the meaning of a local average treatment effect varies depending upon the instrument that is used, when treatment effects are heterogeneous, allows scholars to obtain a variety of estimates for parameters that are meant to measure a structural response to a particular treatment, and to potentially reconcile these across different studies. That is, an IV estimate can be unexpectedly large if the group of compliers as determined by the instrument is different – in one way or the other – from the larger population of firms. Often, however, the LATE interpretation of an instrumental variables estimator is used as a potential disclaimer to the results, in the sense that it is mentioned that, under heterogeneity of the treatment effect, the IV estimators is

---

[8] Similar to our discussion about weak instruments in Subsection 3.4.2, the first stage in (7.45) should not be "too close to zero" to obtain valid statistical inference.

estimating the local average treatment effect for those that are affected by the instrument. For example, Bernstein et al. (2019) write "the instrumental variables estimates only capture the local average treatment effect on the sensitive firms and should be interpreted as such".

Extensions

So far, we discussed the case of a single binary instrument, a binary treatment variable and no control variables. All of this can be relaxed. According to Angrist and Pischke (2009), the "econometric tool remains 2SLS and the interpretation remains fundamentally similar to the basic LATE result, with a few bells and whistles".

If we have two alternative binary instruments, one can estimate two different LATEs, or combine the instruments in a two-stage least squares approach, where the fitted value from the reduced form (explaining treatment from the two instruments) is used as an instrument. In this case, 2SLS provides a weighted average of the instrument-specific LATEs, weighted by the strengths of the instruments. In the general case of 2SLS with multiple instruments for a single treatment, the causal interpretation as a weighted average of local average treatment effects is justified only under a monotonicity condition, which is less trivial with multiple instruments (see Mogstad et al., 2021).

When the instrument z_i is continuous, things are a bit more complicated. To illustrate this, consider the case where z_i can only take on three different values, say $z_i = 0$, $z_i = 1$ and $z_i = 2$. Now one can determine the local average treatment effect for any pair of values by exploiting a binary instrument. These can be combined into a weighted average and the monotonicity condition is more complicated.

It is possible to allow treatment to be non-binary, so as to accommodate variable treatment intensity (see Angrist and Imbens, 1995). In a linear model, it is straightforward to include covariates (control variables) in the analysis. In this case, all assumptions become conditional upon the vector of control variables x_i, and this may help to defend the exogeneity of the instrument z_i. See Angrist and Krueger (2001) for details and additional references. Deuchert and Huber (2017) critically evaluate the strategy of including control variables to justify conditional independence of the instrument and the potential outcomes, and warn for biases when using post-instrument variables.

Shock-based instruments

In the presence of panel data, instruments often rely on shocks, which are arguably exogenous. For example, Duchin et al. (2010) exploit the fact that some firms were forced to increase the number of outsiders on their boards in response to regulations adopted between 1999 and 2003. Their key model of interest relates changes in firm value (or profitability) to change in board independence, where the letter is instrumented by an indicator whether or not the firm complied with the requirement to have a fully independent audit committee (prior to it being mandated by the Sarbanes-Oxley Act of 2002). Giannetti and Laeven (2009) analyse the causal effects of institutional ownership on firm performance and corporate governance, by exploiting an exogenous shock to institutional ownership caused by the Swedish pension reform in 2000.

Atanasov and Black (2016, 2021) provide a critical discussion of the use of shock-based instrumental variables in finance. A key problem, often overlooked, is that of covariate imbalance. This connects to the assumption of independence. Independence requires that the instrument is as good as randomly assigned and that the instrument affects the outcome only through r_i. The latter also implies there are no other shocks at the same time that affect firm characteristics. If the pre-treatment outcomes (of y_{it}) differ widely between the control and treatment groups, or the values of other firm characteristics, this challenges the assumption that the two groups should be similar. Among other things, Atanasov and Black advocate the use of extensive covariates to assess common support and improve pretreatment balance. If the inclusion of additional covariates greatly affects the estimates, this challenges the assumption that the shock is truly clean.

Another critical discussion of instrumental variables estimates and the role of local average treatment effects is given in Jiang (2017). Although an exogenous shock may substantially affect the probability of treatment, it is typically not assigned completely randomly. Whether or not a firm responds to the shock is, to some extent, up to the firm. Firms that gain most from treatment, or whose constraints to participation were most relaxed by the shock, are more likely to choose treatment. As a result, the estimated LATE tends to be relatively high, because it is based on the compliers (which may be quite different from the larger population of interest).

7.6 Difference-in-differences

In the standard difference-in-differences (DiD) set-up there are two groups of units and two time periods (see, e. g., Card and Krueger, 1994). One group of firms receives treatment in the second period (e. g., is subject to a regulatory change), whereas the other group receives no treatment. Such cases are frequently investigated in the financial literature. For example, Gilje and Taillard (2017) exploit an exogenous change in basis risk in the oil and gas industry in 2012 that affected Canadian oil producers (treatment firms) but not US oil producers (control group). Dimmock and Gerken (2016) investigate the impact of a (temporary) change in 2004 in hedge fund registration upon misreporting by comparing newly regulated funds (treatment group) with those that were not affected by the SEC rule change (control group). Diether et al. (2009a) and Fang et al. (2016), among others, investigate the effects of a pilot programme of the SEC in 2004 in which one-third of the Russell 3000 index were arbitrarily chosen to be exempted from short-sale price tests. The sample in this experiment consists of about 1000 pilot stocks (treatment group) – which started trading without short-sale price tests – and about 2000 control stocks. Importantly, stocks were randomly selected to be in the pilot.

7.6.1 The basic difference-in-differences approach

Denoting the outcome of interest as y_{it}, and the control group by C and the treatment group by T, the standard DiD estimator can be obtained from a simple regression with three dummy explanatory variables

$$y_{it} = \beta_0 + \beta_1 d_{1i} + \gamma d_{post,t} + \delta d_{1i} d_{post,t} + u_{it}, \quad t = 1, 2, \tag{7.46}$$

where $d_{1i} = 1$ if firm i is member of the treatment group T (and 0 otherwise), and where $d_{post,t}$ indicates the post treatment period (i. e., $t = 2$). Assuming that $E(u_{it} \mid d_{1i}) = 0$ for both $t = 1$ and $t = 2$, this structure implies that

$$E(y_{it} \mid d_{1i} = 0, d_{post,t} = 0) = \beta_0,$$
$$E(y_{it} \mid d_{1i} = 0, d_{post,t} = 1) = \beta_0 + \gamma,$$
$$E(y_{it} \mid d_{1i} = 1, d_{post,t} = 0) = \beta_0 + \beta_1,$$
$$E(y_{it} \mid d_{1i} = 1, d_{post,t} = 1) = \beta_0 + \beta_1 + \gamma + \delta.$$

The parameter of interest is the treatment effect, δ, which corresponds to the average treatment effect on the treated (ATT) (see Athey and Imbens, 2006). We can summarise the above parameters in the following table, which highlights the interpretation of δ as a difference-in-differences.

	post	pre	difference
treatment (T)	$\beta_0 + \beta_1 + \gamma + \delta$	$\beta_0 + \beta_1$	$\gamma + \delta$
control (C)	$\beta_0 + \gamma$	β_0	γ
difference	$\beta_1 + \delta$	β_1	δ

The advantage of being able to compare a firm before and after treatment in combination with a control group observed in the same periods is obvious. If we would simply compare the treatment group before and after treatment, the expected difference is $\gamma+\delta$, which captures the true treatment effect only if there is no trend in y_{it} between the pre- and post-treatment periods ($\gamma = 0$). This means that, on average, all changes in y_{it} in group 1 are attributed to the treatment, which is correct if there is no systematic difference across periods (i. e., there is no trend in y_{it}). Alternatively, if we only compare cross-sectionally, and focus on the cross-sectional difference between the treatment and control groups in period 2, the expected difference is $\beta_1 + \delta$, which corresponds to the true treatment effect if there is no systematic difference between the treatment and control groups ($\beta_1 = 0$). The DiD approach eliminates these two potential problems, and isolates δ by differencing away any systematic differences between the two groups and by differencing away any common trend affecting both groups.

The OLS estimator for δ in (7.46) produces the **difference-in-differences estimator**. Straightforward algebra shows that it can be written as

$$\hat{\delta} = (\bar{y}_2^T - \bar{y}_1^T) - (\bar{y}_2^C - \bar{y}_1^C) = \Delta\bar{y}_2^T - \Delta\bar{y}_2^C, \tag{7.47}$$

where $\bar{y}_t^g$ denotes the sample average in group g in period t ($g = C, T$). This expression corresponds to the average change in the outcome variable y_{it} for the treatment group minus that for the control group.[9] With panel data, this estimator can be obtained by applying OLS to

$$\Delta y_{it} = \beta_0 + \delta\Delta r_{it} + \Delta u_{it}, \quad t = 2, \tag{7.48}$$

where β_0 denotes an overall intercept and r_{it} is a treatment indicator, equal to $d_{1i}d_{post,t}$. In the current case, $\Delta r_{it} = r_{it}$ for $t = 2$ because $r_{i1} = 0$ for all firms. This first-differenced equation can also be derived from a model in levels given by

$$y_{it} = \mu_t + \delta r_{it} + \alpha_i + u_{it}, \quad t = 1, 2, \tag{7.49}$$

where μ_t captures aggregate time effects and α_i captures time-invariant firm-specific heterogeneity, both considered as fixed effects. In the two-period case, the fixed effects estimator applied to this equation (with time dummies) reproduces the DiD estimator.[10] This equation shows that the average level of y_{it} of any firm can depend upon a time-invariant unobservable firm-specific component, which is eliminated by the first-difference or within transformation. This allows treatment r_{it} to correlate with unobserved firm-specific heterogeneity, as long as the heterogeneity does not vary over time. This is an attractive property. It allows that selection into treatment depends upon (observed and unobserved) *time-invariant* firm characteristics.

Note that, in comparison to the richer econometric models we have seen earlier in this text, the specification in (7.49) may seem misspecified, as it excludes any time-varying variables that may affect the outcome y_{it}. For the purpose of estimating the

---

9 This estimator, or the OLS estimator in (7.46), can also be calculated in the case of repeated cross-sections, that is, when the same firms are not observed twice. This imposes stronger conditions. Among other things it should already be clear in the pre-treatment period whether any given firm belongs to group C or T, even though it is not observed in period 2. Below, we focus on the panel data case. Attrition from the panel may also affect the availability of post-treatment observations for all firms (see, e. g., Hausman and Wise, 1979).

10 Note that, in general, the fixed effects (within) estimator and the first-difference estimator are different for $T > 2$. See also Chapter 2.

treatment effect, this issue does not matter. Estimating (7.49) with fixed firm effects simply reproduces the DiD estimator given in (7.47). The regression specification may be helpful to appreciate some of the assumption underlying its estimation, particularly so when there are multiple periods and treatment takes place at different points in time for different groups. For example, the usual requirement that the explanatory variables should be strictly exogenous in a fixed effects model (see Section 3.6) requires that r_{it} is uncorrelated with u_{is} for any s. For the purpose of estimating δ, the inclusion of firm fixed effects is not essential. Including a group fixed effect, for the treatment and control groups, leads to exactly the same estimator (and this is often how the regression is written; see, for example, Bertrand et al., 2004). This is because the explanatory variables in (7.49) do not vary across firms, only across groups.[11] Another advantage of the regression framework is that it provides a convenient way to obtain standard errors.

The key assumption behind the difference-in-differences approach is that, in the absence of treatment, the average change in y_{it} would have been the same for both the treated and untreated firms. This is referred to as the **parallel trends assumption**, which is a variation of the unconfoundedness assumption discussed earlier. It says that the trends in y_{it} are similar across both groups. In the language of the alternative outcomes framework, we can formulate this as

Assumption (parallel trends) : $E(\Delta y_{0,it} \mid d_{1i} = 1) = E(\Delta y_{0,it} \mid d_{1i} = 0)$.

This states that the average outcomes for treated and controls would have followed parallel trends in the absence of treatment. In the context of the regression model (7.49), the parallel trends assumption implies that u_{is} is uncorrelated with r_{it}. That is, treatment is not allowed to depend upon unobservable time-varying characteristics (affecting the outcomes y_{is}). Importantly, the treatment indicator r_{it} may be correlated with time-invariant characteristics in α_i, because these are eliminated in the first-differencing. It is also allowed that an overall time shift affects y_{it}, as long as it is invariant across groups, because these differences are eliminated in the second differencing (captured by the fixed time effects in the regression).

Challenges to validity: the parallel trends assumption

The presence of parallel trends in the treatment and control groups is highlighted in Figure 7.2. Parallel trends simply says that, in the absence of treatment, the aggregate development of the outcome variable follows a common time trend across both the treatment and control groups. In the figure, this means that the difference between the aggregate line of the control group and the counterfactual line of the treatment group is constant over time. Although the assumption only relates to the two time periods

---

11 Angrist and Pischke (2009) refer to this as a saturated model.

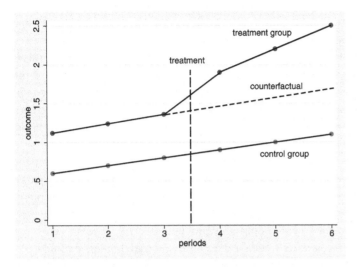

Figure 7.2: Parallel trends.

used to estimate the treatment effect, its validity if often investigated by expanding the time window, as is done in Figure 7.2. The important aspect here is not that the time trend is linear; there is no reason to impose linearity. The important aspect is that the trend is additive. That is, the time effects μ_t in (7.49), in both the treatment and control groups, shift aggregate outcomes by the same amount. This makes the assumption sensitive to the functional form chosen for the dependent variable. For example, it often matters whether the level or the log of a variable is used. Athey and Imbens (2006) have developed a model that is immune to this critique.

To illustrate this, assume there is no genuine effect of treatment. However, treatment is allocated relatively more to larger firms. If the outcome variable is, for example, company sales, and sales exhibit a constant growth rate across both treated and control firms, the growth in sales in $ will be larger for the treatment group than for the control group, simply because treatment is not allocated randomly. (For example, the probability of treatment depends upon α_i.) As a result, a difference-in-difference analysis will mistakenly interpret the higher growth (in $) in the treatment group as the result of the treatment. It therefore makes sense to think about possible differences in composition between the treatment and control groups, and, in relation to this, how the outcome variable would change over time if there was no treatment.

The parallel trends assumption is violated in case there are non-parallel dynamics across the treatment and control groups, and when treatment is not allocated completely randomly. There are many cases where this may arise. For example, treatment may relate to time-varying (observed or unobserved) variables affecting the outcome y_{it}. This can occur if treatment is the outcome of a decision process by the firm (or individual), as this may lead to a selection bias. For example, in labour economics, it has been documented that participants in training programmes experience a decline in earnings prior to the training period (Ashenfelter, 1978), popularly referred to as **Ashenfelter's dip**. Note that, in the context of the two-way fixed effects model, this is a violation of the strict exogeneity of r_{it}. Alternatively, a selection bias may arise if the treatment is endogenous because it targets a group of firms that have experienced unusual values of y_{it} in the pre-treatment period, or a group of firms that is likely to benefit most from treatment. For example, a state may introduce a law to support firms, after firms in this state have done unusually poorly (relative to other states).

To check the validity of the parallel trends assumption, we do not observe the counterfactual outcomes. Thus, we cannot really determine whether there are parallel trends exactly at the point where it matters: just before and after the treatment. Therefore, it is not possible to test the parallel trends assumptions. This, of course, is characteristic of any fundamental endogeneity problem. Instead, scholars rely upon arguments to defend the parallel trends assumption. Such arguments can relate to the way the treatment is allocated to firms, or to the way in which states have implemented regulatory changes. In addition, there are several tests one could do to give more credibility to the parallel trends assumption, or – more generally – to the design of the difference-in-differences set-up. Roberts and Whited (2013) advocate the use of a falsification test by investigating the existence of parallel trends before the treatment takes place. This requires the availability of multiple pre-treatment periods of data, so that one can compare the time trends in y_{it} in the treatment and control groups, well before a treatment actually takes place. This comparison can be based upon a visual inspection, or by means of a formal test. An easy way to do this is by including leads of the treatment indicator in the model; see Heider and Ljungqvist (2015) for an example. This is similar to the test for strict exogeneity (in this case of r_{it}) discussed in Section 3.6. Tests like these are often referred to as **Granger causality tests** (Granger, 1969). Unfortunately, while similar pre-treatment trends are comforting, they are not sufficient to ensure that the endogeneity problem is solved. It is also possible to do a placebo test by means of a difference-in-difference analysis using only pre-event periods (where no effect of the treatment should be present) or using otherwise placebo outcomes that are not supposed to be affected by the treatment. If these placebo tests indicate a nonzero treatment effect, the original DiD estimate is likely to be biased.

The treatment and control groups should be reasonable similar, which would be guaranteed if assignment to treatment is completely random. An example of this is given in Diether et al. (2009a) and other studies, where stocks were randomly selected for a pilot to trade without short-sale price tests. However, in many cases it is likely that some differences exist between the two groups. For example, if the treatment is some law being passed at the state level, firms in the treatment state may have a different industry composition, size distribution, etcetera, compared to firms in the control state. Although one can, to some extent, control for this by including control variables in the difference-in-differences regression, the concern is that any significant differences in observed firm characteristics is also present in unobserved characteristics that affect the outcome variable. Atanasov and Black (2021) stress the need for **pre-treatment balance** between treated and control firms, and challenge the validity of the results in some recent papers. Abadie (2005) proposes a semi-parametric alternative that allows for a common trend, conditional upon one or more covariates.

Inference

Because the difference-in-differences approach is effectively based on a reasonably standard panel regression, much of the discussion on obtaining valid standard errors in Chapter 2 translates to the current setting. For example, adjusting standard errors for heteroskedasticity is easy and often important (see Siegel and Choudhury, 2012, for an example). In addition, it is important to allow for serial correlation in the error term of the equation. This is because the typical outcome variable tends to be quite highly correlated over time, in combination with the fact that the explanatory variables in the model change very little over time (Bertrand et al., 2004). To address the serial correlation problem, one attractive approach, in a multi-period setting, is to collapse the data into two effective periods: before and after. This effectively ignores the time-series variation in the data and analyses averages over all periods before, and all periods after treatment.

Finally, it may be important to allow for some cross-sectional correlation in the error terms. For example, there could be group effects in u_{it}. An obvious choice seems to be to apply clustered standard errors, where clustering is done at the group level, where the group is either the treatment group or the control group. However, this is problematic, because the number of clusters is very small, whereas the validity of clustered standard errors relies upon the number of clusters going to infinity. Donald and Lang (2007) and MacKinnon (2019) elaborate upon this point in the context of DiD estimators. It may be better to impose a more restrictive structure by defining a larger number of clusters, and assuming zero correlation between clusters. In this case, the number of clusters may be sufficiently large (say, 50 or more), but the price one pays is that many cross-sectional correlations are restricted to be zero. See Cameron and Miller (2015) and MacKinnon (2019) for more discussion and alternative approaches.

Including controls

There are several potential reasons why one would include additional controls in the equation to estimate the treatment effect in a difference-in-differences setup. The first is that the inclusion of controls helps to eliminate some of the noise in the equation, and thus leads to a more accurate estimate of the treatment effect. For example, in a model explaining firm leverage from state-level tax changes, it makes sense to control for the usual variables that are found to affect leverage (Heider and Ljungqvist, 2015). If this is the purpose of including control variables, one should not expect the estimated treatment effect to change materially. A second reason is that there are concerns that the assignment to treatment is not sufficiently random. If there are compositional changes in the treatment and control groups, adding (strictly exogenous) control variables can help to alleviate this concern. In this case, the parallel trends becomes a conditional parallel trends assumption. It states that, conditional on the firm characteristics x_{it}, the average outcomes for treated and untreated groups would have followed parallel paths in the absence of treatment. For example, Heider and Ljungqvist (2015) include industry $\times$ year fixed effects, to control for unobserved time-varying industry shocks in leverage. Third, it is possible that the treatment effect is not constant but varies with one or more covariates. This can be accommodated by including interaction terms between the treatment indicator and the relevant covariates.

Note that one should be careful including additional explanatory variables in the model as they may potentially be endogenous and affected by the treatment themselves. Thus, the inclusion of time-varying covariates should be done with care.

7.6.2 Extensions

The double difference-in-difference approach can be extended in a variety of ways. This includes treatments over multiple periods, where treatment may be staggered (e. g., if a particular regulation is imposed sequentially across different locations). The regression framework is also convenient for cases where treatment is not binary, and treatment intensity can vary (as long as the assumption of linearity is appropriate).

It is also possible to perform a triple difference analysis. With multi-period extensions, the assumptions of parallel trends and treatment effects being constant become more challenging. For example, Figure 7.2 illustrates a case where the effect of a treatment gradually increases as time since treatment passes. (Of course, it is also possible that the effect of treatment declines in later periods.) In the absence of counterfactual observations, it becomes more challenging to argue that the time trend of the treatment group is parallel to that of the control group over multiple post-treatment periods. When there are multiple groups receiving treatment at different points in time, which may also experience a different magnitude of the treatment effect, things become even more complex.

Multiple periods and staggered treatments

When multiple periods of data are available, equation (7.49) is extended over multiple periods $t = 1, 2, \ldots, T$, and treatment can take place at different points in time for different groups. A policy change may be effective at different dates across states in the United States, or an exogenous shock may affect firms at different points in time. For example, Derrien and Kecskés (2013) investigate the causal impact of analyst coverage on corporate investment and financing by focusing on firms that lose analyst coverage due to broker closures and mergers between 1994 and 2008. Heider and Ljungqvist

(2015) use a staggered corporate income tax change to investigate how a firm's lever-age is affected by tax increases or decreases; Karpoff and Wittry (2018) explore the effects of state-level antitakeover laws, and argue that a firm's institutional and legal context matter for a correct specification and interpretation.

The above approach then results in a standard two-way fixed effects regression model, that is,

$$y_{it} = \mu_t + \delta r_{it} + \alpha_i + u_{it}, \quad t = 1, \ldots, T. \tag{7.50}$$

It is typically chosen to set $r_{it} = 1$ as long as a particular treatment is "active" for firm i.[12] That is, treatment, for example, a regulatory change, is expected to have a permanent effect of the same magnitude on treated firms. Alternatively, it is possible that the treatment indicator is equal to one only in the treatment period, for example, when a policy is being announced, and zero afterwards. This means that treatment only has a temporary impact on the dependent variable. In this multiple periods set-ting, it is no longer the case that $\Delta r_{it} = r_{it}$. If the treatment indicator r_{it} starts at 0 for all firms, and then changes to 1 at some later time (and remains 1 afterwards), $\Delta r_{it} = 1$ only for the period when the change happens and 0 otherwise. This means that, in the first-difference equation, the relevant indicator is 1 in only one period. For exam-ple, Heider and Ljungqvist (2015) estimate this model for leverage in first differences, including two separate indicators for tax increases and decreases, respectively, or a more general set of variables characterising the tax change. The indicators correspond to whether there was a tax increase (or decrease) in year $t - 1$ and 0 otherwise.

Essentially (7.50) is a standard (two-way) fixed effects model with only one ex-planatory variable, the treatment indicator. Accordingly, for a fixed number of time periods T, the treatment effect δ can be estimated consistently under the condition that r_{it} is *strictly exogenous*. This is restrictive. In the 2×2 case ($T = 2$), where treatment only takes place in period 2, strict exogeneity requires that the treatment indicator is uncorrelated with current and past unobservables in u_{it}. However, with multiple peri-ods available, strict exogeneity also requires that r_{it} is uncorrelated with future values of u_{it}. These requirements also apply if treatment takes place at different points in time across the panel. Consider a policy or regulatory change that is implemented at the state level. It could be that states change their regulations in response to changes in the outcome variable of interest (of the firms in their state), or it could be that firms change their behaviour if they expect that a regulatory change is coming. It may also occur that interested parties are lobbying or otherwise trying to influence legislation if they anticipate to suffer or benefit much from a regulatory change, making the legis-lation process potentially endogenous. For example, based upon earlier studies, Kar-poff and Wittry (2018) provide an overview of state-level antitakeover laws that were

---

[12] This makes being treated an absorbing state.

passed in part because they were promoted by particular firms. In most cases, a firm that was a target of an actual or rumoured takeover bid, lobbied so as to get the antitakeover law approved quickly. For these firms, the enactment of state antitakeover laws is clearly endogenous.

When there is variation in treatment timing, the simple division of the sample into treatment sample and control sample is lost. For example, if group A is not treated, group B experiences treatment in period 2, and group C experiences treatment in period 3, there are three groups of firms (untreated, early treatment, and late treatment) and there are four 2×2 difference-in-differences one could consider (Goodman-Bacon, 2021). For firms that experience early treatment ($t = 2$), the late treatment group also acts as a control group because their treatment status does not vary until $t = 3$. Similarly, firms that are already treated act as controls for firms that experience later treatment. As long as the treatment effect is homogeneous among the different groups, and the parallel trends assumption (which is now somewhat more complicated) is satisfied, this is not a problem. However, with heterogeneous treatment effects, it is not necessarily the case that the two-way fixed effects estimator estimates a sensible average of the individual treatment effects.

For this more general case, the within estimator for δ based on (7.50) can be written as

$$\hat{\delta}_{FE} = \left(\sum_{i,t} \tilde{r}_{it}^2 \right)^{-1} \left(\sum_{i,t} \tilde{r}_{it} \tilde{y}_{it} \right), \tag{7.51}$$

where $\tilde{r}_{it} = (r_{it} - \bar{r}_i) - (\bar{r}_t - \bar{r})$ denotes the treatment indicator after the fixed effects have been removed, $\bar{r}_t = N_t^{-1} \sum_i r_{it}$ denotes the period-specific average, and $\bar{r}$ denotes the overall sample average. While this estimator is easily obtained as a standard panel estimator, it does not easily match to the group means of the different groups that experience treatment at different points in time. Goodman-Bacon (2021) and De Chaisemartin and D'Haultfoeuille (2020) show that the fixed effects estimator in (7.51) is a weighted average of all possible 2×2 difference-in-differences estimators. When the treatment effects vary over groups and time, such weights can become negative. De Chaisemartin and D'Haultfoeuille (2020) show that in exceptional cases, the linear regression coefficient may even be negative while all the ATEs are positive, and propose an alternative estimator that solves this issue. This problem also extends to cases where the model is estimated in first-differences.[13]

A simple example of this is the pattern in Table 7.1, based on De Chaisemartin and D'Haultfoeuille (2020). Treatment is non-stochastic, so there is no selection bias. Group 1 is untreated in period 1 and treated in both periods 2 and 3, while group 2 is

---

13 The *twowayfeweights* package in Stata provides information on the proportion of postive and negative weights, and their averages.

Table 7.1: Staggered treatment with heterogeneous effects.

group	$t = 1$	$t = 2$	$t = 3$
treatment (T1)	0	δ_{12}	δ_{13}
treatment (T2)	0	0	δ_{23}

only treated in period 3. If the three group-specific treatment effects δ_{jt} are not identical, the two-way fixed effects estimator in (7.51) estimates a weighted average, where the weights are different from the proportion that each cell accounts for in the population of treated observations. As a result, $\hat{\delta}_{FE}$ tends to be biased for the overall average treatment effect. Even worse, the weights may become negative. In this example this arises because treated observations of group 1 are used as controls for group 2 in period 3. As stressed by Goodman-Bacon (2021), this "does not imply failure of the design, but it does caution against summarising time-varying effects with a single coefficient". In case of staggered treatment, if the treatment effects vary across units, but not over time (i. e., $\delta_{12} = \delta_{13}$), $\hat{\delta}_{FE}$ provides a variance-weighted average treatment effect. Groups of firms treated in the middle of the sample period receive relatively higher weights compared to groups treated near the beginning or end of the period (Goodman-Bacon, 2021).

Baker et al. (2021) investigate the problem of staggered treatments with treatment effect heterogeneity in the context of finance and accounting applications. Their empirical analysis shows that the problems associated with staggered DiD designs are not just of a theoretical nature, but can have a disturbing impact on the inferences. They also discuss several remedies to eliminate these biases. Most importantly, alternative approaches avoid the use of already treated units as controls for units that are treated later.

Time-varying treatment effects and event studies

In many applications, the impact of a treatment may depend upon how much time has passed since the treatment was experienced. This can be captured by extending the regression model in (7.50) to include lagged values of the treatment indicator. That is,

$$y_{it} = \mu_t + \delta_0 r_{it} + \delta_1 r_{i,t-1} + \cdots + \delta_S r_{i,t-S} + \alpha_i + u_{it}, \tag{7.52}$$

where $r_{i,t-k}$ is an indicator for the treatment group where treatment occurred k periods ago (typically with $r_{is} = 0$ for all $s < 0$). In this case, δ_0 captures the immediate policy effect, and δ_s captures the additional effect s periods after treatment. For this interpretation, it is assumed that the treatment is absorbing so that r_{it} remains 1 in each period after treatment. If $\delta_0 > 0$ and $\delta_1 < 0$, the effect of treatment diminishes after the first period. This model is equivalent to

$$y_{it} = \mu_t + \sum_{k=0}^{S} \gamma_k I(k = t - E_i) + \alpha_i + u_{it}, \tag{7.53}$$

where E_i denotes the time when unit i initially receives the absorbing treatment, and where $\gamma_k = \delta_0 + \cdots + \delta_k$. The indicator functions $I(k = t - E_i)$ indicate that a unit is k periods from the start of treatment (with $k = 0$ corresponding to the treatment period).

Table 7.2 presents the treatment effect parameters from equation (7.53), where time and group fixed effects have been removed. It shows that the treatment effects are homogenous across units and calendar time periods, and depend only on k. Note that, at each point in time one can compare the group that is treated with the group that is never treated (control group C), or with all groups that are not yet treated. (In some applications, the control group C may be empty, as all units are eventually treated.) An important restriction in Table 7.2 is that γ_k does not depend upon the timing of the first treatment. This requires that each cohort experiences the same path of treatment effects. Sun and Abraham (2021) stress that this is a strong assumption, which can be violated for several reasons. For example, units that benefit most from treatment may select their initial treatment earlier in time. Heterogeneity may also be due to cohorts having different characteristics, or because of calendar time effects (such as macroeconomic conditions or stock market sentiment). Callaway and Sant'Anna (2021) provide a more general framework where average treatment effects may vary per cohort and time period, including a discussion of the different treatment effects one could identify, and how these could be summarised in one aggregate ATT (e. g., by calendar time, relative event time, or by the length of the exposure to treatment).

Table 7.2: Staggered treatment with dynamic effects.

group	$t = 1$	$t = 2$	$t = 3$	$t = 4$	$t = 5$
control (C)	0	0	0	0	0
treatment (T1)	0	γ_0	γ_1	γ_2	γ_3
treatment (T2)	0	0	γ_0	γ_1	γ_2
treatment (T3)	0	0	0	γ_0	γ_1

The specification in (7.52) can also be extended to incorporate anticipation effects by including leads of r_{it} in the model, for example, $r_{i,t+1}$. As discussed above, leads of the treatment indicator are also included to test for the existence of differential trends before treatment (to provide ammunition for the validity of the parallel trends assumption). Even though the model is formulated in calendar time this can be thought of as an **event study**. Borusyak et al. (2021) investigate the design of such event studies with dynamic treatment effects and pre-trends, and document some identification issues (if the specification is "too rich"). For example, when firm fixed effects are included and there are no untreated firms, it is not possible to separate calendar time from relative event time.

It is also possible to incorporate separate indicators for the announcement of a regulatory change and the date it becomes effective (see, e,g., Diether et al., 2009a, for an example). Another variant is where the treatment effect is immediate but its magnitude depends upon calendar time. In this case the model specification becomes

$$y_{it} = \mu_t + \delta_t r_{it} + \alpha_i + u_{it}, \quad t = 1, \ldots, T, \tag{7.54}$$

which can be implemented by interacting the treatment indicator by calendar time dummies. Alternatively and equivalently, the treatment effect could vary across the groups being treated. For example, groups that are exposed later to treatment may react differently than those that were exposed before. When the treatment effect δ_t in (7.54) varies with t, the simple estimator in (7.50) is based on a misspecified model and is therefore biased.

Triple differences

In a triple difference or difference-in-difference-in-differences (DDD) model,[14] another differencing step is added to the analysis. There are three reasons for doing this. First, as a means of a robustness check to formally compare the results of the standard DiD analysis with those of a situation where no effect should be present. Second, because there may be a bias in the standard DiD approach, due to a violation of the parallel trends assumption. If it can be argued that this bias is the same in the second difference-in-differences step, doing a triple difference eliminates the bias. Third, because it is expected that the effect of the treatment is different between two subgroups that are treated. On the negative side, triple differencing is likely to lead to increased standard errors of the estimated treatment effect, so one should not use DDD when it is not necessary.

To illustrate the latter, consider Gilje and Taillard (2017), who investigate a quasi-natural experiment in which Canadian light oil producers experience a plausibly exogenous increase in basis risk relative to US light oil producers. Basis risk refers to a hedging friction caused by the fact that the standardised asset used in a financial derivatives contract does not correspond exactly to the underlying risk a firm is exposed to. In early 2012, several events resulted in an unexpected shock in basis risk that affected Canadian firms, but not US firms. The paper estimates a standard DiD model to estimate how treated firms (based in Canada) respond relative to control firms (based in the United States), once their ability to hedge effectively has been curtailed. Because they hypothesise that a negative shock to the effectiveness of hedging

---

14 Sometimes also referred to as triple difference-in-differences.

instruments affect firms with higher ex ante leverage relatively more, they also employ a triple differencing approach by splitting both the treatment and control groups into firms with high and low ex ante leverage. Extending (7.46), the full specification now reads

$$y_{it} = \beta_0 + \beta_1 d_{1i} + \gamma_1 d_{post,t} + \delta_1 d_{1i} d_{post,t} + \beta_2 d_{Hi}$$
$$+ \gamma_2 d_{post,t} d_{Hi} + \beta_3 d_{1i} d_{Hi} + \delta_2 d_{1i} d_{post,t} d_{Hi} + u_{it}, \quad t = 1, 2, \tag{7.55}$$

where d_{Hi} is an indicator for being a high leverage firm, and $d_{1i} = 1$ indicates a treatment firm. The coefficient of interest is δ_2, the coefficient on the triple interaction term. It estimates whether the difference between the differential response of the ex ante highly levered treated firms relative to their highly levered control group and the differential response of the low leverage treated firms relative to their low leverage control group is significant after the basis risk shock. The equation in (7.55) is the standard specification for a DDD analysis, where d_{Hi} can indicate any subgroup that is subject to treatment. The resulting estimator for δ_2 can be shown to equal the difference in two standard DiD estimates; see Atanasov and Black (2016) for more discussion and some concerns with triple differencing.

A recent application making extensive use of the triple difference design is Vuille-mey (2020), who estimates the effect of the introduction of central clearing in 1882 on coffee trade flows in Le Havre, France. The paper exploits the variation between Le Havre and other European markets where clearing is not introduced as well as within Le Havre, between coffee and other commodities. This makes the approach robust against commodity-specific and harbour-specific demand and supply shocks.

Other extensions

The difference-in-differences approach can be combined with other techniques. In cases where there are concerns about the parallel trends assumption, one could combine the DiD regression with the use of instrumental variables, where the instruments should affect treatment but not the group-specific trends. An illustration is Tsoutsoura (2015), who employs DDD in combination with instrumental variables. It is also possible to combine the DiD methods with matching, so as to achieve a sample of treatment and control units that are more similar in terms of covariates (see Lemmon and Roberts, 2010 and Foucault et al., 2011 for some examples).

Finally, the logic of difference-in-differences can also be extended to nonlinear models, such as those discussed in Chapter 6. For example, Jaud et al. (2018) employ a DiD specification in a duration model, where the dependent variable corresponds to an export spell of a particular product. The model is fully specified in the sense that a complete set of explanatory variables is included.

Bibliography

Abadie, A. (2005). Semiparametric Difference-in-Differences Estimators. *Review of Economic Studies 72*, 1–19.

Abadie, A. (2021). Using Synthetic Controls: Feasibility, Data Requirements, and Methodological Aspects. *Journal of Economic Literature 59*, 391–425.

Abadie, A., S. Athey, G. W. Imbens, and J. M. Wooldridge (2017). When Should You Adjust Standard Errors for Clustering? NBER Working Paper 24003.

Abadie, A. and M. D. Cattaneo (2018). Econometric Methods for Program Evaluation. *Annual Review of Economics 10*, 465–503.

Abadie, A., A. Diamond, and J. Hainmueller (2010). Synthetic Control Methods for Comparative Case Studies: Estimating the Effect of California's Tobacco Control Program. *Journal of the American Statistical Association 105*, 493–505.

Abadie, A. and G. W. Imbens (2006). Large Sample Properties of Matching Estimators for Average Treatment Effects. *Econometrica 74*, 235–267.

Abadie, A. and G. W. Imbens (2011). Bias-Corrected Matching Estimators for Average Treatment Effects. *Journal of Business and Economic Statistics 29*, 1–11.

Abrevaya, J. and S. G. Donald (2017). A GMM Approach for Dealing with Missing Data on Regressors. *Review of Economics and Statistics 99*, 657–662.

Acemoglu, D., S. Johnson, A. Kermani, J. Kwak, and T. Mitton (2016). The Value of Connections in Turbulent Times: Evidence from the United States. *Journal of Financial Economics 121*, 368–391.

Acemoglu, D., S. Johnson, and J. A. Robinson (2001). The Colonial Origins of Comparative Development: An Empirical Investigation. *American Economic Review 91*, 1369–1401.

Acharya, S. (1988). A Generalized Econometric Model and Tests of a Signalling Hypothesis with Two Discrete Outcomes. *Journal of Finance 43*, 413–429.

Acharya, S. (1993). Value of Latent Information: Alternative Event Study Methods. *Journal of Finance 48*, 363–385.

Acharya, V. V., H. Almeida, and M. Campello (2013). Aggregate Risk and the Choice between Cash and Lines of Credit. *Journal of Finance 68*, 2059–2116.

Adams, J., D. Hayunga, and S. Mansi (2018). Diseconomies of Scale in the Actively-Managed Mutual Fund Industry: What Do the Outliers in the Data Tell Us? *Critical Finance Review 7*, 1–48.

Adams, J., D. Hayunga, S. Mansi, D. Reeb, and V. Verardi (2019). Identifying and Treating Outliers in Finance. *Financial Management 48*, 345–384.

Adams, R. B., H. Almeida, and D. Ferreira (2005). Powerful CEOs and Their Impact on Corporate Performance. *Review of Financial Studies 18*, 1403–1432.

Adams, R. B., B. E. Hermalin, and M. S. Weisbach (2010). The Role of Boards of Directors in Corporate Governance: A Conceptual Framework and Survey. *Journal of Economic Literature 48*, 58–107.

Afonso, A., P. Gomes, and P. Rother (2009). Ordered Response Models for Sovereign Debt Ratings. *Applied Economics Letters 16*, 769–777.

Agarwal, V., R. Vashishtha, and M. Venkatachalam (2018). Mutual Fund Transparency and Corporate Myopia. *Review of Financial Studies 31*, 1966–2003.

Aghion, P., J. Van Reenen, and L. Zingales (2013). Innovation and Institutional Ownership. *American Economic Review 103*, 277–304.

Ahern, K. R. and A. K. Dittmar (2012). The Changing of the Boards: The Impact of Firm Valuation of Mandated Female Board Representation. *Quarterly Journal of Economics 125*, 137–197.

Ai, C. and E. Norton (2003). Interaction Terms in Logit and Probit Models. *Economics Letters 80*, 123–129.

Almeida, H. and M. Campello (2007). Financial Constraints, Asset Tangibility, and Corporate Investment. *Review of Financial Studies 20*, 1429–1460.

https://doi.org/10.1515/9783110660739-008

Almeida, H., M. Campello, and A. F. Jr. Galvao (2010). Measurement Errors in Investment Equations. *Review of Financial Studies 23*, 3279–3328.

Almeida, H., I. Cunha, M. A. Ferreira, and F. Restrepo (2017). The Real Effects of Credit Ratings: The Sovereign Ceiling Channel. *Journal of Finance 72*, 249–290.

Almeida, H., V. Fos, and M. Kronlund (2016). The Real Effects of Share Repurchases. *Journal of Financial Economics 119*, 168–185.

Alvarez, J. and M. Arellano (2003). The Time Series and Cross-Section Asymptotics of Dynamic Panel Data Estimators. *Econometrica 71*, 1121–1159.

Amemiya, T. (1984). Tobit Models: A Survey. *Journal of Econometrics 24*, 3–61.

Anderson, R. C. and D. M. Reeb (2003). Founding Family Ownership and Firm Performance: Evidence from the S&P 500. *Journal of Finance 58*, 1301–1328.

Anderson, T. and C. Hsiao (1981). Estimation of Dynamic Models with Error Components. *Journal of the American Statistical Association 76*, 598–606.

Anderson, T. W. and H. Rubin (1949). Estimation of the Parameters of a Single Equation in a Complete System of Stochastic Equations. *Annals of Mathematical Statistics 20*, 46–63.

Andrews, I., J. H. Stock, and L. Sun (2019). Weak Instruments in Instrumental Variables Regression: Theory and Practice. *Annual Review of Economics 11*, 727–753.

Ang, A., J. Liu, and K. Schwarz (2020). Using Stocks or Portfolios in Tests of Factor Models. *Journal of Financial and Quantitative Analysis 55*, 709–750.

Angerer, X. and P.-S. Lam (2009). Income Risk and Portfolio Choice: An Empirical Study. *Journal of Finance 64*, 1037–1055.

Angrist, J. D. and G. W. Imbens (1995). Two-Stage Least Squares Estimates of Average Causal Effects in Models with Variable Treatment Intensity. *Journal of the American Statistical Association 90*, 431–442.

Angrist, J. D. and A. B. Krueger (1991). Does Compulsory School Attendance Affect Schooling and Earnings? *Quarterly Journal of Economics 106*, 979–1014.

Angrist, J. D. and A. B. Krueger (2001). Instrumental Variables and the Search for Identification: From Supply and Demand to Natural Experiments. *Journal of Economic Perspectives 15*, 69–85.

Angrist, J. D. and J.-S. Pischke (2009). *Mostly Harmless Econometrics: An Empiricist's Companion.* Princeton University Press.

Angrist, J. D. and J.-S. Pischke (2015). *Mastering 'Metrics: The Path from Cause to Effect.* Princeton University Press.

Appel, I. R., T. A. Gormley, and D. B. Keim (2021). Identification Using Russell 1000/2000 Index Assignments: A Discussion of Methodologies. *Critical Finance Review* (forthcoming).

Arellano, M. (1987). Computing Robust Standard Errors for Within-Group Estimators. *Oxford Bulletin of Economics and Statistics 49*, 431–434.

Arellano, M. (1989). A Note on the Anderson-Hsiao Estimator for Panel Data. *Economics Letters 31*, 337–341.

Arellano, M. (2003). *Panel Data Econometrics.* Oxford University Press, Oxford, UK.

Arellano, M. and S. Bond (1991). Some Tests of Specification for Panel Data: Monte Carlo Evidence and an Application to Employment Equations. *Review of Economic Studies 58*, 277–294.

Arellano, M. and S. Bonhomme (2016). Nonlinear Panel Data Estimation via Quantile Regressions. *Econometrics Journal 19*, C61–C94.

Arellano, M. and O. Bover (1995). Another Look at the Instrumental Variable Estimation of Error Components Models. *Journal of Econometrics 68*, 29–51.

Ashbaugh-Skaife, H., D. W. Collins, and R. LaFond (2006). The Effects of Corporate Governance on Firms' Credit Ratings. *Journal of Accounting and Economics 42*, 203–243.

Ashenfelter, O. (1978). Estimating the Effect of Training Programs on Earnings. *Review of Economics and Statistics 60*, 47–57.

Atanasov, V. and B. Black (2016). Shock-Based Causal Inference in Corporate Finance and Accounting Research. *Critical Finance Review 5*, 207–304.

Atanasov, V. and B. Black (2021). The Trouble with Instruments: The Need for Pretreatment Balance in Shock-Based Instrumental Variable Designs. *Management Science 67*, 1270–1302.

Athey, S. and G. W. Imbens (2006). Identification and Inference in Nonlinear Difference-in-Differences Models. *Econometrica 74*, 431–497.

Bach, L. and D. Metzger (2019). How Close Are Close Shareholder Votes? *Review of Financial Studies 32*, 3183–3214.

Bae, K.-H. and V. K. Goyal (2009). Creditor Rights, Enforcement, and Bank Loans. *Journal of Finance 64*, 823–860.

Baker, A. C., D. F. Larcker, and C. C. Y. Wang (2021). How Much Should We Trust Staggered Difference-in-Differences Estimates? Working paper 736, European Corporate Governance Institute.

Balestra, P. and M. Nerlove (1966). Pooling Cross Section and Time Series Data in the Estimation of a Dynamic Model: The Demand for Natural Gas. *Econometrica 34*, 585–612.

Ball, R. and L. Shivakumar (2005). Earnings Quality in UK Private Firms: Comparative Loss Recognition Timeliness. *Journal of Accounting and Economics 39*, 83–128.

Baltagi, B. H. (2013). *Econometric Analysis of Panel Data* (5th ed.). John Wiley and Sons, Chichester, UK.

Baltagi, B. H. and G. Bresson (2015). *Robust Panel Data Methods and Influential Observations*, Chapter in: Oxford Handbook of Panel Data (edited by B. H. Baltagi), pp. 418–452. Oxford University Press, Oxford, UK.

Baquero, G., J. R. ter Horst, and M. Verbeek (2005). Survival, Look-Ahead Bias and Persistence in Hedge Fund Performance. *Journal of Financial and Quantitative Analysis 35*, 327–342.

Barber, B. M., X. Huang, and T. Odean (2016). Which Factors Matter to Investors? Evidence from Mutual Fund Flows. *Review of Financial Studies 29*, 2600–2642.

Barber, B. M., A. Morse, and A. Yasuda (2021). Impact Investing. *Journal of Financial Economics 139*, 162–185.

Barclay, M. J., C. G. Holderness, and J. Pontiff (1993). Private Benefits from Block Ownership and Discounts on Closed-End Funds. *Journal of Financial Economics 33*, 263–291.

Barro, R. J. (2006). Rare Disasters and Asset Markets in the Twentieth Century. *Quarterly Journal of Economics 121*, 823–866.

Bazdresch, S., R. J. Kahn, and T. M. Whited (2018). Estimating and Testing Dynamic Corporate Finance Models. *Review of Financial Studies 31*, 322–361.

Bazzi, S. and M. A. Clements (2013). Blunt Instruments: Avoiding Common Pitfalls in Identifying the Causes of Economic Growth. *American Economic Journal: Macroeconomics 5*, 152–186.

Beaver, W. H., M. F. McNichols, and J.-W. Rhie (2005). Have Financial Statements Become Less Informative? Evidence from the Ability of Financial Ratios to Predict Bankruptcy. *Review of Accounting Studies 10*, 93–122.

Beck, T., R. Levine, and N. Loayza (2000). Finance and the Sources of Growth. *Journal of Financial Economics 58*, 261–300.

Becker, B. and P. Strömberg (2012). Fiduciary Duties and Equity-Debtholder Conflicts. *Review of Financial Studies 25*, 1931–1969.

Bellemare, M. F., T. Masaki, and T. B. Pepinsky (2017). Lagged Explanatory Variables and the Estimation of Causal Effect. *Journal of Politics 79*, 949–963.

Bena, J., M. A. Ferreira, P. Matos, and P. Pires (2017). Are Foreign Investors Locusts? The Long-Term Effects of Foreign Institutional Ownership. *Journal of Financial Economics 126*, 122–146.

Bennedsen, M., K. Nielsen, F. Perez-Gonzalez, and D. Wolfenzon (2007). Inside the Family Firm: The Role of Family in Succession Decisions and Performance. *Quarterly Journal of Economics 122*, 647–691.

Bennedsen, M., F. Pérez-González, and D. Wolfenzon (2020). Do CEOs Matter? Evidence from Hospitalization Events. *Journal of Finance 75*, 1877–1911.

Berg, T. (2015). Playing the Devil's Advocate: The Causal Effect of Risk Management on Loan Quality. *Review of Financial Studies 28*, 3367–3406.

Berg, T., M. Reisinger, and D. Streitz (2021). Spillover Effects in Empirical Corporate Finance. *Journal of Financial Economics* (forthcoming).

Berk, J. and R. Green (2004). Mutual Fund Flows and Performance in Rational Markets. *Jounal of Political Economy 112*, 1269–1295.

Berndt, E., B. Hall, R. Hall, and J. Hausman (1974). Estimation and Inference in Nonlinear Structural Models. *Annals of Economic and Social Measurement 3*, 653–665.

Bernstein, S., E. Colonnelli, X. Giroud, and B. Iverson (2019). Bankruptcy Spillovers. *Journal of Financial Economics 133*, 608–633.

Bertrand, M., E. Duflo, and S. Mullainathan (2004). How Much Should We Trust Differences-in-Differences Estimates? *Quarterly Journal of Economics 119*, 249–275.

Bertrand, M. and S. Mullainathan (2003). Enjoying the Quiet Life? Corporate Governance and Managerial Preferences. *Journal of Political Economy 111*, 1043–1075.

Bertrand, M. and A. Schoar (2003). Managing with Style: The Effect of Managers on Firm Policies. *Quarterly Journal of Economics 118*, 1169–1208.

Bester, C., T. Conley, and C. Hansen (2011). Inference for Dependent Data Using Cluster Covariance Matrix Estimators. *Journal of Econometrics 165*, 137–151.

Bhagat, S. and B. Bolton (2008). Corporate Governance and Firm Performance. *Journal of Corporate Finance 14*, 257–273.

Bhargava, A., L. Franzini, and W. Narendranathan (1982). Serial Correlation and the Fixed Effects Model. *Review of Economic Studies 49*, 533–549.

Billett, M. T. and H. Xue (2007). The Takeover Deterrent Effect of Open Market Share Repurchases. *Journal of Finance 62*, 1827–1850.

Biørn, E. (2000). Panel Data With Measurement Errors: Instrumental Variables and GMM Procedures Combining Levels And Differences. *Econometric Reviews 19*, 391–424.

Black, D. A., M. C. Berger, and F. A. Scott (2000). Bounding Parameter Estimates with Nonclassical Measurement Error. *Journal of the American Statistical Association 95*, 739–748.

Black, S. E., P. J. Devereux, P. Lundborg, and K. Majlesi (2017). On the Origins of Risk-Taking in Financial Markets. *Journal of Finance 72*, 2229–2277.

Bland, J. R. and A. C. Cook (2019). Random Effects Probit and Logit: Understanding Predictions and Marginal Effects. *Applied Economics Letters 26*, 116–123.

Blume, M. E., F. Lim, and A. C. MacKinlay (1998). The Declining Credit Quality of U.S. Corporate Debt: Myth or Reality? *Journal of Finance 53*, 1389–1413.

Blundell, R. and S. Bond (1998). Initial Conditions and Moment Restrictions in Dynamic Panel Data Models. *Journal of Econometrics 87*, 115–143.

Blundell, R., S. Bond, M. Devereux, and F. Schiantarelli (1992). Investment and Tobin's Q: Evidence from Company Panel Data. *Journal of Econometrics 51*, 233–257.

Bollinger, C. R. (1996). Bounding Mean Regressions When a Binary Regressor is Mismeasured. *Journal of Econometrics 73*, 387–399.

Bonaparte, Y., G. M. Korniotis, and A. Kumar (2014). Income Hedging and Portfolio Decisions. *Journal of Financial Economics 113*, 300–324.

Bond, S. (2002). Dynamic Panel Data Models: A Guide to Micro Data Methods and Practice. *Portuguese Economic Journal 1*, 141–162.

Bonhomme, S. and E. Manresa (2015). Grouped Patterns of Heterogeneity in Panel Data. *Econometrica 83*, 1147–1184.

Boone, A. L. and J. T. White (2015). The Effect of Institutional Ownership on Firm Transparancy and Information Production. *Journal of Financial Economics 117*, 508–533.

Born, B. and J. Breitung (2016). Testing for Serial Correlation in Fixed-Effects Panel Data Models. *Econometric Reviews 35*, 1290–1316.

Borusyak, K., X. Jaravel, and J. Spiess (2021). Revisiting Event Study Designs: Robust and Efficient Estimation. Working paper, University College London.

Bound, J., D. Jaeger, and R. Baker (1995). Problems with Instrumental Variables Estimation when the Correlation between the Instrument and the Endogenous Variable is Weak. *Journal of the American Statistical Association 90*, 443–450.

Bowen, D. E., L. Frésard, and J. P. Taillard (2017). What's Your Identification Strategy? Innovation in Corporate Finance Research. *Management Science 63*, 2529–2548.

Boyson, N. M., N. Gantchev, and A. Shivdasani (2017). Activism Mergers. *Journal of Financial Economics 126*, 54–73.

Bradley, M., A. Brav, I. Goldstein, and W. Jiang (2010). Activist Arbitrage: A Study of Open-Ending Attempts of Closed-End Funds. *Journal of Financial Economics 95*, 1–19.

Brennan, M. J., T. Chordia, and A. Subrahmanyam (1998). Alternative Factor Specifications, Security Characteristics, and the Cross-Section of Expected Stock Returns. *Journal of Financial Economics 49*, 345–373.

Breusch, T. and A. Pagan (1980). A Simple Test for Heteroskedasticity and Random Coefficient Variation. *Econometrica 47*, 1287–1294.

Brockman, P. and E. Unlu (2009). Dividend Policy, Creditor Rights, and the Agency Costs of Debt. *Journal of Financial Economics 92*, 276–299.

Brodeur, A., N. Cook, and A. Heyes (2020). Methods Matter: *p*-Hacking and Publication Bias in Causal Analysis in Economics. *American Economic Review 110*, 3634–3660.

Brodeur, A., M. Lé, M. Sagnier, and Y. Zylberberg (2016). Star Wars: The Empirics Strikes Back. *American Economic Journal: Applied Economics 8*, 1–32.

Brooks, C. (2019). *Introductory Econometrics for Finance* (4th ed.). Cambridge University Press.

Brown, J. R., N. Liang, and S. Weisbenner (2007). Executive Financial Incentives and Payout Policy: Firm Responses to the 2003 Dividend Tax Cut. *Journal of Finance 62*, 1935–1965.

Bruno, G. S. F. (2005). Approximating the Bias of the LSDV Estimator for Dynamic Unbalanced Panel Data Models. *Economics Letters 87*, 361–366.

Bun, M. J. G. and V. Sarafidis (2015). *Dynamic Panel Data Models*, Chapter in: Oxford Handbook of Panel Data (edited by B. H. Baltagi), pp. 76–110. Oxford University Press.

Bun, M. J. G. and F. Windmeijer (2010). The Weak Instrument Problem of the System GMM Estimator in Dynamic Panel Data Models. *Econometrics Journal 13*, 95–126.

Callaway, B. and P. H. C. Sant'Anna (2021). Difference-in-Differences with Multiple Time Periods. *Journal of Econometrics* (forthcoming).

Calonico, S., M. D. Cattaneo, M. H. Farrell, and R. Titiunik (2017). rdrobust: Software for Regression-Discontinuity Designs. *Stata Journal 17*, 372–404.

Calonico, S., M. D. Cattaneo, and R. Titiunik (2014). Robust Nonparametric Confidence Intervals for Regression-Discontinuity Designs. *Econometrica 82*, 2295–2326.

Cameron, A. C., J. B. Gelbach, and D. L. Miller (2008). Bootstrap-Based Improvements for Inference with Clustered Errors. *Journal of Business and Economic Statistics 90*, 414–427.

Cameron, A. C., J. B. Gelbach, and D. L. Miller (2011). Robust Inference With Multiway Clustering. *Journal of Business and Economic Statistics 29*, 238–249.

Cameron, A. C. and D. L. Miller (2015). A Practitioner's Guide to Cluster-Robust Inference. *Journal of Human Resources 50*, 317–372.

Cameron, A. C. and P. K. Trivedi (2005). *Microeconometrics. Methods and Applications*. Cambridge University Press.

Cameron, A. C. and P. K. Trivedi (2013). *Regression Analysis of Count Data* (2nd ed.). Cambridge University Press.

Cameron, A. C. and P. K. Trivedi (2015). *Count Panel Data*, Chapter in: Oxford Handbook of Panel Data (edited by B. H. Baltagi), pp. 233–256. Oxford University Press.

Cameron, A. C. and P. K. Trivedi (2021). *Microeconometrics Using Stata* (2nd ed.). Stata Press, Texas.

Campa, J. M. and S. Kedia (2002). Explaining the Diversification Discount. *Journal of Finance 57*, 1731–1762.

Campbell, J. Y., A. W. Lo, and A. C. MacKinlay (1997). *The Econometrics of Financial Markets*. Princeton University Press.

Canay, I. A. (2011). A Simple Approach to Quantile Regression for Panel Data. *The Econometrics Journal 14*, 368–386.

Card, D. and A. B. Krueger (1994). Minimum Wages and Employment: A Case Study of the Fast-Food Industry in New Jersey and Pennsylvania. *American Economic Review 84*, 772–793.

Cattaneo, M. D., N. Idrobo, and R. Titiunik (2020). *A Practical Introduction to Regression Discontinuity Designs: Foundations*. Elements in Quantitative and Computational Methods for the Social Sciences. Cambridge University Press. doi:10.1017/9781108684606.

Cattaneo, M. D., M. Jansson, and X. Ma (2018). Manipulation Testing Based on Density Discontinuity. *Stata Journal 18*, 234–261.

Cerulli, G. (2014). ivtreatreg: A Command for Fitting Binary Treatment Models with Heterogeneous Response to Treatment and Unobservable Selection. *Stata Journal 14*, 453–480.

Cerulli, G. (2015). *Econometric Evaluation of Socio-Economic Programs: Theory and Applications*. Springer.

Chakravarty, S., H. Gulen, and S. Mayhew (2004). Informed Trading in Stock and Option Markets. *Journal of Finance 59*, 1235–1257.

Chamberlain, G. (1980). Analysis of Covariance with Qualitative Data. *Review of Economic Studies 47*, 225–238.

Chava, S. and M. R. Roberts (2008). How Does Financing Impact Investment? The Role of Debt Covenants. *Journal of Finance 63*, 2085–2121.

Chen, H. J. and S. J. Chen (2012). Investment-Cash Flow Sensitivity Cannot Be a Good Measure of Financial Constraints: Evidence from the Time Series. *Journal of Financial Economics 105*, 393–410.

Chen, J., H. Hong, M. Huang, and J. D. Kubik (2004). Does Fund Size Erode Mutual Fund Performance? The role of Liquidity and Organization. *American Economic Review 94*, 1276–1302.

Chen, N.-F., R. Roll, and S. A. Ross (1986). Economic Forces and the Stock Market. *Journal of Business 59*, 383–403.

Chen, Q., I. Goldstein, and W. Jiang (2008). Directors' Ownership in the U.S. Mutual Fund Industry. *Journal of Finance 63*, 2629–2677.

Choe, H., B. Kho, and R. M. Stulz (2005). Do Domestic Investors Have an Edge? The Trading Experience of Foreign Investors in Korea. *Review of Financial Studies 18*, 795–829.

Christiansen, C., J. Schröter Joensen, and J. Rangvid (2007). Are Economists More Likely to Hold Stocks? *Review of Finance 12*, 465–496.

Christopherson, J. A., W. E. Ferson, and D. A. Glassman (1998). Conditioning Manager Alphas on Economic Information: Another Look at the Persistence of Performance. *Review of Financial Studies 11*, 111–142.

Cleves, M., W. W. Gould, and Y. V. Marchenko (2016). *An Introduction to Survival Analysis Using Stata* (Revised 3rd ed.). Stata Press, Texas.

Cochrane, J. H. (2005). *Asset Pricing* (Revised ed.). Princeton University Press.

Cole, S., T. Sampson, and B. Zia (2011). Prices or Knowledge? What Drives Demand for Financial Services in Emerging Markets? *Journal of Finance 66*, 1933–1967.

Coles, J. L., N. D. Daniel, and L. Naveen (2006). Managerial Incentives and Risk-Taking. *Journal of Financial Economics 79*, 431–468.

Colla, P., F. Ippolito, and K. Li (2013). Debt Specialization. *Journal of Finance 68*, 2117–2141.

Conley, T., S. Goncalves, and C. Hansen (2018). Inference with Dependent Data in Accounting and Finance Applications. *Journal of Accounting Research 56*, 1139–1203.

Conley, T., C. Hansen, and P. Rossi (2012). Plausibly Exogenous. *Review of Economics and Statistics 94*, 260–272.

Cook, T. D. (2008). "Waiting for Life to Arrive": A History of the Regression-Discontinuity Design in Psychology, Statistics and Economics. *Journal of Econometrics 142*, 636–654.

Cooper, M. J., H. Gulen, and P. R. Rau (2005). Changing Names with Style: Mutual Fund Name Changes and Their Effects on Fund Flows. *Journal of Finance 60*, 2825–2858.

Correia, S. (2015). Singletons, Cluster-Robust Standard Errors and Fixed Effects: A Bad Mix. Working paper, Duke University.

Correia, S. (2016). Linear Models with High-Dimensional Fixed Effects: An Efficient and Feasible Estimator. Working paper, http://scorreia.com/research/hdfe.pdf.

Coval, J. D. and T. Shumway (2005). Do Behavioral Biases Affect Asset Prices? *Journal of Finance 60*, 1–34.

Cox, D. R. (1972). Regression Models and Life-Tables. *Journal of the Royal Statistical Society, Series B (Methodological) 34*, 187–220.

Crane, A. D., S. Michenaud, and J. P. Weston (2014). The Effect of Institutional Ownership on Payout Policy: Evidence from Index Thresholds. *Review of Financial Studies 29*, 1377–1408.

Cuñat, V., M. Gine, and M. Guadalupe (2012). The Vote Is Cast: The Effect of Corporate Governance on Shareholder Value. *Journal of Finance 67*, 1943–1977.

Cunningham, S. (2021). *Causal Inference: The Mixtape.* Yale University Press.

Dang, V. A., M. Kim, and Y. Shin (2015). In Search of Robust Methods for Dynamic Panel Data Models in Empirical Corporate Finance. *Journal of Banking and Finance 53*, 84–98.

Dardanoni, V., S. Modica, and F. Peracchi (2011). Regression with Imputed Covariates: A Generalized Missing-Indicator Approach. *Journal of Econometrics 162*, 362–368.

Dass, N. and M. Massa (2011). The Impact of a Strong Bank-Firm Relationship on the Borrowing Firm. *Review of Financial Studies 24*, 1204–1260.

Davidson, R. and J. MacKinnon (2004). *Econometric Theory and Methods.* Oxford University Press, Oxford, UK.

Davidson, R. and J. G. MacKinnon (1993). *Estimation and Inference in Econometrics.* Oxford University Press, Oxford, UK.

De Chaisemartin, C. and X. D'Haultfoeuille (2020). Two-Way Fixed Effects Estimators with Heterogeneous Treatment Effects. *American Economic Review 110*, 2964–2996.

DeAngelo, H., L. DeAngelo, and R. M. Stulz (2006). Dividend Policy and the Earned/Contributed Capital Mix: A Test of the Life-Cycle Theory. *Journal of Financial Economics 81*, 227–254.

Deaton, A. (2010). Instruments, Randomization, and Learning about Development. *Journal of Economic Literature 48*, 424–455.

Dehejia, R. H. and S. Wahba (2002). Propensity Score-Matching Methods for Nonexperimental Causal Studies. *Review of Economics and Statistics 84*, 151–161.

Denis, D. J. and I. Osobov (2008). Why Do Firm Pay Dividends? International Evidence on the Determinants of Dividend Policy. *Journal of Financial Economics 89*, 62–82.

Derrien, F. and A. Kecskés (2013). The Real Effects of Financial Shocks: Evidence from Exogenous Changes in Analyst Coverage. *Journal of Finance 68*, 1407–1440.

Deuchert, E. and M. Huber (2017). A Cautionary Tale About Control Variables in IV Estimation. *Oxford Bulletin of Economics and Statistics 79*, 411–425.

Diether, K. B., K.-H. Lee, and I. M. Werner (2009a). It's SHO Time! Short-Sale Price Tests and Market Quality. *Journal of Finance 64*, 37–73.

Diether, K. B., K.-H. Lee, and I. M. Werner (2009b). Short-Sale Strategies and Return Predictability. *Review of Financial Studies 22*, 575–607.

Dimmock, S. G. and W. C. Gerken (2016). Regulatory Oversight and Return Misreporting by Hedge Funds. *Review of Finance 20*, 795–821.

Dittmar, A. K. (2000). Why Do Firms Repurchase Stock? *Journal of Business 73*, 331–355.

Dittmar, A. K. (2004). Capital Structure in Corporate Spin-Offs. *Journal of Business 77*, 9–43.

Dittmar, A. K. and J. Mahrt-Smith (2007). Corporate Governance and the Value of Cash Holdings. *Journal of Financial Economics 83*, 599–634.

Dittmar, A. K. and A. Thakor (2007). Why Do Firms Issue Equity? *Journal of Finance 62*, 1–54.

Donald, S. G. and K. Lang (2007). Inference with Difference-in-Differences and Other Panel Data. *Review of Economics and Statistics 89*, 221–233.

Driscoll, J. and A. C. Kraay (1998). Consistent Covariance Matrix Estimation with Spatially Dependent Data. *Review of Economics and Statistics 80*, 549–560.

Duchin, R., J. G. Matsusaka, and O. Ozbas (2010). When Are Outside Directors Effective? *Journal of Financial Economics 96*, 195–214.

Duflo, E. and E. Saez (2003). The Role of Information and Social Interactions in Retirement Plan Decisions: Evidence from a Randomized Experiment. *Quarterly Journal of Economics 118*, 815–842.

Dyakov, T., H. Jiang, and M. Verbeek (2020). Trade Less and Exit Overcrowded Markets: Lessons from International Mutual Funds. *Review of Finance 24*, 677–731.

Edmans, A., I. Goldstein, and W. Jiang (2012). The Real Effects of Financial Markets: The Impact of Prices on Takeovers. *Journal of Finance 67*, 933–971.

Ellul, A. and V. Yerramilli (2013). Stronger Risk Controls, Lower Risk: Evidence from U.S. Bank Holding Companies. *Journal of Finance 68*, 1757–1803.

Elsas, R. and D. Florysiak (2015). Dynamic Capital Structure Adjustment and the Impact of Fractional Dependent Variables. *Journal of Financial and Quantitative Analysis 50*, 1105–1133.

Engelberg, J. E. and C. A. Parsons (2011). The Causal Impact of Media in Financial Markets. *Journal of Finance 66*, 67–97.

Erickson, T., C. H. Jiang, and T. M. Whited (2014). Minimum Distance Estimation of the Errors-in-Variables Model Using Linear Cumulant Equations. *Journal of Econometrics 183*, 211–221.

Erickson, T. and T. M. Whited (2000). Measurement Error and the Relationship between Investment and q. *Journal of Political Economy 108*, 1027–1057.

Erickson, T. and T. M. Whited (2012). Treating Measurement Error in Tobin's q. *Review of Financial Studies 25*, 1286–1329.

Falkenstein, E. G. (1996). Preferences for Stock Characteristics as Revealed by Mutual Fund Portfolio Holdings. *Journal of Finance 51*, 111–135.

Fama, E. F. and J. D. MacBeth (1973). Risk, Return, and Equilibrium: Empirical Tests. *Journal of Political Economy 81*, 607–636.

Fama, E. F. and K. R. French (1988). Permanent and Temporary Components of Stock Prices. *Journal of Political Economy 96*, 246–273.

Fama, E. F. and K. R. French (1992). The Cross-Section of Expected Returns. *Journal of Finance 47*, 427–465.

Fama, E. F. and K. R. French (1993). Common Risk Factors in the Returns on Stocks and Bonds. *Journal of Financial Economics 33*, 3–56.

Fama, E. F. and K. R. French (2001). Disappearing Dividends: Changing Firm Characteristics or Lower Propensity to Pay? *Journal of Financial Economics 60*, 3–43.

Fama, E. F. and K. R. French (2002). Testing Trade-Off and Pecking Order Predictions About Dividends and Debt. *Review of Financial Studies 15*, 1–33.

Fang, L. H. (2005). Investment Bank Reputation and the Price and Quality of Underwriting Services. *Journal of Finance 60*, 2729–2761.

Fang, V. W., A. H. Huang, and J. M. Karpoff (2016). Short Selling and Earnings Management: A Controlled Experiment. *Journal of Finance 71*, 1251–1293.

Fee, C. E., C. J. Hadlock, and J. R. Pierce (2013). Managers with and without Style: Evidence Using Exogenous Variation. *Review of Financial Studies 26*, 567–601.

Fich, E. M. and A. Shivdasani (2006). Are Busy Boards Effective Monitors? *Journal of Finance 61*, 689–724.

Flammer, C. (2015). Does Corporate Social Responsibility Lead to Superior Financial Performance? A Regression Discontinuity Approach. *Management Science 61*, 2549–2568.

Flannery, M. J. and K. Rangan (2006). Partial Adjustment toward Target Capital Structures. *Journal of Financial Economics 79*, 469–506.

Flannery, M. J. and K. W. Hankins (2013). Estimating Dynamic Panel Models in Corporate Finance. *Journal of Corporate Finance 19*, 1–19.

Foucault, T., D. Sraer, and D. J. Thesmar (2011). Individual Investors and Volatility. *Journal of Finance 66*, 1369–1406.

Frank, M. Z. and V. K. Goyal (2008). *Trade-off and Pecking Order Theories of Debt*, Chapter in: Handbook of Corporate Finance, Volume 2 (edited by B. E. Eckbo), pp. 135–202. North-Holland, Elsevier.

Gallen, T. and B. Raymond (2020). Broken Instruments. Working paper, available at SSRN, https://ssrn.com/abstract=3671850.

Gelman, A. and G. W. Imbens (2019). Why High-Order Polynomials Should Not Be Used in Regression Discontinuity Designs. *Journal of Business and Economic Statistics 37*, 447–456.

Gerard, F., M. Rokkanen, and C. Rothe (2020). Bounds on Treatment Effects in Regression Discontinuity Designs with a Manipulated Running Variable. *Quantitative Economics 11*, 839–870.

Gézky, C., B. A. Minton, and C. Schrand (1997). Why Firms Use Currency Derivatives. *Journal of Finance 52*, 1323–1354.

Giannetti, M. and L. Laeven (2009). Pension Reform, Ownership Structure, and Corporate Governance: Evidence from a Natural Experiment. *Review of Financial Studies 22*, 4092–4127.

Gibbons, M. R., S. A. Ross, and J. Shanken (1989). A Test of the Efficiency of a Given Portfolio. *Econometrica 57*, 1121–1152.

Gilje, E. P. and J. P. Taillard (2017). Does Hedging Affect Firm Value? Evidence from a Natural Experiment. *Review of Financial Studies 30*, 4083–4132.

Giroud, X., H. M. Mueller, A. Stomper, and A. Westerkamp (2012). Snow and Leverage. *Review of Financial Studies 25*, 680–710.

Goergen, M., L. Renneboog, and L. Correia da Silva (2005). When Do German Firms Change Their Dividends? *Journal of Corporate Finance 11*, 375–399.

Gompers, P., J. Ishii, and A. Metrick (2003). Corporate Governance and Equity Prices. *Quarterly Journal of Economics 118*, 107–156.

Goodman-Bacon, A. (2021). Difference-in-Differences with Variation in Treatment Timing. *Journal of Econometrics* (forthcoming).

Gormley, T. A. and D. A. Matsa (2014). Common Errors: How to (and Not to) Control for Unobserved Heterogeneity. *Review of Financial Studies 27*, 617–661.

Gormley, T. A. and D. A. Matsa (2016). Playing It Safe: Managerial Preferences, Risk, and Agency Conflicts. *Journal of Financial Economics 133*, 431–455.

Gourieroux, C. and J. Jasiak (2001). *Financial Econometrics: Problems, Models, and Methods*. Princeton University Press.

Gourieroux, C., A. Monfort, E. Renault, and A. Trognon (1987). Generalised Residuals. *Journal of Econometrics 34*, 5–32.

Graham, J. R., S. Li, and J. Qiu (2012). Managerial Attributes and Executive Compensation. *Review of Financial Studies 25*, 144–186.

Granger, C. W. (1969). Investigating Causal Relations by Econometric Models and Cross-Spectral Methods. *Econometrica 37*, 424–438.

Granja, J., G. Matvos, and A. Seru (2017). Selling Failed Banks. *Journal of Finance 72*, 1723–1784.

Greene, W. H. (2004a). Fixed Effects and Bias Due to the Incidental Parameters Problem in the Tobit Model. *Econometric Reviews 23*, 125–147.

Greene, W. H. (2004b). The Behaviour of the Maximum Likelihood Estimator of Limited Dependent Variable Models in the Presence of Fixed Effects. *Econometrics Journal 7*, 98–119.

Greene, W. H. (2011). *Econometric Analysis* (7th ed.). Prentice Hall International.

Grieser, W. and C. J. Hadlock (2019). Panel Data Estimation in Finance: Testable Assumptions and Parameter (In)Consistency. *Journal of Financial and Quantitative Analysis 54*, 1–29.

Griliches, Z. and J. A. Hausman (1986). Errors in Variables in Panel Data. *Journal of Econometrics 31*, 93–118.

Gropp, R., C. Gruendl, and A. Guettler (2014). The Impact of Public Guarantees on Bank Risk-Taking: Evidence from a Natural Experiment. *Review of Finance 18*, 467–488.

Guimarães, P. and P. Portugal (2010). A Simple Feasible Procedure to Fit Models with High-Dimensional Fixed Effects. *Stata Journal 10*, 628–649.

Guthrie, K., J. Sokolowsky, and K.-M. Wan (2012). CEO Compensation and Board Structure Revisited. *Journal of Finance 67*, 1149–1168.

Hahn, J., J. A. Hausman, and G. Kuersteiner (2007). Long Difference Instrumental Variables Estimation for Dynamic Panel Models with Fixed Effects. *Journal of Econometrics 140*, 574–617.

Hamilton, J. D. (1994). *Time Series Analysis*. Princeton University Press.

Hansen, C. B. (2007). Asymptotic Properties of a Robust Variance Matrix Estimator for Panel Data When T is Large. *Journal of Econometrics 141*, 597–620.

Hansen, L. P. (1982). Large Sample Properties of Generalized Methods of Moments Estimators. *Econometrica 50*, 1029–1054.

Hansen, L. P., J. Heaton, and A. Yaron (1996). Finite Sample Properties of Some Alternative GMM Estimators. *Journal of Business and Economic Statistics 14*, 262–280.

Hansen, L. P. and R. J. Hodrick (1980). Forward Exchange Rates as Optimal Predictors of Future Spot Rates: An Econometric Analysis. *Journal of Political Economy 88*, 829–853.

Harvey, C. R. (2017). Presidential Address: The Scientific Outlook in Financial Economics. *Journal of Finance 72*, 1399–1440.

Harvey, C. R., Y. Liu, and H. Zhu (2016). ... and the Cross-Section of Expected Returns. *Review of Financial Studies 29*, 5–68.

Hausman, J. A. (1978). Specification Tests in Econometrics. *Econometrica 46*, 1251–1271.

Hausman, J. A., A. W. Lo, and A. C. MacKinlay (1992). An Ordered Probit Analysis of Transaction Stock Prices. *Journal of Financial Economics 31*, 319–379.

Hausman, J. A. and D. F. McFadden (1984). A Specification Test for the Multinomial Logit Model. *Econometrica 52*, 1219–1240.

Hausman, J. A. and W. E. Taylor (1981). Panel Data and Unobservable Individual Effects. *Econometrica 49*, 1377–1398.

Hausman, J. A. and D. A. Wise (1978). A Conditional Probit Model for Qualitative Choice: Discrete Decisions Recognizing Interdependence and Heterogeneous Preferences. *Econometrica 46*, 403–426.

Hausman, J. A. and D. A. Wise (1979). Attrition Bias in Experimental and Panel Data: The Gary Income Maintenance Experiment. *Econometrica 47*, 455–473.

Hayes, R. M., M. L. Lemmon, and M. Qiu (2012). Stock Options and Managerial Incentives for Risk Taking: Evidence from FAS 123R. *Journal of Financial Economics 105*, 174–190.

Heckman, J. J. (1976). The Common Structure of Statistical Models of Truncation, Sample Selection and Limited Dependent Variables and a Simple Estimator for Such Models. *Annals of Economic and Social Measurement 5*, 475–492.

Heckman, J. J. (1978a). Dummy Endogenous Variables in a Simultaneous Equations System. *Econometrica 46*, 931–960.

Heckman, J. J. (1978b). Simple Statistical Models for Discrete Panel Data Developed and Applied to Test the Hypothesis of True State Dependence Against the Hypothesis of Spurious State Dependence. *Annales de l'INSEE 30/31*, 227–269.

Heckman, J. J. (1979). Sample Selection Bias as a Specification Error. *Econometrica 47*, 153–161.

Heckman, J. J. (1981). *The incidental Parameters Problem and the Problem of Initial Conditions in Estimating a Discrete Time-Discrete Data Stochastic Process*, Chapter in: The Structural Analysis of Discrete Data (edited by C. Manski and D. F. McFadden). MIT Press, Cambridge, MA.

Heckman, J. J. (1997). Instrumental Variables: A Study of Implicit Behavioral Assumptions Used in Making Program Evaluations. *Journal of Human Resources 32*, 441–462.

Heckman, J. J. (2010). Building Bridges Between Structural and Program Evaluation Approaches to Evaluating Policy. *Journal of Economic Literature 48*, 356–398.

Heckman, J. J. and S. Urzúa (2010). Comparing IV with Structural Models: What Simple IV Can and Cannot Identify. *Journal of Econometrics 156*, 27–37.

Heider, F. and A. Ljungqvist (2015). As certain as Debt and Taxes: Estimating the Tax Sensitivity of Leverage from State Tax Changes. *Journal of Financial Economics 118*, 684–712.

Helwege, J. and N. Liang (1996). Is There a Pecking Order? Evidence from a Panel of IPO Firms. *Journal of Financial Economics 40*, 429–458.

Hendricks, D., J. Patel, and R. Zeckhauser (1993). Hot Hands in Mutual Funds: Short-Run Persistence of Relative Performance. *The Journal of Finance 48*, 93–130.

Henriksson, R. D. and R. C. Merton (1981). On Market Timing and Investment Performance. II. Statistical Procedures for Evaluating Forecasting Skills. *Journal of Business 54*, 513–533.

Hernán, M. A. and J. M. Robins (2020). *Causal Inference: What If*. Chapman and Hall/CRC, Boca Raton.

Hertzberg, A., J. M. Liberti, and D. Paravisini (2010). Information and Incentives Inside the Firm: Evidence from Loan Officer Rotation. *Journal of Finance 65*, 795–828.

Himmelberg, C. P., R. G. Hubbard, and D. Palia (1999). Understanding the Determinants of Managerial Ownership and the Link Between Ownership and Performance. *Journal of Financial Economics 53*, 353–384.

Hirano, K., G. W. Imbens, and G. Ridder (2003). Efficient Estimation of Average Treatment Effects Using the Estimated Propensity Score. *Econometrica 71*, 1161–1189.

Hjalmarsson, E. (2008). The Stambaugh Bias in Panel Predictive Regressions. *Finance Research Letters 5*, 47–58.

Hjalmarsson, E. (2010). Predicting Global Stock Returns. *Journal of Financial and Quantitative Analysis 45*, 49–80.

Hoberg, G. and G. Phillips (2016). Text-Based Network Industries and Endogenous Product Differentiation. *Journal of Political Economy 124*, 1423–1465.

Hoechle, D. (2007). Robust Standard Errors for Panel Regressions with Cross-Sectional Dependence. *Stata Journal 7*, 281–312.

Hoechle, D., M. Schmid, I. Walter, and D. Yermack (2012). How Much of the Diversification Discount can be Explained by Poor Corporate Governance? *Journal of Financial Economics 103*, 41–60.

Hollifield, B., R. A. Miller, P. Sandås, and J. Slive (2006). Estimating the Gains from Trade in Limit-Order Markets. *Journal of Finance 61*, 2753–2804.

Holtz-Eakin, D., W. K. Newey, and H. S. Rosen (1988). Estimating Vector Autoregressions with Panel Data. *Econometrica 56*, 1371–1395.

Honoré, B. (1992). Trimmed LAD and Least Squares Estimation of Truncated and Censored Regression Models with Fixed Effects. *Econometrica 60*, 533–565.

Honoré, B. and M. Weidner (2020). Moment Conditions for Dynamic Panel Logit Models with Fixed Effects. Cemmap working paper.

Hou, K., C. Xue, and L. Zhang (2020). Replicating Anomalies. *Review of Financial Studies 33*, 2019–2133.

Hovakimian, G. and S. Titman (2006). Corporate Investment with Financial Constraints: Sensitivity of Investment to Funds from Voluntary Asset Sales. *Journal of Money, Credit and Banking 38*, 357–374.

Hsiao, C. (2014). *Analysis of Panel Data* (3rd ed.). Cambridge University Press.

Hsu, D. H. (2004). What Do Entrepreneurs Pay for Venture Capital Affiliation? *Journal of Finance 59*, 1805–1844.

Hu, A. and H. Spamann (2020). Inference with Cluster Imbalance: The Case of State Corporate Laws. Working paper, Yale School of Management.

Huang, P., H.-Y. Huang, and Y. Zhang (2019). Do Firms Hedge with Foreign Currency Derivatives for Employees? *Journal of Financial Economics 133*, 418–440.

Huang, R. and J. R. Ritter (2009). Testing Theories of Capital Structure and Estimating the Speed of Adjustment. *Journal of Financial and Quantitative Analysis 44*, 237–271.

Hurd, M. (1979). Estimation in Truncated Samples When There Is Heteroskedasticity. *Journal of Econometrics 11*, 247–258.

Hyslop, D. R. and G. W. Imbens (2001). Bias From Classical and Other Forms of Measurement Error. *Journal of Business and Economic Statistics 19*, 475–481.

Ibragimov, R. and U. K. Müller (2010). t-Statistic Based Correlation and Heterogeneity Robust Inference. *Journal of Business and Economic Statistics 28*, 453–468.

Ibragimov, R. and U. K. Müller (2016). Inference with Few Heterogeneous Clusters. *Review of Economic and Statistics 98*, 83–96.

Imbens, G. W. (2004). Nonparametric Estimation of Average Treatment Effects under Exogeneity: A Review. *Review of Economics and Statistics 86*, 4–29.

Imbens, G. W. (2015). Matching Methods in Practice: Three Examples. *Journal of Human Resources 50*, 373–419.

Imbens, G. W. and J. Angrist (1994). Identification and Estimation of Local Average Treatment Effects. *Econometrica 62*, 467–475.

Imbens, G. W. and K. Kalyanaraman (2012). Optimal Bandwidth Choice for the Regression Discontinuity Estimator. *Review of Economic Studies 79*, 933–959.

Imbens, G. W. and M. Kolesár (2016). Robust Standard Errors in Small Samples: Some Practical Advice. *Review of Economics and Statistics 98*, 701–712.

Imbens, G. W. and T. Lemieux (2008). Regression Discontinuity Designs: A Guide to Practice. *Journal of Econometrics 142*, 615–635.

Imbens, G. W. and D. B. Rubin (2015). *Causal Inference for Statistics, Social, and Biomedical Sciences: An Introduction*. Cambridge University Press.

Imbens, G. W. and J. M. Wooldridge (2009). Recent Developments in the Econometrics of Program Evaluation. *Journal of Economic Literature 47*, 5–86.

Ioannidou, V., S. Ongena, and J.-L. Peydró (2015). Monetary Policy, Risk-Taking, and Pricing: Evidence from a Quasi-Natural Experiment. *Review of Finance 19*, 95–144.

Jagannathan, R. and Z. Wang (1998). An Asymptotic Theory for Estimating Beta-Pricing Models Using Cross-Sectional Regression. *Journal of Finance 53*, 1285–1309.

Jaggia, S. and S. Thosar (1993). Multiple Bids as a Consequence of Target Management Resistance: A Count Data Approach. *Review of Quantitative Finance and Accounting 3*, 447–457.

Jaud, M., M. Kukenova, and M. Strieborny (2018). Finance, Comparative Advantage, and Resource Allocation. *Review of Finance 22*, 1011–1061.

Jegadeesh, N. (1990). Evidence of Predictable Behavior of Security Returns. *Journal of Finance 45*, 881–898.

Jegadeesh, N., J. Noh, K. Pukthuanthong, R. Roll, and J. Wang (2019). Empirical Tests of Asset Pricing Models with Individual Assets: Resolving the Errors-in-Variables Bias in Risk Premium Estimation. *Journal of Financial Economics 133*, 273–298.

Jensen, M. C. and K. J. Murphy (1990). Performance Pay and Top-Management Incentives. *Journal of Political Economy 98*, 225–264.

Jiang, W. (2017). Have Instrumental Variables Brought Us Closer to the Truth. *Review of Corporate Finance Studies 6*, 127–140.

Jones, M. P. (1996). Indicator and Stratification Methods for Missing Explanatory variables in Multiple Linear Regression. *Journal of the American Statistical Association 91*, 222–230.

Kahn, R. and T. M. Whited (2017). Identification Is Not Causality, and Vice Versa. *Review of Corporate Finance Studies 7*, 1–21.

Kang, J. and C. E. Pflueger (2015). Inflation Risk in Corporate Bonds. *Journal of Finance 70*, 115–162.

Karpoff, J. M., R. J. Schonlau, and E. W. Wehrly (2017). Do Takeover Defense Indices Measure Takeover Deterrence? *Review of Financial Studies 30*, 2359–2412.

Karpoff, J. M. and M. D. Wittry (2018). Institutional and Legal Context in Natural Experiments: The Case of State Antitakeover Laws. *Journal of Finance 73*, 657–714.

Keane, M. P. (1993). *Simulation Estimation for Panel Data Models with Limited Dependent Variables*, Chapter in: Handbook of Statistics, Volume XI (edited by G. S. Maddala, C. R. Rao and H. D. Vinod), pp. 545–571. North-Holland, Elsevier.

Keane, M. P. (2010). Structural vs. Atheoretic Approaches to Econometrics. *Journal of Econometrics 156*, 3–20.

Kerr, W. R., J. Lerner, and A. Schoar (2014). The Consequences of Entrepreneurial Finance: Evidence from Angel Financings. *Review of Financial Studies 27*, 20–55.

Kézdi, G. (2004). Robust Standard Error Estimation in Fixed-Effects Panel Models. *Hungarian Statistical Review 9*, 95–116.

Kiefer, N. M. (1980). Estimation of Fixed Effect Models for Time Series of Cross-Sections with Arbitrary Intertemporal Covariance. *Journal of Econometrics 14*, 195–202.

Kiviet, J. F. (1995). On Bias, Inconsistency, and Efficiency of Various Estimators in Dynamic Panel Data Models. *Journal of Econometrics 68*, 53–78.

Kleibergen, F. and R. Paap (2006). Generalized Reduced Rank Tests Using the Singular Value Decomposition. *Journal of Economic Literature 133*, 97–126.

Kmenta, J. (1986). *Elements of Econometrics*. McMillan, New York.

Knez, P. J. and M. J. Ready (1997). On the Robustness of Size and Book-to-Market in Cross-Sectional Regressions. *Journal of Finance 52*, 1355–1382.

Koenker, R. (2004). Quantile Regression for Longitudinal Data. *Journal of Multivariate Analysis 91*, 74–89.

Koenker, R. (2005). *Quantile Regression*. Cambridge University Press.

Koh, P.-S., D. M. Reeb, E. Sojli, W. W. Tham, and W. Wang (2021). Deleting Unreported Innovation. *Journal of Financial and Quantitative Analysis* (forthcoming).

Koh, P.-S., D. M. Reeb, and W. Zhao (2018). CEO Confidence and Unreported R&D. *Management Science 64*, 5725–5747.

Kothari, S. P., J. S. Sabino, and T. Zach (2005). Implications of Survival and Data Trimming for Tests of Market Efficiency. *Journal of Accounting and Economics 39*, 129–161.

Kraft, A., A. J. Leone, and C. Wasley (2006). An Analysis of the Theories and Explanations Offered for the Mispricing of Accruals and Accrual Components. *Journal of Accounting Research 44*, 297–339.

Lahiri, K. and L. Yang (2013). *Forecasting Binary Outcomes*, Chapter in: Handbook of Economic Forecasting, Volume 2A (edited by G. Elliott and A. Timmermann), pp. 1025–1105. Elsevier Science BV.

Lancaster, T. (1990). *The Econometrics of Transition Data*. Cambridge University Press.

Lancaster, T. (2000). The Incidental Parameters Problem since 1948. *Journal of Econometrics 95*, 391–413.

Larcker, D. F. and T. O. Rusticus (2010). On the Use of Instrumental Variables in Accounting Research. *Journal of Accounting and Economics 49*, 186–205.

Leamer, E. (1978). *Specification Searches*. John Wiley and Sons, Hoboken, NJ.

Lee, D. S. and T. Lemieux (2010). Regression Discontinuity Designs in Economics. *Journal of Economic Literature 48*, 281–355.

Lee, J. H., C. Trzcinka, and S. Venkatesan (2019). Do Portfolio Managers Contracts Contract Portfolio Management? *Journal of Finance 74*, 2543–2577.

Lee, M.-J. (1999). A Root-N Consistent Semiparametric Estimator for Related-Effect Binary Response Panel Data. *Econometrica 67*, 427–433.

Lee, M.-J. (2005). *Micro-Econometrics for Policy, Program and Treatment Effects*. Oxford University Press.

Lei, J., J. Qiu, and C. Wan (2018). Asset Tangibility, Cash Holdings, and Financial Development. *Journal of Corporate Finance 50*, 223–242.

Lel, U. and D. P. Miller (2008). International Cross-Listing, Firm Performance, and Top Management Turnover: A Test of the Bonding Hypothesis. *Journal of Finance 63*, 1897–1937.

Lemmon, M. L. and M. R. Roberts (2010). The Response of Corporate Financing and Investment to Changes in the Supply of Credit. *Journal of Financial and Quantitative Analysis 45*, 555–587.

Lemmon, M. L., M. R. Roberts, and J. F. Zender (2008). Back to the Beginning: Persistence and the Cross-Section of Corporate Capital Structure. *Journal of Finance 63*, 1575–1608.

Lennox, C., J. Francis, and Z. Wang (2012). Selection Models in Accounting Research. *The Accounting Review 87*, 589–616.

Lewellen, J. (2015). The Cross-Section of Expected Stock Returns. *Critical Finance Review 4*, 1–44.

Lewellen, J., S. Nagel, and J. Shanken (2010). A Skeptical Appraisal of Asset Pricing Tests. *Journal of Financial Economics 96*, 175–194.

Li, K. and N. Prabhala (2007). *Self-Selection Models in Corporate Finance*, Chapter in: Handbook of Empirical Corporate Finance, Volume 1 (edited by B. E. Eckbo). Elsevier North-Holland.

Liesenfeld, R. and J.-F. Richard (2010). Efficient Estimation of Probit Models with Correlated Errors. *Journal of Econometrics 156*, 367–376.

Linton, O. (2019). *Financial Econometrics: Models and Methods*. Cambridge University Press.

Ljungqvist, A. and W. J. Wilhelm, Jr. (2005). Does Prospect Theory Explain IPO Market Behavior? *Journal of Finance 60*, 1759–1790.

Lo, A. W. and A. C. MacKinlay (1990). Data-Snooping Biases in Tests of Financial Asset Pricing Models. *Review of Financial Studies 3*, 431–467.

Lou, Y. and C. A. Otto (2020). Debt Heterogeneity and Covenants. *Management Science 66*, 70–92.

Loutskina, E. (2011). The Role of Securitization in Bank Liquidity and Funding Management. *Journal of Financial Economics 100*, 663–684.

Love, D. A. (2010). The Effects of Marital Status and Children on Savings and Portfolio Choice. *Review of Financial Studies 23*, 385–432.

Lovell, M. C. (1983). Data Mining. *Review of Economics and Statistics 65*, 1–12.

Ma, Y. (2019). Nonfinancial Firms as Cross-Market Arbitrageurs. *Journal of Finance 74*, 3041–3087.

MacKinnon, J. G. (2019). How Cluster-Robust Inference Is Changing Applied Econometrics. *Canadian Journal of Economics 52*, 851–881.

MacKinnon, J. G., M. Ø. Nielsen, and M. D. Webb (2020). Testing for the Appropriate Level of Clustering in Linear Regression Models. Working paper 1428, Economics Department, Queen's University.

MacKinnon, J. G., M. Ø. Nielsen, and M. D. Webb (2021a). Cluster-Robust Inference: A Guide to Empirical Practice. Working paper, Queen's University.

MacKinnon, J. G., M. Ø. Nielsen, and M. D. Webb (2021b). Wild Bootstrap and Asymptotic Inference With Multiway Clustering. *Journal of Business and Economic Statistics 39*, 505–519.

MacKinnon, J. G. and H. White (1985). Some Heteroskedasticity Consistent Covariance Matrix Estimators with Improved Small Sample Properties. *Journal of Econometrics 29*, 305–325.

Maddala, G. S. (1983). *Limited-Dependent and Qualitative Variables in Econometrics*. Cambridge University Press.

Maddala, G. S. (1987). Limited Dependent Variable Models Using Panel Data. *Journal of Human Resources 22*, 307–338.

Maddala, G. S. and K. Lahiri (2009). *Introductory Econometrics* (4th ed.). John Wiley and Sons, Chichester, UK.

Madhavan, A. and M. Cheng (1997). In Search of Liquidity: Block Trades in the Upstairs and Downstairs Markets. *Review of Financial Studies 10*, 175–203.

Maksimovic, V. and G. Phillips (2002). Do Conglomerate Firms Allocate Resources Inefficiently across Industries? Theory and Evidence. *Journal of Finance 57*, 721–767.

Maksimovic, V., G. Phillips, and L. Yang (2013). Private and Public Merger Waves. *Journal of Finance 68*, 2177–2217.

Malenko, N. and Y. Shen (2016). The Role of Proxy Advisory Firms: Evidence from a Regression-Discontinuity Design. *Review of Financial Studies 29*, 3394–3427.

Malmendier, U. and G. Tate (2005). CEO Overconfidence and Corporate Investment. *Journal of Finance 60*, 2661–2700.

Malmendier, U. and G. Tate (2009). Superstar CEOs. *Quarterly Journal of Economics 124*, 1593–1638.

Manski, C. F. (1987). Semiparametric Analysis of Random Effects Linear Models from Binary Panel Data. *Econometrica 55*, 357–362.

Manski, C. F. (1989). Anatomy of the Selection Problem. *Journal of Human Resources 24*, 243–260.

Marin, J. M. and J. P. Olivier (2008). The Dog That Did Not Bark: Insider Trading and Crashes. *Journal of Finance 63*, 2429–2476.

Massa, M. (2003). How Do Family Strategies Affect Fund Performance? When Performance-Maximization is Not the Only Game in Town. *Journal of Financial Economics 67*, 249–304.

McCrary, J. (2008). Manipulation of the Running Variable in the Regression Discontinuity Design: A Density Test. *Journal of Econometrics 142*, 698–714.

McFadden, D. F. (1974). *Conditional Logit Analysis of Qualitative Choice Analysis*, Chapter in: Frontiers in Econometrics (edited by P. Zarembka), pp. 105–142. Academic Press, New York.

Meling, T. G. (2021). Anonymous Trading in Equities. *Journal of Finance 76*, 707–754.

Menzly, L. and O. Ozbas (2010). Market Segmentation and Cross-Predictability of Returns. *Journal of Finance 65*, 1555–1580.

Meyer, B. D. (1990). Unemployment Insurance and Unemployment Spells. *Econometrica 58*, 757–782.

Miller, M. and F. Modigliani (1961). Dividend Policy, Growth and the Valuation of Shares. *Journal of Business 34*, 411–433.

Mitton, T. (2021). Methodological Variation in Empirical Corporate Finance. *Review of Financial Studies* (forthcoming).

Modigliani, F. and M. H. Miller (1958). The Cost of Capital, Corporation Finance and the Theory of Investment. *American Economic Review 48*, 261–297.

Mogstad, M., A. Torgovistky, and C. R. Walters (2021). The Causal Interpretation of Two-Stage Least Squares with Multiple Instrumental Variables. *American Economic Review* (forthcoming).

Montiel Olea, J. L. and C. E. Pflueger (2013). A Robust Test for Weak Instruments. *Journal of Business and Economic Statistics 31*, 358–369.

Moon, H. R. and P. C. B. Phillips (2000). Estimation of Autoregressive Roots Near Unity Using Panel Data. *Econometric Theory 16*, 927–997.

Moulton, B. R. (1986). Random Group Effects and the Precision of Regression Estimates. *Journal of Econometrics 32*, 385–397.

Mundlak, Y. (1961). Empirical Production Function Free of Management Bias. *Journal of Farm Economics 43*, 44–56.

Mundlak, Y. (1978). On the Pooling of Time Series and Cross Section Data. *Econometrica 46*, 69–85.

Murphy, K. J. (1985). Corporate Performance and Managerial Renumeration: An Empirical Analysis. *Journal of Accounting and Economics 7*, 11–42.

Myers, S. (1984). The Capital Structure Puzzle. *Journal of Finance 39*, 575–592.

Nash, R. and A. Patel (2019). Instrumental Variables Analysis and the Role of National Culture in Corporate Finance. *Financial Management 48*, 385–416.

Newey, W. K. (1985). Generalized Method of Moments Specification Testing. *Journal of Econometrics 29*, 229–256.

Newey, W. K. and K. D. West (1987). A Simple Positive-Definite Heteroskedasticity and Autocorrelation-Consistent Covariance Matrix. *Econometrica 55*, 703–708.

Newey, W. K. and K. D. West (1994). Automatic Lag Selection in Covariance Matrix Estimation. *Review of Economic Studies 61*, 631–653.

Nickell, S. (1981). Biases in Dynamic Models with Fixed Effects. *Econometrica 49*, 1417–1426.

Offenberg, D. and C. Pirinsky (2015). How Do Acquirers Choose between Mergers and Tender Offers? *Journal of Financial Economics 116*, 331–348.

Ohlson, J. A. (1980). Financial Ratios and the Probabilistic Prediction of Bankruptcy. *Journal of Accounting Research 18*, 109–131.

Ongena, S. and D. C. Smith (2001). The Duration of Bank Relationships. *Journal of Financial Economics 61*, 449–475.

Ouimet, P. and G. Tate (2020). Learning from Coworkers: Peer Effects on Individual Investment Decisions. *Journal of Finance 75*, 133–172.

Pagano, M., F. Panetta, and L. Zingales (1998). Why Do Companies Go Public? An Empirical Analysis. *Journal of Finance 53*, 27–64.

Palia, D. (2001). The Endogeneity of Managerial Compensation in Firm Valuation: A Solution. *Review of Financial Studies 14*, 735–764.

Pástor, L., R. F. Stambaugh, and L. A. Taylor (2015). Scale and Skill in Active Management. *Journal of Financial Economics 116*, 23–45.

Pástor, L. and P. Veronesi (2003). Stock Valuation and Learning about Profitability. *Journal of Finance 58*, 1749–1789.

Pérez-González, F. and H. Yun (2013). Risk Management and Firm Value: Evidence from Weather Derivatives. *Journal of Finance 68*, 2143–2176.

Pesaran, M. H. (2015). *Time Series and Panel Data Econometrics*. Oxford University Press, Oxford, UK.

Petersen, M. A. (2009). Estimating Standard Errors in Finance Panel Data Sets: Comparing Approaches. *Review of Financial Studies 22*, 435–480.

Pontiff, J. (1996). Costly Arbitrage: Evidence from Closed-End Funds. *Quarterly Journal of Economics 111*, 1135–1151.

Powell, J. L. (1984). Least Absolute Deviations Estimation for the Censored Regression Model. *Journal of Econometrics 25*, 303–325.

Powell, J. L. (1986). Symmetrically Trimmed Least Squares Estimation for Tobit Models. *Econometrica 54*, 1435–1460.

Powers, E. A. (2005). Interpreting Logit Regressions with Interaction Terms: an Application to the Management Turnover Literature. *Journal of Corporate Finance 11*, 504–522.

Puhani, P. (2000). The Heckman Correction for Sample Selection and its Critique. *Journal of Economic Surveys 14*, 53–67.

Puri, M. and R. Zarutskie (2012). On the Life Cycle Dynamics of Venture-Capital- and Non-Venture-Capital-Financed Firms. *Journal of Finance 67*, 2247–2293.

Pustejovsky, J. E. and E. Tipton (2018). Small-Sample Methods for Cluster-Robust Variance Estimation and Hypothesis Testing in Fixed Effects Models. *Journal of Business and Economic Statistics 36*, 672–683.

Ramadorai, T. (2012). The Secondary Market for Hedge Funds and the Closed Hedge Fund Premium. *Journal of Finance 67*, 479–512.

Reed, W. R. (2015). On the Practice of Lagging Variables to Avoid Simultaneity. *Oxford Bulletin of Economics and Statistics 77*, 897–905.

Reiss, P. C. (2016). Just How Sensitive are Instrumental Variable Estimates? *Foundations and Trends in Accounting 10*, 204–237.

Rivers, D. and Q. H. Vuong (1988). Limited Information Estimators and Exogeneity Tests for Simultaneous Probit Models. *Journal of Econometrics 39*, 347–366.

Roberts, M. R. and T. M. Whited (2013). *Endogeneity in Empirical Corporate Finance*, Chapter 7 in: Handbook of the Economics of Finance (edited by G. M. Constantinides, M. Harris and R. M. Stulz), pp. 493–572. Elsevier Science BV.

Robinson, P. (1982). On the Asymptotic Properties of Estimators of Models Containing Limited Dependent Variables. *Econometrica 50*, 27–41.

Roll, R. (1988). R^2. *Journal of Finance 43*, 541–566.

Roodman, D. (2009a). A Note on the Theme of Too Many Instruments. *Oxford Bulletin of Economics and Statistics 71*, 135–158.

Roodman, D. (2009b). How to Do xtabond2: An Introduction to Difference and System GMM in Stata. *Stata Journal 9*, 86–136.

Roodman, D., J. G. MacKinnon, M. Ø. Nielsen, and M. D. Webb (2019). Fast and Wild: Bootstrap Inference in Stata Using boottest. *Stata Journal 19*, 4–60.

Rosenbaum, P. R. and D. B. Rubin (1983). The Central Role of the Propensity Score in Observational Studies for Causal Effects. *Biometrika 70*, 41–55.

Ross, S. A. (1976). The Arbitrage Theory of Capital Asset Pricing. *Journal of Economic Theory 13*, 341–360.

Rousseeuw, P. J. and A. M. Leroy (2003). *Robust Estimation and Outlier Detection*. John Wiley and Sons, Hoboken, NJ.

Rubin, D. B. (1974). Estimating Causal Effects of Treatments in Randomized and Nonrandomized Studies. *Journal of Educational Psychology 66*, 688–701.

Rubin, D. B. (1976). Inference and Missing Data. *Biometrika 87*, 581–592.

Sarafidis, V. and T. J. Wansbeek (2012). Cross-Sectional Dependence in Panel Data Analysis. *Econometric Reviews 31*, 483–531.

Seru, A., T. Shumway, and N. Stoffman (2010). Learning by Trading. *Review of Financial Studies 23*, 705–739.

Shanken, J. (1992). On the Estimation of Beta Pricing Models. *Review of Financial Studies 5*, 1–34.

Shanken, J. and G. Zhou (2007). Estimating and Testing Beta Pricing Models: Alternative Methods and their Performance in Simulations. *Journal of Financial Economics 84*, 40–86.

Shumway, T. (2001). Forecasting Bankruptcy More Accurately: A Simple Hazard Model. *Journal of Business 74*, 101–124.

Siegel, J. and P. Choudhury (2012). A Reexamination of Tunneling and Business Groups: New Data and New Methods. *Review of Financial Studies 25*, 1763–1798.

Siriwardane, E. N. (2019). Limited Investment Capital and Credit Spreads. *Journal of Finance 74*, 2303–2347.

Sirri, E. R. and P. Tufano (1998). Costly Search and Mutual Fund Flows. *The Journal of Finance 53*, 1589–1622.

Skoulakis, G. (2008). Panel Data Inference in Finance: Least-Squares vs Fama-MacBeth. Working paper, available at SSRN, https://ssrn.com/abstract=1108865.

Słoczyński, T. (2021). Interpreting OLS Estimands When Treatment Effects Are Heterogeneous: Smaller Groups Get Larger Weights. *Review of Economic and Statistics* (forthcoming).

Smith, J. A. and P. E. Todd (2005). Does Matching Overcome LaLonde's Critique of Nonexperimental Estimators? *Journal of Econometrics 125*, 305–353.

Sojli, E., W. W. Tham, and W. Wang (2021). Time-Varying Group Unobserved Heterogeneity in Finance. Working paper, available at SSRN, https://ssrn.com/abstract=3258048.

Spiegel, M. and H. Zhang (2013). Mutual Fund Risk and Market Share-Adjusted Fund Flows. *Journal of Financial Economics 108*, 506–528.

Stambaugh, R. F. (1999). Predictive Regressions. *Journal of Financial Economics 54*, 375–421.

Stock, J. H. and M. W. Watson (2007). *Introduction to Econometrics* (2nd ed.). Addison-Wesley, Boston, MA.

Stock, J. H. and M. W. Watson (2008). Heteroskedasticity-Robust Standard Errors for Fixed Effects Panel Data Regression. *Econometrica 76*, 155–174.

Stock, J. H., J. H. Wright, and M. Yogo (2002). A Survey of Weak Instruments and Weak Identification in Generalized Method of Moments. *Journal of Business and Economic Statistics 20*, 518–529.

Stock, J. H. and M. Yogo (2005). *Testing for Weak Instruments in Linear IV Regression*, Chapter in: Identification and Inference for Econometric Models: Essays in Honor of Thomas Rothenberg (edited by D. W. K. Andrews and J. H. Stock), pp. 80–108. Cambridge University Press.

Strebulaev, I. A. and T. M. Whited (2011). Dynamic Models and Structural Estimation in Corporate Finance. *Foundations and Trends in Finance 6*, 1–163.

Sullivan, R., A. G. Timmermann, and H. L. White (2001). Dangers of Data-Driven Inference: The Case of Calender Effects in Stock Returns. *Journal of Econometrics 105*, 249–286.

Sun, L. and S. Abraham (2021). Estimating Dynamic Treatment Effects in Event Studies with Heterogeneous Treatment Effects. *Journal of Econometrics* (forthcoming).

Sun, L. and M. Teo (2019). Public Hedge Funds. *Journal of Financial Economics 131*, 44–60.

Sun, Y., P. C. Phillips, and S. Jin (2008). Optimal Bandwith Selection in Heteroskedasticity-Autocorrelation Robust Testing. *Econometrica 76*, 175–194.

Sun, Z., A. Wang, and L. Zheng (2012). The Road Less Traveled: Strategy Distinctiveness and Hedge Fund Performance. *Review of Financial Studies 25*, 96–143.

Ter Horst, J. R. and M. Verbeek (2000). Estimating Short-Run Persistence in Mutual Fund Performance. *Review of Economics and Statistics 82*, 646–655.

Tetlock, P. C., M. Saar-Tsechansky, and S. Macskassy (2008). More Than Words: Quantifying Language to Measure Firms' Fundamentals. *Journal of Finance 63*, 1437–1467.

Thompson, S. B. (2011). Simple Formulas for Standard Errors that Cluster by Both Firm and Time. *Journal of Financial Economics 99*, 1–10.

Tobin, J. (1958). Estimation of Relationships for Limited Dependent Variables. *Econometrica 26*, 24–36.

Tsoutsoura, M. (2015). The Effect of Succession Taxes on Family Firm Investment: Evidence from a Natural Experiment. *Journal of Finance 70*, 649–688.

Van den Berg, G. J. (2001). *Duration Models: Specification, Identification and Multiple Durations*, Chapter in: Handbook of Econometrics, Volume V (edited by J. J. Heckman and E. Leamer), pp. 3381–3460. Elsevier North-Holland.

Vella, F. and M. Verbeek (1999a). Estimating and Interpreting Models with Endogenous Treatment Effects. *Journal of Business and Economic Statistics 17*, 473–478.

Vella, F. and M. Verbeek (1999b). Two-Step Estimation of Panel Data Models with Censored Endogenous Variables and Selection Bias. *Journal of Econometrics 90*, 239–263.

Verbeek, M. (1995). Alternative Transformations to Eliminate Fixed Effects. *Econometric Reviews 14*, 205–211.

Verbeek, M. (2017). *A Guide to Modern Econometrics* (5th ed.). John Wiley and Sons, Hoboken, NJ.

Verbeek, M. and T. E. Nijman (1992). Testing for Selectivity Bias in Panel Data Models. *International Economic Review 33*, 681–703.

Verbeek, M. and T. E. Nijman (1996). *Incomplete Panels and Selection Bias*, Chapter in: The Econometrics of Panel Data. A Handbook of the Theory with Applications (edited by L. Mátyás and P. Sevestre). Kluwer Academic Publishers.

Vogelsang, T. (2012). Heteroskedasticity, Autocorrelation and Spatial Correlation Robust Inference in Linear Panel Models with Fixed Effects. *Journal of Econometrics 166*, 303–319.

Vuillemey, G. (2020). The Value of Central Clearing. *Journal of Finance 75*, 2021–2053.

Wald, A. (1940). The Fitting of Straight Lines if Both Variables are Subject to Error. *Annals of Mathematical Statistics 11*, 284–300.

Wansbeek, T. J. and A. Kapteyn (1989). Estimation of the Error-Components Model with Incomplete Panels. *Journal of Econometrics 41*, 341–361.

Wardlaw, M. (2020). Measuring Mutual Fund Flow Pressure as Shock to Stock Returns. *Journal of Finance 75*, 3221–3243.

Wasserstein, R. L. and N. A. Lazar (2016). The ASA's Statement on *p*-Values: Context, Process and Purpose. *The American Statistician 70*, 129–133.

Wei, W. and A. Young (2021). Selection Bias or Treatment Effect? A Re-Examination of Russell 1000/2000 Index Reconstitution. *Critical Finance Review* (forthcoming).

White, H. L. (1980). A Heteroskedasticity-Consistent Covariance Matrix Estimator and a Direct Test for Heteroskedasticity. *Econometrica 48*, 817–838.

White, H. L. (1982). Maximum Likelihood Estimation of Misspecified Models. *Econometrica 50*, 1–25.

Whited, T. M. (2006). External Finance Constraints and the Intertemporal Pattern of Intermittent Investment. *Journal of Financial Economics 81*, 467–502.

Windmeijer, F. (2005). A Finite Sample Correction for the Variance of Linear Efficient Two-Step GMM. *Journal of Econometrics 126*, 25–51.

Wintoki, M. B., J. S. Linck, and J. M. Netter (2012). Endogeneity and the Dynamics of Internal Corporate Governance. *Journal of Financial Economics 105*, 581–606.

Wooldridge, J. M. (1995). Selection Corrections for Panel Data Models Under Conditional Mean Independence Assumptions. *Journal of Econometrics 68*, 115–132.

Wooldridge, J. M. (2005). Simple Solutions to the Initial Conditions Problem in Dynamic, Nonlinear Panel Data Models with Unobserved Heterogeneity. *Journal of Applied Econometrics 20*, 39–54.

Wooldridge, J. M. (2010). *Econometric Analysis of Cross-Section and Panel Data* (2nd ed.). MIT Press, Cambridge, MA.

Wooldridge, J. M. (2014). Quasi-Maximum Likelihood Estimation and Testing for Nonlinear Models with Endogenous Explanatory Variables. *Journal of Econometrics 182*, 226–234.

Wooldridge, J. M. (2019). Correlated Random Effects Models with Unbalanced Panels. *Journal of Econometrics 211*, 137–150.

Wu, J. (2004). The Choice of Equity-Selling Mechanisms. *Journal of Financial Economics 74*, 93–119.

Yermack, D. L. (1996). Higher Market Valuation of Companies with a Small Board of Directors. *Journal of Financial Economics 40*, 185–211.

Yoon, H.-J. and K. Lee (2019). A Weighted Fama-MacBeth Two-Step Panel Regression Procedure. *Applied Economics Letters 26*, 677–683.

Zhou, Q., R. Faff, and K. Alpert (2014). Bias Correction in the Estimation of Dynamic Panel Models in Corporate Finance. *Journal of Corporate Finance 25*, 494–513.

Zhu, M. (2018). Informative Fund Size, Managerial Skill, and Investor Rationality. *Journal of Financial Economics 130*, 114–134.

Zmijewski, M. E. (1984). Methodological Issues Related to the Estimation of Financial Distress Prediction Models. *Journal of Accounting Research 22*, 59–82.

Index